# Ethics in 1 Peter

# Ethics in 1 Peter

The *Imitatio Christi* and the Ethics of Suffering in 1 Peter and the Gospel of Mark—A Comparative Study

Elritia Le Roux

FOREWORD BY
Friedrich W. Horn

◆PICKWICK *Publications* • Eugene, Oregon

ETHICS IN 1 PETER
The *Imitatio Christi* and the Ethics of Suffering in 1 Peter and the Gospel of Mark—A Comparative Study

Copyright © 2018 Elritia Le Roux. All rights reserved. Except for brief quotations in critical publications or reviews, no part of this book may be reproduced in any manner without prior written permission from the publisher. Write: Permissions, Wipf and Stock Publishers, 199 W. 8th Ave., Suite 3, Eugene, OR 97401.

Pickwick Publications
An Imprint of Wipf and Stock Publishers
199 W. 8th Ave., Suite 3
Eugene, OR 97401

www.wipfandstock.com

PAPERBACK ISBN: 978-1-5326-1948-9
HARDCOVER ISBN: 978-1-4982-4577-7
EBOOK ISBN: 978-1-4982-4576-0

*Cataloguing-in-Publication data:*

Names: Le Roux, Elritia, author | Horn, Friedrich W., foreword.

Title: Ethics in 1 Peter : the imitatio christi and the ethics of suffering in 1 Peter and the gospel of Mark—a comparative study / Elritia Le Roux ; foreword by Friedrich W. Horn.

Description: Eugene, OR: Pickwick Publications, 2018. | Includes bibliographical references.

Identifiers: ISBN 978-1-5326-1948-9 (paperback) | ISBN 978-1-4982-4577-7 (hardcover) | ISBN 978-1-4982-4576-0 (ebook).

Subjects: LCSH: Bible. Peter, 1st—Criticism, interpretation, etc. | Bible. Mark—Criticism, interpretation, etc.

Classification: BS2795.52 L47 2017 (print). | BS2795.52 (ebook).

Manufactured in the U.S.A.      04/17/18

Dedicated to Prof. Gert J. Steyn

υἱέ ἐμῇ σοφίᾳ πρόσεχε ἐμοῖς δὲ λόγοις παράβαλλε σὸν οὖς ἵνα φυλάξῃς ἔννοιαν ἀγαθήν αἴσθησιν δὲ ἐμῶν χειλέων ἐντέλλομαί σοι

Motto:

τοῦτο γὰρ χάρις εἰ διὰ συνείδησιν θεοῦ ὑποφέρει τις λύπας πάσχων ἀδίκως. ποῖον γὰρκ λέος εἰ ἁμαρτάνοντες καὶ κολαφιζόμενοι ὑπομενεῖτε; ἀλλ᾽ εἰ ἀγαφοποιοῦντες καὶ πάσχοντες ὑπομενεῖτε, τοῦτο χάρις παρὰ θεῷ. εἰς τοῦτο γὰρ ἐκλήθητε, ὅτι καὶ Χριστὸς ἔπαθεν ὑπὲρ ὑμῶν ὑμῖν ὑπογραμμὸν ἵνα ἐπακολουθήσητε τοῖς ἴχνεσιν αὐτοῦ

# Contents

*Foreword by Friedrich W. Horn* | ix
*Preface* | xiii
*Acknowledgments* | xv
*Abbreviations* | xviii

1. Introduction, History of Research on 1 Peter, Methodology, and Hypothesis | 1
2. The Relation between Peter and Mark: The Presence of Petrine Traditions and Memories in Rome | 88
3. Christology as Foundation for Ethics | 137

*Bibliography* | 277

# Foreword

ELRITIA LE ROUX HAT diese Dissertation als Stipendiatin im Rahmen des von der Johannes Gutenberg-Universität Mainz eingerichteten Projektes ProGeisteswissenschaften geschrieben, das auf die Initiative PRO Geistes- und Sozialwissenschaften der Johannes Gutenberg-Universität Mainz zurückgeht. Sie war als Stipendiatin in den Jahren 2010-2012 zugleich Mitglied der von Prof.Friedrich W. Horn, Prof. Ulrich Volp und Prof. Ruben Zimmermann, zeitweise auch Junior-Prof. BlossomStefaniw, geleiteten Doktorandengruppe „Begründungszusammenhänge der christlichen Ethik in Neuem Testament und Alter Kirche," in der Doktorandinnen und Doktoranden aus den Fächern Neues Testament und Kirchengeschichte/ Alte Kirche zusammengefasst waren. Gemeinsam mit Elritia le Roux promovierten in dieser Zeit aus der Doktorandengruppe Dr. Esther Verwold im Fach Kirchengeschichte/Patristik, Dr. Fredrik Wagener im Fach Neues Testament und Dr. Karl Weyer-Menkhoff im Fach Neues Testament. Im Anschluss daran trat Elritia le Roux zum Ende des Jahres 2012 eine Anstellung als Pfarrerin bei der *Nederduitsch Hervormde Gemeente Otjiwarongo* in Namibia an und brachte die Dissertation in dieser Zeitunter bisweilen schwierigen Umständen im Pfarramt zu Ende. Das Rigorosum vor der Evangelisch-Theologischen Fakultät der Johannes Gutenberg-Universität Mainz fand im Jahr 2016 in allen theologischen Disziplinen in deutscher Sprache statt.

Als Dissertationsprojekt war mit der Ausschreibung einer Doktorandengruppe von mir das Arbeitsthema „Begründung einer Ethik differenzierter gesellschaftlicher Partizipation im 1. Petrusbrief" ausgegeben worden. Gedacht war an eine Beschreibung der im 1. Petrusbrief erkennbaren unterschiedlichen Reaktionen auf die gesellschaftlichen und politischen Bedrängungen der christlichen Gemeinden in ihrer Minoritätsposition sowie eine Darstellung der vom Verfasser dieses Briefs angedachten gesellschaftlichen Verortung der Gemeinden zwischen missionarischer Offenheit, gesellschaftlichem Tatzeugnis, politischem Kalkül und Rückzug in den binnenkirchlichen Bereich. Elritia le Roux hat diese Vorgabe nur partiell aufgenommen, da sich für sie in der Beschäftigung mit dem 1. Petrusbrief Beobachtungen aufdrängten, die ihre Darstellung in eine andere Richtung führten. Ihre Arbeit geht von der Hypothese aus, dass das Markusevangelium und der 1. Petrusbrief in Rom entstanden seien. Auf dieser Hypothese aufbauend, vielleicht auch sie nachträglich begründend, werden die Gemeinsamkeiten beider Schriften vor allem in der Leidensethik ausgearbeitet. Le Roux erklärt diese nicht durch gegenseitige literarische Abhängigkeit oder gar durch persönliche Bekanntschaft der uns unbekannten Autoren, sondern durch eine spezifische Theologie in der römischen Gemeinde unter Vespasian, auf die beide Autoren zurückgreifen. Ich habe diesen Ansatz mitgetragen, auch wenn ich die Zielsetzung einer Comparative Study zwischen dem 1. Petrusbrief und dem Markusevangelium seinerzeit nicht für ertragreich hielt, da die These einer Petrus-Schule in Rom zunehmend an Plausibilität einbüßte.

In Vielem überschreitet die Arbeit den üblichen Rahmen einer Dissertation. Nicht nur seitenmäßig, sondern auch dadurch, dass Elritia le Roux etliche Schwerpunkte bearbeitet (Markusevangelium, 1. Petrusbrief, Christologie, Leidenstheologie, römische Zeitgeschichte u.a.), die je für sich bereits ein Thema darstellen. Auch zeichnet sich die Arbeit durch einen entschlossenen und entschiedenen direkten Zugriff auf die Texte aus und sie gewinnt dadurch ein klares theologisches Profil. Überhaupt vermittelt die Dissertation den untrüglichen Eindruck, dass der Herzschlag ihrer Autorin bei theologischen Fragen liegt. Das spezifische Anliegen, die Leidenstheologie des 1. Petrusbriefs von einer in Rom ansässigen, auch im Markusevangelium zu findenden Theologie her abzuleiten, ist der eigene, so in dieser Breite in der Forschung bisher nicht ausgeführte Beitrag. Er fußt freilich auf etlichen Hypothesen wie derjenigen einer spezifischen Petrus-Gruppe in Rom oder derjenigen einer stadtrömischen Herkunft des Markusevangeliums. Doch weiß le Roux um die Anfechtbarkeit dieser Hypothesen und bewegt sich in ihrer Darlegung mit der nötigen Vorsicht und Zurückhaltung.

Ich habe hohen Respekt vor der Gesamtleistung. Elritia le Roux legt eine theologisch dichte und diskutable Perspektive für den 1. Petrusbrief vor und die Verfasserin überzeugt durch breites und sicheres theologisches Urteilsvermögen. Ich habe gleichfalls Respekt vor dem Mut, als Stipendiatin in eine Doktorandengruppe in Mainz zu gehen, ein fremdes Wissenschaftssystem kennenzulernen, in kurzer Zeit die deutsche Sprache zu erlernen und eine Dissertation in diesen neuen und anfänglich fremden Kontexten abzuschließen. Die Publikation dieser Studie ist ein wichtiger Beitrag für die neutestamentliche Forschung und für eine Theologie, die Antworten auf die Frage des gesellschaftlich und politisch verursachten Leides und seiner Bewältigung sucht.

Prof. Dr. Friedrich W. Horn<br>
Johannes Gutenberg-Universität Mainz<br>
Mainz, im Februar 2017

# Preface

WHEN I STARTED THE preliminary reading of First Peter, freshly after completing a Magister thesis on discipleship and ethics in the Gospel of Mark, I had a distinct hunch that there is a theological affinity between the two New Testament writings. The more my research deepened, I became aware of more and more similarities especially in the two authors' handling of the subject of suffering, the passion of Jesus Christ, Christology, and the ethics that flows from it. I started formulating the hypothesis in my head of a possible correlation between the two texts. The early Christian tradition according to Papias, although not historically reliable, that Mark acted as Peter's secretary, suggested that at least in the early Christian memory there is some association between Peter and Mark. Furthermore, the association of both texts with Rome as a plausible place of origin provided some grounds for further enquiry. The breakthrough came when John H. Elliott, in his 1985 article "Backward and Forward 'In His Steps': Following Jesus from Rome to Raymond and Beyond: The Tradition, Redaction and Reception of 1 Peter 2:18-25," suggested an affinity between the texts that demanded further exploring. I hope that this study succeeds in providing such an exploration. I would not like to argue for a historical or literal dependence of the one upon the other, but rather a dependence on the same traditions and theological thoughts that originated from Rome and was associated with the apostle Peter. In my opinion Mark and Peter display a similar Christology, especially as far as the passion of Christ is concerned, and use this Christology as foundation for the development of an ethic of suffering.

# Acknowledgments

A STUDY OF THIS compass would not have been possible without the support and assistance of the following persons, whom I consider to be *sine qua non*.

First and foremost is Prof. Gert Steyn, to whom this book is dedicated. Prof. Steyn believed in my potential when I was still a pre-graduate student of the New Testament. Under his guidance and with his motivation, I delivered my first official academic paper at a conference of the New Testament Society of South Africa. When the opportunity of a scholarship in Germany to complete a PhD in New Testament landed on his desk, he, in consultation with the highly acclaimed and revered scholar of the New Testament in South Africa, Prof. Andrie du Toit, put me in correspondence with the Germans in Mainz and the rest, as they say, is history. Therefore, my sincerest thanks to Gert Steyn and Andrie du Toit.

From the capable and nurturing hands of Gert Steyn I was transferred into the hands of Prof. Dr. Friedrich Wilhelm Horn, whom I have the distinct honour of calling my *Doctorvater*. That indeed he was. It was an honor and privilege to study under the guidance of an academic who enjoys the admiration and respect of his colleagues and peers as well as his students. Prof. Horn is the rare combination of academic excellence and compassionate fatherly guidance. I have great appreciation.

Prof. Horn's colleague in the New Testament Department at Johannes Gutenberg University, Prof. Ruben Zimmermann, went to great lengths to expose his students to acclaimed New Testament scholars from all over the world. For these initiatives, especially the annual Mainz Moral Meetings, I am sincerely grateful. Prof. Zimmermann also invited me to publish in his grandiose project, *Die Wunder Jesu Kompendium*, an opportunity for which I have tremendous appreciation.

It was clear from the word go that a proper knowledge of Latin was a prerequisite for a PhD in theology in Germany. As a firm believer in the doctrine of the Providence of the Almighty, I came to realize that my years of dedication and *dilligentia* (as my Latin teacher called it) to the subject which was my first love finally came to pass in something meaningful and even triumphant. Therefore, I thank my Latin teachers Rita Irene Wiesemann and Corrie Schumann for creating an unrivalled enthusiasm in the depths of my being for the ancient world and the history and language thereof, which turned me into an ardent lover of the classics and the New Testament.

Upon arrival in Mainz, Germany, I was cordially welcomed by the assistant of Prof. Ruben Zimmermann, Dr. Susanne Luther, who played an exceptional role in accommodating me, helping me to settle in and feel at home and providing me with excellent advice. Without Susanne I would have been lost and therefore I am very much obliged for her unique and indispensible input. Susanne's compassion was extended by the acquaintance of Drs. Anna Zernecke and Eckardt Schmidt, who became dear friends and theatre companions. Our deep theological and cultural conversations gave me command over the German language which enriched my being tremendously.

Back home, from the following scholars within my beloved church of origin, the Nederduitsch Hervormde Kerk van Afrika, I enjoyed the support, pastoral care and academic motivation of Prof. P. A. Geyser, Prof. Natie van Wyk, Dr. Wouter van Wyk and especially Dr. Johann Beukes. The value of these conversations and words of comfort, wisdom and encouragement can hardly be exaggerated. I have overflowing appreciation. I would also like to thank the Nederduitsch Hervormde Kerk for their financial support during my studies. For the financial and moral support I received from Dr. Marina Muller I am extremely grateful. I also owe a great word of thanks to my colleague in the congregation of Middelburg, Rev. N. J. S. Steenekamp, for his love, support, and motivation during my doctoral examination.

I would like to thank Yolande Steenkamp for undertaking the huge effort of editing this book and for sacrificing many hours bringing the raw materials to academic perfection.

On a personal level, and this is probably the most decisive contribution: the love and support of my family and friends. Melanie Galliart and Antje Kozempel, my German girlfriends, who supported me with tea and coffee, dinners, Christmas festivities, *Mädelsabend und Mädelswochende*, lifted my spirits and carried me through the toughest hours.

I owe much of my success to Wouter van Wyk, Petrus Dreyer, and Josef Oosthuizen, who are closer than brothers, for they are my brothers in Christ. They believed in me, gave me wings when I needed to fly and returned the faith, which forever binds us to one another, when I lost it. This is as much your accomplishment as it is mine.

My loving and supportive parents, Frank and Edrie le Roux, who held my hand throughout this journey, hopefully look back upon their investment in their only child and smile with enormous gratitude to our heavenly Father.

# Abbreviations

## Ancient Works

| | |
|---|---|
| *A.J.* | *Antiquitates judaicae*, by Josephus |
| *Ann.* | *Annales*, by Tacitus |
| *Apol.* | *Apologia*, by Justin |
| *Apol.* | *Apologia*, by Plato |
| *Apol.* | *Apologeticus*, by Tertullian |
| *B.J.* | *Bellum judaicum*, by Josephus |
| *C. Ap.* | *Contra Apionem*, by Josephus |
| *Cels.* | *Contra Celsum*, by Origen |
| *Ep.* | *Epistulae*, by Pliny the Younger |
| *Ep.* | *Epistulae morales*, by Seneca |
| *Epig.* | *Epigrams*, by Martial |
| *Eryx.* | *Eryxias*, by Plato |
| *Eth. nic.* | *Ethica nichomachea*, by Aristotle |
| *Geogr.* | *Geographica*, by Strabo |
| *Gorg.* | *Gorgias*, by Plato |
| *Haer.* | *Adversus haereses*, by Irenaeus |
| *Hist.* | *Historiae*, by Herodotus |
| *Hist. eccl.* | *Historia ecclesiastica*, by Eusebius |
| *Ios.* | *De Iosepho*, by Philo |
| *Ira* | *De ira*, by Seneca |
| *Legat.* | *Legatio ad Gaium*, by Philo |

| | |
|---|---|
| *Leg.* | *Leges*, by Plato |
| *[Lib. ed.]* | *De liberis educandis*, by Plutarch |
| *[Mag. mor.]* | *Magna moralia*, by Aristotle |
| *Metaph.* | *Metaphysica*, by Aristotle |
| *Mil. glor.* | *Miles gloriosus*, by Plautus |
| *Mor.* | *Moralia*, by Plutarch |
| *Oct.* | *Octavius*, by Minucius Felix |
| *Ordin.* | *Sermo cum presbyter fuit ordinatus*, by Chrysostom |
| *Prof in Virt* | *De Profectibus in Virtute* by Plutarch |
| *Somn.* | *De somniis*, by Philo |
| *Spec.* | *De specialibus legibus*, by Philo |
| *Strom.* | *Stromata*, by Clement |
| *Tusc.* | *Tusculanae disputationes*, by Cicero |
| Val. Max. | Valerius Maximus |
| *Vit.* | *Vitellius*, by Suetonius |

## Modern Works

| | |
|---|---|
| AB | Anchor Bible |
| *ABD* | *Anchor Bible Dictionary*. Edited by David Noel Freedman. 6 vols. New York: Doubleday, 1992 |
| ABG | Arbeiten zur Bibel und ihrer Geschichte |
| ACNT | Augsburg Commentaries on the New Testament |
| AGJU | Arbeiten zur Geschichte des antiken Judentums und des Urchristentums |
| AnBib | Analecta biblica |
| ATANT | Abhandlungen zur Theologie des Alten und Neuen Testaments |
| AthenMTh | Athenäums Monographien, Theologie |
| BBB | Bonner biblische Beiträge |
| BBET | Beiträge zur biblischen Exegese und Theologie |
| *Bib* | *Biblica* |
| BibInt | Biblical Interpretation |

| | |
|---|---|
| *BibLeb* | *Bibel und Leben* |
| BNTC | Black's New Testament Commentaries |
| *BTB* | *Biblical Theology Bulletin* |
| BThS | Biblisch–theologische Schwerpunkte |
| BZNW | *Beiheftezur Zeitschrift für die neutestamentliche Wissenschaft und die* |
| | *Kunde der älteren Kirche* |
| *CBQ* | *Catholic Biblical Quarterly* |
| CD | Karl Barth, *Church Dogmatics*. Translated by G. T. Thomson et al. Edinburgh: T. & T. Clark, 1936–77 |
| ConBNT | Coniectanea neotestamentica or Coniectanea biblica: New Testament Series |
| EKKNT | Evangelisch-katholischer Kommentar zum Neuen Testament |
| *ExAud* | *Ex Auditu* |
| DNTC | Doubleday New Testament Commentary Series |
| ETL | *Ephemerides theologicae lovanienses* |
| EuroH | Europäische Hochschulschriften |
| *ExpTim* | *Expository Times* |
| FB | Forschung zur Bibel |
| FTS | Freiburger Theologische Studien |
| GNT | Grundrisse zum Neuen Testament |
| HBB | Herold Biblical Booklets |
| HBC | *Harper's Bible Commentary*. Edited by James Luther Mays et al. San Francisco: Harper & Row, 1988. |
| *Historia* | *Historia: Zeitschrift für alte Geschichte* |
| HNT | Handbuch zum Neuen Testament |
| *Hom. Luc.* | *Homilae in Lucam*, by Origen |
| HTS | Harvard Theological Studies |
| *HvTSt* | *HervormdeTeologiese Studies/Theological Studies* |
| HvTStSup | Hervormde Teologiese Studies / Theological Studies Supplements |

| | |
|---|---|
| *IDB* | *The Interpreter's Dictionary of the Bible.* Edited by George Arthur Buttrick. 4 vols. Nashville: Abingdon, 1962 |
| ISJ | Institucion San Jeronimo |
| *JAAR* | *Journal of the American Academy of Religion* |
| *JBL* | *Journal of Biblical Literature* |
| *JJS* | *Journal of Jewish Studies* |
| *JSNT* | *Journal for the Study of the New Testament* |
| JSNTSup | Journal for the Study of the New Testament: Supplement Series |
| *JTS* | *Journal of Theological Studies* |
| KEK | Kritisch-exegetischer Kommentar über das Neue Testament (Meyer-Kommentar) |
| LD | Lectio Divina |
| LEC | Library of Early Christianity |
| *LTQ* | *Lexington Theological Quarterly* |
| *LV* | *Lumen Vitae* |
| MJT | Marburger Jahrbuch Theologie |
| MThSt | Marburger Theologische Studien |
| NABPRSS | National Association of Baptist Professors of Religion Special Studies Series |
| NCB | New Century Bible |
| *Neot* | *Neotestamentica* |
| NIGTC | New International Greek Testament Commentary |
| NovTSup | Novum Testamentum Supplements |
| NTD | Das Neue Testament Deutsch |
| NTM | New Testament Message |
| *NTS* | *New Testament Studies* |
| *PEQ* | *Palestine Exploration Quarterly* |
| *Ph&R* | *Philosophy & Rhetoric* |
| ProcC | Proclamation Commentaries |
| *RB* | *Revue Biblique* |
| *ResQ* | *Restoration Quarterly* |
| *RevExp* | *Review & Expositor* |

| | |
|---|---|
| *RevistB* | *Revista biblica* |
| RVV | Religiongeschichtliche Versuche und Vorarbeiten |
| SANT | Studien zum Alten und Neuen Testaments |
| *Sat.* | *Satirae*, by Juvenal |
| SBLDS | Society of Biblical Literature Dissertation Series |
| SBLSP | Society of Biblical Literature Seminar Papers |
| SBLSymS | Society of Biblical Literature Symposium Series |
| SBS | Stuttgarter Bibelstudien |
| SBT | Studies in Biblical Theology |
| SCL | Sather Classical Lectures |
| *ScrHier* | *Scripta hierosolymitana* |
| SHCT | Studies in the History of Christian Thought |
| *SJT* | *Scottish Journal of Theology* |
| SNTSMS | Society for New Testament Studies Monograph Series |
| ST | *Studia theologica* |
| SUNT | Studien zur Umwelt des Neuen Testaments |
| TBC | Torch Bible Commentaries |
| *TBT* | *The Bible Today* |
| TDNT | *Theological Dictionary of the New Testament*. Edited by Gerhard Kittel and Gerhard Friedrich. Translated by Geoffrey W. Bromiley. 10 vols. Grand Rapids, 1964–1976 |
| TNTC | Tyndale New Testament Commentaries |
| *Tru* | *Theologische Rundschau* |
| *TWNT* | *Theologische Wörterbuch zum Neuen Testament*. Edited by Gerhard Kittel and Gerhard Friedrich. Stuttgart: Kohlhammer, 1932–1979 |
| WBC | Word Biblical Commentary |
| WUNT | Wissenschaftliche Untersuchungen zum Neuen Testament |
| *TSK* | *Theologische Studien und Kritiken* |
| *ZNW* | *Zeitschrift für die neutestamentliche Wissenschaft und die Kunde der älteren Kirche* |
| *ZTK* | *Zeitschrift für Theologie und Kirche* |

# 1

# Introduction, History of Research on 1 Peter, Methodology, and Hypothesis

## Introduction

### Preliminary Remarks

MARTIN LUTHER (1522) VIEWED 1 Peter among "the true and noblest books of the New Testament," the "true kernel and marrow of all the books." Luther had the following to say about 1 Peter, which he included with the Gospel and the First Epistle of John, the letters of Paul to the Romans, Galatians and Ephesians:

> These are the books that show you Christ and teach you all that is necessary and salvatory for you to know, even if you were never to see or hear any other book or doctrine. For in these you do not find many works or miracles of Christ described, but you do find depicted in masterly fashion how faith in Christ overcomes sin, death and hell, and gives life, righteousness and salvation. This is the real nature of the gospel as you have heard.[1]

In recent times 1 Peter received a prominent place in liturgy. Selwyn called it "a microcosm of Christian faith and duty, model of pastoral change."[2] J. N. D. Kelly viewed it as "one of the most pastorally attractive and vigorously confident documents of the New Testament."[3] S. Neil was of the opinion that 1 Peter is "a storm-centre of New Testament studies."[4]

Howard Marshall mentioned that "if one were to be shipwrecked on a deserted island and allowed to have only one of the New Testament

---

1. Luther, *Luther's Works* 35.361–62.
2. Selwyn, *St. Peter: Greek Text*, 1.
3. Kelly, *Peter and Jude*, 1.
4. Neil, *Interpretation*, 343.

letters as a companion, then 1 Peter would be the ideal choice, so rich in its teaching, so warm in its spirit, and so comforting its message in a hostile environment."[5] According to Hiebert the epistle conveys the triumph of faith over suffering by proclaiming the Christ-centred hope amidst an antagonistic society.[6]

According to Elliott, 1 Peter was regarded as less important by New Testament scholars in comparison to the attention received by the Synoptic Gospels, the Johanine corpus, and the epistles attributed to Paul.[7] The reason for this state of affairs may be the fact that 1 Peter was regarded for a long time to be a Deutero-Pauline document, and therefore dependent on Paul for its authority. However, 1 Peter was one of the first writings to be included in the Christian canon. Christian authors such as Clement of Rome and Polycarp of Smyrna were inspired by 1 Peter's words of consolation, exhortation and hope. In following centuries it was embraced in the East and the West as an indisputable statement of Christian faith, teaching and practice.[8] First Peter soon received great appreciation as a creative synthesis of multiple strands of early Christian thought, an eloquent voice of Roman Christianity and a moving call to steadfastness and hope in the face of hostility.

Horrell notes that 1 Peter is a "non-polemical" letter, by which he means that there are no traces of differences among Christians or heretical teachings that needed to be addressed.[9] Instead, the letter is remarkably theological.[10] According to Marshall all the categories of Christian belief are present in 1 Peter.[11] These include worship and praise of God, opposition to evil and salvation which will be perfectly completed in the future. Horrell adds that 1 Peter is a rich example of how Jewish traditions and sacred scriptures and christological traditions of the early Christian movement were employed in shaping the new Christian identity.[12] According to Horrell, "1 Peter contains some of the most memorable and splendid declarations of the glorious identity of the people of God found in the New Testament."[13] Therefore, 1 Peter is regarded as a significant contribution to

---

5. Marshall, *1 Peter*, 12.
6. Hiebert, *First Peter*, 1.
7. Elliott, "Rehabilitation," 3; cf. Michaels, *1 Peter*, xxxi.
8. Elliott, *1 Peter: New Translation*, 4.
9. Horrell, *1 Peter*, 100.
10. Marshall, *New Testament*, 657; cf. Martin, "1 Peter," 104.
11. Marshall, *New Testament*, 648.
12. Horrell, *1 Peter*, 101.
13. Ibid, 101.

the development of Christian identity and especially defining this identity in terms of important Christian images and ideas.[14]

Additionally, 1 Peter may be described as a letter of hope—the hope of believers's certain salvation in the death and resurrection of Christ, which may serve as a means of encouragement in their current adverse circumstances. It should be noted, however, that although the letter speaks of their perfect salvation in future, 1 Peter is not an example of a delayed or imminent eschatology. It is much rather an example of a realised eschatology, as will be argued later in this study.

Horrell also tries to move beyond the Elliott-Balch debate,[15] where Elliott suggests that the author urged his audience to maintain a very distinctive identity and not become too involved in the surrounding culture, and Balch argues that the author suggested that believers should conform to the practices of the surrounding culture, in order not to provoke further hostility, especially from the Roman authorities. Horrell argues that it is not a situation of the one or the other, but rather a situation of both. The audience ought to promote a balance between quiet conformity and simultaneously establishing a distinctive Christian identity. Horrell convincingly argues that the author's purpose is to comfort and motivate the addressees by describing their new identity and the accompanying salvation and hope they have in Christ, as well as to encourage them to endure suffering in the same way Christ did.[16] Therefore 1 Peter becomes an important letter in confronting the situation of suffering in the early Christian Church. It gives an example of how the early church applied the acts of Jesus and the writings of the Old Testament in order to address their contemporary situation of suffering.[17]

In the same way the author wants them to live blameless and righteous lives in order to avoid further hostility from the outside world. In the words of Horrell, "the strategy of quiet conformity, within limits, makes sense *as a survival strategy* in the situation where a powerless minority is oppressed due to both public and imperial hostility."[18] This strategy is radically different from that found in Revelation, which was composed in more or less the same timeframe and addressed to the same audience. The author of Revelation, contrary to that of 1 Peter, encourages definite separation from the greater society and resistance to the Emperor, whom he is demonizing (cf. Rev 13:17–18).

14. Cf. Feldmeier, *Der erste Brief*, 18.
15. Horrell, *1 Peter*, 102.
16. Ibid., 109.
17. Cf. Davids, *First Epistle*, 3.
18. Author's italics. Horrell, *1 Peter*, 109.

First Peter offers, as Feldmeier describes, a theology as a reflective account of faith.[19] Feldmeier finds it refreshing that a letter written primarily to console and to encourage is so rich in doctrine, and argues that the content of the Apostolic Creed could all be found in 1 Peter.[20]

## History of Research

### Authorship of 1 Peter

Bacon argues that as far as early Christian tradition is concerned, the dating of writings is rather vague and not really of significance.[21] However, as far as the name of the author is concerned, it is a totally different matter. Tradition, as will be indicated below, has the danger of becoming absolute truths, beyond question or doubt and it the words of Bacon "bold in proportion to its consciousness of the general ignorance."[22] Tradition names the author of any ancient anonymous document to meet the requirements of those who want to employ it in substantiating their theological agendas. The receivers on the other hand are comforted by this, since the document originates from a reliable source. Therefore tradition holds that the Pentateuch was written by Moses and the Psalms by David, while the critical scholar is uncomfortable with these bold claims. But the critical scholar is then confronted with the problem that if the Pentateuch was not written by Moses and the Psalms not by David, who then was responsible for these documents? The same holds true for 1 Peter, written in the name of the Apostle Peter.

Some scholars are still of the opinion that it is indeed the case that 1 Peter was written by the Apostle Peter,[23] since the letter makes the claim in the opening greeting and it was accepted undoubtedly by the early church.[24] Eusebius, writing in the late third and early fourth century, lists 1 Peter among the New Testament writings of which there is no doubt as far as canonicity is concerned.[25] Further, the content of the letter also does not suggest another author. Rather there is evidence in the letter that would support authorship by the Apostle, e.g., the prominence of the "stone"-metaphor, which could be linked with Matt 16:18 and Peter being an eyewitness to the

---

19. Feldmeier, *Der erste Brief*, 29.
20. Ibid., 30.
21. Bacon, *Is Mark?*, 8.
22. Ibid.
23. Guthrie, *New Testament*, 762–81; Marshall, *1 Peter*, 22–24.
24. Horrell, *1 Peter*, 20; cf. Elliott, *1 Peter: New Translation*, 148–49.
25. Horrell, *Epistles*, 5.

suffering of Christ. Dschulnigg makes the interesting observation that the letter is not ascribed to Simon,[26] *id est* the Apostle's first name, but to his nickname, meaning "stone" or "rock." Peter is, however, depicted throughout the New Testament as the most prominent among the disciples and the first of the disciples to see the resurrected Christ. As such he also receives the special mandate to proclaim the gospel of Jesus Christ. Michaels gives a different perspective.[27] According to the Synoptic Gospels Peter, although recognizing Jesus as the Christ, the Son of the living God, misunderstood his own confession. Jesus ironically gave Peter the nickname "rock," because his character turned out to be flawed. He eventually denied Jesus. The depiction of Peter by the evangelists is not one of a hero, but rather someone who failed Jesus, but who was also pardoned by Christ.

It is generally accepted however, by recent New Testament scholars, that 1 Peter was not written by the Apostle Peter.[28] Primarily this position is held because the strategy and content of the letter indicate a period after the death of the Apostle and rather attest to the situation of the Christians in Asia Minor in the decades following the death of the apostle.

Further reasons for this conclusion include the following:

a. The high quality of the Greek and classical vocabulary,[29] as well as the masterly rhetorical composition places 1 Peter among the more sophisticated New Testament writings. It is therefore highly implausible that a Galilean fisherman, whose mother tongue was Aramaic and was described by the author of Acts as "unschooled" (Acts 4:13), could be capable of such fine Greek. He could have mastered a primitive form of Greek, due to the Hellenization of Galilee, but even so, it would not be compatible with the high quality of the Greek encountered in 1 Peter.[30] Although the language of the New Testament is often described as the everyday Greek heard on the streets and in the marketplace, Brox describes the language of 1 Peter as "above average."[31] According to Schelke the author was capable of "rhetorical artistry,"[32]

26. Dschulnigg, *Petrus*, 172.

27. Michaels, *1 Peter*, lv–lvii.

28. Cf. Schnelle, *History and Theology*; Schelkle, *Die Petrusbriefe*; Neugebauer 1980; Goppelt, *Commentary*; Dschulnigg, *Petrus*, 173.

29. Elliott, *1 Peter: New Translation*, 120; cf. Davids, *First Epistle*, 4; Schnelle, *History and Theology*, 400; Selwyn, *St. Peter: Greek Text*, 499–500.

30. Cf. Achtemeier, *1 Peter*, 1; Horrell, *1 Peter*, 2; Feldmeier, *Der erste Brief*, 23; Boring, *1 Peter*, 30–31.

31. Brox, *Petrusbrief* (1st ed.), 45.

32. Schelkle, *Die Petrusbriefe*, 13.

and it is regarded as some of the best prose of the New Testament.[33] Achtemeier highlights several literary characteristics of the style in which the letter was written that indicate that the author composed it with great care.[34] These include the frequent use of comparison (1 Pet 1:7, 13; 2:2, 16, 25; 3:4–5; 5:8), the use of homophones (1 Pet 1:4, 19; 3:18), the use of synonyms (1 Pet 1:8, 10; 2:25; 3:4), the use of anaphora to introduce parallel phrases (1 Pet 4:11), the use of the synthetic (1 Pet 2:22–23; 4:11; 5:2–3) and the antithetic (1 Pet 2:14; 3:18; 4:6) parallelism, parallel expressions mentioning first the negative, then the positive to communicate the same idea (1 Pet 1:14–15, 18–21, 23; 2:16; 5:2–3), the employment of a rhythmic structure (1 Pet 1:3–12), the use of conjunctive participles (e.g., 1 Pet 1:8, 9, 11, 23) and relative clauses which could lead to long sentences (e.g., 1 Pet 1:17–21). Radermacher notes the absence of Semiticisms[35] and Bigg the absence of Latinisms.[36] Achtemeier ascribes the employment of participles to function as imperatives—a practice not known to Classical or Hellenistic Greek—not to Hebraic influences, as often used by Rabbinic writings to indicate continuous or habitual actions, but to the use of common Christian tradition, which originated in the Hebrew language.[37] According to Achtemeier the author uses "distinctively Christian language."[38] Although Greek might not have been the author's mother tongue,[39] Lampe and Luz are confident that the author enjoyed a formal education in rhetoric and philosophy, along with arithmetic, geometry, music, and the reading of Classical Greek, stating that the linguistic quality of the letter could be sufficiently explained if the author completed grammar school.[40] Wifstrand argues that the author's use of Greek goes beyond a mere acquaintance "with carelessly spoken Greek." If these scholars are followed, authorship by the apostle Peter, a Galilean fisherman with limited education, becomes almost impossible—a view supported by this study.

---

33. See Bigg, *St. Peter and St. Jude*, 4.
34. Achtemeier, *1 Peter*, 3.
35. Radermacher, "Der erste Petrusbrief," 290.
36. Bigg, *St. Peter and St. Jude*, 3.
37. Achtemeier, *1 Peter*, 4.
38 Ibid., 4.
39. Cf. Bigg, *St. Peter and St. Jude*, 5.
40. Lampe and Luz, "Nachpaulinisches Christentum," 188; see also Wifstrand, "Stylistic Problems," 178.

b. The quotations from the Old Testament in 1 Peter are cited from the Septuagint and not from the Hebrew or Aramaic Targums with which Peter would have been familiar. The numerous allusions to Old Testament texts bear witness that the author thought in terms of the LXX.[41] Once again the masterly interweaving of LXX texts could hardly be the product of a Galilean fisherman, whose Scripture was in Hebrew and whose language of worship was Aramaic. Additionally, it is highly unlikely that a Galilean with a primary mission to the Jews and depicted by Paul as the pillar of the Jerusalem church (Gal 2:9) would have such an interest in the gentile Christians and could so easily apply the promises to and identity of Israel as God's elect and holy people to the Christians. Christian identity in 1 Peter thus indicates an evolution beyond the time of the apostles Peter and Paul.[42]

c. First Peter contains very little of the actual teachings of Jesus, except for a few sayings that is not pertinently ascribed to Jesus. The words of Jesus that are alluded to in 1 Peter only indicate that the author was familiar with the early Christian tradition, particularly the Gospel traditions.[43] If the sayings of Jesus reflected in the letter were indeed the memories of the apostle Peter, it must have been in the original Aramaic, which Peter would have translated into Greek, instead of drawing from the established Greek in the Gospel tradition. Boring-notes—and this is perhaps the most important reason for disregarding authorship by the Apostle Peter—that the Christology reflected in the Gospels is completely different from that which is found in 1 Peter.[44] In the Gospels we still find traces of the historical Jesus, but in 1 Peter the focus is completely on the post- Easter Jesus of the kerugma. The author cites Scripture instead of Jesus and therefore implies that it is indeed Christ of whom the Scriptures speak. The Christ-event is not only located in the "historical" Jesus, but in God's universal activity and involvement with creation. The proclaimed post-Easter Christ transcends the earthly Jesus, for the Scriptures, inspired by the Holy Spirit, attest to the pre-existent Christ.[45] Special prominence to the Gospel of Mathew and allusions to the other Gospels clearly indicate

---

41. Elliott, *1 Peter: New Translation*, 120; cf. Best, *1 Peter*, 49–50; Achtemeier, *1 Peter*, 1; Horrell, *1 Peter*, 21; Feldmeier, *Der erste Brief*, 23; Boring, *1 Peter*, 31; Schnelle, *History and Theology*, 400.

42. Horrell, *Epistles*, 7.

43. Cf. Achtemeier, *1 Peter*, 10.

44. Boring, *1 Peter*, 36.

45. Boring, "Narrative Dynamics," 37.

that the author was a representative from the mainstream Christian tradition.⁴⁶ The fact that the letter is attributed to Peter is significant in this respect, as Peter is representative of the authentic apostolic faith. Nothing is mentioned of Jesus's ministry, or actual deeds which would be strange for an eyewitness and one of Jesus's closest disciples to omit.⁴⁷ Furthermore, the author never makes any references to his personal experiences of being a disciple of Christ. The letter's reference to the passion of Christ is more dependent on Isaiah 53 than an actual account of an eyewitness, and if anything, only proves the author's knowledge of Old Testament Scripture.⁴⁸ The use of Peter's name by the author is much rather again a strategy of giving authority to the writing. The evidence about the disciples obtained from the Gospels cannot be accepted as historical, for the writers of the gospels also structured their material for theological purposes. The portrayal of Peter as the spokesperson of the disciples and an authoritative figure, led to the fact that the church in Jerusalem had a significant influence on the early church. Since the church in Rome has become more prominent and Peter has been associated with Rome, it made sense to write the letter in Peter's name.⁴⁹ Peter was the disciple to recognise Jesus as the Christ, and although the evangelists depict Peter as not grasping the significance of his own confession, he becomes the first to confess Jesus as the Christ. In the memory of the early church Peter therefore becomes the ultimate witness to the gospel.

According to Elliott, the fact that the author refers to himself as a "witness" μάρτυς does not necessarily imply an "eyewitness," but merely someone who testifies to Christ's suffering and glory.⁵⁰ Zwierlein, quoting from the first letter of *Clemens*, indicates that the word μάρτυς, or derivatives thereof, occurs forty-six times in this letter and could in each instance be interpreted as bearing witness, rather than referring to martyrdom.⁵¹ Μαρτυρέω in *1 Clement* has the same meaning as in Acts 23:11, where it explicitly means to testify. Böttrich confirms this.⁵² According to him Clemens, as the Bishop of Rome, writes to the congregation in Corinth in order to address the issue of some members seeking to elevate themselves above others. "Vermutlich geht

---

46. See Brox, *Petrusbrief* (2nd ed), 45; Best, "Gospel Tradition," 95.
47. Cf. Achtemeier, *1 Peter*, 1, 9; Boring, *1 Peter*, 35; see also Beare, *First Epistle*, 44.
48. Achtemeier, *1 Peter*, 9; cf. Boring, *1 Peter*, 35.
49. Brown, Donfried, and Reumann, *Der Petrus der Bibel*, 139.
50. Elliott, *1 Peter: New Translation*, 120.
51. Zwierlein, *Petrus in Rom*, 17.
52. Böttrich, *Petrus*, 215–16.

es dabei um einen Generationenkonflikt und Autorität der Amtsträger. Deshalb präsentiert Clemens gleich zu Beginn eine ganze Kette von Beispielen zum Beleg für die destructive Wirkung von 'Eifersucht', 'Neid' und 'Streit.'"[53] He further emphasises that μαρτυρέω should only be understood in the sense of testifying. This becomes evident in what Clement writes in 1 Clem. 5:4.7 that Paul and Peter leave this world and enter the everlasting glory *after* they "testified." Zwierlein indicates that Polycarp, writing between AD 120 and 140, is the first to use the word in the sense of martyrdom, but prior to that it simply did not have that meaning.[54]

Zwierlein therefore concludes that the composer of 1 Clemens knows nothing about a martyrdom of Peter and Paul in Rome, simply about their bearing witness of their faith in Christ.[55] The earliest sources to attest to a martyrdom of Peter and Paul in Rome date from AD 180–190 in the *Acta Petri*.

Furthermore, it is known that Paul travelled to Rome, since as a Roman citizen he could be referred to the emperor for his trial. However, there exists no historical evidence that the fisherman, Peter, who was primarily situated in Jerusalem and worked in Syria and Antioch, ever travelled to Rome. This gives rise to the question why Peter was associated with Rome in the first place. This tradition probably originated from the *Acta Petri* which contains an episode in which Peter, during the reign of Claudius, was called by the Lord to follow Simon Magus, the magician he expelled from Jerusalem (cf. Acts 8:18–24) and who is also known as the father of Gnosticism, to Rome.[56] This tradition seems to have been developed in opposing Gnosticism. Peter, as the Apostle and representative of the true Christian faith, is summoned by the Lord himself to travel to Rome in order to combat this despicable heresy.[57] According to this tradition, which was also followed by Ambrose, Nero was befriended with Simon Magus and therefore sought to have Peter killed. It seems as though the death of Peter and Paul was not only the result of Nero's persecution of the Christians as scapegoats for the fire, but that the Apostles were engaged in *personal* conflict with the emperor.[58] The story then develops that Peter was arrested by the soldiers of the prefect, Agrippa, in order to be crucified and that he was crucified upside down, for he did not view himself worthy as to die in the same manner

---

53. Ibid., 215; cf. Michaels, *1 Peter*, lx.
54. Zwierlein, *Petrus in Rom*, 22; cf. Böttrich, *Petrus*, 216.
55. Zwierlein, *Petrus in Rom*, 30.
56. Cf. Ibid., 129.
57. Cf. Eusebius, *Hist. eccl.* 2:14, 4–6.
58. Cf. Böttrich, *Petrus*, 219.

as Christ did.⁵⁹ Irenaeus of Lyon also interpreted the letter of Clemens as referring to martyrdom, because it suited his writing against the heresy of Gnosticism that Peter as the authoritative representative of the Church in Rome undertook the journey to Rome to combat Simon Magus, the father of Gnosticism.⁶⁰ It was important for the early church to claim authority as to be representative of the true faith. Traditions associated with an apostle were viewed as irreproachable.⁶¹ This tradition is however in conflict with what is known from the New Testament about the historical Apostle Peter, who is depicted as the Apostle of the Jews *par excellence*. Ambrose, however, tries to link his story with the text in John 21:18, which he views as a prediction of Peter's martyrdom. Michaels is concerned with the uncritical acceptance of this verse, viewed as a prediction of Peter's martyrdom.⁶² This tradition has no historical foundation and is often used by scholars when the authorship or dating of 1 Peter is discussed. Even if John 21:18 is taken at face value, it could very well only refer to the difference between youth and old age. This description could easily be applied to an old man being dependent on others because he is no longer capable of taking care of himself. If the tradition of Peter's martyrdom solely relies on this verse it is highly problematic. Tertullian, however, later follows the same path in his Apology, which was written in AD 197.⁶³ The question arises whether there exists anything historical in these early Christian writings. When compared to the canonised Acts of the Apostles nothing is known about the death of neither Peter nor Paul and there is no account of Peter travelling to Rome. The legend about Peter and Paul's martyrdom in Rome originated from AD 185 to 195. This tradition, however, was firmly enforced in the Christian memory from the second century onwards and was accepted even by scholars in a very uncritical manner. Böttrich mentions how Henryk Sienkiewicz's acclaimed film, *Quo Vadis*, engraved this story into the minds of Christians.⁶⁴ The tradition was however challenged by Karl Heussi, who asked the question of whether Peter was in Rome at all.⁶⁵ Furthermore, if Paul's letter to the Romans, in which he writes that he is still planning to visit Rome, is dated around AD 58 and Paul only arrived in Rome around AD 62, Simon Magus could not have been active there in the time of Claudius. According to Bruce

---

59. Ibid., 226.
60. Cf. Zwierlein, *Petrus in Rom*, 141–46.
61. Boring, *1 Peter*, 26.
62. Michaels, *1 Peter*, lvii.
63. Cf. Zwierlein, *Petrus in Rom*, 119.
64. Böttrich, *Petrus*, 220.
65. Heussi, *Die römische Petrustradition*, 35–104.

and Güting the Roman historian, Suetonius, in AD 120, wrote a biography on the first twelve emperors of Rome and about Claudius he stated that he expelled the Jews from Rome and that the "Chrestos" who were taken up with Christ constantly caused uproar in the city.[66] The expulsion of the Jews from Rome also influenced Christian growth in the city negatively.

   d. No historical evidence points to the fact that Peter ever travelled to Asia Minor for missionary purposes.[67] Neither does anything in the letter indicate a personal relationship between Peter and the addressees. Instead, the author rather emphasizes that the ties that bound him to his audience were spiritual. As a means of consolation he stresses that both the author and the addressees are part of the worldwide brotherhood connected by their faith in Christ and they share the condition of being strangers and aliens in a hostile world, experiencing similar suffering and afflictions (1 Pet 1:1; 5:8–9; 5:11; 5:12–13). However, according to Elliot this argument is uncertain,[68] since the Apostle Paul also wrote to communities that he never visited and post New Testament tradition testified to Peter's missionary activity in Asia Minor, stating that he often visited Pontus and Bithynia.[69] It is of significance, however, that the name of Peter was known in this region and that it had authority associated with it.

   e. Achtemeier mentions that the many allusions to Pauline literature and the similarities in both content and language give reason to believe that the author drew from early Christian traditions (as will also be argued below).[70] This is hard to reconcile with a person who knew Christ personally and who would have had his own very specific understanding of the person of Christ.

   f. The author introduces himself as the "co-elder" συμπρεσβύτερος (1 Pet 5:1), a title used nowhere else in the New Testament to refer to the Apostle Peter.[71] However, Peter does serve as the perfect example of how an elder should act. Peter, although an authoritative apostle became a martyr and not someone seeking his own honor. The imagery

---

66. Bruce and Güting, *Außerbiblische Zeugnisse*, 12.

67. Cf. Dschulnigg, *Petrus*, 173; Davids, *First Epistle*, 5.

68. Elliott, *1 Peter: New Translation*, 120, cf. also Brown, Donfried, and Reumann, *Der Petrus der Bibel*, 131.

69. See Origen in Eusebius, *Hist. eccl.* 3.1

70. Achtemeier, *1 Peter*, 2; cf. Boring, *1 Peter*, 31.

71. Elliott, *1 Peter: New Translation*, 121; cf. Dschulnigg, *Petrus*, 173; Brown, Donfried, and Reumann, *Der Petrus der Bibel*, 132–33; Schnelle, *History and Theology*, 400.

of the shepherd is also associated with Peter, evoking the Gospel of John (John 21:15–19), probably written from Ephesus and therefore a tradition possibly known to the audience, in which Peter was specifically assigned to feed the lambs and the sheep. This is again not a literary dependence, but a tradition used by the author in association with the legacy of Peter.[72]

g. Krodel notes that if the letter is written from Rome (as will be indicated later in this study) and one wants to argue for authorship by the Apostle Peter, it must have been written during the period when Paul was also active in Rome.[73] Yet since there is no mention of Paul in the letter, such an argument would not be possible.

h. Several factors, which will be indicated later, point to a later dating of the letter, definitely post AD 70, and possibly even later than AD 90, which eliminates the possibility of authorship by the Apostle Peter.[74] One of the most convincing being the fact that 1 Peter attests to no tension between Gentile and Jewish Christians or what the Gentile Christians attitude towards the Jewish law should be.[75] The letter was written during a time when Christianity significantly expanded throughout Asia Minor and that Christianity already infiltrated all spheres and strata of the population.[76]

According to early Church tradition Peter died during Nero's persecution of the Christians in Rome ca. AD 65–67.[77] This tradition, as previously indicated, is questionable. Zwierlein mentions that everyone agrees that there exists a grave of the Apostle Peter,[78] somewhere beneath the St. Peter's Basilica in Rome. Archeological excavations, however, produced no such grave underneath the St. Peter Basilica which could be dated to the first century AD. Dinkler states that there did however exist a cult in the memory of the Apostles on the Via Appia since AD 260,[79] and archeology proved the cultic activity around the belief that the bones of the Apostles Peter and Paul were present there. No graves were discovered on the Via Apia as well, but graffiti indicated the belief that this is the place where the

---

72. Brown, Donfried, and Reumann, *Der Petrus der Bibel*, 133.
73. Krodel, "1 Peter," 64.
74. Cf. Horrell, *Epistles*, 6, Feldmeier, *Der erste Brief*, 23.
75. Horrell, *1 Peter*, 22.
76. Feldmeier, *Der erste Brief*, 23; cf. Dschulnigg, *Petrus*, 174.
77. Origen in Eusebius, *Hist. eccl.* 3.1.3.
78. Zwierlein, *Petrus in Rom*, 4; cf. Böttrich, *Petrus*, 227–31.
79. Dinkler, "Die Petrus-Rom Frage," 305.

bones of the Apostles Peter as well as Paul rest. The earliest of these inscriptions, according to Dinkler dates back to the year AD 258 and attest to the presence of a cult around Peter and Paul.[80] Archeological evidence shows that it was only from the end of the third century beginning of the fourth century AD that a cult was formed at the place where the St. Peter Basilica was erected. Zwierlein,[81] who dates the *Letter of Clement*, who seemed to have known 1 Peter, around the year AD 125, argues that patristic tradition does not stand the test of critical scientific research.

Regardless of whether Peter was martyred in Rome or not, Achtemeier argues that the internal and external historical evidence of the letter points to a period later than the time in which the apostle lived.[82] Michaels adds that Peter's death as such cannot be used in arguing for a certain date of the composition of the letter, since historical evidence of the time, place and circumstances of Peter's death is corrupted by early Church traditions and legendary tales about the apostles in order to build authority around their personalities.[83]

i. Irenaeus, ca. AD 180 is the first of the early Church Fathers to mention Peter as the author of the letter. However, 1 Peter was known to Clement of Rome and Polycarp and none of them mentions Peter as the author.[84]

### 1 Peter as a Pseudonymous Letter

For Achtemeier it is a logical consequence that if authorship by the apostle Peter is rejected the letter must be pseudonymous.[85] Danker explains that the terms pseudonymity and pseudography are morally neutral and refer to a common practice in Greco-Roman philosophical circles as well as in biblical communities.[86] It simply meant that the writing was ascribed to someone other than the actual author. As far as biblical texts are concerned this practice was employed because biblical literature presumes divine inspiration and should therefore be authoritative. Authority gained further weight if the particular writing could be associated or ascribed to authoritative

---

80. Ibid., 40.
81 Zwierlein, *Petrus in Rom*, 13.
82. Achtemeier, *1 Peter*, 2.
83. Michaels, *1 Peter*, lxi.
84. Elliott, *1 Peter: New Translation*, 121.
85 Achtemeier, *1 Peter*, 2, cf. Schnelle, *History and Theology*, 401.
86. Danker, *Invitation 4*, 129.

figures, even if they were known to be deceased. The actual authors viewed themselves as to be a continuation of the tradition or religious current of the person under whose name they wrote.[87] Achtemeier also mentioned the notion in antiquity to attribute the writing of a student to the master of whose teachings such a writing owes its origin.[88] Many rabbis were of the opinion that the name of the teacher and not that of the student validated the authority of the writing.[89] From this perspective it becomes clear that pseudographic writers gave the name of the apostle in whose tradition they stood the name of their writing in order to actualize that authoritative tradition in a later situation.

Although the majority of scholars agree on the pseudonymity of 1 Peter, they differ on the purpose and reason for ascribing it to the Apostle Peter.[90] Some argue for the origin of the letter from a Pauline circle because of the correlations in theological thought. These scholars would also argue for a literal dependency on Pauline literature and erroneously identify the addressees of the letter with the Christian communities that emerged because of Paul's missionary activity. They however fail to recognise the undeniable differences between 1 Peter and Pauline as well as Deutero-Pauline writings. Goppelt particularly emphasises the general character of 1 Peter in contrast to the *ad hoc* writings of Paul.[91] A dependency on Pauline thought and theology fails to recognise the distinctive Petrine mission with distinctive objectives.

Brox, who extensively discussed the pseudonymity of 1 Peter,[92] agrees with Beare that the mentioning of Silvanus and Mark by name is simply part of the "device of pseudonymity."[93] Brox, however, considers the possibility that Silvanus and Mark are mentioned because of their association with the Apostolic council in Acts 15 and Mark as the co-worker of Peter in Jerusalem (Acts 12:12).[94] We could argue for an author who played a prominent role in the church in Rome and who wrote in the name of Peter and mentioned the co-workers of Paul. The question however arises why the letter was written in the name of Peter and not of Paul. This could be answered by arguing

---

87. Elliott, *1 Peter: New Translation*, 125.
88. Achtemeier, *1 Peter*, 40.
89. See Gerhardsson, *Memory*, 131.
90. Brox, "Zur pseusodographischen Rahmung," 78–69; cf. Dschulnigg, *Petrus*, 174.
91. Goppelt, *Commentary*, 47–56.
92. Brox, "Zur pseusodographischen Rahmung"; Brox, "Der erste Petrusbrief in der literarischen Tradition"; Brox, "Tendenz"; Brox, *Petrusbrief* (2nd ed), 43–47.
93. Beare, *First Epistle*, 48–50.
94. Brox, "Zur pseusodographischen Rahmung," 85–86.

for Rome as the place of the origin of the letter and the prominence Peter enjoyed in the Roman church. This idea is further developed with the early Christian tradition of Peter's martyrdom in Rome and Peter's position as the first bishop of Rome.[95] The use of Peter's name was thus a specific strategy of the author to provide the epistle with apostolic authority.[96] It was important for the Christian church at the time that the letter should be "apostolic" and thus that the content thereof could be traced back to the apostolic origins of the church. In this sense, there was no better person than Peter, since he was the first of the disciples to see the resurrected Christ, he played the most prominent role among the disciples as depicted by the Gospel writers, he denied Christ, yet recovered and ultimately followed in the footsteps of Christ and he was recognised by Paul as a leading figure in the early church.

## 1 Peter as the Product of a Petrine Circle in Rome

John H Elliott is the primary exponent of the view that 1 Peter originated from a Petrine circle in Rome, written in the name of its leading figure, the Apostle Peter.[97] Identifying the pseudonymous writer of the letter with Silvanus or another unnamed person does not consider the possibility of the letter originating from a group rather than a single individual. This theory gained significant support and will also be argued in this study. It is highly plausible that there existed a Petrine circle in Rome to which Silvanus, Mark and the unnamed συνεκλεκτή (1 Pet 5:12-13) belonged. This circle owned its existence to the legacy of Peter being associated with Rome. The following arguments substantiate this. This group identified and perpetuated the ideas, theology and views on social reality held by the Apostle Peter, preserved and developed it and eventually conveyed it to Asia Minor. In the light of the above mentioned reasons for attributing the letter to Peter and emphasizing the apostolic authenticity thereof, the situation could be explained if 1 Peter was the product of a group who regarded themselves as the continuation of the traditions and teachings they received from Peter.[98]

---

95. Horrell, *Epistles*, 7; see also Brown et al. 1973; Perkins 1994. Brown et al.

96. Horrell, *Epistles*, 7; cf. Achtemeier, *1 Peter*, 41–42.

97. Elliott, *1 Peter: New Translation*, 127; cf. Elliott, *Estrangement*, 32–36; Elliott, "Peter, Silvanus and Mark"; Elliott 1981, 267–95; Elliott, "Salutation," 66; Eliott & Martin, *James, 1-2 Peter*, 277–78; cf. also Senior, *1&2 Peter*, xiv–xv; Best, *1 Peter*, 62–63; Green, *1 Peter*, 10.

98. Achtemeier, *1 Peter*, 42; cf. Elliott, "Rehabilitation," 9.

This group, situated in Rome, intended the letter to convey the social view and kerygma they derived from Peter.[99]

    a. All missionaries did not operate alone, but had several co-workers. The existence of a group around the Apostle Peter is therefore socially and practically highly plausible. Literary evidence from the New Testament also attest to this fact, e.g., Peter's prominent place among the disciples (Mark 3:13–19 and Mark 1:36). Elliott further states that this group activity was not simply the result of family ties (e.g., Andrew) or geographical location (e.g., Galilee, Jerusalem, Antioch or Corinth), but *par excellence* relations with missionary co-workers and circles of support.[100] Although the New Testament—and Acts in particular—attest more to the activities of the Apostle Paul and his associates, there is no reason why the Apostle Peter would not have acted in a similar way. The early Christian movement was precisely established because of group activities and inter-provincial support and hospitality bestowed on itinerant missionaries.[101]

    b. That Peter worked in a group is also highly possible from a sociological point of view. Religious and social movements are defined by shared experiences, thoughts, visions and actions. According to Elliott only influential and persuasive collective movements had an effect on the course of history.[102] The Jesus movement progressed beyond Palestine and expanded through the activity of missionary networks, household churches and social support groups.

    c. Elliott is of the opinion that the explicit mentioning of Silvanus and Mark in 1 Pet 5:12–13 can be explained if they were actually associated with the Apostle Peter and known to the community where the letter originated from.[103]

    d. The author of the letter does not mention Peter, Silvanus or Mark more than once, which could lead to the conclusion that these persons were known to the addressees by reputation. First Peter 1:1 clearly refers to the Apostle Peter, one of the earliest persons called to follow Jesus, a witness to the suffering of Christ and his resurrection, a prominent representative of the earliest post-Easter Christian movement.[104] It is

---

99. See Elliott, "Peter, Silvanus and Mark," 257.
100. Elliott, *A Home*, 273.
101. Ibid., 273; cf. Messelken "Zur Durchsetzung," 262–63.
102. Elliott, *1 Peter: New Translation*, 128
103. Ibid., 128.
104. Elliott, *A Home*, 274.

possible that some of the recipients of the letter were present on the first Pentecost in Jerusalem and heard the actual preaching of Peter and that the movement thereby spread to Asia Minor (cf. Acts 2:9).

It is, however, important to note that the author of the letter does not only employ Peter's name to establish the authority of the writing but also to convey the solidarity of Peter with the suffering communities in Asia Minor. Therefore the reference to Peter as the συμπρεσβύτερος "fellow elder." This is in accordance with the communal bond between different Christian communities which the letter wants to underscore (cf.κοινωνεῖτε 1 Pet 4:13;κοινωνός 1 Pet 5:1). The fact that 1 Peter mentions the same persons who played active parts at the council of Jerusalem, especially Peter and Silvanus, attests to a cohesion between the church in Jerusalem, now Rome (where the letter probably originated from) and the communities in Asia Minor to whom the letter was addressed. A universal ethnic and geographical diversity made the universal grace and salvation of God a touchable experience. The addressees could identify with each other's suffering as well as with the memory of the tradition of the Apostle Peter who suffered martyrdom in Rome. This gave meaning to their suffering.

Elliott argues that the attribution of the letter to the Apostle Peter has specific theological and strategic purposes.[105] The letter is identified with the person whose theological legacy is reflected in the letter and which inspired the composers thereof. It further functions to create a personal relationship between the significant Roman Christian community and the communities across the Mediterranean. It also plays an important role in the identity that the author wants to convey to his audience: they share in the same faith tradition and message with the prominent Apostle Peter, which again becomes a source of inspiration to them. Peter being witness to the gospel of Christ, and according to the early church tradition, witness in his martyrdom, serves as an example to these Christians to endure their suffering, following in the footsteps of Christ. As far as sharing in the eternal glory of Christ is concerned, Peter also becomes an inspiration, for he was the first of the disciples to have seen the resurrected Christ.[106]

Elliott explains that the only Mark and Silvanus who could have been so well known by reputation, must have been the Silvanus and Mark associated with the church in Jerusalem, which was in contact with at least some of the communities in Asia Minor.[107] The majority of scholars of the New Testament are of the opinion that it is the same Silvanus and (John) Mark

---

105. Ibid., 275.
106. Brown, Donfried, and Reumann, *Der Petrus der Bibel*, 133.
107. Elliott, *1 Peter: New Translation*, 129.

who is mentioned elsewhere in the New Testament. Elliott argues that if this was indeed the case and if these people now belonged to the Petrine circle in Rome, the mentioning of their names would add to the authority as well as the theological strategy of the letter.[108] Mark had a favourable association with Peter, while Silvanus (Silas) was more associated with the missionary activity of Paul, but this need not indicate that Silvanus' theology was solely shaped by Pauline influences. Silvanus described by Acts 15 as a man who enjoyed the honor and respect of the faithful and who was even regarded as a prophet, took part in the meeting gathered in Jerusalem to discuss the Christian mission to the Gentiles.[109] According to the report in Acts of this meeting, Peter and Silvanus played important roles and it is the only other place in the New Testament, apart from 1 Peter, where Peter, Silvanus and Mark (by implication) are mentioned together. They originate from the community in Jerusalem, and they carried this tradition to the new kernel of the Christian church situated in Rome. It is interesting to note that in Acts 15 as well, Silvanus had the function of being the messenger, the bearer of the letter, rather than the secretary.[110] Personal encounters of the recipients with these figures, as Elliott suggests, could be possible, but this is mere speculation.[111]

- e. Of significance for the theology contained in the letter is the mentioning of personal names. Unlike Hebrews and 1John, the author of 1 Peter emphasises the personal bond that exists between him and the recipients of the letter by mentioning the names of persons probably known to the addressees. The mentioning of the names promotes and communicates a personal bond between the senders and the recipients.[112] Further it is important to note that Silvanus is referred to as "brother" ἀδελφοῦ and Markus as "my son" ὁ υἱός μου which corresponds with the strong family imagery which the letter wants to convey, e.g., the believing community is characterised as a "brotherhood" ἀδελφότητι (1 Pet 2:17, 5:9), family or household of God οἶκος (1 Pet 2:5, 4:17). It is argued by the author that the brother and son of Peter, part of the brotherhood in Rome, shared the same experiences as their brothers in Asia Minor.[113] According to Goppelt the mentioning of personal

---

108. Elliott, *A Home*, 276.
109. See Wilson 1973, 178–95.
110. Elliott, *A Home*, 279.
111. Ibid., 273.
112. Ibid., 274.
113. Elliott, *1 Peter: New Translation*, 129.

names add to the authority of the epistle.¹¹⁴ These three persons and their reputations are associated with the earliest Jesus movement, crucial decisions and the initial mission to the Gentile world. Theologically it emphasises the universal message of the grace of God that transgresses ethnical and geographical boundaries. The fact that these persons are associated with the Mother Church in Jerusalem, the antiquity of the traditions they represent gives further weight to the theology of the letter. This argument is in accordance with the letter originating from Rome, "Babylon" (see below), as a melting pot of diverse Christian traditions.¹¹⁵ This group functioned around Peter as the central figure. His name carries the most authority since he was known by the recipients as the primary disciple and eye witness to the ministry and suffering of Christ. Elliott states that "attribution of the letter to Peter appropriately identifies the one within the Roman community to whom its content and theology most owned its origin and inspiration."¹¹⁶ However, this study disagrees with Elliott's view that the Petrine circle bears witness to the Apostle Peter's martyrdom in Rome, since such a martyrdom is not historically conclusive.¹¹⁷

Should all three these names be viewed as fictive because of the pseudographical nature of the letter, the theological significance for the addressees would remain. These persons and their missionary careers and reputations bacame part of the Christian tradition that became known to new converts and their names were associated with crucial moments and developments within their collective memory. They already testified with their own lives to that what they are asking the addressees of the letter to do.

The author(s) of 1 Peter displayed a particular interest in the solidarity and familiar bond which existed between different Christian communities. Therefore they stressed internal harmony and a supportive reaction towards conflict from the outside. The author(s) employed well known figures, the crux of the univerality proclaimed gospel, commonly known liturgical, catechetical and paraenetic traditions, shared experiences of suffering and ostracism and the new identity of the members of the household of God and the accompanying hope in order to emphasise the bond between the senders and the recipients.¹¹⁸ The Petrine circle also used Rome as a location to enhance the authority of the Christian movement. If they were to

114. Goppelt, *Commentary*, 50–52.
115. See Vanhoye, "1 Pierre."
116. Elliott, *1 Peter: New Translation*, 130.
117. Elliott, *A Home*, 273.
118. Ibid., 280.

succeed and the theology of the Petrine circle in Rome could influence the communities in Asia Minor, their prominence would increase.

Horrell is cautious to make final decision about the authorship of the letter, since none of the arguments, for Petrine authorship or against it, are decisively conclusive and he therefore suggest that the question should remain open.[119] To a certain extend, this study agrees with Horrell's view, although authorship by the Apostle seems unconvincing. Yet it could be stated that the identity of the author or group of authors remains unknown.

From this perspective the person who actually wrote the letter is of less importance than the person in whose name the letter was written. Elliott argues that the letter was ascribed to the Apostle Peter because the group responsible for its composition was proclaiming the perspectives, traditions, teaching and theology of the Apostle.[120] It should be noted that Peter is portryed by early Christian literature as the prototype disciple, the one assigned by Christ to proclaim the gospel to take care of the herd. Peter was one of the three elected disciples to witness the glorification of Jesus on the mount. Therefore he received a unique revelation. As previously mentioned, he was the first to confess Jesus as the Christ, the son of the living God. This could even be historically plausible.[121] Since he received the mandate to be the shepherd of the faithfull, he could be seen as the protector of the true and orthodox faith, which explains why the early church composed their writings against heresy around his character. Historical facts about the Apostle Peter are not easily discerned from the tradition that originated around his person and his significance within the early church. Even if some undisputed facts about his career could surface, this will not solve the question of his significance to the early church. The writings of the New Testament and the early church fathers merely gives us an image of Peter, which they used to further their own agendas. Boring notes: "After the church became a worldwide institution within which Peter was an accepted authority figure, material was associated with him or attributed to him that had no connection with the life and ministry of Simon Peter."[122]

In order to address the circumstance of Christians suffering in a hostile world, it was important for the author that his letter is representative of the true Christian faith and the true Christian worldview. More importantly, the letter's Christology is not shaped by narratives of the historical Jesus, but

---

119. Horrell, *1 Peter*, 22–23.

120. Elliott, *1 Peter: New Translation*, 130; cf. Feldmeier, *Der erste Brief*, 26; Horrell, *1 Peter*, 23.

121. Brown, Donfried, and Reumann, *Der Petrus der Bibel*, 145; Boring, *1 Peter*, 20.

122. Boring, *1 Peter*, 26.

by incorporating the meaning of Jesus in the greater worldview. Important for this study is that the works of the *weak, suffering*[123] Jesus became the saving act of God.[124]

Additionally, as Vanhoye argues, the letter of 1 Peter does not only contain the legacy of the Apostle Peter, but also the theology of the church in Rome as the letter's place of composition (as will be argued below).[125]

It should be stated that no final and clearcut conclusion can be reached regarding the authorship of 1 Peter. However, this study agrees with the view of Achtemeier that an anonymous pseudographic author, located in Rome, who drew on traditions associated with the apostle Peter and other early Christian traditions, especially the Pauline writings, is at this stage the "best working hypothesis."[126]

## Date of Composition

Elliott handles the question of the dating of the epistle by establishing a date before which it had to be written (*terminus ad quem*) and a date after which it had to be written (*terminus a quo*).[127] According to available external evidence Irenaeus[128] was the first to cite 1 Peter.[129] However allusions to 1 Peter are already found in the writings of Papias,[130] the letter of Polycarp to the Philippians and the letter ascribed to *1 Clement*, from Rome to the church in Corinth at ca. AD 95. It is however more plausible that these authors were familiar with the same early Christian traditions.[131] *First Clement* for example is also concerned with the problem of elders in the congregation in Corinth establishing a hierarchy and therefore emphasises the importance of unity and equality (cf. 1 Pet 5:1–3). Elliott argues for a composition prior to AD 95, assuming that Clement and Polycarp were familiar with 1 Peter. Achtemeier however notes that if Polycarp did indeed quote 1 Peter, he did so without any reference to a specific passage and when examined in detail proves less convincing.[132] Demonstrable literary quotations from 1 Peter

---

123. My emphasis.
124. Boring, *1 Peter*, 36; 49-72.
125. Vanhoye, "1 Pierre."
126. Achtemeier, *1 Peter*, 43; cf. Boring, *1 Peter*, 29–30.
127. Elliott, *1 Peter: New Translation*, 134–136.
128. Irenaeus, *Haer.* 4.9.2, ca. AD 180.
129. Cf. Hiebert, *First Peter*, 2.
130. Eusebius, *Hist. eccl.* 3.39.17, ca. AD 140.
131. Cf. Osiek, "Apostolic Fathers," 507.
132. Achtemeier, *1 Peter*, 44, cf. Hiebert, *First Peter*, 2.

only occurred in the writings of Irenaeus, Clement from Alexandria and Tertullianus by the end of the second century. Achtemeier also mentions that as far as dating is concerned, one needs to take into consideration that no unanimous church doctrine existed prior to the fourth century and that it is therefore difficult to discern whether a certain doctrine is an earlier or a later development.

Elliott further proposes that a date prior to AD 95 corresponds with the letter of Pliny,[133] written to the Emperor Trajan concerning the Christians in Pontus (ca. AD 111–112). Elliott is of the opinion that although 1 Peter abundantly mentions suffering and harassment, there is no mentioning of people renouncing their faith as Plinius indicates. Therefore Elliott argues for that these denouncements must have occurred after the composition of 1 Peter.

Elliott further substantiates his argumentation for the latest dating of 1 Peter ca. AD 95,[134] by the different situations reflected by 1 Peter and Revelation. By the time of the composition of Revelation (post AD 95) the situation of the Christians in Asia Minor radically deteriorated. First Peter mentioned no Christians being martyred, whereas Revelation mentions that several Christians died.[135] Additionally Elliott argues that the author of 1 Peter exhibits a much more moderate position towards the Roman Empire than the author of Revelation. This study, however, rather follows Achtemeier's argument that the priority of 1 Peter over Revelation cannot be argued on the basis of their different attitudes towards the Roman Empire and especially the Emperor.[136] It could very well be that these documents, addressed to the same geographical area, originated in the same timeframe. Although this study argues for a dating of 1 Peter even later than Revelation by the end of the first century or the beginning of the second, it is concluded that the different views on the Emperor reflected in 1 Peter and Revelation respectively are the result of different theologies held by the authors and therefore does not aid us in determining the dating of 1 Peter. Achtemeier argues for a five year later *terminus ad quem* in order to entertain the possibility that the correspondence between Pliny and Trajanus could describe the exact circumstances addressed in 1 Peter.[137] Yet, Achtemeier is not convinced because of a lack of internal evidence from 1 Peter that actual matyrdom took place and also because there is no citations of 1 Peter in the works

---

133. Pliny, *Ep.* 10.96.
134. Elliott, *1 Peter: New Translation*, 135.
135. Cf. Rev 2:13; 6:9–10; 16:6; 18:24; 19:2.
136. Achtemeier, *1 Peter*, 48.
137. Ibid., 49.

of Ignatius. Therefore Achtemeier concludes that 1 Peter must have been written before Pliny's letters to Trajan. This study, however does not agree. There is no reason to believe that the "suffering" described in 1 Peter could not also include capital punishment and sporadic leathal persecution even though it was not the official policy of the Empire at the time. Zwierlein is of the opinion that it is plausible that 1 Peter could have been composed during the time of Trajan, *id est* around AD 110.[138]

Elliott argues for a composition prior to AD 95 because of the "early character of the letter's theology, its vibrant eschatology and expectation of an imminent coming of Christ."[139] This study completely disagrees with this statement and would rather argue (as will be the case later in the study) that we find in 1 Peter a very highly developed theology and much rather a realised than an imminent eschatology. This argument is also weakened by the fact that the author of 1 Peter knew the traditions of Pauline and deutero-Pauline writings and shows similarities with James, Hebrews and the Gospels of Matthew and Luke, which are all later writings and shows advanced theological thinking.[140]

Elliott is of the opinion that the letter's lack of mentioning internal conflict or conflict with Gnosticism, typical of later New Testament writings, e.g., the Pastoral letters (1–3 John, Jude and 2 Peter) also attests to this earlier dating.

As far as the *terminus a quo* is concerned, Elliott suggests a date after AD 70 on the following grounds.[141]

a. The content of 1 Peter suggests that the author was fimiliar with the Apostle Paul's letter to the Romans, which would require a date after the composition of Romans (ca. AD 56–58).[142]

b. The author refers to Rome as Babylon (1 Pet 5:13). The regarding of Rome as a next Babylon, the destroyer of Jerusalem and the Temple, is found only in documents after AD 70.[143] The composition of 1 Peter after AD 70 also attests to the author being someone else than the Apostle Peter.[144]

---

138. Zwierlein, *Petrus in Rom*, 315.
139. Elliott, *1 Peter: New Translation*, 135.
140. Dschulnigg, *Petrus*, 173.
141. Elliott, *1 Peter: New Translation*, 136–137.
142. Cf. Davids, *First Epistle*, 4.
143. Boring, *1 Peter*, 34.
144. Cf. Zwierlein, *Petrus in Rom*, 7; Michaels, *1 Peter*, lxiii.

c. The fact that the letter is addressed to such a large and wide spread audience,[145] and that Bithynia, Pontus and Cappadocia were not reached by Paul, leads to the conclusion that sufficient time has elapsed in order for Christianity to spread into areas beyond Paul's missionary activity in the fifties.[146] The date of the letter must therefore be at least two to three decates after Paul's missionary activity. First Peter was addressed to Christians living in remote rural areas, not only in the cities, where the Pauline mission was focused.

d. The occurance of πρεσβυτέρους in 1 Peter 5:1 indicates a time of significant growth within the church and a period during which the church became more institutionalised. Boring adds that in the undisputed letters of Paul church leaders are not referred to as "elders."[147]

e. First Peter contains no evidence of inner-conflict between Jewish and Gentile Christians concerning the observance of the Mosaic Law, circumcision anddietary laws. Michaels mentions that the "opponents" of the Christians in 1 Peter are the Gentiles and not the Jews.[148] First Peter 2:4–8 states that it was not the Jews that rejected Christ as the true cornerstone, but people in general. Neither is the law an issue in 1 Peter, and no traces are found of a conflict between the law and the grace of God as in the Pauline epistles. This is an indication of a different situation which requires different theological reflection.[149] The main concern of 1 Peter is rather the conflict of the Christian sect with a hostile outside world. The term "Christian," Χριστιανός, is a concept not used, and probably not known to Paul. Christianity developed as a discernable entity different from Judaism. The earliest apostles, who still were Jews (e.g., James, Peter, John and Paul) already died and their work was continued by circles of disciples and associates who used their names in order to give authority to their writings and to communicate that they stand in the line of a certain tradition.[150] The addressees displayed a mixed ethnic character, and Christianity's break with Judaism had to be justified. Elliott therefore notes that the situation of the recipients is more comparable to that of the audiences who received the Gospels, which focussed on the development of the

145. Elliott, *A Home*, 85.
146. Cf. ibid., 64; cf. Siker, "Christianity," 240.
147. Boring, *1 Peter*, 34.
148. Michaels, *1 Peter*, xlix.
149. Elliott, *A Home*, 85; cf. Achtemeier, *1 Peter*, 39; Boring, *1 Peter*, 34; Davids, *First Epistle*, 25.
150. Elliott, *A Home*, 85.

new Christian identity.¹⁵¹ Siker argues that by the second century AD the concern was no longer establishing a Christian identity different from the Jewish identity, but rather conflict between the Jews and the Christians emerged from Christians viewing themselves as the true Israel and that the Jews who did not confess Christ as the Messiah lost their status as God's elect.¹⁵² Christians also rejected the Jewish religious practices of the day as unpleasing to God.

f. The provinces mentioned in 1 Pet 1:1 attest to the realignment of these provinces by the Roman Emperor, Vespasian in AD 72.¹⁵³

g. The period after AD 72 until the last years of the reign of Domitian (AD 93–96) seemed to be a period of relative stability, tranquillity and prosperity which would provide a situation ideal for the expansion of Christianity over Asia Minor.¹⁵⁴ The moderate stance towards the Roman Empire reflected in 1 Pet 2:13–17 corresponds with this argument, which advocated peaceful social and civic coexistece.

h. Although 1 Peter was probably known by *1 Clement* (circa AD 96),¹⁵⁵ there is no reason to argue for literary dependence.

As Michaels mentions, none of the above is conclusive in itself, but taken together a later date is more plausible.¹⁵⁶ This study would argue an even later dating beyond the turn of the first century AD when Christianity was established as an entity clearly discernable from Judaism which could very likely experienced hostily exactly because of their new identity. This would cohere with 1 Pet 4:12–16, indicating that Christians suffered for "the name of Christ." Again the Pliny-Trajan correspondence illuminates the historical circumstances of charges brought against Christians and them being condemned simply for believing in Christ. There exists no internal evidence from the letter which completely disagrees with a dating beyond the reign of Trajan. Michaels mentions that similarities occur between the situation presupposed in 1 Peter and that presupposed in other sources of the second century, e.g., the Apology of Justin Martyr.¹⁵⁷ Most scholars also agree that 1 Peter does not deal with official Roman persecution, rather with

---

151. Ibid., 85.
152. Siker, "Christianity"; cf. Osiek, "Apostolic Fathers," 516.
153. See Filson, "Peter"; Elliott, *A Home*, 60, 91.
154. Cf. Elliott, *A Home*, 84–87; Green, *1 Peter*, 8–9; Boring, *1 Peter*, 33; Michaels, *1 Peter*, lxiii.
155. Hiebert, *First Peter*, 2; see Hagner 1973, 239–46.
156. Michaels, *1 Peter*, lxvi.
157. Ibid., lxv.

social hostility which could lead to sporadic charges and convictions which sometimes resulted in capital punishment.[158]

This study rather prefers a later dating which would imply that 1 Peter is a Christian writing originating from the second century AD. Siker notes that the second and third century Christian writings have great significance in depicting the development of Christianity from the time of Jesus and the Apostles to Eusebius.[159] The second century further shows an additional Christian canon developing alongside the Septuagint, since the letters and Gospels were also read in the services of the congregations. A new collection of writings became authoritative.[160] Second Peter is a clear example that the Pauline letters were already regarded as Scripture (cf. 2 Pet 3:15–17). The apostles and eyewitnesses to the ministry of Christ were no longer alive and it became increasingly important for the early Christian church to preserve the traditions linked to Jesus and the apostles.

## Sources

### *The Citation and Use of Sacred Scripture*

The Old Testament is one of the author's most prominent sources and is by far the source to which explicit reference is most frequently made. According to Boring, 1 Peter is only second to Revelation as the book in the New Testament which relies the most on the Old Testament.[161] It is remarkable how the author has no difficulty to apply Jewish sacred Scripture to the Christian church. He often gives a Christological interpretation of Old Testament literature.[162] Christ becomes the "corner stone of Zion" (1 Pet 2:4–6) and is automatically viewed as the suffering servant of Isaiah 53 (1 Pet 2:22–25). Cited consistently according to the Greek version (LXX), the Old Testament supplied the author with a rich variety of direct quotations, allusions and motifs. On the whole 1 Peter seems to contain at least forty-six citations from the Old Testament (LXX).[163] Four books of the Pentateuch (Genesis, Exodus, Leviticus, Deuteronomy), four of the latter Prophets (Isaiah, Hosea, Ezekiel, Malachi) and three of the writings (Psalms, Proverbs, Job) are

---

158. Cf. Horrell, *Epistles*, 9.
159. Siker, "Christianity," 231.
160. Cf. Gamble, *Canon*; McDonald, *Formation*; Metzger, *Canon*.
161. Boring, *1 Peter*, 39, cf. Best, *1 Peter*, 29; Davids, *First Epistle*, 23–24.
162. Michaels, *1 Peter*, xl.
163. Cf. Elliott, *1 Peter: New Translation*, 15; Horrell, *Epistles*, 12; see also Best 1969, 217–75; Schutter, *Hermeneutic*;.

represented and with a concentration on three writings in particular (Pss 33, 34 in 3:10–12—Psalms 11x, Isaiah 21x, Proverbs 6x).[164] Achtemeier further notes that the author draws all his imagery from the Old Testament.[165] Lohse also notes that early Christian paraenetic literature was especially fond of Wisdom Psalms and Proverbs.[166]

Linking the eschatological community with the history of God's covenant people, this material served to stress the social estrangement and oppression of God's people as resident aliens in Diaspora (1:1, 17–18; 2:11; 3:6 [Gen 23:4; cf. Gen 12:1–20; 20:1–18; Isa 52:3, 5] 3:10–12 [Ps 33[34]; 5:8–9, 13 [Jer 50–1]); their election to holiness (1:15–16 [Lev 19:2]; 2:5, 9 [Exod 19:6; Isa 43:20; Hos 1:6, 9 2:1, 3, 25]); the rejection, suffering and exaltation of the Messiah-Servant (2:4–8 [Isa 8:14; 28:16; Ps 117 [118]:22]; 2:22–24 [Isa 53:4, 6, 9]; divine redemption of the righteous oppressed (1:13 [Exod 12:11], 1:17–19; cf. 1:2 [Exod 12–15; Isa 52:3, 5]); the examples of Sarah (3:5–6 [Gen 18:12]) and Noah (3:20 [Gen 6–8]); fear of God rather than man (2:17 [Prov 24:21]; 3:6 [Prov 3:25]; 3:14–15 [Isa 8:12–13]); moral conduct (3:10–12 [Ps 33:13–17 (34:12–16)]; 4:8 [Prov 10:12]; the imminence of divine judgment (2:12[Isa 10:3]; 4:17 [Ezek 9:6]; 4:18 [Prov 11:31 LXX]; 5:7 [Ps 54[55]:23]). Motifs and themes of the Exodus and Passover tradition also figure prominently (sprinkling the blood of the Passover Lamb, 1:2, 19; inheritance, 1:4; 3:7, 9 girding of lions, 1:13; redemption, 1:18; Exodus covenant and election, 2:4–10; cf. 1:1 and 5:13; alien residence, 1:17, 2:11, mighty hand of God, 5:6).[167]

The Petrine author makes abundant use of the OT; but the letter as a whole is no discernable "homily" on any particular Old Testament text or combination of texts. Its primary focus is not an Old Testament text to be interpreted but a suffering community to be consoled and encouraged.[168] The letter employs a diversity of Old Testament texts, motifs and themes in order to illustrate the ancient heritage to which the Christian brotherhood is heir and to provide scriptural and hence authoritative substantiation for its message of affirmation and exhortation.[169] Davids mentions that the author weaves allusions to the Old Testament into his text in order to strengthen

---

164. Cf. Achtemeier, *1 Peter*, 12, Feldmeier, *Der erste Brief*, 18.
165. Achtemeier, *1 Peter*, 12.
166. Lohse, "Parenesis," 55.
167. Cf. Elliott, *1 Peter: New Translation*, 17.
168. Schutter, *Hermeneutic*, 172–76.
169. Cf. Feldmeier, *Der erste Brief*, 18.

his letter with the authority of the Old Testament.[170] The quotations on the other hand serve to enhance and reinforce the argument.

### *Other Literature and Traditions of Israel*

First Peter contains no explicit citation of the writings of Qumran, or the works of Philo and Josephus. On the whole, however, the author is clearly familiar with concepts, terminology, traditions and perspectives which occurred in this diverse body of literature.[171]

Although not quoted explicitly in 1 Peter, 1 Enoch (especially chapters 6–36, 65–67, 106–108) is one important representative of a broad Israelite tradition concerning the Noachic flood and its surrounding events. This tradition contains several motifs, concepts and themes which the Petrine author employed in 3:19–20 and illustrates as well the cosmology presumed in these verses, as Spitta indicated.[172]

The Qumran writings and 1 Peter reveal a similar eschatological perspective in their use of the OT, their conception of a community as an elect and holy people of the covenant in conflict with outsiders, their ethical exclusivity concerning admissions to the community, and their distinctive behaviour within the community.[173] However, substantial differences exist, especially regarding the conceptualization and identification of the Messiah and the community's engagement with society. Whereas the Qumran community embraced an ascetic lifestyle and geographical withdrawal from society, 1 Peter suggests a distinctive identity and ethic, yet with an attractive openness to non-believers. Achtemeier adds that it should be remembered that the Qumran community and early Christianity shared the same thought world and that the one is not necessarily dependent on the other for general ideas such as election, baptism, the fulfillment of prophecies, the eschatological punishment of the wicked and the deliverance of the faithful.[174] However, a more specific point of agreement would be the reference to "strangers" and "exiles" as a means to describe the situation of the members of the movement and their experience of the outside world. According to Achtemeier these descriptions point to a similarity in self-understanding.[175] Achtemeier also notes the remarkably different outcome of both these

170. Davids, *First Epistle*, 25.
171. Elliott, *1 Peter: New Translation*, 17.
172. Spitta, *Christi Predigt*.
173. Cf. Boring, *1 Peter*, 40.
174. Achtemeier, *1 Peter*, 13.
175. Ibid., 13.

understandings: the Qumran community completely isolated itself from the outside world and disengaged with society, whereas the addressees of 1 Peter are encouraged to continue living in the society with the possibility of transforming it. Feldmeier adds that the Diaspora-motif plays a central role in the theology of 1 Peter, and he refers to the self-understanding of the community as "foreigners," the motif of re-birth and the description of their salvation as imperishable.[176] This shows a clear influence of Hellenistic Judaism. Davids argues, and this study agrees, that these themes were influencing the general thought world of the author and his addressees.[177] These would have been recognised by his audience.

On the whole the similarities between 1 Peter and Philo of Alexandria are of a general nature and do not require an insistence on literary dependence. The writings of Philo illustrate the perspectives of a Diaspora Jew on the social and cultural conventions of the age of a tense relation between Judaism and secular society, a situation that offered an analogy for the dilemma of the Jesus movement. One remarkable analogy between Peter and Philo, however involves their common appeal to and similar exposition of the covenant formula of Exod 19:3–6. Like Philo, the Petrine author also knew and adapted the Hellenistic household management (*oikonomia*) tradition in 2:13—3:7, 5:1–5a.[178] Both authors also shared social perspectives typical of Diaspora Judaism and its familiarity with Greco-Roman social, cultural and ethical traditions.

### Greco-Roman Thought, Diction and Culture

The author of 1 Peter nowhere exactly cites an ancient secular text, although he appears to be familiar with the language, rhetoric, diction, literary conventions and moral exhortation contained in virtues, vices and household codes. This familiarity is a result of the cultural heritage and the prominence of Hellenistic culture at the time of composition.[179] However it is much rather the Septuagint, Israelite and early Christian traditions that took form in a Hellenistic context that influenced the author, than Greco-Roman literature as such.[180] However the key first century Mediterranean values, honor and shame, the gender constructions, reciprocity, etc., are reflected in 1 Peter.

---

176. Feldmeier, *Der erste Brief*, 19.
177. Davids, *First Epistle*, 25.
178. Elliott, *A Home*, 208–20; Prostmeier, *Handlungsmodelle*, 278–99.
179. Cf. Boring, *1 Peter*, 41.
180. Cf. Elliott, *1 Peter: New Translation*, 19.

## New Testament and Early Christian Tradition

Elliott argues for the employment of a common Christian tradition by the various authors of the New Testament rather than exact literary dependence.[181] Horrell indicates that there occur no explicit citations of the Gospel tradition in 1 Peter.[182] References exist in the form of allusions.[183] Of these the allusions to the Sermon on the Mount are the clearest[184]. This became evident with the rise of redaction criticism during the 1920s.[185] The history of the transmission and alterations to commonly used material and the specific interests of the various authors came into focus. Thorough exegesis of New Testament text demonstrated an underlying tradition that influenced the different writings of the New Testament. These oral traditions took different literal forms as illustrated by form criticism. These included kerugmatik, exhortatory, liturgical and catechetical traditions and were employed in different contexts to instruct, console, serve as apologies or polemics, or in early Christian worship. Carrington[186] especially emphasised the catechetical tradition, employed for the instruction of new converts to the Christian movement which was associated with baptism. The four main themes included in this catechism included the departure of the evil ways of the past, subjection, watchfulness and the resistance of temptations. The catechism was introduced by a prayer for knowledge and wisdom and the acceptance of the Word of truth.[187] This catechism was used in the fifties AD in the Gentile mission.

Selwyn on the other hand discerned four different traditions employed in 1 Peter including liturgical and hymnal material, persecution, catechism and *Verba Christi*.[188] Elliott elaborates on these themes by adding the following:[189]

a. Christological and kerygmatic formulas which existed in hymns and creeds or which still circulated independently. These formulas display

---

181. Elliott, *1 Peter: New Translation*, 21.

182. Horrell, *Epistles*, 12.

183. See Thompson *Clothed with Christ*, 37–63.

184. See examples below.

185. Cf. Selwyn, *St. Peter: Greek Text*, 363–466; Lohse, "Paraenesis"; Kelly, *Peter and Jude*, 11–15; Best, *1 Peter*; Elliott, 1976; Millauer, *Leiden als Gnade*; Brox 1978a; Brox, *Petrusbrief* (2nd ed); Cothenet, "Les Orientations"; Vanhoye, "1 Pierre"; Michaels, *1 Peter*, xi–xl; Goppelt, *Commentary*, 33–55.

186. Carrington, *The Primitive*.

187. Ibid., 31.

188. Selwyn, *St. Peter: Greek Text*, 17–24; cf. Achtemeier, *1 Peter*, 22.

189 Elliott, *1 Peter: New Translation*, 30.

the following features: They are about Jesus Christ, who was foreknown by God before the foundation of the world (1 Pet 1:20), who in his lifetime did no wrong (1 Pet 2:22), who was rejected by humans, but honored by God (1 Pet 2:4), who suffered for the sake of others (1 Pet 2:21), who did not insult when he was insulted (1 Pet 2:23), who endured his suffering committed to God as the One who judges righteously (1 Pet 2:23), who was crucified ( 1 Pet 2:24), through whose wounds the believers were healed (1 Pet 2:24), who received complete salvation for the sins of the faithful (1 Pet 3:18), who was righteous, but suffered for the unrighteous (1 Pet 3:18), who died in the flesh, but was resurrected by the spirit (1 Pet 3:18, 4:1), who was raised from the grave by God and received glory (1 Pet 1:3, 22), who ascended to heaven (1 Pet 3:22), who sits at the right hand of God (1 Pet 3:22), who has authority over angels and powers (1 Pet 3:22), whose glory will be revealed in full (1 Pet 1: 7, 13; 5:4). These Christological kerygmatic formulas served as a model for Christian believe, hope, behaviour and trust in God. These formulas explained indicatives and grounded consequent imperatives.[190]

b. Traditions associated with Baptism, e.g., the technical term used for baptism, βάπτισμα, occurs in 1 Pet 3:21, metaphorical references to baptism like to be "born again" in 1 Pet 3:22 and "new born babies" in 1 Pet 2:2, baptism as a means to become "children of God" in 1 Pet 1:14, baptism brought in relation with hearing the truth of the word in 1 Pet 1:12, 22–25; 4:17, baptism as transformation expressed in "formerly/now" in 1 Pet 1:14–17, 2:9, 25, 4:2–4 and baptism's moral obligations to renounce the former and embrace the new in 1 Pet 2:1, 11; 3:9, and 4:2–4, 15. Elliott states that although "baptism" is explicitly mentioned only once in the letter, the author presupposes the baptism of the addressees and uses it as the grounds for moral instruction.[191]

c. Liturgical tradition. Although most scholars do not consider 1 Peter to be a baptismal liturgy, traditions from early Christian liturgies are evident. In 1 Pet 1:2 there is the trinitarian formula related to baptism. In 1 Pet 1:3–5 the blessing with hymnic predicate for God is found as well as in 1 Pet 1:6, 8, and 4:13, which was typical of cultic texts. First Peter 4:11 and 5:11 contain doxologies and an "amen." The liturgical traditions functioned to emphasise the themes and traditions that were known to the senders of the letter as well as to the recipients,

---

190 Cf. Lohse, "Parenesis."
191 Elliott, *1 Peter: New Translation*, 34.

d. Hortatory Tradition. The Qumran writings contained moral instructions and regulations regarding behaviour within the community and exponents of Diaspora Judaism, e.g., Philo, documented ethical instructions. In the Greco-Roman world catalogues containing lists of vices and virtues and moral instructions regarding the management of the household were widely known. Christian authors employed these moral instructions, although they re-interpreted them in terms of their obedience to the will of God. The author of 1 Peter used phrases and formulas commonly associated with moral instruction. Fifty-one finite imperatives occur in 1 Peter in the present and aorist tenses, as well as seven participles used imperatively. The author also employed the Old Testament wisdom tradition in 1 Pet 3:10–12 (Ps 33[34]:13–17); 1 Pet 4:8 (Prov 10:12 from the Masoretic Text); 1 Pet 4:18 (Prov 11:31 from the Septuagint); 1 Pet 5:5 (Prov 3:34 from the Septuagint) and 1 Pet 5:6 (Ps 54 [55]:23 from the Septuagint). Lists of vices and virtues are found in 1 Pet 2:1, 3:8, 4:3, 15, 4:8–11. First Peter also contains an example of the *Haustafel*,[192] frequently occurring in the New Testament concerning the relations of husbands and wives, parents and children, slaves and masters, the old and the young in 1 Pet 2:18—3:7 and 5:1–5. *Verba Christi* are cited in 1 Pet 2:12 (Matt 5:16); 1 Pet 2:19–20 (Luke 6:32–34); 1 Pet 3:14 (Matt 5:10); 1 Pet 5:1–5 (Matt 20:20–28 / Mark 10:35–45 / Luke 22:24–27). Davids mentions that the author does not simply copy the *Haustafel* from Paul, but he employs a common tradition to his unique situation.[193] Michaels notes that a distinctive difference is that the author starts his section on the house hold duties with a more universal approach, including the responsibility towards the authorities as well as to every human being outside of the Christian community.[194] According to Michaels the author employs much more of the sayings of Jesus than from the traditional house hold codes and he applies these sayings to concrete situations.

e. Selwyn argued that the author of 1 Peter relied on the passion tradition in order to give the audience a positive perspective on the suffering that they are experiencing.[195] Nauck agrees with this by stating that 1 Peter is the New Testament writing that relies on this tradition the

---

192. Cf. Davids, *First Epistle*, 11.
193. Ibid., 12; cf. Schnelle, *History and Theology*, 410.
194. Michaels, *1 Peter*, xlii–xliii.
195. Selwyn, *St. Peter: Greek Text*, 439–458.

most.[196] Imagery of rejoicing in suffering, solidarity with the suffering Christ who will be glorified by God and enduring faith characterises the letter from beginning to end (1 Pet 1:6–8; 2:18–25, 3:13–4:1; 4:12–16; 5:8–9, 10–11).[197]

From this abundance of early Christian traditions and teachings New Testament authors drew in order to compose their writings.[198] First Peter shows similarities with other New Testament writings, since they drew from the same tradition. This is much more plausible than trying to argue for one New Testament document being literary depended upon another. Achtemeier convincingly argues that the author of 1 Peter was well established within the early Christian tradition and employed individual elements which he applied to a particular situation.[199] He further adds that the early Christian tradition was "linguistically stabilised" and represented a fusion between Synoptic and Pauline elements.[200] In addition, this tradition originated from the Palestinian church, grounded in the Old Testament and influenced by the gentile Hellenistic churches.[201]

Therefore, the similarities between 1 Peter and other New Testament writings are the consequence of these common traditions rather than a literary dependence.[202] The author of 1 Peter displays a particular affinity for traditions also reflected in Paul's letter to the Romans and the Deutero-Pauline letter to the Ephesians.[203] Similarities between 1 Peter and Romans include the following: 1 Pet 1:14–16 (Rom 12:2); 1 Pet 1:21 (Rom 4:24); 1 Pet 1:22, 3:8–9 (Rom 12:9–19); 1 Pet 2:4–10 (Rom 9:25, 32–33); 1 Pet 2:5 (Rom 12:1, 15:16, 31), 1 Pet 2:6–8 (Rom 9:33 [Isa 28:6; Ps 117:22, Isa 8:14] Rom 14:13); 1 Pet 2:13–17 (Rom 13:1, 3, 7); 1 Pet 3:22 (Rom 8:34); 1 Pet 4:1 (Rom 6:7, 10); 1 Pet 4:8–11 (Rom 12:3–13). Achtemeier draws attention to the similarities being mostly from Rom 9–13 and in Rom 9, Paul also quoted from the Old Testament, and in Rom 13 the similarity occurs in the Christians responsibility to the state.[204] This again strengthens the

---

196. Nauck, "Probleme," 80.

197. See Lohse, "Parenesis"; Thomas, "First Epistle"; and De Villiers, "Joy in Suffering."

198. Cf. Lohse, "Parenesis," 42.

199. Achtemeier, 1 Peter, 21.

200. Cf. Johnson "Asia Minor," 117; Boring, 1 Peter, 39.

201. Cf. Goppelt, Commentary, 54, 56.

202. Horrell, 1 Peter, 35–40; cf. Davids, First Epistle, 26.

203. Cf. Achtemeier, 1 Peter, 15–16; Schnelle, History and Theology, 410–411; Michaels, 1 Peter, xliv.

204 Achtemeier, 1 Peter, 16.

argument that the author of 1 Peter was not literary dependent on Paul, but that both authors drew from the early Christian tradition's exhortation and catechetical materials.

Affinities with Ephesians include: 1 Pet 1:2, 20 (Eph 1:4–5); 1 Pet 1:3 (Eph 1:3, 18–19); 1 Pet 1:13 (Eph 6:14); 1 Pet 1:14–18, 4:2–3 (Eph 4:17–18, 5:8); 1 Pet 1:20 (Eph 1:4); 1 Pet 2:1 (Eph 4:25; 31); 1 Pet 2:4–6 (Eph 2:19–22); 1 Pet 2:18–20 (Eph 6:5–9); 1 Pet 3:1 (Eph 5:22); 1 Pet 3:7 (Eph 5:25–33); 1 Pet 3:18, 22 (Eph 1:20–21, 4:8–10); 1 Pet 5:8–9 (Eph 6:11–13). As far as correlation between 1 Peter and Ephesians is concerned, Achtemeier is also of the opinion that it is the result of the use of common Christian tradition and citations from the Old Testament.[205] Furthermore, the epistles were indented to address different theological aspects.

In general the writing of 1 Peter reflects the same structure as a typical Pauline epistle, including the greeting mentioning the sender and the addressees, the division of the letter body and the final greetings. The author of 1 Peter used typically Pauline language, e.g. ἐν Χριστῷ, ἀποκαλύψει, διακονέω, χάρισμα. First Peter echoes the same Pauline theology of God who takes the initiative in human salvation through the passion and resurrection of Jesus Christ, in which new life and freedom from sin is given to those who believe.[206]

Elliott, however, emphasised the significant differences between 1 Peter and the Pauline writings.[207] According to Elliott these differences "constitute incontestable evidence" that although the Pauline writings might have been known to the author of 1 Peter, both authors drew from the same tradition, because 1 Peter is remarkably different. Arguments that the author of 1 Peter depended on Paul, was an exponent of Pauline theology, a member of the Pauline circle or that there was a polemic between the two authors are unconvincing.[208] Horrell agrees that 1 Peter is not simply a pseudo-Pauline document reflecting a later stage in the development of early Christianity.[209] The fact that two to three decades passed since Paul's missionary activity in Asia Minor and the composition of 1 Peter, as well as the spread of Christianity to vast and remote rural areas like Cappadocia, provides significant evidence not to associate 1 Peter with a Pauline circle as

---

205. Ibid., 17.
206. Achtemeier, *1 Peter*, 18, cf. Schelkle, *Die Petrusbriefe*, 5.
207. Elliott, *1 Peter: New Translation*, 40; cf. Elliott, "Rehabilitation," 7–8; Boring, *1 Peter*, 42.
208. Cf. Elliott, "Rehabilitation," 9.
209. Horrell, *1 Peter*, 2.

far as origin, intentand address are concerned.[210] Achtemeier also indicates significant differences between 1 Peter and Paul as far as language and content are concerned.[211] There is no mentioning in 1 Peter of the "old" and the "new Adam" and the author of 1 Peter expresses the atonement in terms of the Suffering Servant imagery drawn from Isaiah 53, which does not occur in Paul. Paul employs the "cross" whereas the author of 1 Peter speaks about "passion." This is a significant difference which will receive more attention later in this study.

Some other prominent Pauline imagery are also absent from 1 Peter. These include: the church as the body of Christ, the work of the Holy Spirit, the emphasis on justification by faith and not by law and very importantly the absence of any tension between the Jews and the Christians. In 1 Peter imagery used to describe Israel's exclusive status as God's elect is simply applied to the Christian church.

The common Christian tradition employed by both authors explains the similarities between them; however each author applied these traditions differently, since they each had their own theology and addressed Christian communities in different social contexts. This would explain the "Pauline flavour" of 1 Peter.[212] It is also difficult to determine whether the author of 1 Peter was familiar with the Pauline writings, actually read them, or if so much time already passed that Pauline material became well established in the early Christian tradition. Achtemeier also concludes that although the author used and developed certain Pauline ideas,[213] 1 Peter was not an attempt to "defend Paulinism" or to simply reflect on the theology of Paul. Boring even suggests that 1 Peter represents the acknowledgement of the Roman church as Peter's prominence over Paul.[214] Pauline traditions rather serve the Petrine tradition. Achtemeier emphasises that the similarities between Pauline literature and 1 Peter exist more on a linguistic level than as far as the content is concerned. The theological distinctiveness of 1 Peter is much bigger than linguistic similarities. Therefore Horrell also emphasises the distinctive character of 1 Peter and the unique literal and rhetorical strategy employed by the author.[215] Boring even suggest a distinctive Petrine tradition and stream of theological development. This view will be developed further in the existing study. Boring is adamant that a general

---

210. Elliott, *A Home*, 65.
211. Achtemeier, *1 Peter*, 18.
212. Ibid., 18–19; cf. Brown, Donfried, and Reumann, *Der Petrus der Bibel*, 132.
213. Achtemeier, *1 Peter*, 19.
214. Boring, *1 Peter*, 43.
215. Horrell, *1 Peter*, 2; cf. also Boring, *1 Peter*, 33.

Christian tradition does not exist.[216] There rather was a variety of traditions including the Markan, Pauline and Johanine traditions. Peter shows very few contact or knowledge of the Johanine tradition, but gives more prominence to Gospel traditions and especially the Pauline tradition.

Likewise 1 Peter and James are both general letters intended for an audience in the Diaspora. Both drew from the wisdom tradition and display a hortatory tone. They are concerned with emphasizing the distinctiveness of the Christian community against the outside world. Yet, they also demonstrate significant differences. James has the life within the Christian community in view, while the focus of 1 Peter is primarily on the relation of the Christian community towards the hostile outside world which caused the Christians to endure suffering.[217]

First Peter also shows considerable similarities with Hebrews, e.g., 1 Pet 1:1, 2:11 (Heb 11:13); 1 Pet 1:2 (Heb 12:24); 1 Pet 1:23 (Heb 4:12); 1 Pet 2:25, 5:4 (Heb 13:20); 1 Pet 3:9 (Heb 12:17); 1 Pet 3:18 (Heb 9:28); 1 Pet 4:14 (Heb 13:13). Both these writings address the themes of social alienation and solidarity with the suffering Christ and it could also be argued that the situation of the recipients corresponded in how they were ostracised from society.[218]

According to Elliot commonalities between 1 Peter and the Synoptic Gospels emerged from the employment of the sayings of Jesus and the tradition of the passion of Christ.[219] Horrell adds similarities between 1 Peter and the Sermon on the Mount (1 Pet 2:12 / Matt 5:16, 1 Pet 2:19–20 / Luke 6:32–34, 1 Pet 3:14 / Matt 5:10 / Luke 6:22, 1 Pet 4:13–14 / Matt 5:11–12).[220] Again, Davids notes that these traditions are not literary citations, but rather allusions—the reference is clear, but the author uses them for his unique purpose. Michael also notes that it becomes clear that the author used the pre-synoptic tradition rather than the finished Gospels.[221] This will become important for the purpose of this study.

Related motifs and themes with the Gospel of John include rebirth (1 Pet 1:3, 23 / John 3:3, 7); mutual love (1 Pet 1:22, 3:8, 4:8 / John 13:14, 15:12); Jesus as the Shepherd and the command to the shepherd to attend to the flock (1 Pet 2:25, 5:4 / John 10:11, 14; 1 Pet 5:2 / John 21:15–17).

---

216. Boring, *1 Peter*, 41–42.

217. Elliott, *1 Peter: New Translation*, 23–24.

218. Brox, "Der erste Petrusbrief in der literarischen Tradition," 185; Michaels, *1 Peter*, xliv.

219. Elliott, *1 Peter: New Translation*, 25; cf. Davids, *First Epistle*, 27.

220. Horrell, *1 Peter*, 35; cf. Green, *1 Peter*, 231.

221. Michaels, *1 Peter*, xli.

Achtemeier argues that these similarities are so familiar to the broader Christian teaching, and often goes back to the person or teaching of Jesus himself, that no argument for a literal dependency would endure.[222] The rebirth-imagery would rather point to a shared spiritual climate.

The similarities between 1 Peter and the speeches of Peter in Acts also rather suggest common Christian tradition than support for authorship by the Apostle. However, Elliott advocates the probability of the existence of a Petrine circle, within which certain theological themes and traditions associated with the Apostle Peter circulated.[223]

Similar to 1 Peter and Jude is their employment of the flood tradition, which they linked with condemnation and salvation and themes including election, holiness, the expectation of the return of Christ and prophecy. However, the two writings display completely different vocabulary, styles, sources, situations and theology.[224]

First Peter barely corresponds with Revelation. Although both writings are concerned with innocent Christian suffering, are addressed to the same geographical area, refer to Rome as Babylon and originated after AD 70, the theologies and particularly the authors' view of the Roman Empire differ significantly.

Many New Testament scholars therefore viewed 1 Peter as a melting pot of Christian traditions which came together at the church in Rome.[225] Feldmeier is of the opinion that it is typical of the "catholic" epistles to integrate the various Christian traditions drawn from the very foundational earliest oral traditions, the Jesus traditions from the various Gospels and the Pauline traditions and then process it to unique and independent theology.

According to Goppelt, diverse early Christian traditions were woven into a new form of theology.[226] However, the author did not simply summarize various Christian traditions into one letter. The author rather had a specific aim in arranging his data in a particular way which correlated with his own theological agenda. Marks of the author's unique literal creativity are also visible throughout the letter.[227] Green elaborates on these by mentioning the author's emphasis on the suffering of Christ, his emphasis

---

222. Achtemeier, *1 Peter*, 21.
223. Elliott, *1 Peter: New Translation*, 25.
224. Ibid., 27.
225. Cf. Feldmeier, *Der erste Brief*, 19.
226. Goppelt, *Commentary*, 22.
227. Horrell, *1 Peter*, 42, cf. Green, *1 Peter*, 232.

on hope, his response to the authorities and to the hostile outsiders and his concern with the identity of the church.[228]

## Place of Origin

Rome as the place of origin of 1 Peter is preferred by most scholars.[229] Internal evidence from the letter itself also attests to this fact. Early church tradition identifies both Mark and Peter with Rome, a theory that will be developed further in this study. Green is so convinced of this that he views Rome as the author of 1 Peter's main concern.[230] It is the *Roman*[231] paganistic religions, the *Roman* imperialistic practices, the presense of *Roman* governors and armies, the *Roman* worldview that everyone is being subjected to and the *Roman* law that dictates matters of law and order. According to Green, Rome is the enemy and the cause of all the suffering experienced by Christians.[232] By referring to Rome as "Babylon," the author also reminds his audience of the suffering endured by the Judeans because of the destruction of Jerusalem in 586 BC and the Babilonian exile. This hostility is relived through Rome as another oppressive world power.

"Babylon" is explicitly mentioned as the place where the letter was sent from, which as mentioned above, is associated with Rome afer AD 70. Elliott,[233] in agreement with Goppelt,[234] rejects the idea that Babylon is used as a "codename" for Rome, to insure secrecy surrounding the geographical position of the author as is the case in Revelation. Distinctively different from the author of Revelation, the author of 1 Peter does not view the Roman Empire in a negative way, nor is he attributing the suffering and harassment of the recipients to Rome. When the letter refers to Roman authority (1 Pet 2:14, 17), the audience is urged to respect the Emperor. Furthermore, the author instructs his addressees to maintain honorable conduct and not to engage in revolutionary activity. Concealing the name of the place of origin would therefore be unnecessary. It is rather a case of symbolism, just as

---

228. Green, *1 Peter*, 160.

229. Cf. Horrell, *1 Peter*, 23; Horrell, *Epistles*, 7; Achtemeier, *1 Peter*, 64; Feldmeier, *Der erste Brief*, 27; Böttrich, *Petrus*, 222; Boring, *1 Peter*, 38; Schnelle, *History and Theology*, 402–403; Hiebert, *First Peter*, 18; see Zwierlein, *Petrus in Rom*, 7–11.

230. Green, *1 Peter*, 1.

231. My emphasis.

232. Green, *1 Peter*, 1.

233. Elliott, *1 Peter: New Translation*, 132; cf. Horrell, *Epistles*, 8; Feldmeier, *Der erste Brief*, 28; Boring, *1 Peter*, 38.

234. Goppelt, *Commentary*, 375.

Babylon was the world power which destroyed Jerusalem and the Temple in 586 BC, Rome is now the next world power which also suppressed Judea, destroyed the Temple and scattered the Judeans all over the Mediterranean world, continuing the Diaspora.[235] Felmeier also mentions that Babylon is linked with the Diaspora and the experience of the Judean exiles of being "foreigners and sojourners" and therefore evokes powerfull associations among the audience.[236]

According to 1 Peter the Christians in Rome and in Asia Minor experience the same suffering and are therefore a supportive brotherhood to one another. Horrell seems to agree with this view by referring to similarities that exist between 1 Peter and other New Testament writings connected with Rome, e.g., Paul's letter to the Romans.[237] Although, as indicated above, the similarities between Romans and 1 Peter are not to be ascribed to literary dependence but rather to a conglomoration of ideas and knowledge of the same traditions. Also, as will be argued below, it was in the interest of the church in Rome to compose a letter of a circular nature, and consequently the Roman church increased its influence in early Christianity.

Elliott further argues that Rome makes sense from a geographical point of view.[238] In the sequence of the mentioning of the provinces in 1 Pet 1:1, Pontus is mentioned first, an ideal place of departure for Silvanus, the bearer of the letter, on his journey from the West by ship. Bithynia is mentioned last, would indicate that he then departed from the port of Puteoli or Ostia on his return to Rome. Although this argument is not conclusive, it does have merit. Pliny the Younger took a similar route on his departure from Rome to Bithynia Pontus.[239] The route proposed also makes sense when it is considered that Cilicia, Lycia and Pamphylia, which lie to the south of the Taurus range, are not included in the addressees.[240]

Additionally, Peter, Mark and 1 Peter are all associated with Rome (an argument that will be developed later in this study), which is attested by *1 Clement* (5:1–7) and Ignatius (*Rom. 4.3*). Papias and Clement of Alexandria also attested to 1 Peter originating from Rome.[241] Tradition also maintains that Peter was martyred in Rome during Nero's persecution of

---

235. Cf. Achtemeier, *1 Peter*, 63, Feldmeier, *Der erste Brief*, 27.
236. Cf. Green, *1 Peter*, 1.
237. Horrell, *1 Peter*, 24.
238. Elliott, *1 Peter: New Translation*, 133.
239. Pliny, *Ep*. 10.15–17.
240. Elliott, *1 Peter: New Translation*, 91.
241. Eusebius, *Hist. eccl.* 2.15.2; cf. Achtemeier, *1 Peter*, 63, see also Böttrich, *Petrus*, 222–223.

the Christians as the scapegoats of the catastrophic fire of AD 64. However, as indicated above, this tradition is legendary rather than historical. But, having said that, it remains that the Church in Rome could very possibly be the conflux of Markan, Pauline and Petrine traditions and theology, since it was already a place where many cultures, traditions, religions and theologies met.[242] If Elliott's theory of a Petrine circle in Rome, as accepted by this study, is taken into account it would be highly unlikely that a Christian community in the heart of the Roman Empire, at the centre of political, economical and cultural power, would not take advantage of its location. From Rome they could excercise significant influence on other Christian communities elsewhere in the Roman Empire.[243] This influence was answered with the respect with which other Christian communities regarded the Chrurch in Rome. Therefore Elliott argues that 1 Peter could be regarded as the first document attesting to the Roman Christians' attempt to establish a greater influence and bridge with the communities in Asia Minor.[244] Both words *influence* and *bridge* need to be stressed although respectively. The Roman Church indeed excircised significant influence on other Christian communities in such a way that it became the ecclesiastical capitol of Christianity. Their *influence*, although maybe not intended originally, later became a powerplay. The *bridge* on the other hand they wanted to establish was not a way to keep a one-way hirarchy from Rome in tact, but rather a road which could be travelled in both directions: Support and brotherhood from Rome to the Christians in Asia Minor, but also from the Christians in Asia Minor to Rome. This idea of solidarity among Christians was not only the concern of the Christians at Rome but of the greater Christian movement. The early Church father, Irenaeus, also wants to strengthen this authority of Rome as the centre of the true faith, associated with the Apostle Peter. The legend of the grave of Peter situated in Rome made Rome the place many a Christian pilgrim visited.[245]

The author of 1 Peter's familiarity with Paul's letter to the Romans and Mark (also associated with Rome as will be indicated later in this study), as demonstrated by the corresponding formulas, terminology and theological ideas, cannot conclusively be attributed to literary dependency. Therefore it is much more plausible that these similarities are the result of Rome being a gathering point of traditions which many authors employed. This argument

---

242. Horrell, *Epistles*, 8; cf. Cothenet, "Les Orientations," 27–36; Vanhoye, "1 Pierre"; Boring, *1 Peter*, 28.

243. Cf. Elliott, *A Home*, 281.

244. Ibid., 282.

245. Cf. Zwierlein, *Petrus in Rom*, 174.

receives further support by the fact that Rome was the capitol and largest city of the Roman Empire, which was inhibited by approximately 1 million persons, of whom the majority consisted out of foreign slaves or former slaves. Goppelt also argues that the Church in Rome, as the capitol of the world, was the ideal place for 1 Peter to be composed.[246] Many displaced Christians were present in Rome, and could identify with the situation of suffering and harassment experienced by their brothers and sisters in Asia Minor. In the salutation in 1 Pet 5:12–13 Mark is described as "my son," Μᾶρκος ὁ υἱός μου, and Silvanus as "a faithful brother," Σιλουανοῦ ὑμῖν τοῦ πιστοῦ ἀδελφοῦ. According to Elliott, this forms part of the author's family imagery, linking the Roman Christian community, from where the letter originates with the communities in Asia Minor to whom it is addressed as all part of the larger community in Christ. Thereby solidarity among Christians across the Roman world is also emphasised.[247]

Judeans were a significant group among these foreigners as the existence of eight synagogues in Rome indicates. Christianity was initially a Jewish sect, which later completely departed ways with Judaism. At first, however, Christians still formed part of synagogue communities, which provided a basis for the spread of Christianity to other parts of the Empire.

Brown states that after the fall of Jerusalem in AD 70, with the result that many Jewish Christians became scattered all over the Mediterranean, Rome took the place of Jerusalem as the centre where Jewish Christianity was observed.[248]

Additionally, in the Apostle Paul's letter to the Christians in Rome, at least five distinctive households are mentioned.[249] It should also be taken into consideration that there did not exist a central synagogue, which lead to diversity among Jewish communities. Rome, already being the melting pot of diverse cultures, religions and ideas and also the location of several Jewish synagogues, clearly allows for the possibility of the existence of a distinctive Petrine circle to which Silvanus and Mark could have belonged.[250]

According to Elliott some scholars previously suggested Antioch in Syria as a place where the letter originated from.[251] This position is probably derived from the legend that Origen (*Hom. Luke* 6.1) and Eusebius (*Hist. eccl.* 3.36.2) was familiar with and identified Peter as the first bishop

246. Goppelt, *Commentary*, 48.
247. Elliott, *A Home*, 274.
248. Brown, "First Epistle," 132.
249. Rom 16:3–16 cf. Lampe, "Roman Christians."
250. Elliott, *1 Peter: New Translation*, 133.
251. Ibid., 131; Hunzinger, "Babylon als Deckname."

of Antioch, prior to Ignatius.[252] Ignatius, however never mentioned Peter as his predecessor, which indicates that the legend only developed after Ignatius and therefore lacks historical evidence. Furthermore, 1 Peter displays distinctively different theology than that presented by Ignatius. First Peter is not concerned with typical problems of the church in the East such as conflict with Israel and Gnosticism. First Peter could rather be associated with Western writings, e.g., Mark and *1 Clement*.[253]

Scholars like Knopf, Streeter, Hunzinger, Vielhauer, Marxsen and Reichert suggested Asia Minor as the place where 1 Peter originated.[254] Although Papias and Polycarp were familiar with the letter, this is rather due to the fact that the letter was addressed to Asia Minor than the possibility that it originated from there. Hunzinger and Vielhauer were of the opinion that due to the apocalyptic nature of the letter, the place of origin and the address would have been the same.[255] This, however, as Elliott also confirms, is an unsubstantiated oversimplification,[256] and furthermore, 1 Peter could barely be considered as apocalyptic as Michaels and Schutter proposed.[257]

It could therefore be concluded that the letter was ascribed to Peter as a continuation of the Petrine legacy. It also reflects the ideas and views of the Christian group situated in Rome which shows concern for their brothers and sisters experiencing similar suffering and harassments in Asia Minor. Theologically it emphasises a common hope in the deliverance of God, trust in the grace of God and expectation of the final revelation of the glory of God in which they have part. This theology receives historicity if the Church at the centre of the Roman Empire expresses concern for their co-heirs of the grace, salvation and glory of God in Christ, in other parts of the Roman world. The bond between Christians were also strengthened by the authority given to certain writings, e.g., the Gospels and the letters of Paul.[258] Siker states: "When Christians in different locales gathered to worship and read from the same new (and old) scriptures, this practice allowed the formation of a common Christian identity."[259] Although it should be taken into

252. Origen, *Hom. Luc.* 6.1; and Eusebius, *Hist. eccl.* 3.36.2.

253. Goppelt, *Commentary*, 48.

254. Knopf, *Die Briefe*, 25; Streeter, "Church in Asia," 131–134; Hunzinger, "Babylon als Deckname," 71; Vielhauer, "Die Apokryphen," 587–88; Marxsen, "Der Mitälteste," 389, 391; Reichert, *Eine urchristeliche Praeparatio*, 525–29.

255. Hunzinger, "Babylon als Deckname," 77 and Vielhauer, "Die Apokryphen," 588.

256. Elliott, *1 Peter: New Translation*, 131.

257. Michaels, *1 Peter*, xlvi–xlix; and Schutter, "1 Peter 4:17."

258. Siker, "Christianity," 253

259. Ibid., 253.

consideration that the early Christian church was very diverse and that the authority given to different writings largely varied, the Gospels, the letters of Paul, 1 John and 1 Peter established a certain unity. Viewing Rome as the place of composition of 1 Peter, Rome certainly also played an important role in the decision about the authority of traditions and writings associated with them. It attests to the Roman Church later becoming the most influential and supportive of Christian communities all over the world.

## Addressees and *Sitz im Leben*

### *Social Profile of the Addressees*

It is important for the exegete to take cognisance of the historical, geographical, political, religious and cultural diversity of the addressees of 1 Peter. What these diverse groups share with one another is their communal faith in Christ and their new identity as the people of God. Therefore the letter stresses the bond that exists between Christians in different parts of the world by employing family imagery and urging them to solidarity, rooted in their solidarity with Christ, and ardent love for one another. Their social situation necessitates the establishment of a sense of singular social identity. Hostile reactions from the outside world and pressure to conform and assimilate with the dominant culture intensified the crisis experienced by the recipients.

As far as the population profile of these provinces is concerned, it was indeed very diverse. At this point Achtemeier mentions that because of the vast geographical area that the letter is addressed to, the situation in one area might be totally different from a situation in the next.[260] Furthermore, since it is unlikely that the author ever visited the congregations personally, one must take into account that he made certain assumptions about the demographic composition of these communities.[261] As also mentioned above, the daily circumstances in the cities was quite different than that of the countryside. Therefore Achtemeier argues that the letter intented to address its audience in the broadest possible terms so that it could be inclusive and relevant.[262] This study evaluates this point of view as more plausible than the argument of Elliott (which will be discussed below) that the terminology used in the greeting of the letter refers to the official status of the addressees.

260. Achtemeier, *1 Peter*, 50.
261. Michaels, *1 Peter*, xlv.
262. Achtemeier, *1 Peter*, 50.

Natives, including local aristocrats, administrators and ordinary citizens were present. The addressees also included foreigners or *perigrini* ( technical term that will be explained below) as well as slaves and freed slaves.²⁶³ This is also confirmed by the letter of Pliny that Christians included people from every social class, every gender and every age.²⁶⁴

Given the vast geographical area that the letter addresses, enormous diversity concerning peoples and cultures is a natural consequence. It is thus clear that Elliott's argument for an official legal status of the recipients as "strangers, aliens and sojourners," as will be elaborated below is not convincing. Elliott contradicts himself when he emphasises "religious peculiarity and strangeness."²⁶⁵ This means separation from the dominant culture, distinctiveness and absolute dedication to the will of God. Due to their conversion to Christianity they became strangers in a hostile world.

The author's application of the term διασπορᾶ, a term coined by the LXX to refer to Jews no longer living in the geographical area of Palestine, to the Christian communities is also problematic. The Christian communities were already mixed and diverse and consisted of Jews as well as Gentiles. Διασπορᾶcould thus no longer refer to Jews living outside the borders of Israel but had to have obtained a different meaning which could include the many Gentile Christians.²⁶⁶ Goppelt agrees with this view and adds that it could also not be interpreted solely as referring to the addressees' strangeness on earth and that their true home is in heaven.²⁶⁷ Goppelt rather applies διασπορᾶto the concrete social situation of the Christian communities. Elliott himself states that the author wants to emphasise the distinctive character of the Christian community contrary to the non-believers, whether they were Jewish or Gentile.²⁶⁸

Among them were also freed persons (*liberti*), who were slaves previously and an enormous amount of slaves. As a result of the Diaspora and the displacement of many people throughout the Roman world, the population also included a significant amount of foreigners and sojourners, as defined by the official Roman social term. Among these sojourners and foreigners there was a considerable amount of Judean communities, living in urban as well as in rural areas, who enjoyed a certain degree of religious freedom concerning the observation of the Mosaic Law and a protected right to send

263. Cf. Horrell, *1 Peter*, 48.
264. Pliny, *Ep*. 10.96.
265. Elliott, *A Home*, 36.
266. Cf. Horrell, *1 Peter*, 47.
267. Goppelt, 1978, 286.
268. Elliott, *A Home*, 43.

an annual tax to the Temple in Jerusalem.²⁶⁹ First Peter is therefore addressing an audience which consisted of Jews and Gentiles, although the latter were the majority.²⁷⁰ This could be derived from the fact that the letter refers to the former pagan lifestyles of the Gentiles, from which they now need to distance themselves (1 Pet 4:3–5). Schnelle re-inforces this argument by showing that in 1 Pet 3:1 the husbands of Christian wives are described as Gentiles, since they have no knowledge of the Word.²⁷¹ Elliott²⁷² also mentions the contact that these Gentiles could have had previously with Jews in the synagogues, which would also explain why the author alludes and cites so much from the Septuagint. If these Gentiles attended the synagogues, they were familiar with the Jewish Scriptures. Some of them might even have been Jewish proselytes.²⁷³ Horrell further argues that although the author employs destinctive Jewish imagery in the opening of the letter (e.g. διασπορᾷ ἐκλεκτοῖς παρεπιδήμοις), used to describe the people of Israel in the Jewish sacred scriptures, this imagery is now being applied to a predominantly Gentile audience, as indicated by 1 Pet 1:14, 1 Pet 1:18, 1 Pet 2:10, 1 Pet 4:3–4.²⁷⁴ In the words of Michaels: "For the sake of Jesus the Jew, and the Jewish heritage they valued so highly, these Gentile Christians were taking on themselves both the praise and the contempt that the Jews experienced in Roman society."²⁷⁵ This statement is, however, debatable, since a distinctive Christian identity was being developed and Christianity also experienced hostility from their Jewish neighbours.

Green adds that it should be remembered that the Septuagint was the sacred Scripture of early Christian converts and that they continuously progressed in their knowledge thereof.²⁷⁶ It should also be taken into consideration that due to Hellenisation and the great influence it had on the entire first century Mediterranean world, it is an oversimplification to speak about "Jews" and "Gentiles" in terms of exclusive compartments.²⁷⁷ It could also not be known by the author to what extent the communities

---

269. Josephus, *A.J.* 14.16.

270. Cf. Elliott, *A Home*, 65; Achtemeier, *1 Peter*, 51; Green, *1 Peter*, 5; Boring, *1 Peter*, 43; Schnelle, *History and Theology*, 403; Hiebert, *First Peter*, 16; Michaels, *1 Peter*, xlvi.

271. Schnelle, *History and Theology*, 404.

272. Elliott, *A Home*, 66.

273. Horrell, *1 Peter*, 48.

274. Ibid., 47, cf. Achtemeier, *1 Peter*, 51, Bechtler, *Following in His Steps*, 61–64; Hiebert, *First Peter*, 16.

275. Michaels, *1 Peter*, li.

276. Green, *1 Peter*, 6.

277. Boring, *1 Peter*, 24.

he addressed were familiar with Jewish Scriptures. In is however evident that this was his assumption.

As in every Roman province Roman soldiers were present to maintain order and to suppress revolutionary initiatives against the Empire. Asia Minor was also a location where war veterans received land.

Elliott argues that "strangers" and "sojourners" παρεπιδήμοις refer to the political, legal and social situation of the audience, who did not enjoy the privileges of citizenship. This would mean that παροικίας, "by-dwellers," indicates the institutionalised rank of people who were below citizens, yet above freed-persons and slaves.[278] This distinctive social class included those who were deprived of their land which was annexed by the world powers as well as strangers from other regions who resided there for more than 30 days. They were not allowed to vote or to poses land, to occupy civic offices or to receive honors. Legally, they were only partially protected, and matters such as marriage, commerce, transfer of property and occupation of land were restricted. They could be forced into military service and received severer forms of civil and criminal punishment. Although they could not occupy priestly offices, they were allowed to participate in cultic activities, but again with certain limitations. They were not excluded, however, from the financial burdens and still had to pay tribute, taxes and production quotas.[279]

Elliott made a strong argument for the Hellenistic context in which the term πάροικοι was employed.[280] To him, it refers undoubtedly to an official social condition and calls it a "technical term" which he translates as "dwelling beside, neighbouring, sojourning, alien or stranger." This indicated that these people are removed from their homes, they do not have native roots, and they are foreign to the language, customs, and culture of the world in which they lived.

Elliott regards this as a political-legal term, which meant that these people had no civil rights. This is substantiated by Schaefer's elaborate study which noted the abundant appearance of the word in legal documents indicating city residents in Asia Minor during the Hellenistic period.[281] This was an official status recognised by the state, used to refer to a particular stratum of the population different from full citizens as well as inferior. Schaefer further indicated that this status did include certain advantages, however they could not be treated in the same way as full citizens, since they

---

278. Cf. Dickey, "Some Economic," 406; Rostovtzeff, *Social and Economic*, 236–237.
279. Elliott, *A Home*, 35–37, 67–69.
280. Ibid., 23.
281. Schaefer, "Paroikoi," 1695.

were passersby and often, at least partly, from a "barbaric origin."²⁸² Therefore they were still subjected to political and economical exploitation and viewed with suspicion by the citizens. Those belonging to even lower social strata were again envious of them. The amount of actual πάροικοι in the late Hellenistic and early Empirical period remains uncertain, but according to Schaefer it was significant. Among these were travelling merchants and craftsmen who primarily resided in the cities. As such they were Roman subjects.²⁸³ A foreigner or stranger, *perigrinus* in Latin, was viewed by Roman law as a person who was not a citizen of Rome. According to Berger a large part of the population residing in Rome and the Roman Empire were *perigrini*, and subjected to Rome after their home countries were conquered by Rome.²⁸⁴ As the Empire expanded, more *perigrini* were added to the population. *Perigrini* did enjoy certain legal rights and were regarded as so-called "free persons," and therefore were not considered as slaves. When an agreement existed between Rome and their country of origin they enjoyed the rights guaranteed by the agreement. Such an agreement could allow them to become legally married, if they obtained the *ius conubii* and such a marriage (called a *iustia nuptial*) would be recognised by the state. However, they had no political rights and could not serve in public assemblies or in official positions. They could not write a testament or act as a witness to such a document, nor could they become heirs of Roman citizens. They could only engage in legal trade with Roman citizens if they were granted the *ius commercii*. Transactions between foreigners of the same country of origin could be concluded in occurrence with the general legislation regarding trade. Disputes could also be settled according to their own laws. They did however enjoy protection by the Roman courts, and were protected by the praetor over the *perigrini* from the third century BC.

Elliott further substantiates his theory by referring to the occurrence of the word πάροικοι in the Septuagint.²⁸⁵ He argues that once again this referred to an official legal status, and rejects any notion that it could have a "spiritual" meaning referring to the condition of the faithful living on earth. This study completely also discards a "spiritual" interpretation. The spiritual interpretation of these terms was simply the consequence of misinterpretation that led to erroneous translations. Beare is a particular exponent of this view.²⁸⁶ He argued that Christians are "strangers and so-

---

282. Ibid., 1701.
283. Rostovtzeff, *Social and Economic*, 655.
284. Berger, *Encyclopaedic Dictionary*, 626–27; cf. Elliott, *A Home*, 37.
285. Elliott, *A Home*, 27.
286. Beare, *First Epistle*, 135.

journers" on earth and that their true home is in heaven. They will never be at home on earth since that is not their place of belonging. Their heavenly home also becomes the reason for their distinctive way of conduct. Such an interpretation also linked with the body/soul dualism, which made its influential, although debatable, entrance into Christian thought. The ways of the flesh had to be discarded and a complete spiritual existence, orientated towards heaven, was desired. This would entail a total withdrawal from the outside world, which this study will argue was not in the mind of the author of 1 Peter at all. Elliott also rejected this view, but on the grounds of his emphasis on the actual legal and official interpretation of πάροικοι and παρεπίδημοι, which he found evidence for in secular as well as religious literature around the time of the composition of 1 Peter.[287] A further legitimate objection of Elliott toward this "spiritual" interpretation is the letter's undeniable involvement with the actual social situation of the addressees. The moral instructions are always grounded in the distinctiveness of the Christian community from the outside world. Their social alienation and conflict with non-believers are central themes in the letter of 1 Peter. Elliott also notes that πάροικοι is often used together with διασπορά and that these terms could even be used interchangeably (cf. Gen 23:4 and Ps. 38:12).[288] Διασπορά was also a technical term, used in the LXX, referring to the displacement of the Jews and the fact that they were scattered across the Mediterranean and resided among the Gentiles.[289] The term παρεπίδημοι, which occurs less frequently, was a more general term referring to a transgressing visitor. Al three terms however, also originated from the legal citizen's point of view and attested to the suspicion with which these people were regarded. They therefore remained vulnerable outsiders.

Further evidence of the official occurrence of the term is provided by Josephus and the rabbinic Jewish writings. In these cases however, the term was used from a Jewish perspective discerning the statuses of a full proselyte, half proselyte, god fearer and resident alien.[290] The resident alien only lived in the land of Israel but did not conform to the Jewish faith at all. He had however social and economical obligations.[291] Elliott therefore maintains that these legal and political terms apply to the addressees of 1 Peter since it is explicitly employed by the author in 1 Pet 1:1, 17 and 2:11

---

287. Elliott, *A Home*, 42.
288. Ibid. Cf. Schmidt, Schmidt & Meyer "Paroikos," 842.
289. Ibid, 842.
290. Elliott, *A Home*, 32.
291. Schmidt, Schmidt, and Meyer, "Paroikos," 850.

and would therefore immediately be interpreted as such by the audience.²⁹² Elliott places them in the same category as the thousands of Jews scattered across the Roman Empire. Elliott maintains that it is as a result of their different languages, clothing, customs, traditions and foreign roots that they are regarded with hostility and charges of wrongdoing by the native population.²⁹³ Their behaviour could be harmful for the prosperity of the areas in which they lived, since they aggravated the gods. This is, according to Elliott, the suffering which the letter wants to address. This study however, disagrees. Horrell calls Elliott's view of the addressees' official social status as παροίκους and παρεπιδήμους "questionable."²⁹⁴ The implication of this view would be that the addressees already had this status prior to their conversion. Elliott wants to stress that this is their official socio-political categorisation. In agreement with Horrell, this study challenges such a view.²⁹⁵ In the light of the extreme diversity of the addressees, coming from all strata of the population and all sorts of ethnic and religious backgrounds, it would make more sense to argue that παροίκους and παρεπιδήμους have a more "figurative" though not "spiritual" meaning. This study would suggest that these terms rather refer to the audience's new situation as a result of their conversion to Christianity. This also complies with the emphasis that the epistle has on the new identity of the addressees as the "people of God."

The recipients were converts of the Jesus movement. They believed in Christ, entered the believing community through baptism and anticipated the final revelation of the glory of Christ. They are distinctively called "Christians" Χριστιανός (1 Pet 4:16). They heard the gospel due to the missionary activity of others prior to the senders of the letter (cf. 1 Pet 1:12, 25).

Reicke estimates the amount of Christians being present in Asia Minor by AD 67 at approximately 40,000, which increased to more than 80,000 by AD 100.²⁹⁶ It is therefore clear that the Jesus movement had an early and significant presence in Asia Minor, which laid the foundation for missionary and supportive networks which enabled this rapid growth.²⁹⁷ According to Bruce and Gütling there were also economic reasons for people's conversion to Christianity, since the animals that they had to bring to their temples for offerings placed an additional burden on their already severe poverty.²⁹⁸

292. Elliott, *A Home*, 35.
293. Elliott, *1 Peter: New Translation*, 94.
294. Horrell, *1 Peter*, 50.
295. Ibid., 51.
296. Reicke, *New Testament Era*, 302–4.
297. Elliott, *1 Peter: New Translation*, 89.
298. Bruce and Güting, *Außerbiblische Zeugnisse*, 18.

Some scholars might argue that the audience of 1 Peter did not include the slave owning class, since no instruction is given to masters. The view of this study, however, is that the omission of slave owners rather has a theological purpose as will be elaborated later. Although a specific instruction to slave owners is absent, it does not mean that they were not among the addressees. The employment of the term πρεσβυτέρους according to Campbell,[299] refers to those who were household leaders and therefore automatically became the leaders of the churches which originated in their households. Horrell states that although it cannot explicitly be derived from the text, it is highly possible that there were whole households among the addressees, which included husbands, wives, masters and slaves.[300]

From the contents of 1 Peter it is established that the letter addresses a primary Gentile audience, which experienced the difficulties of departing from their previous pagan ways as well as the temptation to relapse into their former way of living (cf. 1 Pet 1:14–16, 18–19; 2:9–10, 11–12, 4:1–6, 12–19). This, however, does not exclude Jewish Christians from the audience. Elliott notes that the word "Gentile" (ἔθνεσιν) does not indicate that the author and the audience were of exclusive Judean origin. This collective term, formally used to indicate everyone that did not belong to Israel, the people of God, is used by the author in order to refer to those who did not convert to Christianity. They now became the "outsiders." The author draws from Israelite and Hellenistic traditions, which corresponds with the statement that the letter is addressing a diverse audience. It is also clear from the content of the letter that the author presupposed knowledge of the Scriptures and the Christian faith and values among the recipients. In addition the author also presupposed that the figures of Mark and Silvanus were known to the audience, albeit only by reputation, as well as the authority of the Apostle Peter, to whom the letter is ascribed. The fact that the author refers to the audience as "Christians,"Χριστιανός, supports the notion that the addressees already belonged to a new religious movement, discernable from Judaism. This had the implication that the Judeans among them became divorced from their previous social and ideological identity.

As also mentioned by Elliott and in the view of this study more correctly,[301] the alienation that the addressees experienced was a result of their conversion to Christianity.[302] According to 1 Peter, the audience was

299. Campbell, *Honour, Shame*.
300. Horrell, *1 Peter*, 49.
301. Elliott, *1 Peter: New Translation*, 97.
302. Cf. Elliott, 1981; Brox, "Situation und Sprache"; Brox, *Petrusbrief* (2nd ed); Goppelt, *Commentary*.

subjected to hostility, verbal abuse and humiliating shaming from ignorant (1 Pet 2:15) outsiders (1 Pet 2:12, 15; 3:9, 13, 16; 4:4, 14; 5:8–9). This harassment lead to innocent suffering (1 Pet 1:6; 2:12, 19–20, 3:14, 17, 18; 4:1, 2, 13, 16, 19; 5:8–9, 10). The letter also alludes to knowledge among the addressees of the suffering of fellow Christians in other parts of the world.

### Sitz im Leben

The coined historical critical term *Sitz im Leben* could be translated with "situation" of the addressees, which could be defined as Elliott states: "the set of circumstances, as perceived, described and diagnosed."[303] The author of 1 Peter's handling of the "situation" of the addressees evolves around their undeserved suffering as inflicted by their non-believing hostile neighbours. Previously, scholars associated the suffering experienced by the recipients as the result of official Roman persecution, which started with Nero in the mid sixties.[304] These scholars wanted consequently wanted to correspond the dating of 1 Peter either with Nero's persecution (ca. 54–68), that of Domitian (81–96) or that of Trajan (98–117). This approach proved to be wrong, based on the fact that no official Roman persecution is noted by historians prior to that of Decius in AD 250.[305] However sporadic persecution of Christians did occur prior to the third century AD, but these persecutions were, as described by Elliott, "mob-initiated, locally restricted and unsystematic."[306] Hostile neighbours often accused members of the Christian movement as being a threat to local law and order and provoking the gods by not honoring them, which could cause misfortune to the entire society. Local Roman governors usually had to judge these accusations.[307] Christians could be charged by other citizens and then had to appear in front of the local magistrate. This sometimes lead to trials and executions, although it was not the official Roman policy at the time. The correspondence between Pliny and Trajan might shed some light on the matter. As Michaels notes, the letters between Pliny and Trajan are not so significant

---

303. Elliott, *1 Peter: New Translation*, 97.

304. Cf. Windisch, *Katolishe Briefe*, 80; Knox, "Pliny and Peter"; Beare, *First Epistle*, 30–34, 188; Schrage and Balz, "Der erste Petrusbrief," 63; Downing, "Pliny's Persecution"; Molthagen, "Die Lage."

305. See Eusebius, *Hist. eccl.* 6.39.1–42.6; 7.1.

306. Elliott, *1 Peter: New Translation*, 98.

307. Schnelle, *History and Theology*, 405; see Colwell, "Popular Reactions"; Krodel, "Persecution and Toleration."

in order to pinpoint a date for the compostition of 1 Peter.[308] It rather illustrates the situation these Christian communities found themselves in and also that it was a situation that has been going on for some time. In his letter to Trajan, Pliny consults the Emperor regarding the situation of the ever increasing amount of Christians:[309]

> It is customary to me, my lord, to refer to you all about which I doubt; for who can better guide my hesitence or instruct my ignorance? I never attended the prosecution of Christians, therefore I do not know what is punished, and to what extent it is punished, and what ought to be investigated. I am very hesitent about whether there is any distinction concerning age and to what extent the young should be treated differently from the more robust, whether pardon should be given to repentence, whether a person who was a Christian in some sense, should not benefit by having renounced it and whether the name itself, if no crimes occurred, or the crimes accompanied by the name should be punished.
>
> Meanwhile, in the cases brought before me as Christians, this is the procedure I followed. I asked them whether they were Christians. Those who confessed I asked a second and a third time, threatening them with execution. Those who persevered, I ordered to be condemned. Because I did not doubt that, whatever it was that they professed, that their obstinacy and inflexible stubborness should be punished regardlessly. There were others of the same insanity who were Roman citizens, whom I noted as to be sent back to Rome.
>
> Later, during the trials, as often happens, the charges expanded and more cases occurred. An anonymous document was presented which contained the names of many. Those who denied that they were or had been Christians, and called after me upon the gods and your statue, which I ordered to be brought along together with images of the gods for this purpose, and worshiped them with incence and wine and furthermore those who cursed Christ (it is said that those who are true Christians cannot be forced into any of these things) I ordered to be dismissed. Others, who were named by an informant, said that they were Christians, but they denied the faith, some three years ago, some many years earlier and a few even twenty years

---

308. Michaels, *1 Peter*, lxvi.

309. Pliny, *Ep.* 10.96, my trans. Cf. Sherwin-White, *Fifty Letters*; Walsh, *Pliny the Younger*.

# INTRODUCTION, HISTORY, METHODOLOGY AND HYPOTHESIS

ago. All of these also venerated your statue and the statues of the gods and cursed Christ.

They affirmed, however, that what their guilt or error entailed was that they had the custom to, on a fixed day, convene before sunrise to sing a song to Christ as God and to bind themselves to an oath not to engage in any criminal activity, but that they will not commit theft, robbery or adultery, that they will not be dishonest and that they will not withhold any money deposited with them when it is required. When these rituals were completed it was customary for them to depart and then to convene again to eat together which was common and harmless. They ceased to do this after my edict, by which according to your instructions, I prohibited the existence of secret societies. I believed it was necessary to obtain what the truth was from two maid servants, who were called deaconesssses, by using torture. I discovered nothing but a low and undesirable supersition. Therefore, I postponed the hearing and hastened to consult you, because it seemed to me that the matter is worthy of your attention. Even more so, because of the number indicated: Because many of every age, of every social ranking and of both sexes were summoned or will be summoned shortly. The contamination of this superstition has extended not only to the cities but to the villages and farms as well, but it seems that it can be stopped and corrected. It is adequately certain that temples which were abandoned began to be celebrated again and that the holy rituals that have been abandoned were continued. And the meat for the offerings, for which up to now only rarely a buyer was found, is now selling in many places. It could therefore easily be concluded that a great crowd of people can be ammended if there is an opportunity for penetence.

Trajan replied to Pliny as follows:[310]

You followed the procedure you should have, my Secundus, in examining the cases of those who are Christians that were brought before you, because there is not something universal that can be constituted, which would entail a certain formula. Christians are not to be sought out. If they are prosecuted and convicted, they should be punished, but in such a way that a person who denies that he is a Christian and he acts accordingly—that is by worshipping our gods—my receive pardon on the grounds of his penetence, even if he was previously suspected.

---

310. Trajan, *Epistle* 10.97, my trans.

Anonymous documents should have no place in any accusation, for they set the worst example, and does not belong to our age.

Pliny arrived in Pontus in AD 110 and then he discovered documents to the effect of Christians being charged. Pliny's uncertainty about these matters attest to the fact that no official Roman policy concerning the Christians existed at the time.[311] He even hopes that the Emperor would agree with him to display mercy to those Christians who were willing to renounce their faith. The problem with Christians not adhering to the Roman gods and participating in the Emperor cult, was the fear that their deviant behaviour would provoke the gods and cause disfavour to the community. This could threaten political stability and prosperity and could even be interpreted as religious or political rebellion.[312]

Furthermore, Nero's attack on the Christians in Rome in the mid sixties, according to Roman historian Tacitus (ca. AD 117) was as a result of the catastrophic fire in AD July 64, which destroyed four fifths of the city, and which Nero wanted to blame the Christians for. Nero sought to divert attention from himself as probably responsible for the fire, which he caused in order to have a new palace build. He therefore charged the *Christiani* with arson and they were burned on the Vatican Hill.[313] Tacitus mentions the sadistic nature of this persecution: some were devoured by wild animals in the arena, some were nailed to crosses and others covered with tar were set alight to serve as street lamps. Tactitus admits that this brutality evoked the sympathy of the masses.[314] This persecution however, was restricted only to Rome, and did not lead to a policy of Christian persecution across the Roman Empire. Schnelle adds that there exists no documentation of a Christian persecution during the same periode affecting Asia Minor.[315] This is confirmed by Suetonius, another Roman historian and contemporary of Tacitus, who wrote that Nero attacked the Christians,[316] however not in relation with the fire, but because they were a "novel and malicious superstition."[317] For Suetonius, it is a matter of certainty that Nero was responsible for the fire. Tacitus and Suetonius agree that Nero's

---

311. Schnelle, *History and Theology*, 405.

312. Cf. Horrell, *1 Peter*, 57.

313. Tacitus, *Ann.* 15.44;cf. Eusebius, *Hist. eccl.* 2.25.1–8.

314. Cf. Böttrich, *Petrus*, 218.

315. Schnelle, *History and Theology*, 406.

316. Suetonius, *Nero* 16.

317. Cf. Elliott, *1 Peter: New Translation*, 99; Bruce and Güting, *Außerbiblische Zeugnisse*, 13.

# INTRODUCTION, HISTORY, METHODOLOGY AND HYPOTHESIS 55

local persecution of the Christians in Rome did not initiate an Empire wide Christian persecution.

The reign of the Flavian emperors marked a period of general stability and prosperity. No evidence indicates that either Vespasian (AD 69-79) or Titus (AD 79-81) undertook an official persecution. According to Suetonius, Domitian (AD 81-96) had his conflicts with the senatorial aristocracy and philosophers in Rome, especially during the final years of his reign (AD 93-96).[318] Although he had his difficulties with some senators and although he executed his cousin Flavius Clemens and had his wife Flavia Domitilla exiled on the charge of atheism because she favoured the Judean rituals, this do not prove that he ordered an official world wide Christian persecution.

As far as Trajan is concerned, his elaborate correspondence with Pliny the Younger, his delegate in the province of Bithynia-Pontus (as discussed above) clearly indicates that no official Roman policy regarding the Christians existed at the time. The lack of an official Roman policy concerning the handling of the Christians in fact necessitated Pliny to inquire the emperor on how he should address the situation. In addition, Trajan unambiguously stated that Christians should not be sought out or punished on any other grounds than criminal behaviour.[319] This rather attests to a leniency and toleration regarding the official Roman position towards the Christians. Once again the situation in focus occurred in a specific province, which attests to the accusations brought before Pliny as being instigated by local non-believers.[320]

Elliott also states that the fact that provinces like Cappadocia and Galatia were not really affected by Roman urbanisation, limited the importance of Rome in these areas.[321] The Romans had little success in unifying these people into a common allegiance with Rome. Therefore it cannot be assumed that the Christians residing in Cappadocia, Galatia, Pontus and Bithynia experienced consistent conflict with Rome.

There is thus no external evidence that points to an official Roman persecution, which would have caused the suffering so frequently mentioned in 1 Peter. Elliott notes that neither does any evidence from the content of the letter indicate an official Roman persecution.[322] The letter contains only one specific reference to Roman rule in 1 Pet 2:13-27, which explicitly states that the Emperor should be honored, and the governors whose task it was

---

318. Suetonius, *Dom.* 10-15.
319. Pliny, *Ep.* 10.97.
320. Cf. Horrell, *1 Peter*, 58.
321. Elliott, *A Home*, 62.
322. Elliott, *1 Peter: New Translation*, 100.

to maintain law and order and to punish wrongdoers should be respected. It would be problematic to reconcile this instruction with a period when the Christians were subjected to severe persecution. The suffering that the addressees of the letter experienced is much rather the result of social ostracism and local harassment as will be indicated by this study. This problem was intesified by the fact that the audience already displayed a diverse character and comprised of different backgrounds, religions and cultures. Conforming to the dominant culture would therefore be very attractive and it was also desired by the Romans.[323] Colwell also emphasises that, prior to Decius (AD 249–51), no empire-wide persecution of Christians took place.[324] According to Colwell it is not certain whether the Roman courts condemned Christians simply on because of their identity as Christians, the Roman mob certainly did. They were ignorant of the practices and beliefs of the Christian movement, but their distinctive character and their identity as a contra-community in particular raised opposition. Since Green views Rome and everything associated as the cause of the suffering that the addressees of 1 Peter experience,[325] the question arises how the author wants them to respond to Rome. Available options would be either to withdraw and to move to the margins of city centers, or to become an underground revolutionary movement or even to acquire political power and positions to the advantage of their movement. The Jews often opted for the latter and had all kinds ot tactics for engagement with Rome, often to the disadvantage and even persecution of Christians.

For the historical critical exegete to take cognisance of the fact that the Greek word πάσχω "to suffer" and derivatives thereof occur more in the letter of 1 Peter than in any other New Testament writing (12x) (1 Pet 2:19, 20, 21, 23; 3:14, 17, 18; 4:1 [2x], 15, 19; 5:10) and the related noun πάθημα τος "suffering" in 1:11; 4:13, 5:1, 9. Terms associated with suffering, e.g., λυπέω "pain, grieve, injure" occur in 1:6 and 2:19. Reference is also made frequently to the suffering of Christ in 1:2, 19; 2:4, 23–24. The innocent suffering of Christ is compared to the undeserved suffering of the addressees, for they did no wrong (2:19, 21–25; 3:28; 4:1). From the contents of the letter the suffering is also described as continuous slander and abuse by non-believers who shamed the Christians and brought them into discredit with the local authorities. Neugebauer therefore defines the nature of the suffering as being verbal rather than physical (cf. καταλαλέω "speak evil of" 2:12, 3:16; ἐπηρεάζω "mistreat, insult" 3:16; βλασφημέω "speak against

---

323. Elliott, *A Home*, 65.
324. Colwell, "Popular Reactions," 53.
325. Green, *1 Peter*, 1.

slander, insult" 4:4; ὀνειδίζω "reproach" 4:14; λοιδορέω "curse, speak evil of, insult" and ἀντιλοιδορέω "reply with a curse" 2:23; κακός, ἡ, όν "evil, bad, wrong; injury, harm (as a noun)," 3:9, and κακόω "treat badly, harm; be cruel and force," 3:13).[326] The non-believers outside the Christian communities, partly because of ignorance towards the Christian movement accused the Christians of wrongdoing (1 Pet 2:12, 15, 19–20; 3:15). This underscores the continuous estrangement of the believers from the non-believers. Christians were regarded with suspicion because they withdrew from previous associations (4:4) and referred to as Χριστιανός (4:16), an abusive name meaning "Christ lackeys,"[327] because of their confessing of Jesus Christ. This form of address had a dangerous connotation in the Roman world, since it provoked the imagery of the revolutionist Jesus, who called himself the Christ, which was crucified in Jerusalem. Those associated with him, might also have revolutionist ideas and therefore posed a threat to the stability of the society. This term also discerned them from the Judeans, which exposed them to the charge in the words of the Roman historian Suetonius: *nova prava superstitio* "a new perverse superstition."[328]

Christians all over the world experienced the same suffering (1 Pet 5:9). Therefore, Elliott suggests that the causes for the suffering experienced by the Christians should be sought rather in the general interaction, and conflict that arose from this interaction, within the larger society of Asia Minor.[329] This study would thus suggest that the address of the recipients of the letter as παροίκους "resident aliens" (1 Pet 2:11) by the author, is rather a reference to their alienation from the society in which they were quite at home prior to their conversion. Elliott, however, maintains that the term literary refers to their official legal and social status, which already place them in a vulnerable position as indicated above.[330] Elliott underscores this argument by referring to the same term used in the Septuagint to indicate a literal official social status as experienced by Moses and Abraham. This is, however problematic, as Elliott himself indicated that the residents of the provinces mentioned in the opening verse of the letter also included citizens, government officials, Roman soldiers and war veterans.[331] This study however agrees with Elliott that the παροίκους does not refer to a spiritual state of being indicating that the addressees are strangers on the earth because their true home is in heaven.

326. Neugebauer, "Zur Deutung," 62.
327. Elliott, *1 Peter: New Translation*, 101; cf. Boring, *1 Peter*, 44.
328. Suetonius, *Nero* 16.2.
329. Elliott, *A Home*, 62.
330. Elliott, *1 Peter: New Translation*, 101.
331. Ibid., 90.

It is rather a case of the addressees becoming estranged from their pagan environment and having to find a new place of belonging, acceptance and social security. Therefore the author of 1 Peter emphasises their new identity, and also employs family imagery in order to create this new identity into a concrete reality.[332] As Beskow also indicates, the newly established Christian communities had to become a hospitable place of refuge for other Christian missionaries passing through their region.[333] The author of 1 Peter wants to convey the universal brotherhood that exists between followers of the Jesus movement across the world.

It can therefore be concluded that the situation of the audience of 1 Peter was one of suffering, however not suffering as a result on an official Roman persecution, but rather as the result of increasing social, political, cultural and above all religious tension with their non-believing neighbours.[334] The local harassment from non-believers of the same social ranking could of course also lead to accusations being made at the local authorities that could lead to trials and punishment. These however occurred sporadically and were not the result of any official Roman persecution known to historians. In addition, the author of 1 Peter displays a positive attitude towards Roman authority that would be difficult to reconcile with a period of official Roman persecution. Elliott states: "The letter presupposes a situation where the addressees were not being treated as 'enemies of the state' but were made victims of social discrimination."[335] The letter of 1 Peter thus gives a perspective on a later stage in Christianity, where conflict arised because of Christians now becoming an entity distinctive from Judaism, struggling to find its way through a hostile world. The initial conflict that Christianity experienced with Judaism as reflected in the letters of Paul, is no longer a concern in 1 Peter. Yet this separation of Judaism became a further cause of suffering, for as long as Christianity was only a phenomenon within Judaism, the privileges and protection Rome vested to Judaism, could also be enjoyed by Christians.[336] The final separation of Christianity from Judaism occurred during the first Jewish-Roman war (AD 66–70), and this had serious consequences for the Christian movement. The distinctive identity of Christianity removed them from the protection enjoyed by their Jewish counterparts. This separation is also attested explicitly by the text of 1 Peter in 4:16. Χριστιανός indicates that the distinctive identity was also

---

332. Cf. Horrell, *1 Peter*, 51.
333. "Mission, Trade and Emigration in the Second Century."
334. Cf. Horrell, *1 Peter*, 56–58.
335. Elliott, *1 Peter: New Translation*, 103.
336. Elliott, *A Home*, 72.

acknowledged by the greater society. This break with previous alliances, whether guilds or Judaism, caused the Christian converts to become aliens and strangers with no place of belonging. Elliott emphasised that this new status increased their vulnerability.[337] Green also mentions the archaeological discovery of a graffiti cartoon of a man worshipping a donkey-headed figure on a cross dating from the early second century. The Greek heading to the drawing states: "Alexamenos worships his god." This is a clear example of the animosity and slandering Christians had to endure. The fact that the Christians no longer attended public religious festivals caused their neighbours to view their behaviour as atheistic. This behaviour could be regarded as a provocation of the gods.

Another important perspective on the conditions of many of the early Christian converts, which also resulted in continuous suffering, was their inescapable and inevitable poverty. Rural farming communities were always captivated by the city elite, for the land was owned by the elite and crops went directly to the cities and to the Roman army. Furthermore these peasants were subjected to high taxation. This situation, argued by Dickey, prepared the audience for an apocalyptic message, and made the Christian movement a very attractive alternative:[338]

> During the first three centuries the general economic status of the labour classes went from bad to worse. There was no permanent alleviation, and there seemed no hope of it by ordinary processes. Therefore, when Christianity entered with its promises of a "new age" of righteousness inaugurated by divine power which included "feeding the hungry with good things" and "exalting those of low degree," it could not help get a hearing.[339]

Elliott also states that this weak economic condition the lower social classes in Asia Minor experienced stimulated the interest in Christianity, since it promised salvation and a unique hope (cf. 1 Pet 1:3, 9, 13, 21; 3:15, 21).[340] Salvation is required when a form of suffering or distress is experienced. Social and economic oppression therefore necessitates salvation.[341]

---

337. Ibid., 73; cf. Green, *1 Peter*, 6.
338. Dickey, "Some Economic," 411.
339. Ibid, 411.
340. Elliott, *A Home*, 72.
341. Weber, "Religion," 107; cf. Hiebert, *First Peter*, 15.

## A Sectarian Religious Identity

Elliott emphasises that the distinctive character required by Christianity caused their non-believing neighbours to be suspicious and hostile towards them.[342] They became social deviants. Elliott identifies seven characteristics of sectarian religious movements:[343]

1. It originates from objection to current circumstances
2. It does not confirm to the worldview of the greater society
3. It propagates equality
4. It is a place of belonging, brotherhood (sisterhood) where love is shared among equals and there is no discrimination toward new converts
5. Converts join the community by free will
6. Commitment and adherence are required by members
7. It displays apocalyptic expectations

Wilson gives a more elaborate definition:[344]

> The sect is a clearly defined community; it is of a size which permits only a minimal range of diversity of conduct; it seeks itself to rigidify a pattern of behaviour and to make coherent its structure of values; it contends actively against any other organization of values and ideals and against any other social context possible for its adherents, offering itself as an all-embracing, divinely prescribed society. The sect is not only an ideological unit, seeking to enforce behaviour on those who accept belief, and seeking every occasion to draw the faithful apart from the rest of society and into the company of each other . . . The sect as a protest group has always developed its own distinctive ethic, belief and practices, against the background of the wider society; its own protest is conditioned by the economical, social, ideological and religious circumstances prevailing at the time of its emergence and development.[345]

Textual evidence linking the letter of 1 Peter with these descriptions is abundant. The recipients of the letter are a defined, divinely ordained community—the elect and holy people of God (1 Pet 1:3—2:10). They were

342. Elliott, *A Home*, 73.
343. Ibid., 74.
344. Wilson, *Sects and Society*, 1.
345. Ibid., 1; see also Wilson, *Patterns of Sectarianism*; Wilson, *Religious Sects*; and Wilson, *Magic*, 1973.

established by God the Father, the Holy Spirit and Jesus Christ (1 Pet 1:1–2). They became distinctive from the rest of the society through a voluntary break with familial, social and religious alliances (1 Pet 1:3–5, 10–12, 18–21; 2:4–10). They established a new family, a new brotherhood, defined by communal faith in Christ, salvation and living hope (1 Pet 1:22; 2:5, 17; 5:9; 1:2–3, 6–8, 13, 18–21; 2:3, 4–10). Their ethic was defined as commitment to the will of God and to one another (1 Pet 1:17; 2:17; 3:6, 14; 2:8; 3:20, 4:17; 2:15; 3:17, 4:2, 19). They are co-heirs of salvation in Christ and divine grace, and which will reach its pinnacle with the return of Christ (1 Pet 1:5, 9, 10; 2:2; 3:21; 4:18; 1:2, 10, 13; 3:7; 4:10; 5:5, 10, 12; 1:5, 7, 13; 4:13; 5:1). They are to maintain their discernable ethical character, should not be tempted to return to their former futile pagan ways (1 Pet 1:22; 2:1; 3:8; 4:7–11; 5:1–5; 1:14–16, 18–21; 2:11; 3:9, 13–17; 4:1–6, 12–19; 5: 8–9).

It is inevitable that sectarian communities will engage in conflict with the rest of society, but the way they conduct themselves amidst this conflict is the important factor.[346] The author uses the paraenetic genre to specifically address this conflict situation. The communities addressed in 1 Peter were not allowed to let this conflict manifest in revolutionary activity or in a total withdrawal from society. Because of social and religious movements being intertwined in the ancient Mediterranean world, Christianity also belonged to both spheres.[347] As a social movement Christianity was especially attractive to the social outcast. They were accepted unconditionally. The living hope of salvation which manifested in a community of equals appealed in particular to the socially marginalized, with no political or economic protection.

### *The Christian Community's Engagement with Non-Believers*

Elliott is of the opinion that it was the tension of the Christian communities with their non-believing neighbours that necessitated the composition of the letter.[348] Christianity's disagreement with society implied a reaction from non-believers. Since they parted with former social alliances and religious activities, their civic loyalty was doubted and they were regarded as provoking the gods to withdraw their favour from society. As such they were regarded as a threat to public order and stability. Although no official Roman persecution of Christians took place, they were always treated with suspicion because of their association with the crucified Judean

---

346. Wilson, *Magic*, 20, cf. Schnelle, *History and Theology*, 404.
347. Elliott, *A Home*, 77.
348. Ibid., 78.

revolutionary and the memory of their involvement with the fire in Rome in AD 64. Christianity had a different view of God—no longer a *do ut des* cultic activity which entailed that the gods had to be pleased in order to bestow favour upon the society. Christians already achieved favour with God through the saving activity of Christ.[349] Christians were regarded as the "strangers and aliens" socially as well as religiously.

This is evident from the text in 1 Peter. Ignorance (1 Pet 2:15), suspicion of wrongdoing (1 Pet 2:12; 4:14–16) and aggressive hostility (1 Pet 3:13–14, 16; 4:4) were some of the reactions of the outside world towards the Christian communities.[350] This ignorance and suspicion eventually manifested in slander and condemnation.

For the Jewish community it was also important to distance themselves from the messianic movement and they had to convince the local authorities that they were not in the least associated with this movement that originated from the crucified revolutionary Jesus.

On the other hand, pagan contempt of the Jews was also projected upon the Christians. They viewed the Jews to be "strange and inferior."[351] The Jews were also not in accord with the Roman state religion and cults and were therefore regarded as primitive and superstitious. Their ethnical exclusivity and monotheism were also frowned upon. This pagan contempt of Judaism and Christianity lead to continuous social ostracism. Elliott emphasises quite correctly that the admonitions of the author of 1 Peter indicates that what he prescribes ethically was not yet realised in their practices.[352] The temptation to return to their former alliances was ever present (1 Pet 1:14, 18; 2:11; 4:1–4). Similarly they could yield to the temptation of reacting to the slandering with violence, criminality and civic disobedience or even total social separation (1 Pet 2:13–17). As a way of maintaining their identity of a contra-community, the author also stressed internal unity and love among one another within the community (1 Pet 1:22; 3:7, 8–9; 4:8; 5:14).

## Purpose of Composition

Goppelt calls 1 Peter the only New Testament writing which systematically and thematically addressed the issue of Christian alien residence within the ancient Mediterranean society.[353]

349. Wilson, *Magic*, 41–42.
350. Elliott, *A Home*, 79.
351. Daniel, "Anti-Semitism," 65.
352. Elliott, *A Home*, 83.
353. Goppelt, *Der erste Petrusbrief*, 71.

The situation described above could easily lead to the newly converted becoming disillusioned and experiencing despair. If the situation persisted or was simply ignored, the believers would become discouraged. Many of them would consider deserting the Christian movement to avoid this suffering. Since the believers became estranged as a result of their conversion to Christianity, a simple return to the former ways and a re-assimilation into the society which they belonged to would put an immediate end to this experience. This would ultimately lead to the disappearance of the Christian movement in Asia Minor. Therefore the audience required a persuasive word of consolation in order to remain firm in their new faith and commitment to God, Christ and one another and to resist the temptation of returning to previous pagan practices.[354] The letter confronts the issue of the addressees' innocent suffering, which is the consequence of them being ostracised by the societies they belonged to by emphasizing their moral distinctiveness and solidarity with fellow-Christians, even elsewhere in the world. Therefore 1 Pet 5:12 could be regarded as stating the purpose of the letter in a nutshell: παρακαλῶν καὶ ἐπιμαρτυρῶν ταύτην εἶναι ἀληθῆ χάριν τοῦ θεοῦ εἰς ἣν στῆτε. Horrell agrees with this stating that "the author's main concern was to instruct and encourage Christians who, because of their faith, were experiencing hostility, persecution and suffering."[355] Horrell particularly emphasises the suffering of women and slaves who converted to Christianity independently of the master of the household and consequently became the object of increasing suspicion (cf. 1 Pet 2:18—3:6). In spite of these suspicions, continuous hostility and slandering, the author encourages his audience to maintain good conduct and not to engage in criminal activity. The author wants his audience to remain hopeful because of their unique identity as God's elect. *First Clement* echoes the same sentiments of the church of Rome to act as the "voice of encouragement"[356] to Christians spread throughout the Empire and subjected to the same suffering. It could also be suggested that 1 Peter marks the development of the dominance of the church in Rome as a centre influencing Christian congregations throughout the Roman Empire.[357] According to Boring the problematic passage in 1 Pet 3:18–22 describing Christ's decent to the spirits in prison to preach to them should also be understood as moral

---

354. Cf. Elliott, *1 Peter: New Translation*, 103.
355. Horrell, *Epistles*, 11.
356. Ibid.
357. See Brown and Maier, 1983; Brown, Donfried, and Reumann, *Der Petrus der Bibel*, 132.

instruction.[358] Just as Christ proclaimed the gospel in a dark and hopeless situation, the Christians should remain faithful to the gospel in adverse circumstances. This explanation of Boring could very well make sense within the context of the letter. The preceding sentence explicitly states that Christians should rather suffer for doing right than for doing wrong and then the paragraph is introduced by ὅτι indicating that a motivational sub clause is about to follow. Many scholars therefore view 1 Peter as an answer to these congregations in the midst of suffering to encourage and console them.[359] This consolation is founded in the eschatological hope which the letter describes in 1 Pet 1:3–5. Dryden, however, disagrees that consolation was the author's main motivation for writing his letter.[360] Although consolation is indeed a strong motive in the letter, Dryden views the paraenetic nature of the letter with its purpose to encourage moral development and character growth among those who recently converted from their Gentile ways to Christianity and are now estranged from their former pagan practices as the main purpose for writing the letter.[361] Schlatter already had the view that the author was prompted to write the epistle in order to instruct his audience on "how to suffer."[362]

The proposed hypothesis of this study agrees with this approach. Lohse further notes that the unit in 1 Pet 2:11—3:12, in which the *Haustafel* is employed, stands out as the centre of the epistle urging the addressees to endure and maintain a life of good conduct, in spite of the slandering that they are subjected to, so that the non-believers will see their good works and praise God.[363] The church is also encouraged to be obedient to the authorities. According to Lohse the *Haustafel* traditions, which also occur in other New Testament writings, is used here to serve the main purpose of the epistle, namely that the suffering Christians should through their good deeds "silence the ignorance of foolish men" (cf. 1 Pet 2:15). Balch, with his emphasis on the *Haustafel*, argues that the author wanted his audience to reduce social tension with their non-believing neighbours by proper conduct in the household.[364] Partially, this study agrees, however, Balch's view that the author wanted to encourage assimilation and conformation cannot be accepted. The author places too much stress on the distinctiveness of

---

358. Boring, *1 Peter*, 45.
359. E.g., Lohse, "Parenesis," 42.
360. Dryden, *Theology and Ethics*, 40.
361. See also Lohse, "Parenesis," 42–43.
362. Schlatter, *Petrus und Paulus*, 13.
363. Lohse, "Parenesis," 43.
364. Balch, *Let Wives*, 81.

the Christian community. Achtemeier correctly states that assimilation into Hellenistic culture was what the author wanted to discourage the most.[365] For Elliott, as mentioned above, the author was adamant that the Christian community should maintain their distinctive Christian character and identity and that to re-assimilate would be a form of regression with the ultimate outcome that the Christian communities would cease to exist.

The eschatology of 1 Peter is indeed not a delayed or imminent eschatology, but a *realised* eschatology. It could therefore not be argued that the author is encouraging his audience to persevere through their suffering since the end of all things is at hand. The eschatological motif in 1 Peter much rather serves as a motivation for certain moral conduct.

The epistle's emphasis on conversion, especially in 1 Peter 1:13—2:3, fits with the paraenetic agenda, describing life before and after conversion in order to promote the virtues of the new and eradicate the vices of the former. Here the birth and baptism imagery plays an important role. It is not possible to be "unborn"; therefore it is impossible to return to their former way of life.[366] In the words of Beare, ". . . the writer is concerned with to set forth the manner of life to be followed by the Christian in the Church and in the world and he refers to the doctrines of the faith only as to principles held in common by him and the readers, to which they may appeal with confidence in seeking their to direct their conduct."[367]

The question arises, however, why the author responds with a paraenetic letter to the suffering that his audience is experiencing. Why does he encourage them to strive for excellence in moral conduct while they are suffering? The answer that Dryden provides is that the author responds to the "moral challenge" of suffering.[368] The human reaction towards suffering would be revolution, retribution, violence and vengeance, yet the author requires them to maintain the moral higher ground. Dryden, very importantly, notes that they are confronted with two temptations. The first is to retaliate and to re-assimilate to their previous ways and the second is to respond with revolutionary activity and violence.

The newly converted are not only faced with the challenges of adapting to their new status and the accompanying estrangement, they are also subjected to suffering that could lead to persecution. Therefore the author does not simply write to them in order to comfort them and the aid them in surviving these troubling times, he urges them towards character

365. Achtemeier, "Newborn Babes," 219, cf. Elliott, "Situation and Strategy," 72–73.
366. Dryden, *Theology and Ethics*, 43–44.
367. Beare, *First Epistle*, 50.
368. Dryden, *Theology and Ethics*, 44.

development amidst these circumstances. In the words of Dryden: "In fact, the author interprets their situation of suffering as a means of bringing about growth. Persecution is not something to be endured but an *opportunity for growth*."[369] This character growth is not simply manifested in good and virtuous conduct but also in growing faith and dependence upon God. This is an important aspect of the author's agenda because of the universal human response to suffering. Questions about God's apparent absence or God lacking to intervene with radical cataclysmic actions always arise. The faithful do not experience God as loving or caring, but they feel abandoned, struggling with the universal theodicy question. The author of 1 Peter seems to be aware of this doubt in the minds of his audience and therefore emphasises God's grace and continuous love for them (cf. 1 Peter 1:3–12). The author wants them to interpret their suffering and God's apparent neglect in another way: to be unified with Christ in this unique way through sharing in his suffering and ultimately sharing in his glory should be viewed as a grace of God (1 Pet 5:10).

This also illustrates how 1 Peter's application of theology (indicative) and moral instructions (imperative) are inseparable and employed both to serve the purpose of the letter. Moral ideals which are not rooted in faith have no substance and nothing concrete to serve as motivation. Therefore Dryden, and this study seeks to follow him, argues for the classical Reformation principle that good works could only be the result of faith, and faith therefore has priority over good works.[370] The character growth and good conduct that the author seeks to promote is only possible through dependence upon God in faith. Boring indicates that the evangelisation of the addressees and their rebirth was the initiative of God, who called them out of the darkness into a marvellous light (cf. 1 Pet 1:15; 2:9).[371] God's initiative will be brought to a *grand finale* when He reveals his eschatological glory and the humble will be exalted (cf. 1 Pet 5:6).

Green adds that the author is against Christians seeking to form alliances with Romans in powerful positions.[372] God should be seen as the only One on whom they can depend and therefore they should refuse to conform to Roman conventions and to the Roman worldview. Rather, they should adapt the values of the merciful God who elected and valued what the world has rejected. To a certain extend the author writes an invitation to adapt one's worldview to God's view of the world. In the words of Green, 1 Peter

---

369. Ibid., 45, my italics.
370. Ibid., 47.
371. Boring, "Narrative Dynamics," 31.
372. Green, *1 Peter*, 3.

"offers not so much an invitation as an exercise in formation in the character and ways of God."[373] Their conduct should be modelled on that of Christ, who also rejected the politics of his day and suffered on a *Roman* cross. The Christian communities were struggling with finding and maintaining their identity as God's holy people in a hostile world. This struggle is alleviated by identifying with the suffering Christ in the hope that they will also share in his glorification certified by the resurrection of Christ.

A further important aim of the letter is the missionary ethic that it proposes. Elliott argues that it was an important concern for the early Christian communities to be attractive for outsiders.[374] They were attractive, precisely because of their distinctiveness, they formed an alternative community. To the same extent as they have a missionary obligation to the rest of the world, they also have a responsibility towards one another, expressed in mutual love, hospitality and ministry (1 Pet 4:7–11).[375] McDonald uses the term "crucible" to refer to the context in which the ethics of the first Christian communities were formed.[376] The Christians should be characterised by respect for everyone, especially those in authoritative positions (1 Pet 2:13–17). Yet the emphasis of the entire letter is on how Christians should respond to their hostile neighbours—they have a missionary obligation towards them (1 Pet 2:11–12) and should persue peace with their neighbours (1 Pet 3:11).[377] This context was influenced by interaction between tradition, context, world view and their situation of living. An ethos had to be created which was to be expressed in their everyday practises and which was in corrolation to their teaching. MacIntyre summarises it as follows:

> What they set themselves out to achieve instead—often not recognising fully what they were doing—was the construction of new forms of community within which the moral life could be sustained so that both morality and civility might survive the coming ages of barbarism and darkness.[378]

Christian communities departed from the social world in which they existed, yet they did not practise asceticism. They were still living *in* this society, although with a radically different world view and accompanying ethos.

---

373. Green, *1 Peter*, 3.
374. Elliott, *1 Peter: New Translation*, 104.
375. Michaels, *1 Peter*, xxxv.
376. McDonald, *Crucible*, 10.
377. Michaels, *1 Peter*, xxxv.
378. MacIntyre, *After Virtue*, 263.

Their social and public lives were now to be determined by their status as Christians or followers of Christ.

The first Christian communities originated amidst conflict. According to McDonald a more stimulating context could not be wished for the origin of a new religious movement.[379] New questions arised which required new answers. The Christian movement became more and more independent and became a context where a new ethos had to be created. Within Christian communities equality existed among its members, or was at least desired, as will be indicated later in this study. Yet these communities were not completely removed from the Greco-Roman world within which they existed. Christians interacted with the unconverted when they travelled to the cities and visited the market squares. Some were slawes, some were wives, some were husbands and some were formar Jews. Lampe's illuminating observation is that Christians operated in two very distinctive contexts.[380] Their everyday lives were still conducted within the worldly Greco-Roman context in which they were slaves, masters, husbands or wives. Yet within the household congregation equality among all members was taught. Unity within Christ transfered boundaries. This however did not change the culturalal influences that shaped their society. These communities belonged to contexts that were established by power cultural influences. Bellah defines the Christian communities as socially interdependent, which means that they largely depended on oneantoher and therefore included everyone in discussions, decisions and practices.[381] These communities, by so doing, formed their own "crucible" within which Christian ethics developed.[382] Their ethics as well as their ethos were shaped by a number of influences from their surrounding environment.

Such an example is the sence of community that was established by *symposia* and *collegia*. Although converted Christians, especially the audience of 1 Peter, were encouraged to part with such organisations, they provided a model on which Christian communities could be built. Within the *symposia* and *collegia* the value of hospitality was indispensable. The convention of these groups was also a source of communial support also entailing religious commitment and/or sacrifices and a communual meal. Communual dining played a key role in the creation of solidarity, but also the maintenance of status, gender roles and power relations. It also reflected the values, norms, attitudes and worldview of a particular group. Dining

---

379. McDonald, *Crucible*, 15.
380. Lampe, "Language of Equality," 79.
381. Bellah, et al., Habits of the Heart, 16–21.
382. McDonald, *Crucible*, 151.

together indicated a bond of faithfulness and intimicy among its members. Borg states that this dining together of people of unequal statusses was one of the most controversial aspects of the early Christian movement.[383]

Koester states that Epicureanism was the philosophical school with the closest parallel to early Christian communities.[384] Inclusiveness and friendship were typical characteristics of the Epicureans. Meeks aggrees with this and states that the Epicureans provides the closest analogy with early Christian communities.[385] The radical difference is however that the Epicureans derived their ethic from Aristotle, which was aimed at personal development rather than mutual relationships. Relationships were only a means to an end, so that an individual would receive the necessary support to realise his or her personal goals.[386]

For the follower of Christ this was different. The closest family ties and solidarity were to be experienced within the Christian community and communian with those who did the will of God. The Christian community became a new family which shared in communal ethos and beliefs. Christian communities were not monastic. Many house churches developed in busy cities and members stil played their roles within the greater society.

Van Eck indicates that the new community in Christ was defined by the radical reversal of roles *inter alia* child/adult, servant/master, first/last, rich/poor.[387] Life inside the Christian communities was characterised by freedom from the self, and by living in the new way as modelled by Christ.[388] The Christian family did not originate from blood ties or from a master-servant relation. Rather it was founded on the principles of voluntary enterance and equality.[389] The only precondition was that idolatry and other paganist religious activities should be terminated. The identity of the Christian communities was characterised by their understanding of themselves as the people of God.[390] Although shaped upon the model of the ancient household, the earliest Christian households were not homogenic.

In order to become part of a Christian community, one had to break with dominant religious ideas. Van Eck further indicates that the new community of equals also became a community of hope for the socially

---

383. Borg, *Conflict*, 78–79.
384. Koester, *History*, 141.
385. Meeks, *Origins*, 26.
386. Nussbaum, "Therapeutic Arguments," 69.
387. Van Eck, *Galilee and Jerusalem*, 28.
388. Waetjen, *Recording of Power*, 100.
389. Barton, *Discipleship and Family*, 85.
390. McDonald, *Crucible*, 153.

marginalised.[391] Membership of the Christian community radically transformed the status of those who formally had no status.

It can be accepted that those who entered these communities had to make radical paradigm shifts. This created friction and was no easy matter indeed. Lampe stated that the fact that Christians remained part of the Greco-Roman social context and at the same time formed part of the Christian communities lead to certain internal conflict, e.g., a Christian bussiness man of high social ranking could find himself in an embarrassing situation with female slaves (which were now considerred to be his equals) or when women played leading roles in the congregation.[392] The ideal of a egaliterian community influenced the Christians' view of their world and changed the way they regarded women and slaves, as will be argued later in this study.[393]

The first Christian communities indeed formed an alternative community based on their new identity in Christ.[394] Barton states that to take part in the new fictional family in Christ was a vocation to the practical manifestation of the values as embodied by the life and works of Christ.[395] These values include love, sacrifice, respect, forgiveness, obedience, faithfulness, friendship and hospitality. These values had to be realised in the everyday lives of the faithful. Barton also argues that these new relations had the potential of transforming the current social structures of the time.[396] According to Barton, the circumstances of the early Christians was not without hope.[397] Although the followers of Jesus were always subjected to social marginalisation, they also lived in the promise of a new eschatological community founded on the authority of Christ. These communities were contra-communities, a new social community which was developing.

If the Christian communities were to subject to the temptation of returning to the former existence and to conform once again to the society from which they separated since their conversion to Christianity, this distinctiveness would be completely lost.[398] The continuation and growth of the Christian movement necessitated their divinely conferred identity and purpose to be emphasised. Balch would argue for assimilation into the

---

391. Van Eck, *Galilee and Jerusalem*, 29.
392. Lampe, "Language of Equality," 80.
393. Cf. ibid., 81.
394. Roloff, *Die Kirche*, 38.
395. Barton, *Life Together*, 35.
396. Ibid., 112.
397. Barton, *Discipleship and Family*, 107.
398. Cf. Elliott, *1 Peter: New Translation*, 104; contra Balch, *Let Wives*, 1986.

greater Greco-Roman culture in order not to provoke further resistance,[399] whereas Elliott has often been criticised as viewing 1 Peter to argue for withdrawal from society in order to live a life of holiness.[400]

## New Testament Ethics

Plutarch was of the opinion that philosophy provides a cure for the weak and the suffering, because through philosophy it is possible to know what is beautiful and what is offensive; what is righteous and what is unrighteous, what should be pursued and what should be avoided; and how one should behave towards the gods, the elderly, the law, the foreigner, the authorities, friends, women, children and slaves. The gods ought to be worshiped, the elderly honored, laws abided by, authorities obeyed, friends loved, women handled with care, children loved and slaves not mistreated, and most importantly, to celebrate good fortune abundantly and not to mourn misfortune too much, not to overindulge in pleasure and not to be too harsh and inhumane in anger.[401]

Before defining ethics *per se*, it is necessary for the purposes of this study to discern between *ethos* and *ethics*. Wolter views *ethos* as a canon of institutionalised behaviour which is valid within a certain society at a certain place at a certain point in time.[402] There is a close relation between the *ethos* practiced by a society and the identity of that particular society, for people from being born into a certain society are raised and educated to conform to the *ethos* of that society. This definition is applicable to understanding the *ethos* of the Christian communities to which 1 Peter is addressed. These communities should be defined by their distinctive "Christian" behaviour and so their identity as Christians will become established. This identity has an internal as well as an external function. Internally, it provides a code of conduct among their fellow Christians and externally it disassociates them from the rest of the society and at the same time provides an established norm for engaging with the outside world. Wolter discerns between an "inclusive" and an "exclusive" *ethos*.[403] The first refers to behaviour that the Christian community shares with the rest of the outside world as normative, e.g., to refrain from theft. The latter is what Wolter calls the "boundary markers," in other words that which is distinctively Christian and defines their unique

399. Balch, *Let Wives*; Balch 1981.
400. Elliott, *A Home*; Elliott, *1 Peter: New Translation*; cf. Green, *1 Peter*, 2.
401. Plutarch, *[Lib. ed.]* 10; cf. Wolter, "Die ethische Identität," 61.
402. Wolter, "Die ethische Identität," 61.
403. Ibid., 64.

identity. Often, it is argued that the Christians are different from the rest of society for they are better, elected by God and therefore has a special status. Furthermore, Wolter notes that Christians should be known by *agape*, their unconditional love for one another.[404] This made the early Christian movement particularly attractive for the marginalised. *Agape* should become the discerning factor in Christian *ethos*, along with an egalitarian reciprocity, which would be the very foundation of the essential Christian ecclesiology. Zimmermann importantly notes that it can never be certain if the *ethos* described by a New Testament author is an actual historical practice or an idealised practice to be desired.[405] He therefore proposes that it is safer to speak of an "ethos remembered" for it has to be reflected within the Christian communities to have an identity building function. There is just a dialectic relation between the community and the text.

*Ethics*, on the other hand, is first defined by Aristotle[406] as the "systematic-theoretical examination of the lived ethos."[407] *Ethics* is therefore a reflective science. It requires into the foundations of the lived ethos, analyses traditions and norms and questions the motives behind morality. Zimmermann argues that as far as the writings of the New Testament is concerned, ethics is rather "implicit."[408] This means that there exists an ethic behind the paraenetic discourse, while the paraenesis itself is more focussed on the *ethos* of the community that it addresses. An "ethical superstructure" could be derived from the New Testament text although it is not explicitly evident from the text itself. Although derived from the text, it is not something that should be imposed on the text, and should therefore never become divorced from the text itself. Ethics can also never be completely separated from the *ethos*, for ethical reflection is embedded within a concretely lived *ethos*. Not only the situation, but especially the text and the acceptance of the text as canonical had an influence on the shaping of Christian ethics.

This study, therefore, concludes that New Testament ethics has a hermeneutical function. The world behind the text, *id est* the historical context and *Sitz im Leben*, the critical exegete and the world in front of the text, *id est* the presuppositions of the exegete—which should always be remembered, engage in an exciting interplay. The science of hermeneutics is *par excellence* a science concerned with giving meaning, thus a science concerned with

---

404. Ibid., 81.
405. Zimmermann, "Ethics of New Testament Writings," 415.
406. See translation by Kilian-Dirlmeier 1984.
407. Cf. Zimmermann, "Ethics of New Testament Writings," 399.
408. Zimmermann, "Ethics of New Testament Writings," 401–404.

existentialism.[409] Heidegger designed the so-called "hermeneutic circle" that is never completed until the reality in front of the exegete meats the reality of the text and the world behind the text. This engagement generates meaning. Ethics is also concerned with inquiring about the meaning of existence and therefore questions to what extent a desired *ethos* is in fact desirable and plausible within a concrete situation. Mouton states that the writings of the New Testament, considered as canonical by the Christian community, have an inherent transformative potential that could be applied to the everyday practical lives of the faithful.[410] Because of the biblical texts being embedded in the patriarchal system of the first century Mediterranean world, a hermeneutic of suspicion becomes a necessity. In the engagement between the biblical text and the contemporary context a creative space originates which requires a consciousness of the preliminary status of our statements.

## Methodology

Van Eck indicated that a literary investigation of the text and the descriptive exegesis of the social contexts in which texts originated were not sufficient in order to shed light on the rethorical strategy[411] of the author and on the objective(s) that the author wanted to accomplish.[412] This is of great importance. A text was designed to function within a particular historical context. It was intended to have an effect of the lifes and behaviour of its recipients. Historical critisism was particularly concerned with the socalled *Sitz im Leben* of biblical texts. This was a descriptive methodology, which attempted at providing answers to the questions of *what happened when and where*. What was not sufficiently dealt with were the questions of *why and how* the circumstances described by the historical criticism necessitated the composition of a particular text and what the author of that text aimed to achieve by such a writing. What needs to be explained is the relation between the biblical text and the social condition it addressed. No text originates in a vacuum. All ideas and therefore also theological ideas are socially formed and need to be explored within the social and historical contexts

---

409. Pieper, *Einführung*, 229.

410. Mouton, "Transformative Potential," 244–53.

411. Elliott, *A Home*, 10, prefers the term "strategy" over "purpose" or "intention," because a strategy would imply the conscious and calculated choice for the employment of word, phrases, quotations, a certain genre, etc., to accomplish the intended effect on the recipients. The way in which a biblical text has been designed thus becomes important.

412. Van Eck, *Galilee and Jerusalem*, 82; cf. Elliott, *A Home*, 3.

that shaped them. There exists an enagement between social realities and religious symbols.[413] Considered in this way, biblical literature becomes products of a reflection on a dynamic social process. Elliott states that a social-scientific reading of the text "compliments and improves" historical critisism, for it also pays attention to the social and the sociological dimentions of a text.[414] Social-scientific exegesis also includes the circumstances that necessitated the writing of a texts and the author's choice of a certain strategy in order to convey his theology.

*Formgeschichte* also has a social interest. Concern for the *Sitz im Leben* of the early Christian movement is per se a concern for the social context in which it originated.[415] A certain *Sitz im Leben* influences the author's choice for a certain *Gattung/Form* as the appropriate vehicle of the message. Ironicly Van Aarde indicates that exegetes in the twentieth century paid more attention to *Formgeschichte* and consequently neglected the social sciences.[416] The dynamics of ideas, concepts and knowledge which are socially determined ought to be considered scientifically.[417] Gager already critisised the overemphasis on the literal reading of the text and the fact that the birth of Christianity was "a social world in the making" is neglected.[418] Exegetes increasingly employ social scientific theories in order to further the understanding, description and explanation of the dynamics of people, groups and cultures in the ancient Mediterranean world.[419] Wayne A. Meeks made a valuable contribution by his book *The First Urban Christians: The Social World of the Apostle Paul*, where he described various social aspects of first century Christians.

The contexts within which texts originate also encompass to the social conduct, social systems, social groups, social institutions and codes of conduct present within that context.[420] Texts are further shaped by the language, context and social perspectives within which they originate. A text is ultimately a way of communication, and always communicates something of the context and social background behind it. Therefore an exegete needs to take cognisance of not only independent historical and social data,

---

413. Elliott, *A Home*, 4.

414. Ibid., 1.

415. Ibid., 3; cf. Osiek, *What Are They Saying*, 3; see also Zimmermann, *Neutestamentliche Methodenlehre*, 145.

416. Van Aarde, "Inleiding," 54.

417. Van Aarde, "*Evangelium Infantium*," 437.

418. Gager, *Kingdom*, 2.

419. Van Aarde, "Inleiding," 50.

420. Van Eck, *Galilee and Jerusalem*, 82

but also the interrelations of ideas, common behaviour, value and cultural systems. Elliott indicated that a social scientific study of a text has two important focusses.[421] Firstly social science is employed in order to construct theories and models which could be applied to annalyse data which could aid the exegete in getting a perspective of the ancient Mediterranean world and the early Christian movement. Secondly the rethorical strategy and the objectives of the author with a particular strategy need to be investigated. Van Aarde states that social scientific exegesis also focuses on the ancient Mediterranean culture and the social interactions which determined this culture.[422] It is concerned with analyzing the social contexts of documents in the Bible and to understand the rethoric within the message in light of the culture. Social scientific exegesis also explores the narrative world of a text and the commentary or criticism of the author on the social context.

Different aspects of social scientific criticism were explored in previous studies, but this study will pay attention to social marginalisation;[423] the symbolic universe;[424] social identity and group formation;[425] "contra community" (in other words the "subversive" nature of Jesus and his first followers)[426] and family values.[427]

Elliott convincingly argued for the combination of literal and social scientific criticism in order to explain texts within their contexts in terms of the original intended communication between the author and the recipients.[428] Social-scientific exegesis wants to determine the rethorical effect of the text on its audience. Already at the beginning of the twentieth century Gustav Adolf Deissmann argued in his book *Licht vom Oosten*, translated in 1927 as *Light from the Ancient East: The New Testament Illustrated by Recently Discovered Texts of the Greaco-Roman World*, that New Testament texts should not only be read literary, but also socially and against the backdrop of the Greek folk literature of the first century AD.

This study agrees with Elliott that the genre, structure, content, themes and message of a text are shaped by social and cultural dynamics which apply within a certain historical context and these presupposes a particular

---

421. Elliott, "Social-Scientific Study," 5–6.
422. Van Aarde, "Inleiding," 50.
423. See Duling, *New Testament*.
424. See Joubert, "Van werklikheid"; Joubert, "Wanneer die onmoontlike."
425. See Malina, *New Testament World*.
426. See Malina and Rohrbaugh, *John*, 7.
427. See Balch and Osiek, *Families*.
428. Elliott, *A Home*, 3.

response.[429] So the intention of a text within its context is determined.[430] The rethorical strategy of a text needs to be discovered.[431]

Peterson also suggests a combination of the literary and social scientific methods since it considers the literary, rethorical and sociological aspects of the text.[432] These two methods, although discernable, are inseperable and essential to a comprehensive understanding of the text. However, a literary analysis should precede a social scientific reading of the text. The reasoning behind this sequence is that the social and historical contexts are not directly accessible to the modern exegete and could at best be constructed by research. Such a construction necessitates a literary analysis.[433] Elliott regards this method be be a more "comprehensive" reading of the text.[434] Van Aarde emphasises that a social scientific reading of the text guards the exegete against an anachronistic reading of the text.[435] Such a reading of a text presupposes phenomena that occured chronologically after the composition of the text as sociological phenomena within the text. The exegete should take into consideration that biblical texts originated millennia ago within a homogenous predominantly agrarian society, far removed from the current idustrialised post-modern global village.[436]

This study will consequently read the selected texts synchronically as well as diachronically as suggested by the methodology of historical criticism. However the study will move beyond historical criticism to social scientific criticism in order to determine the rhetorical function of a text as well as to attempt to discover the author's theology.

Horrell stressed the aspect of ideology critisism of a socail scientific reading of the text.[437] Horrell adds that feminist and liberation theology employed a hermeneutic of suspicion.[438] This kind of hermeneutic refers to the social conditions of the people to whom the text refers as well as the audience of the text and those who are exposed to it. "Social conditions" imply those factors that influence a group and include gender; age; ethicity; social class; status; nationality; language; political, social, and religious af-

---

429. Elliott, "Social-Scientific Study," 6.
430. Cf. Van Aarde, "Inleiding," 65.
431. Van Aarde, "Sosiaal-wetenskaplike," 1123; cf. Elliott, *A Home*, xix,xxii.
432. Peterson, *Rediscovering Paul*, 6.
433. Van Staden, *Compassion*, 33.
434. Elliott, *A Home*, 8.
435. Van Aarde, "Inleiding," 52a.
436. Ibid., 65a.
437. Horrell, *1 Peter*, 22–24.
438. Van Aarde, "Sosiaal-wetenskaplike," 1125.

filiantions.⁴³⁹ Elliott argues that social-scientific exegesis is critical towards ideologies reflected in biblical texts.⁴⁴⁰

A hermeneutic of suspicion together with a growing conscience of gaurding against an ethnocentric reading of the text has ethical implications. Often ancient pre-modern texts are read through the paradigm of current social structures which leads to an ethnocentric and reductionistic reading of the text. The latter means that the total distinctness and strangeness of the biblical text are reduced to that which is commonly known. Consequently the effect of the text on the modern reader, that originates from its distinctness, is lost.⁴⁴¹ Elliott adds that the exegete also brings his or her own presuppositions and self-interests to the text, for the exegete is also a product of his or her history and social context.⁴⁴² What an exegete discovers in a text, is that which his or her social position, political affiliations, experience and gender prepared them to see.

The insight of Peter Berger in his book, *Questions of Faith: A Skeptical Affirmation of Christianity* needs to be noted.⁴⁴³ According to Berger social realities are influenced dialectically through a symbolic world. This symbolic world, he calls the *sacred canopy*, which means that people's social ideas, values, thoughts, emotions and beliefs are influenced by a transcendent world.⁴⁴⁴ This could collectively be called culture—a theoretical abstraction that influences the core of human existence. The symbolic universe leads to the establishment of a social universe where this culture is expressed.⁴⁴⁵

Dialectical thoughts in philosophy, theology and sociology that took cogniscance of the tention that exists between the symbolic universe and the social universe led to the realisation that culture is relative to a certain period, geographical location and frame of reference. Within this dialectical tension a search for control of the symbolic universe originates. This leads to a process of mystification. Through mystification norms become internalised and socialised as canononical.

These norms become generally accepted and aids in defining social identity and are viewed as authoritative since they are divinely sanctioned. This process is easily realised within the socalled "book religions," e.g., Judaism, Islam and Christianity since these norms are considered to be devinely

439. Ibid., 1126.
440. Elliott, *A Home*, 11.
441. Van Aarde, "Sosiaal-wetenskaplike," 1132.
442. Elliott, *A Home*, 12.
443. Berger, *Questions of Faith*; see Berger and Luckmann, 1966, 42–128.
444. Cf. Van Aarde, "Sosiaal-wetenskaplike," 1132.
445. Ibid., 1133; cf. Elliott, *A Home*, 12.

revealed in sacred texts and are therefore absolute.[446] However, when a text is read critical of the culture, it is doubted whether a meaningfull life is necessarily synonymous with social conformity. Berger calls the blind submisiveness to culture with reference to matters of faith *bad faith* since culturaly constructed imperatives are mystified and legitmated as the will of God. Cultural criticism questions the traditional and the conventional and does not simply accept these to be "divine."[447] An ethical study should always challenge traditionally accepted conventions. This approach has its roots in the tradition of the Reformation which displayed the courage to reduce human achievements and to acknowledge the total incompetence of humanity to completely understand the will of God. When theology is apprehended by human culture, the task of theology to challange and criticise is lost and human thoughts and actions are viewed too positively.

This study wants to illustrate that the author of 1 Peter also took a critical stance against the culture of the day and therefore a *prescriptive ethic* could be deduced from the letter. The author was not pleased with the current circumstance of his audience and with the way that they conducted themselves within this environment. The audience was encouraged to form a contra-community and to maintain their radical difference from the rest of the society. Therefore they needed to be devoted to the will of God as proclaimed by the gospel and by imitating Christ.[448]

Thus 1 Peter was composed in order to effect the narrower as well as the wider social contexts of its recipients.[449] Therefore the way in which the author chose to write was not a random choice, but a specific literal, sociological and theological strategy was embedded within the rethorical strategy of the author. The text was designed in such a way that it produced a certain response from the audience. Within this strategy, the self-interests[450] of the author also become apparent. Often, as is the case with 1 Peter, the document does not only reflect the interests of a particular author, but also of a particular group. Therefore the social interests, social class, organisational structures, geographical locations and authority of the author or group needs to be considered.[451] Since a text originated within a particular context, influenced by history and sociology, the world behind the text is more often than not an implicit matter, because it was not necessary for

---

446. Van Aarde, "Sosiaal-wetenskaplike," 1136.
447. Ibid., 1137.
448. Cf. Ibid., 1140–41.
449. Elliott, *A Home*, 8.
450. That which motivated the author to compose the text.
451. Elliott, *A Home*, 11.

the author to explain the social conditions in which they lived. Therefore it is the task of the exegete to construct this world. In order to make such a construction the exegete needs to pay attention to the genre, structure, content and function of a text. The *Wirkungsgesichte* of a text needs to be considered. Biblical texts and their redaction are processes of ongoing social engagement. No biblical text is a static absolute document, universally and timelessly applicable to any given situation. Rather biblical texts engaged in the comparable themes in the different periods of history.[452] It is a hermeneutic task to discover these recurring theological motives which moves from the peculiar to the general.

Horrell rightly notes that every text runs the danger of being used in order to substantuate a particular point of view.[453] Every exegete approaches the text with his or her own prejudices, presuppositions and agendas. Meaning is created by the encounter of the reader with the text. It is thus possible that 1 Peter could be misused in order to legitimise the subjection of slaves and women or that Christianity is superior to Judaism and replaced the true Israel. The aim of this study is to, as far as possible, avoid falling into these traps. Therefore a hermeneutic of suspicion, which exposes the powerplay behind these texts and which gives a voice to the oppressed, could lead to a more inclusive reading of the text and allows the text to still make a moral appeal to the reader. Karl Barth summerised it very well when he stated that the objective of the honest exegete should not be to ask what the prophets or apostles said, but what ought to be said on the basis of what they said.[454] The value of any biblical text is situated in its ability to continue to challenge and discomfort us in every new context.[455]

## Hypothesis

Since 1 Peter is the document in the New Testament which contains the largest occurrence of the Greek word πάσχω or derivatives thereof, it is safe to say that suffering is probably the most important theme in the epistle. When dealing with the "implicit" (see discussion above) ethics of 1 Peter, the question arises as to what the role of suffering is in the author's implied ethical thinking. The *ethos* the author wants his audience to embrace could easily be derived from the extensive paraenetic literature that the letter contains, but as far as the *ethics* that underlies these moral instructions is

---

452. Ibid., 9.
453. Horrell, *1 Peter*, 110.
454 Barth, *CD* 1.1, 16.
455 Horrell, *1 Peter*, 111.

concerned, matters are less clear. However, as previously argued, ethics is never completely separated from its context and especially not from its text, so the text of 1 Peter does provide certain clues as to the ethical thinking of the author. From the text it is clear that suffering is the predominant theme of the letter. Therefore this study would suggest that the author employs an *ethics of suffering*.[456] Suffering ethics is very closely related to an *Imitatio Christi* ethic, which would entail to follow in the footsteps of Christ and to do as Christ has done. However, with suffering ethics, the focus on what ought to be imitated shifts from the general caring, compassionate loving example of Christ to the *suffering* of Christ. In other words, Christ should be followed in his suffering and especially in his suffering. This is illustrated by the author's employment of the suffering servant imagery from Isa 52:13—53:12 in 1 Pet 2:18-24. It is of further significance that the author employs this imagery when addressing the slaves—those in the position with the least power. Not only should the slandering and *malefides* of the outside world be tolerated as the suffering servant quietly endured his suffering, but Christ should be followed even beyond his death.

First Peter 2:21 is part of a larger textual unit which consists of an exhortation of Christian household servants (1 Pet 2:18-20) which is succeeded and supported by an extensive Christological argument (1 Pet 2:22-25). And this unit is in turn part of a line of thought that commences with 1 Pet 2:11 which introduces the second major section of the letter. The social condition and divine vocation of the οἰκέται is typical of the condition of the entire Christian community. The fact that they are exposed to unkind and hostile masters makes them a prototype of the entire Christian community who became vulnerable within a hostile environment. The exhortation aimed at the servants therefore becomes a model or a basis for the conduct of the entire Christian community. Subsequently, the Christological argumentation provides the indicative for the imperative that follows it as well as precedes it. "The innocent suffering of righteous servants, like that of righteous believers (cf. 1 Pet 3:12, 4:18) derives its power and motivation from the vicarious suffering of the Righteous One (1 Pet 3:18), the Servant of God, Jesus Christ."[457]

According to Elliott the first section of the letter, 1 Pet 1:1—2:10, emphasises the distinctive new identity of the believers.[458] Through the grace of God and because of their faithful response to the gospel the believers are incorporated into the household of God. Sanctified by their vocation they

---

456. My italics.
457. Elliott, "Backward and Forward," 188.
458. Ibid., 186.

constitute an elect and holy community who is called to live distinctively and holy within a hostile environment. Because of this identity the letter turns its attention to the conduct of this new community within their hostile environment (1 Pet 2:11—3:12). The believers were to distance themselves from the ways of their non-believing neighbours, and although they were slandered as evil-doers, they were to live such an attractive way of life that non-believers will come to glorify God (cf. 1 Pet 2:12). The author then handles the good social conduct in the different spheres of life.

Christ furthermore preached to the spirits who formerly did not know God, but was saved because of his patience, "through water" just as he saved Noah and his family. So these suffering Christians are to live and preach the gospel to "spirits in captivity"—a dark, godforsaken, threatening and hostile environment in which it seems unlikely that the proclamation of the gospel and the existence of the Christian church will prevail. Christ preached during the same, maybe even worse, circumstances and by the grace of God, which cannot be comprehended by mankind, these "spirits" were saved. By following Christ, by enduring and by taking part in his suffering these Christians ought to become the agents of salvation and "win over" the non-believers among which they live.

The author of 1 Peter is not unique in his application of an *ethics of suffering*. As far as 1 Pet 2:22–25 is concerned, there is a general consensus among scholars that the author used an early Christian liturgical tradition in the form of a "Christ hymn" or "Passion hymn."[459] The use of the tradition is indicated by the occurrence of similar kerygmatic, liturgical and creedal material.[460] In 1 Peter elements of the Christological passion hymn as well as redactional additions were employed to elaborate on the statement made in verse 21 to confirm the vicarious nature and the consequences for salvation that the suffering and death of Jesus Christ had.

This Christ hymn or passion hymn belongs to a tradition upon which the Synoptic Gospels also relied. Goppelt traces it back to the primitive ὑπὲρ formula which is found in the words of Jesus concerning his immanent passion (cf. Mark 10:45; 14:24).[461] The motifs used here are derived from the suffering servant song of Isaiah 53. This Old Testament passage played a key role in the formation of early Christology. It is also the author's reliance upon the Suffering Servant passage, which he uses to unite the suffering righteous believers *passio iustorum* with their suffering righteous Lord

---

459. Cf. Goppelt, *Der erste Petrusbrief*, 204–207.
460. Cf. Deichgräber, *Gotteshymnus*, 142.
461. Goppelt, *Der erste Petrusbrief*, 206–7.

*passio iusti*, which relates 1 Peter with the Gospels and especially with the Gospel of Mark.[462]

The author of Mark, writing thirty to forty years earlier, also from Rome (as will be argued in this study) addresses an audience faced with the same crisis as in 1 Peter. The conflict between Rome and the Jews reached boiling point with the destruction of the temple in Jerusalem and Titus' triumph in Rome and Christians became the unfortunate scapegoats enduring hostility from both sides. An early Christian tradition, strongly influenced by the prominence of the Apostle Peter,[463] led to the composition of the First Gospel in Rome—attributed to Mark, who was regarded by tradition as the secretary of Peter. Although deprived from any historical plausibility, a *tradition* emphasizing the importance of the character of the Apostle Peter for the authentic Christian faith developed in Rome. The author of Mark clearly employs the ethic of suffering as is illustrated by his abundant allusion to the suffering servant imagery in Mark 14:10-11, 18, 21, 24, 41-42, 44, 61; 15:1, 5, 6-15, 39 in his construction of the passion narrative. The Markan author chooses a gospel, a narrative genre. Moral instructions are not so easily deduced from the text as in the case of paraenetic literature. That does not mean however, that the gospels contain no ethics. Ethics are certainly implicit to these writings. The bold statement in Mark 8:34 attest to this. The author of Mark is crystal clear: he, who wants to follow Christ, should be willing to suffer. Marcus contextualises this ethical statement:[464]

> Although Mark's Gospel provides no unequivocal indication, Mark 8:34 does speak of taking up one's cross and following Jesus, thus implying a participation in his sufferings. Mark 13:9-13, moreover, portrays the persecution and suffering experienced by the community as the arena in which its proclamation of the gospel manifests the power of God. If, as seems likely, the martyr church's proclamation of the gospel leads some of its hearers to cast in their lot with Jesus and thus to save their lives (see Mark 8:35-38), then we may say that indirectly, Mark's community is giving its live as ransom for many (see Mark 10:45) and pouring out its blood for their sake (see Mark 14:24). We should emphasise, however, that if indeed the idea of the vicarious suffering of the community is present in Mark, that suffering is only efficacious because of its linkage with the

---

462. Elliott, "Backward and Forward," 191.

463. Cf. The prominence of Peter in the Gospel of Mark will be developed further in this study.

464. Marcus, *Way of the Lord*, 195.

sufferings of Jesus, because it is a suffering "for his sake and the gospel's" (see again Mark 8:34–35).[465]

By following Christ in his suffering, the community testifies to the gospel of Christ, not merely as distant ideals, but as concrete lived realities—they indeed proclaimed the gospel by their blood.

When the Petrine circle composed their epistle ca. AD 100—110 in the name of the Apostle Peter, the same theological tradition was continued.[466] It was even enforced by the tradition, although legendary, of Peter's martyrdom in Rome. Peter himself became the moral exemplar. There are simply too many similarities between the historical context, theology, Christology and ethics in the Gospel of Mark and 1 Peter to be ignored. These similarities will be developed further in this study to propose that the ethics of suffering was the moral reflection behind the ethos of the Christian communities required by both the authors of Mark and 1 Peter. This hypothesis will be further illustrated by both authors' allusion to the suffering servant imagery found in Deutero-Isaiah. The authoritative Old Testament Scriptures spoke of the suffering and eventual glorification of a servant who persevered in his obedience. An appeal is now made to the audiences of Mark and 1 Peter to participate in this unification with Christ. The story of the crucified and glorified Christ becomes the story of the persecuted and divinely vindicated Christian communities, which took of their cross and followed Christ.[467]

"In Mark as well as in 1 Peter the suffering of the righteous community is inseparably linked with and based upon the suffering of Jesus Christ, the righteous One."[468] This study elaborates on the suggestion made by Elliott in reliance upon Nauck that Isaiah 53 together with certain Psalms provided motifs for a primitive Christological tradition upon which 1 Peter also draws.[469] According to Pesch the entire second half of the Gospel of Mark (Mark 8:27–16:8) incorporates a pre-Markan passion narrative and basic to this theme is the suffering righteous one, *Passio Iusti*.[470] This study elaborates on the similarities between Mark and 1 Peter especially in terms of their theologies of suffering which is based upon a larger pre-synoptic tradition.[471] The affinities between Mark and 1 Peter

465. Ibid., 195.
466. Cf. Elliott, *1 Peter: New Translation*, 127
467. Cf. Marcus, *Way of the Lord*, 186.
468. Elliott, "Backward and Forward," 192.
469. Nauck, "Freude im Leidem," 68–80.
470. Pesch, *Markusevangelium 1*, 63–68.
471. Cf. Selwyn, *The First Epistle*; Lohse, *Märtyr*, 182–87 ; Schelkle, *Petrusbriefe*

are not the result of literary dependence, but rather of reliance upon a common tradition which embraces not only the theme of "joy in suffering" but also of "solidarity in suffering."

First Peter 2:21 also has affinities with Mark. The case for the relationship between Mark and 1 Peter is further strengthened by their common origin in Rome.[472] According to Elliott: "If there is merit to this proposal, then local oral tradition shared by various groups in Rome, together with their social situation and socio-religious perspectives, would account for numerous points of contact between both documents, including their interpretation of solidarity in suffering and its link with the calling to follow Jesus."[473]

The phrase ὑπολιμπάνων ὑπογραμμὸν ἵνα ἐπακολουθήσητε τοῖς ἴχνεσιν αὐτοῦ is unique to 1 Peter, however, Mark is familiar with the expression of "following Jesus" as an expression of allegiance and solidarity with Jesus (cf. Mark 1:16–20; 2:14).

The term used by our author, ὑπογραμμός, "example," is often used in a pedagogical sense. According to Schrenk: "for purposes of instruction, a word is proposed which contains all the letters of the alphabet in a form in which is called ὑπογραμμός παιδικός."[474] While the example 1 Peter has in mind refers to the innocent suffering of Jesus, the pedagogical connotations associated with this term calls the mind the relationship between Jesus and his disciples as teacher and pupils. First Peter and Mark further associate the following of Jesus with a vocation or a calling. According to the author of 1 Peter the ultimate origin of the vocation is God Himself, whereas in Mark the calling is done by Jesus. However, in both Mark and 1 Peter the call to follow Jesus inevitably involves suffering.

"Both the Letter (1 Peter) and Gospel (Mark) originated in Rome and reflect, each in its own way, the fluid oral traditions, similar social conditions, and common theological perspectives of the Roman Christian community."[475] In support of this theory which is also held by this study, Elliott notes the following:

1. Both 1 Peter and Mark are products of a marginal, sectarian community intend upon affirming and legitimating its identity over and against Judaism and Greco-Roman society. Both distinguish those who heed the call of Jesus in faith and follow him from those who reject him, the righteous elect from the

---

112–113, Goldstein, "Die Kirche," 38–54.

472. Cf. Elliott, *A Home*, 181–94.
473. Elliott, "Backward and Forward," 194.
474. Schrenk, "Messiah," 772–773.
475 Elliott, "Backward and Forward," 194.

unrighteous sinners, those who live by the will of God from those who follow human ordinances and conventions, insiders and outsiders.

2. Both documents, however, reveal a conservative Christian stance vis-à-vis civil government. As Mark's account of the passion seeks to exonerate the Romans in the case of Jesus's execution and highlights the confession of a Roman soldier (Mark 15:39), so in 1 Peter, Christians are encouraged to be subordinate to civil authority and to regard the emperor and his governors as those charged with maintaining justice (1 Pet 2:13–17).

3. According to both documents, the relation of the elect believers to the non-believing outsiders is one of tension and conflict, resulting in the innocent suffering of both Jesus and believers.

4. Both Mark and 1 Peter describe faith, allegiance and solidarity in terms of response to the call to follow Jesus, the essence of which for both is sharing in his innocent suffering and ultimate divine vindication.

5. Accordingly, both 1 Peter and Mark employ the kerygma of Jesus's passion, death and resurrection (in the form of hymnic material as in 1 Peter, or in the form of a passion narrative as in Mark) to explain or justify the suffering of his followers.

6. In presenting this bond which suffering forges between the Lord and his followers, both documents stress a mutual obedience to God's will and cite the status and behaviour of the servant as illustrative of a proper Christian stance. And in this connection, both depict Jesus as an innocent suffering servant who provides the example for his followers to emulate. In 1 Peter and in the tradition upon which 1 Pet 2:22–25 depends, this portrait has been developed through the use of the suffering servant motif of Isaiah 53. In Mark the influence of this text is less obvious but still possible. Two later documents acquainted with 1 Peter—namely, the Letters of Clement of Rome and Polycarp to the Philippians—further illustrate the course of this Christological tradition and its association with the Isaianic text. If Mark shares the Roman provenance of 1 Peter and *1 Clement*, then it is possible that a sub-stream of local Christological tradition associating the Christ and the suffering servant of Isaiah best explains many features common to, but differently employed by and formulated in, all three Roman writings. In this case, the influence of Isaiah 53 which remains at best implicit in Mark becomes clearer in 1 Peter and more explicit in *1 Clement*.

7. Both 1 Peter and Mark employ similar ecclesial, as well as Christological, motifs and images to depict the community of the faithful. Believers are the "elect" of God, sheep once scattered but eventually gathered, and those who are called to follow the Lord. Chief among such communal metaphors, however, in both 1 Peter and Mark, is the portrayal of the believing community as the new family or household of God. In both documents οἶκος and οἰκία play a major role in locating and indentifying the true family of God. In both, the audiences are addressed as children or favourably compared to children and household servants. In both writings believers are encouraged to see themselves as obedient and humble household servants, called to follow the example of their obedient and suffering Servant-Lord. Moreover, it is important to note that in 1 Peter, Mark, *1 Clement*, and Polycarp it is the household code that provides all four documents with a framework for integrating much of their common material. In the case of 1 Peter and Mark in particular, it is in conjunction with internal household instruction that both documents elaborate on following Jesus or discipleship in terms of sharing in the service and suffering of their Servant-Lord."[476]

If it is accepted that Rome is the place of origin of the Gospel of Mark, 1 Peter, *1 Clement* and Polycarp, it is highly plausible that Rome was the city where such traditions confluxed, circulated and developed. First Peter, as a text written from the Christian community in Rome, exhibits the ecumenical vision of this community but also combines various Old Testament and Diaspora traditions in its message to the Christian community in Asia Minor. This in turn fosters the unity within the worldwide Christian movement.

The text of 1 Peter moves beyond the contours of merely exegetical concerns to that of theology and ethics. Within this text the term "example" calls our attention to the role that *imitatio Christi* piety played in the history and development of Christian theology, ethics and spirituality.[477]

In 1 Peter Christ becomes the example to follow, not merely an ideal to aspire to. The Christ described in 1 Peter is an exemplar of complete and utter obedience to the will of God, but also as an instrument of empowerment. In 1 Peter Jesus Christ is both the model and the means. In his obedience to the will of God without sinning, in doing what is just, in his innocent suffering, in his election and holiness, in his vicarious death and glorious vindication he gave substance to the unity and solidarity which

---

476. Elliott, "Backward and Forward," 196
477. Ibid., 200

exists between him and those who believe in him through the mercy of God. Simultaneously, Christ is unique: he is the only righteous One that can make others righteous; his suffering alone is vicarious, it is only by his suffering, death and resurrection that the powers of evil and sin are conquered and that a new age is inaugurated. Christ is therefore not merely the example, but also the enabler.

# 2

# The Relation between Peter and Mark

*The Presence of Petrine Traditions and Memories in Rome.*

## Introduction

IN AN ARTICLE PUBLISHED on discipleship in 1 Peter Elliott shows interest in the possibility of a relation between 1 Peter and the Gospel of Mark.[1] Most scholars agree that both these documents originated from Rome, but a most interesting feature is that they both attest to the so-called *passio iustiliustorum* tradition which is rooted in the suffering of Jesus as "the righteous One." A hypothesis of a pre-existing and pre-Markan passion narrative deserves intensive attention. The similarities between the theologies of Mark and Peter, especially as far as the suffering of Christ is concerned urged this study to consider the possibility of a pre-synoptic tradition which influenced both these documents. As in the case with similarities 1 Peter shares with other New Testament writings, an argument is not made for the literary dependence of 1 Peter on Mark. It is rather a case of both these documents drawing from a similar tradition, which was most probably present in Rome. Elliott argues that there existed a "local oral tradition shared by the various groups in Rome."[2] Before the Gospel of Mark, we only have the genuine letters of Paul and the pre-synoptic oral tradition. Is it therefore not possible that the prominent role that the person of Peter plays in the Gospel of Mark is indicative of a pre-Markan Petrine tradition? It is even possible that in the pre-Markan oral tradition Peter even played a more significant role which was tempered by the redaction of the author of Mark.[3]

As will be further illustrated in this chapter, Mark and 1 Peter shared the same social conditions and the same socio-religious responses to these

---

1. Elliott, 1990, 191.
2. Ibid., 192.
3. Hengel, *Der Unterschätze*, 62.

conditions. Both these documents emphasise the communities' solidarity with each other amidst the suffering they have to endure and even more importantly, both documents attest to the inseparable link between following Christ and sharing in his suffering (cf. Mark 8:34 and 1 Peter 2:21).

Elliott further maintains that both these documents, although respectively, mirror the conflux of oral traditions in Rome, shared social circumstances and similar theological perspectives which distinctively defined the Roman community. Mark and Peter's communities found themselves in a situation where they had to defend themselves against outside hostility and social ostracism. In both cases it was necessary for these communities to re-affirm their position and their identity both in response to Judaism and in response to the Greco-Roman world.[4]

When the writings of Mark and 1 Peter are compared with each other, astounding similarities especially in terms of Christology, ecclesiology and discipleship become evident. The themes of Christology and ecclesiology and their respective relations with discipleship and ethics will enjoy attention in the chapters to follow. In this chapter the focus will be on the following aspects:

1. The history of the Christian community in Rome and the social conditions which necessitated the composition of these documents

2. The prominence given to the person and character of Peter in the Gospel of Mark

3. The importance of the traditions, reputation and kerygmatic teachings associated with Peter in both these documents

4. The possibility (or not) of the historical presence of Peter in Rome.

## The History of the Christian Community in Rome

According to Lampe it is difficult to determine the presence of Christians in the city of Rome prior to the activity of the apostle Paul.[5]

Christians in Rome consisted of Jews and Gentiles and at least as far as the presence of the Jews is concerned there exists evidence of their inhabitancy since the Diaspora. The region of Putioli and Rome was the main trade route from the east during the first half of the first century. It is therefore highly possible that more Jews and eventually Christianity found its way to

---

4. Elliott, *A Home*, 196.
5. Lampe, *Die Stadtrömische Christen*, 1.

Rome along these trade routes from the east.⁶ Jews established themselves in Rome during the Diaspora because of the economical prospects the city offered, which were not only limited to Italy but to the entire Roman Empire. The presence of "foreigners" in the city evoked diverse reactions. On the one hand, Tacitus reports a speech held in the Senate during the reign of Nero which made clear that certain house owners were uncomfortable with the increasing amount of slaves in their household that practised different religious customs and spoke foreign languages. On the other hand Rome boasted in the fact that the city attracted people from all over the empire, which made the city a home for all the inhabitants of the Empire.

From the second century BC a significant number of Jews lived in Rome and the first evidence of their presence dates back to 139 BC. After Pompey conquered Jerusalem in 61 BC, their numbers dramatically increased due to the fact that he brought many slaves from Jerusalem to Rome.[7]

When Herod the Great died in 4 BC, eight thousand Jews formed part of a delegation from Judea to plead for an end to be put to the dynasty of the Herodians. In AD 19 the army, deployed in Sardinia, included four thousand Jews. Historians therefore estimate the total number of Jews in Rome at about forty to fifty thousand during the first century AD.[8]

In spite of all the hostility and ignorance the Romans had against the Jews, many Romans converted to Judaism. Gentiles who did not embrace the Mosaic Law completely, but who shared their hope of salvation because of the covenant God made with Noah, were regarded as "Godfearers." Godfearers were expected not to eat food offered to idols, not to commit incest, not to work on the Sabbath and to refrain from eating leavened bread during Passover. Most of these Godfearers were members of the upper ranks of society.

According to Josephus the wife of Nero, Poppaea Sabina, was a Godfearer and used her influence to intervene on behalf of the Jews. It is interesting to note that only Josephus mentions her sympathetic attitude towards the Jews. According to the Roman historians, Tacitus and Suetonius, she was promiscuous and scheming and died in a violent manner as Nero kicked her to death.[9]

Not all Jews who lived in Rome belonged to the higher strata of the population which included properly educated and synagogue-attending

---

6. Ibid., 3.
7. Green, *Christianity*, 2.
8. Ibid., 3.
9. Ibid., 14.

people. Many Jews were poor and uneducated and preferred to disguise the fact that they were Jews by assimilating to the Roman culture. Two features of Judaism were viewed as particularly strange by the Romans: the observance of the Sabbath and the custom of circumcision.[10]

Nevertheless, Josephus's report illuminates the fact that Jews enjoyed sympathies even as high as the palace of the emperor. Members of Herod's family lived in Rome and the daughter of Agrippa, Drusilla, married Antonius Felix, the brother of Antonius Pallas, who was the most important civil servant under Claudius.[11]

It can therefore be concluded that well educated Jews did penetrate upper-class Roman circles, which resulted in sympathetic attitudes towards them. These sympathetic attitudes even survived the Jewish War of AD 66 to 73. The Romans successfully silenced the revolt, besieged Jerusalem and destroyed the temple. Vespasian together with his son Titus finally ended the war and this marked the birth of the Flavian dynasty.[12]

In spite of the consequences of the Jewish War in AD 70 and the fact that the Jews had to pay taxes to the temple of Jupiter, Jewish communities in Rome, especially in the upper classes remained remarkably peaceful. The triumph of Vespasian and Titus after the defeat of the Jews and the destruction of the temple and the increasing anti-Semitic climate in Rome certainly deeply offended and humiliated the Jewish community in Rome. However, they did not engage in revolutionary activity. They were wise not to do so, especially in the light of the recent victory the mighty new emperor accomplished against Jewish revolutionists. They did not seek to challenge or aggravate such a powerful man. It is however remarkable to note that the Jewish community in Rome was not fanatical and remained quiet and peaceful even during troublesome times.[13]

Despite the fact that the Jewish community in Rome included the wealthy and the poor, they were still bound by the covenant as one people. New Jewish immigrants to Rome were also welcomed in their midst. Many enjoyed citizen status. They made converts from all the spheres of society, including among the aristocrats. Some hated them and some respected them. Jews were able to preserve their cultural and religious identity for centuries. The Jews in Rome did not display political or nationalistic ambitions and they did not organise themselves under a specific leadership in order to protect their interests. Belonging to a synagogue was also not compulsory in

---

10. Ibid., 11–12.
11. Ibid., 15.
12. Ibid., 16.
13. Ibid., 18.

order to be defined as a Jew. Rather, observing the Mosaic Law was a family matter, including keeping the Sabbath and dietary regulations.

With the edict of Claudius, which is referred to in Acts 18:2, the Christians in Rome for the first time entered the historical scene. From this period the following deductions could be made: the Christians in Rome were Jews who originated from the synagogues in the city; their confession of Jesus as the Messiah resulted in conflict between them and the Jews in the synagogue; this occurred in around AD 40. According to Acts 18:2 Claudius expelled all Jews from Rome and among these were Priscilla and Aquila, who relocated to Corinth. It seems that Priscilla and Aquila did not leave Rome necessarily because they were Jews, but rather because they were Jewish Christians. Suetonius, during the second century AD documented "*Iudaeos impulsore Chresto assidue tumultuantes Roma expulit*." This further attest to the theory that it was Jewish Christians who were expelled from Rome, since they caused uproars in the synagogues. Similar situations occurred all over the Mediterranean as the number of Jews confessing Jesus as Messiah increased. Synagogues in Jerusalem, Antioch, Iconia, Lystra and Corinth experienced the same tension.[14] From a Roman imperial point of view, especially as far as the Jewish religious freedom is concerned, it made sense not to get involved in internal religious conflicts and disputes. Rome required peace and order and did not entertain communities causing disturbances. For the same reason Paul often collided with Roman authorities because he caused disruptions in the synagogues throughout the Empire. Consequently, Paul was continuously forced to depart from the cities he visited in Greece and Asia Minor. Yet he managed to establish Christian communities who continued his work in his absence.

In the case of Rome, although the congregation was not founded by Paul himself, the leaders of the Christian community, Priscilla and Aquila, were expelled. This however seemed not to be a permanent arrangement, because about four years later in Paul's letter to the Romans he mentions Priscilla and Aquila as being the hosts where the Christian community met (cf. Rom 16:3–4).[15]

It is not known how great the number of expelled Jewish Christians was. According to Suetonius it was certainly not all Jews, but those who became followers of Christ. Priscilla and Aquila were among the prominent figures of the early church and are personally commended by Paul in his letter to the Romans (cf. Rom 16:3–5). Therefore it makes sense that they are mentioned in Acts to have been among these Jewish Christians. The author

14. Lampe, *Die Stadtrömische Christen*, 5; cf. Green, *Christianity*, 26.
15. Green, *Christianity*, 27.

of Acts is however not correct in his report that "all Jews" were expelled from the city, because among these Jews were also Roman citizens.[16]

The edict of Claudius most probably marks the departing of Jewish and Christian ways in the city of Rome. Paul's letter to the Romans, dated around AD 50, and Nero's persecution of the Christians in AD 64 attest to the fact that by that time Christians in Rome were already a group distinctive of the Jews.[17]

The first Gentile Christians to associate themselves with the Jews expelled from the synagogues, were people that were attracted to the Christian faith because it offered them a part in salvation without having to subordinate to Jewish purity codes and rituals, especially circumcision. By the time Paul composed his letter to the Romans it is clear that he addressed a predominantly Gentile audience. The addressees were however familiar with the contents of the Old Testament, since they were exposed to it in the synagogues. Opposed to the proselytes, the Gentiles who became sympathetic towards the Christian faith did not only consist of the lower classes of the population and a majority of slaves. These Gentiles also included knights and people from higher social classes.[18] Although the Gentile Christians were in the majority in the Roman church, Jewish Christians were still present and it is quite clear from the letter to the Romans that they were reprimanded for still clinging to their Jewish ways and believes.[19]

When the Jewish Christians returned to Rome it was quite possible that a little turmoil took place about leading positions. The Jewish Christians found that the community managed to survive and even grow under Gentile leadership. This put them in a peculiar position, since there was no going back to the Jewish community either. It is amidst these circumstances that Paul wrote his letter to the Romans.[20]

Paul wanted to introduce himself to a congregation he longed to visit (cf. Rom 1:13; 15:22–23). His planned itinerary was to first visit Jerusalem to deliver the collections he raised in Macedonia and Achaia and then to travel to Spain in order to spread the gospel to the West and travel through Rome on the way (cf. Rom 15:22–29). Paul expressed concern of what was awaiting him in Jerusalem and wanted the support of the Roman congregations but also in aiding his mission to Spain.[21]

16. Lampe, *Die Stadtrömische Christen*, 6.
17. Ibid., 8–9.
18. Ibid., 53–55; cf. Green, *Christianity*, 24.
19. Lampe, *Die Stadtrömische Christen*, 57; cf. Green, *Christianity*, 26.
20. Green, *Christianity*, 28.
21. Ibid., 29.

From the content of the letter it is however abundantly clear that Paul is concerned about the relation between the Jewish and the Gentile Christians in the Roman Christian community especially as far as the interpretation of the Torah is concerned.[22]

Additionally, it should be remembered that the Roman church was a very diverse community including not only Jewish and Gentile Christians, but people from all social levels and economic means, from slaves to business people, from Roman citizens to foreigners and sojourners, from people being part of the community from the start to recent converts. Although one community, it was constituted out of four to five household churches, and these churches most probably also displayed differences.[23]

Paul therefore aims at reaching reconciliation within the church in Rome. This is also clear from the fact that he instructs the people named in the list in Romans 16 to greet each other and does not send them his own regards. It should be kept in mind that Paul did not find the congregation in Rome and therefore handles the situation more officially than paternally. Paul's clear emphasis is on unity (cf. Rom 16:17–20), addressing the conflict between Gentile and Jewish Christians. This is also clear from the rest of the content of the letter. Paul first explains that the gospel is not limited to the Jews, and that it is not by obeying the laws of the Torah, but by faith in Christ that one becomes righteous and part of the people with whom God has a covenant. Paul agrees with the Jewish belief that keeping the laws of the Torah is a response to receiving God's grace. Therefore he also stresses that the law is still relevant.[24]

What does concern him is the fact that the Jews claim to be the exclusive receivers of the grace of God and that the covenant is restricted to those who are circumcised and who keep the dietary laws of the Torah. Paul abolishes the idea that the Law should be abused to keep the Jews' exclusive claim to be God's elect intact. The Jews are further reprimanded for ethnical superiority and hypocrisy. The emphasis should not be on outer signs but on internal faith. Furthermore, both Jew and Gentile were saved by the sacrifice of Christ upon the cross and therefore they should also be reconciled with one another.[25]

Paul seems to express a positive stance towards Roman authorities, since all authority comes from God (cf. Rom 13:1). Shortly after writing these words, Paul is arrested in Jerusalem and taken to Caesarea Philippi

---

22. Ibid., 30.
23. Ibid., 31.
24. Ibid., 36; cf. Lössl, *Early Church*, 62.
25. Green, *Christianity*, 37.

under Roman protective custody, conducted by the procurator Felix, who was assigned to deal with extremists, messianic movements and revolutionary activities in Jerusalem and Galilee. Paul was to be tried by his successor, Porcius Festus, in Jerusalem, but Paul demanded, on grounds of his Roman citizenship, that he ought to be tried in Rome.[26]

On his way to Rome Paul stayed in Puteoli for a while. There he discovered that the Christians in Puteoli shared closed relations with the Christians in Rome and they informed the Roman Christians about Paul's arrival. Acts only mentions that Paul met some Christian travellers on the Appian Way and at the Forum of Appius. The writer of Acts wants to illustrate that within the person of Paul the gospel made its way from Jerusalem to Rome.[27]

It is clear that as far as tradition and theology are concerned; the Christians in Rome were still largely influenced by their Jewish and synagogue traditions and doctrines. This is also the result of the fact that the majority of the first generation Christians in Rome was familiar with synagogue practices and teachings and especially the Old Testament Scripture.[28]

It is not exactly clear how, but the fact remains that within the Roman Christian circles a process was started during which Jewish-Christian teachings were transferred from the first generation to the next. It is possible that we could speak of a Christian "school," similar to those found in Greek philosophical and Jewish spheres. A distinctive ethos and different worldview certainly developed from these circles.[29] Through the widely spoken Greek language and by being part of a greater Hellenistic culture, Jewish communities, especially those who confessed Jesus as the Christ, were open to travellers who shared the same beliefs.

Where Roman authorities still recognised Christians as a Jewish sect in AD 49, they were regarded as a new and subversive superstition by the time Nero placed the blame of the fire on them (ca. AD 64). Nevertheless, the Roman church quickly established itself as an influential Christian community, since it could claim that they were founded upon the teachings of both Peter and Paul. The tradition that both these apostles died in Rome lend further prestige to their position. Although the persecution under Nero had a tremendously horrifying effect on the Church in Rome, they were able to rise

---

26. Ibid., 40.
27. Ibid., 41.
28. Lampe, *Die Stadtrömische Christen*, 60.
29. Ibid., 61.

from the ashes and to establish themselves as probably the most influential Christian community by the turn of the first century.[30]

After Nero's persecution of the Christians in Rome, the earliest written evidence about the Christians in Rome comes from a letter written to the church in Corinth known as *1 Clement* (ca. AD 96), the letter of 1 Peter at the end of the first century AD and a later document called *the Shepherd of Hermas* (ca. AD 104).[31]

These documents clearly indicate that the church in Rome recovered after the persecution under Nero. Especially *1 Clement* is written with such confidence; offering the Roman church and the apostles Peter and Paul, both associated with the Roman church, as examples to be followed by the church in Corinth. This also attests to the fact the church in Rome was ever increasing its influence.

*First Clement* does not indicate any internal conflicts between Jewish and Gentile Christians. It is indicated that the Christians successfully claimed Jewish Holy Scriptures as their own and regarded themselves as the true and elect Israel, with whom the covenant was established.[32] The same could be deduced from the contents of 1 Peter.

Furthermore, *1 Clement* views the Roman community to be one church and should also display unity with the church in Corinth. It attests to a concept of church order and unity derived from the order in the cosmos, an idea inherited from Judaism as well as from Stoicism.[33]

## The Social Conditions in Rome that Necessitated Theological Response

### Introduction

The question that concerns us is the *Sitz im Leben* from which Mark and 1 Peter was written. Texts do not originate in a vacuum, but need to be interpreted within the political, economic, religious and linguistic context which gave birth to them. Appreciation of the above mentioned factors by the exegete makes it possible to understand the dynamic of the text and how the author uses language and rhetoric to convey a certain message.

---

30. Green, *Christianity*, 1.
31. Ibid., 53.
32. Ibid., 54.
33. Ibid., 56.

Apocalyptic or prophetic writings are always necessitated by certain social and cultural factors as well as the current world view.[34]

> In a situation where social and political structures have reduced a segment of society to a status of impotence in terms of power, of moral crisis in terms of unchallenged evil or cynical exploitation of the national leadership, and of questioning the meaning of one's place in the divine purpose at work in the world, there is a yearning for a framework of understanding in which these hostile forces can be comprehended and in which there is hope for transformation and meaning."[35]

This "framework of understanding" usually originates around a prophetic figure, who is also understood to be an ethical figure and a messenger of God. What he teaches is to be interpreted as a revelation of the will of God. Those who become followers or disciples of this figure are especially those of an unprivileged background. What discerns them from mystical movements is that they do not desire a complete withdrawal from society, but rather seeks to transform the world and to reclaim the world as God's possession. With this "messianic eschatology" in mind they wait upon the ultimate social and political transformation of the world.[36]

As a result of this messianic worldview tensions arose with those who do not share in this view. These tensions led to the establishment of new communities where new structures and forms of existence were proclaimed. Within these communities a prophetic figure arose which would have provided moral guidance and offered certainty. Confidence was built around his person and the belief arose that he could transform the ultimate evils of the world as well. The prophetic figure was perceived to be a person of integrity, and although his followers identified with him, he was respected as the unique recipient of divine insight. These figures desired to bring about a new era in which the heavenly realm was made more visible.[37]

Two social contexts come into play as far as the Gospel of Mark is concerned. The first is the social setting of Galilee and Jerusalem in the twenties and thirties which forms the background of the narrative and secondly that of the author and his addressees, *id est* Rome after AD 70. Certain similarities exist between these two contexts. In the first instance during both these periods the Jews experienced a peculiar situation, especially those Jews who became followers of Jesus. In both cases these Jesus-followers did not seek

---

34. Kee, *Community*, 77.
35. Ibid., 78.
36. Ibid., 78.
37. Ibid., 78–79.

solitude or withdrawal from society, but they were rather focused on the drastic reform initiated by Jesus. In each of these periods tension was raising which could have ominous consequences for the followers of the Jesus movement. It could be argued that these two contexts merge during the Jewish War, when Jews and Christians found themselves in an extremely peculiar situation. During this period anti-Semitism became evident, which caused Christians and Jews alike to experience social ostracism and slander. The temple, the centre of the presence of Yhwh was destroyed.[38]

Uncertainty was intensified by the deaths of Paul, Peter and James—great apostles to whom they looked for guidance. These events certainly necessitated the writing of the Gospel of Mark.[39]

The situation in Rome during the sixties and seventies could even be regarded as worse than the situation in Galilee during the twenties and thirties. Christians suffered under the tyranny of Nero and became the victims of rising anti-Semitism, slander and ostracism. Being a Jew or a Christian in these circumstances was indeed unsettling. In a certain sense it was even worse to be a Christian, since proselytism was despised by the Romans and although not prohibited, could lead to ostracism.[40] Under the rule of Nero Christians were extremely vulnerable, since Nero discerned them from the Jews and blamed them for the catastrophic fire in Rome. The Christians did not enjoy the same religious privileges and freedom the Jews did. Therefore the main reason why the Christians were treated with such contempt was because they were regarded as practicing a superstition.[41]

## Nero's Persecution of the Christians in Rome

With Nero's persecution of the Christians in AD 64 the first direct conflict between Christianity and the pagan Empire occurred. This event marked the Christians as a distinctive, hostile and potentially ominous group. The catastrophic fire, which broke out in Rome in July AD 64 and continued to blaze for nine days, destroyed a quarter of the city. The inhabitants of Rome at the time as well as later historians claimed that Nero himself was responsible for the fire and in order to divert the attention from him he blamed the Christians. Tacitus wrote:

---

38. Witherington, *Gospel of Mark*, 31.
39. Ibid., 32.
40. Nanos, *Mystery of Romans*, 66.
41. Witherington, *Gospel of Mark*, 34.

> In order to suppress the rumour, Nero falsely blamed the people, detested for their abominable crimes, who were called Christians by the populace and inflicted exquisite tortures on them. Christus, after whom they were named, suffered the extreme penalty at the hands of the procurator Pontius Pilate when Tiberius was emperor. Though repressed for a time, this pernicious superstition broke out again, not only in Judea, the origin of its evil, but also in Rome to which every sort of crime and evil activity flows from everywhere else and is practised. Accordingly, they first arrested those who pleaded guilty; then a large number denounced by them were convicted, not so much for the crime of incendiarism than for hatred of the human race. Various kinds of mockery were added to their deaths: covered with the skins of beasts, they were executed by being ripped to death by dogs or fixed to crosses or by being set on fire when daylight failed they burned to serve as torches in the night. Nero offered his gardens for the spectacle and he gave circus games, mixing with the people dressed as a charioteer or standing up in a chariot. Hence, even against criminals who deserved the extreme penalty, there arose a feeling of compassion for it was not for the public good but for one man's cruelty that they had been destroyed.[42]

In order for Nero to afflict punishment on the Christians, they had to be a discernable group. At this time they were no longer confused with the Jews or regarded as a Jewish sect. They had their own distinctive identity. They were thought to be guilty of a "superstition" which in Roman terms meant practicing a foreign religion. It should be noted that the Jews no longer considered the Christians to be part of them either. At the time of Nero's persecution the number of Christians also had to be significant enough to create such a spectacle.

The statement by Tacitus that the Roman people were sympathetic towards the Christians should not be understood as their general attitude against the Christians but rather a result of their hatred of Nero.

The Jewish historian, Josephus, who relocated to Rome after the Jewish War and published his report on the event between AD 75 and 79, was reluctant to write about Christianity. There could be various reasons for his doing so: it could be his disapproval of Christianity, his ignorance of the new obscure movement or the ever increasing separation between Jews and

---

42. Tacitus, *Ann.* 15.38–44, translation by Green, *Christianity*, 50.

Christians. It is possible that Josephus shared the general public opinion of the Romans against the Christians.[43]

Christianity was perceived by the Romans to inflict the disfavour of the gods and destroying peace and order in society. Christians were thought to be guilty of criminality and incest. In ancient Rome it was not only expected of the Emperor to undertake the practical rebuilding and reconstruction of the city after such a disaster, he also had to consult the Sibylline books in order to determine whether the disaster was part of the divine plan. Vulcanus, god of fire, Ceres, goddess of agriculture and Juno had to be appeased with sacrifices and prayers. It was the responsibility of the government to ensure *pax deorum* in order to avoid such catastrophes as a result of the gods' anger. The Romans took this task of the government very seriously, since it was associated with their understanding of their transcendental realm that had to be reflected in their social context. Therefore the appointment of government had to be divinely sanctioned. Groups such as the Christians, who refused to take part in the public religion, were regarded as conspiring against the state. The ancient relation between the transcendent, the so-called symbolic universe, and the social universe needs to be understood. These were two sides of the same coin and the latter was to be the reflection of the former. Therefore, the supernatural forces that controlled the transcendent also controlled society and peace and order in society guaranteed peace with the gods. Magical and religious practices other than the official state religion disturbed this relation and could have disastrous consequences for the entire society and were therefore regarded as a conspiracy in order to create chaos in the social domain.[44]

It is especially in this function that Tacitus believed Nero failed the Roman people and his attempt to shift the blame to the Christians was merely a way of covering for his own incompetence.

Accusations of arson were brought against the "Christians" (named after their founder Christ who was crucified in Judea during the reign of Tiberius). Nero went to great lengths to ensure that his persecution of the Christians seemed legit. His guards did not merely seek out Christians and executed them. They were first brought before the praetor, who handled criminal cases. Here they were however tortured into admitting guilt and implicating others which led to the arrest and execution of many. These executions took on many forms. One was to take part in spectacles held in the arena where they were killed by wild animals. The arena was Nero's own personal circus built

---

43. Green, *Christianity*, 54.
44. Brent, *Political History*, 35.

upon the Vatican hill in the vicinity where around AD 160 the place was indentified where the Apostle Peter allegedly died.[45]

Although Tacitus in his account of the fire wants to pardon the Christians of arson and place the blame on Nero, this should not be misunderstood as his, or the rest of Rome's attitude towards the Christians. It should also be taken into account that the general opinion of the Christians during Nero's persecution was indeed very negative. Hatred against Christianity was quite common as the histories of Tacitus also indicate. Although he does not blame the Christians for the fire and is convinced that Nero blamed the Christians in order to divert attention from himself, he agrees with Nero's persecution of the Christians. This attitude is also maintained by his contemporary historian, Seutonius, who described the Christian movement as *maleficae*.[46] Hatred against the Christians were of such a nature that his selection of them to be the scapegoats of the fire was accepted by the Roman population in spite of the fact that Nero was a very unpopular ruler. He was indeed very successful in diverting the attention away from himself.[47]

The word *superstitio*, which he uses to refer to the religion practised by the Christians, indicated a foreign and alien religious practice. These practices had the potential of invoking disaster on the rest of society for it aggravated the gods. Christians were therefore regarded to be in the same category as those who practised black magic and disturbed the *pax deorum*. The Christians were guilty of the same charge because they refused to take part in the public polytheistic Roman worship.[48]

Tacitus does view the Christians to be "guilty of all things shameful and horrible" because of their strange and foreign practices they brought along with them from Judea to Rome. Although he regarded them as being innocent of arson, he did view them as being guilty of hatred against the human race. This charge was clarified by the three general charges against the Christians namely atheism, Thyestian banquets and Oedipopean intercourse. According to the myth of Thyests, he attended a banquet where his children were offered as a meal. The myth of Oedipus tells the story of him marrying his mother after he killed his father. In other words, the Christians were thought to be guilty of cannibalism and incest.[49] Christians were stereotyped as practicing incest and cannibalism, based upon their eating of the body of Christ and drinking his blood and addressing one another

45. Ibid., 33.
46. Feldmeier, *Die Christen als Fremde*, 112.
47. Ibid., 114.
48. Brent, *Political History*, 34.
49. Ibid., 36.

as brother and sister and greeting each other with a kiss. Christians were accused of eating the flesh of new born babies and re-enacting the myth of Oedipus by engaging in incest with their mothers and sisters. These acts were believed to have magical consequences and could disturb natural and social peace and order.[50]

Furthermore, the Romans had a general distrust in religions originating from the East. Christianity was especially suspicious since its founder was a crucified rebellion.[51] Christianity's association of Judaism was another factor impacting negatively on the Romans' regard of them. Although Rome, to a certain extent, permitted religious freedom, it was still expected of subjects in the provinces to pay their respects to the stately cult. The Roman state was after all a divinely sanctioned institution, and refusal to take part in the state cult was regarded as insubordination. The fact that Christians separated themselves from the larger society and did not take part in public festivals was also frowned upon by the Romans.[52] The behaviour of the Christians also led to the perception that they could hold a political threat. They honored a crucified rebel and addressed him as "*kurios*." In the Roman context, religion was no private matter and always had communal and political connotations. Christianity was therefore perceived as an obstinate, new revolutionary movement without any traditional foundation.[53]

From political as well as from communal sides Christian behaviour was regarded as offensive. It seemed to the Romans as though the Christians opposed their attempt to establish the Roman culture and *modus Vivendi* throughout the Empire. The Christian doctrine that their true home was in heaven and that they were actually citizens of the kingdom of God was in sharp contrast with the Roman ideal.[54]

These doctrines reminded the Romans of the Jewish perception of themselves as God's holy elect and the Jews were *par excellence* the people to, on grounds of their religious convictions, rebel the most against Roman authority. Therefore the Romans feared that Christianity was merely a continuation of these apocalyptically sanctioned rebellions.[55]

It seemed as though the same hatred against the Empire was present among Christians as that which led to the Jewish revolts. It should however be noted that there were distinctive differences between the Romans'

---

50. Ibid., 37.
51. Feldmeier, *Die Christen als Fremde*, 113.
52. Ibid., 115–16.
53. Ibid., 121–22.
54. Ibid., 124–25.
55. Ibid., 127.

attitude towards the Jews and that towards the Christians. Although the Jews organised three revolts against Roman subjection, the Romans still regarded them as a homogeneous people with a common history and traditions. Even though their religion was regarded as foreign and despicable, it originated from an age old tradition transferred to each new generation which could be traced back to the great ancestors and founders of the people. This aspect of Judaism was respected by the Romans. Christianity, on the contrary could not claim ancient traditions, nor were they a homogeneous people and they did not originate from the same country or city. Judaism enjoyed the privilege of being a legitimate religion, which Christianity did not have. The Jews had an identity—one could spot a Jew on a distance, and they belonged to a discernable ethnical group.[56]

Contrary to the Jews, the Christians had a missionary dimension, which they took very seriously and pursued almost aggressively. Consequently, Christianity uncontrollably spread through families, households, cities and towns in pursuit of new converts to the belief. They were especially successful among women and slaves which made their penetration even more difficult to detect. Therefore the Romans regarded them as a subversive movement; operating in the shadows. Once they infiltrated families and households they were believed to disturb to peace and harmony within the households.[57]

After the fire, Nero undertook the rebuilding of the city and made provision for more water points and appointed public guards to protect these new buildings against criminal activity. It seemed as though Nero went to great trouble in order to cover his tracks.[58]

## The Impact of the Emperor Vespasian's Propaganda on the Church in Rome

It seemed that Vespasian's propaganda was successful among the Roman citizenry. The people arranged festivals in his honor and conducted prayers and offerings to secure his long and successful reign. He was widely regarded as benefactor of the people and glorified for ending the civil war and ushering a period of prosperity and stability. He also provided money where needed and his triumph was not only a display of his power as the conqueror of the Jews but also of his person being that of a world leader.[59]

56. Ibid., 129; cf. Lössl, *Early Church*, 68.
57. Feldmeier, *Die Christen als Fremde*, 131–32.
58. Brent, *Political History*, 32.
59. Winn, *Purpose of Mark's Gospel*, 167.

This power display had a negative impact on Christianity. Christian beliefs did not welcome the deifying of Roman rulers. The only saviour and prince of peace they recognised was Jesus Christ. This was however not a new experience to the Christians in Rome. By now they were used to the Roman emperors' overestimation of their own persons. The only aspect that discerned Vespasian from what they experienced previously was Vespasian's claim that he was the fulfilment of the messianic prophecy. Former imperial claims were regarded as blasphemous, but this arrogant claim crossed a new boundary. This offensive act of Vespasian was viewed by the Christians as a direct insult to their distinctive beliefs. The fact that the Christians confessed Jesus as the Messiah, the one the prophets spoke of in the Scriptures, was the very essence of their belief that separated them from the Jews.[60]

On the other hand it is quite possible that Vespasian's claim convinced some Roman Christians, especially because of his great military success, and caused them to doubt their commitment to the Christian movement. On grounds of his victory over the Jews and the destruction of the temple this claim could enjoy some historical truth. His divine election and favour certainly manifested in subsequent success and stature—something that could not be said about Jesus, who suffered a rebel's death on the cross.[61]

Contrary to Christ, Vespasian's reign was tangible and visible and manifested in every sphere of Roman everyday lives. Vespasian provided in the physical needs of his people. He secured food, money and the restoration of public buildings. Jesus could not offer these—at least not in such a tangible and immediate manner. This situation was definitely worsened by the delay of the Parousia. The more extravagant and spectacular Vespasian's reign became the more intense the crisis for the church became to hold fast to the belief of a new kingdom about to realise. If the recent fate of the Jews were to be taken as an example, denying the power of Vespasian would have entailed fatal consequences. Within this present situation it made sense to abandon the Christian faith and to follow a leader who was clearly establishing himself as a benefactor and a bringer of peace and stability not to mention extremely powerful.

The impact of the destruction of the temple in Jerusalem and the violent silencing of the Jewish rebellion can hardly be overestimated. Judaism as well as Christianity was faced with an existential crisis which affected the very heart of their beliefs. The consequences of the Roman victory over the Jews certainly casted a shadow over the future of the Christian church in Rome. These included increased anti-Semitism, intolerance towards

---

60. Ibid., 168.
61. Ibid., 168–69.

eschatological movements and an extremely powerful emperor who increasingly gained the favour of the Roman population. In AD 71 Titus shared in his father's triumph in Rome and showed of the temple treasures booted from Jerusalem. These were depicted upon the triumphal arch in the Forum in Rome, including the golden candelabrum and a scroll of the Torah. This action was understood as a hideous sacrilege to the Jews and the highest form of humiliation. After the siege of Jerusalem, the temple was destroyed, never to be rebuilt again. Martin Goodman noted that the refusal to allow the Jews to rebuild the temple was a significant decision by the Romans.[62] Because of the fact that religious, apocalyptic messianic expectations were the case of the war, Vespasian and Titus regarded their victory as a victory over Judaism. Because of the Jews' interconnectedness across the Diaspora and their shared identity grounded in Judaism this state of affairs affected Jews throughout the empire. This sent a powerful message to all the Jews living within the empire. Qumran was completely destroyed and Judea became an imperial province, governed from Caesarea as its capital. Temple taxes were no longer paid to the temple in Jerusalem, but to the temple of Jupiter Capitolinus in Rome. It could be assumed that the apocalyptic hope for the restoration of the temple was still present among the Jews. During the late first century, the second century and even as late as the third century Jewish apocalyptic literature was circulated among Christian churches, which continuously defined themselves as an entity separate from Judaism. Although the churches were relatively small in numbers, they were well organised and began to develop hierarchical structures and produced their own literature.[63]

Although the general climate in Rome at the time evoked fear and uncertainty among Christians, it did not result in actual persecution. The Christian movement, with a few exceptions, enjoyed a relatively quiet period during the reign of the Flavian dynasty.[64] These Gentile Christians formed a minority group and suffered the ostracism of their own communities. Although many Christians were charged and brought before the Roman authorities, anonymous claims against Christians could not be made and Christians were not to be sought out. The person appearing in front of the local magistrate had to be accused of a specific crime. Nevertheless, in an atmosphere where political unrests and rebellions motivated by messianic

---

62. Goodman, *Rome and Jerusalem*, 452–53.
63. Lössl, *Early Church*, 68.
64. Winn, *Purpose of Mark's Gospel*, 172.

expectation could erupt at any moment, the Roman authorities had to act against illegal clubs (*hetaeriae*).[65]

The situation described above provided all the ingredients for a potentially disastrous crisis in the midst of the church in Rome, especially as far as their Christological beliefs are concerned. A response by Christian leadership was urgent and essential.[66]

## The Christian Community in Rome's Response to these Circumstances

According to Kee four possible options existed for the Jews in Palestine prior to the Jewish War (AD 66–70).[67] The first was to completely subject to the Roman authorities and their client-kings, in the case of Judea and Galilee to Herod. Such a position would entail that they conform to Hellenistic culture and practises, which were further enforced upon them by Herod's extravagant building projects including theatres, stadiums and bath houses. The second option would be a passive form of resistance. This would mean that they do not object to Roman rule and the collection of taxes. The Pharisees could be categorised as such. They continuously turned their religious practises inwards into the family sphere. Political and economical liberation from Roman oppression and an increased eschatological hope of the dawn of a new age were not of particular importance to them. For the Pharisees the emphasis was on the cultic purity and ethical behaviour which ought to characterise the people of the covenant according to their interpretation of the Torah.

The third reaction would be that of the Essenes or Qumran community. They shared certain views of the audience of Mark's Gospel including Scriptural interpretation, passive resistance, the covenant community as an entity different from the corrupt Jewish leaders in Jerusalem and an imminent eschatological expectation. They also practised the custom of not taking anything with when embarking on a journey and to solely rely on the hospitality of others (cf. Mark 6:10). There were, however, significant differences. The Essenes radically withdrew from society and lived in the desert in order to remain pure from contamination by the corrupt religious leaders in Jerusalem. They were less open to accept new members into the community and had certain preconditions: a person had to be a true Israelite, had to subject to an ascetic lifestyle and total subjection to the Mosaic Law, as interpreted by the

---

65. Lössl, *Early Church*, 70.
66. Winn, *Purpose of Mark's Gospel*, 169.
67. Kee, *Community*, 97.

community. Contrary to these commands, the Gospel of Mark stresses the inclusive nature of the Christian community and to re-welcome those who were tempted to abandon the faith in the face of danger.

The fourth possibility was that of the Jewish revolutionists who were the instigators of the Jewish revolt against the Romans.[68] These revolutionary activities were not limited to Jerusalem. It also expanded to Hellenised cities such as Alexandria, Jordan and Syria. The brutal slaughtering of Jews in Caesarea, ironically the centre where the most urbanised Jews lived, was the last straw which urged the Jewish revolutionists to take up the sword against their Gentile neighbours.[69]

The audience of the Gospel of Mark (i.e. the Christian community in Rome) took a completely different stance. The fact that they were an open, welcoming and egalitarian community was irreconcilable with the Pharisees' as well as the Essenes' outlook. Jesus is revealed in the Gospel of Mark as the suffering messiah, not a power hungry political revolutionist. In fact Mark stresses in no uncertain terms that Jesus had no political or nationalistic aspirations at all. Jesus supported obedience to Roman rule also as far as the payment of taxes was concerned.

The recipients of Mark's Gospel regarded themselves as a new community grounded upon the values of Christ, whom they viewed as the Messiah of whom the prophets spoke. They were therefore the unique heirs of the promises of God. This perspective led to an ever increasing distance between them and Orthodox Judaism.

The distance that developed between the Christian and the Orthodox Jewish communities led to hostility and suspicion from the Jews, and the Christians were increasingly expelled from the synagogues. On the other hand the Romans, to a certain extent, still identified them as a Jewish sect, at least as far as their messianic expectations and their foundation upon a crucified Jewish rebel were concerned. This placed the Christian community in an unfavoured position from both Jewish and Gentile perspectives and increasing ostracism and slander from both sides. Here an important extra-biblical argument for dating the Gospel of Mark after AD 70 and during the early years of Vespasian's reign comes into play. The destruction of the temple in AD 70 made it abundantly clear that the Jewish expectation of a nationalistic and politically powerful Messiah who would liberate them from the Romans was false. Vespasian, seeking to win the support of the Jews, seized this opportunity to make the messianic prophecy applicable to him. This was however too ironic to be accepted. The Davidic king, whom

---

68. Ibid., 98.
69. Ibid., 99.

the Jews expected to free them from Roman oppression, could under no circumstance be a Roman who declares himself as such after their temple was destroyed. Vespasian hoped that this claim would add to his successful propaganda and would communicate a significant threat to the Jews not to rebel against him. Even though the Jews would never accept that a Roman ruler could be the fulfilment of their messianic prophecy, they were now a defeated nation and not in a position to challenge Roman power.[70]

Another factor that should be taken into account is the persecution and suffering the church recently enjoyed under the reign of Nero. This horrifying event was still fresh in their minds since it only happened five years prior to Vespasian's triumph.[71]

It was this situation that urged the author of the First Gospel to encourage his audience and affirm their beliefs.[72] It could therefore be concluded that the author did not only write from Rome, but he most probably had a Roman audience in mind or at the very least was highly influenced by the current situation of the church in Rome. The major challenges experienced by the Christians in Rome including Christological uncertainty as a result of Vespasian's messianic claims, increased eschatological tension, anti-Semitic sentiments, uncertainty about the new emperor's attitude towards the Christians and general Roman intolerance of messianic movements are all addressed by the content of the Gospel of Mark.[73]

One of the major reactions of the Christian church against these events was the expectation of an imminent Parousia. This is evident from the content of the Gospel of Mark (especially Mark 13). Wars, persecution, famine and natural disasters were all unmistakably associated with the end times and the destruction of the temple, regarded by Jews as well as some Christians as a holy place of God's unique presence was an ominous event. A heightened eschatological tension was experienced by the church.[74]

The only answer the church could provide to the immeasurable impact the reign and accompanying very visible power display of Vespasian was the close return of Christ and the very concrete establishment of his kingdom. Such a belief would not be appreciated by the Romans. They have just brutally suppressed an apocalyptically motivated revolt among the Jews, since they do not tolerate challenges to their divinely sanctioned authority. The more the church resulted to these eschatological beliefs, the

---

70. Winn, *Purpose of Mark's Gospel*, 163.
71. Feldmeier, *Die Christen als Fremde*, 112.
72. Kee, *Community*, 100.
73. Winn, *Purpose of Mark's Gospel*, 173.
74. Ibid., 170.

more vulnerable they actually became by provoking the anger and disfavour of the new emperor. This certainly led to fear and uncertainty among the Roman Christians.[75]

Mark's Gospel attests to the fact that there were false entities around claiming the title of Messiah. Jesus warns against these in Mark 13:21-22. This should not be understood as a future threat, but as a threat experienced by the community that the Gospel addresses. This content once again corresponds to the situation in Rome in the light of Vespasian's pretence to be the fulfilment of the messianic prophecies. Vespasian perfectly fits the profile of a false messiah.[76]

The essence of the Gospel of Mark's message is the emphasis on suffering. Whoever wants to be a disciple of Christ must be prepared to deny himself and follow in the footsteps of Christ, which necessarily includes suffering (cf. Mark 8:34). Although no record of official persecution of Christians exists, room must be allowed for the possibility of sporadic accusations brought before local governors, which could have resulted in the execution of Christians (cf. Mark 13:13). Similarities with the situation in Rome around the time of AD 70 are evident. The Christian community just endured violent persecution under Nero and was subjected to the slandering, hatred and mistrust of the non-believers. The consequences of the Jewish war did not hold many positive prospects in store for the Christian community and uncertainty dominated their expectations about the new emperor's policy regarding Christians.[77]

Their future and their safety were in jeopardy. Their identity as followers of a Jewish rebel crucified in Rome placed them in a peculiar position, especially because messianic movements were very unpleasing to the Romans at the time.

As stated above, it would have made sense to followers of the Jesus-movement to abandon their faith. The success of Vespasian was overwhelming and present all around and the heavenly kingdom of Christ seemed very far removed from their reality. This historical situation is also in tact with the portrayal of discipleship in the Gospel of Mark. The disciples are constantly failing to stay true to the purpose of their calling (cf. Mark 4:35-41; 6:45-52; 8:14-20, 27-38; 10:46-52). This focus, especially with the spotlight on Peter who served as an example to the community in Rome, attests to the fact that Mark's audience needed to be reprimanded for their apostasy. "The problem of disciples wavering in their faith commitments and failing

75. Ibid., 172.
76. Ibid., 174.
77. Ibid., 175.

to recognise Jesus's true identity is consistent with the problems facing the church in Rome circa 70 AD."[78] The struggle of the addressees of Mark seems to be the same of that of the disciples: in fear of persecution they are tempted to abandon their faith. An appeal is being made to those in the community who remained steadfast not to judge these weaker brothers and sisters but to encourage them and to allow them back into the community of faith as Jesus did with Peter. "Mark's portrayal of the disciples who broke under the cross and yet were restored to true discipleship by the Risen Christ was meant to be a potent message of reconciliation to a church torn with recrimination and factions in the wake of persecution and the failure it generated."[79]

The Christian community in Rome suffered a Christological crisis. Not only did Vespasian claim that his rule of the world was divinely ordained, but he also pretended to be the awaited Jewish Messiah, which was the heart of the Christian faith as the confessed Jesus to be the Messiah. This challenged the very existence of the church.[80]

Mark's Gospel seems to be an answer to this situation. He opens his Gospel with the word εὐαγγελίου, an allusion to Deutero-Isaiah's εὐαγγελιζόμενος "the one who proclaims the good news," which is to be understood as the one who announces the Lord's victory over the enemies of Israel. For the Romans the beginning of the good news would be the new age of peace and prosperity inaugurated by their new ruler. Mark explicitly challenges this idea with the opening of his Gospel to establish Jesus as the true Messiah. "The incipit can be read as a bold and carefully crafted response to the claims of Flavian propaganda." With the allusion to Deutero-Isaiah Mark wants to establish that the Jewish Scriptures proclaim Jesus and not the current emperor as the awaited Messiah. More provocative to his Roman audience, which probably consisted of a majority of Gentile Christians, would be Mark's application of the Roman understanding of "good news" to the person of Jesus. Jesus is the true bringer of peace and prosperity, not the emperor, and Jesus and his kingdom are stated to be superior to that of the emperor. Mark is therefore not writing an apology to the Romans on behalf of the Christian movement, he is writing a response to the false messianic claims of the emperor and boldly challenges them.[81] For the Roman world the emperor was the embodiment of the first among humans, the one favoured by the gods. In the Roman world this

---

78. Ibid., 176.
79. Senior, *Passion of Jesus*, 153.
80. Winn, *Purpose of Mark's Gospel*, 178.
81. Ibid., 179.

was a reality to reckon with, for the emperor had absolute power, including power over life and death.

Mark is aiming at constructing an alternative reality in which Jesus Christ is the most powerful and not the emperor. Christ is the manifestation of God's concern for the world and the coming of God's kingdom in the world. Christ as the ultimate world leader is not from royal descent, but originated from a humble peasant family in Galilee. In contrast to the spectacular triumph of Vespasian, Jesus died on a cross. He was not established as the leader of the world as a result of military power or political influence, but he exercised his power to uplift the weak. This was another type of "good news" than that proclaimed by the emperor.[82]

This explains the preference given to Christology in the Gospel of Mark. Mark uses the Christological titles of "Christ," "Son of God," and "Son of Man." All three these express kingship. Jesus was not only established as the ruler of Israel, but of the entire world—therefore superior to the emperor. This corresponds with the Jewish idea of the Messiah. He would not only be the ruler of Israel, but he would conquer the enemies of Israel.[83]

For Mark's Roman readers, the title "Son of God" had a further very significant meaning, since this was the title adapted by the Roman emperors since the reign of August, which also resulted in the imperial cult. Again Mark is challenging the claims of the Roman emperor, that he is the true divinely ordained ruler.

Mark's Christology could therefore be understood as a rejection of Flavian propaganda. However, in the light of the pressing situation of his addressees, Mark cannot make these Christological claims without substantiating them. He does this by Jesus's divine confirmation (cf. Mark 1:11; 9:7). The legends surrounding Vespasian's divine ordination expressed in oracles are made out to be inferior to Jesus's direct divine conformation from the voice of God himself.[84]

It is significant that the evangelist places his bold Christological claim of Jesus as the true Son of God in the mouth of the Roman centurion (Mark 15:39). By doing so, a Roman recognises Jesus's superiority to the emperor.

Of further importance is to note that Vespasian did not claim divinity on the grounds of his family bloodline. He was not a descendent of the Julio-Claudian dynasty. By Mark's emphasis on Jesus being the true Son of

---

82. Bolt, *Jesus' Defeat*, 273.
83. Winn, *Purpose of Mark's Gospel*, 180.
84. Ibid., 181.

God, he exposes a weakness in Vespasian's propaganda. Again, Mark is not being apologetic but he directly confronts Vespasian's false claims.[85]

Mark's portrayal of discipleship displays the following discerning features: a disciple has to recognise Jesus's true identity and have faith in him; a disciple needs to stay steadfast and committed to Jesus and the gospel even if this entails suffering and persecution; a disciple has to abandon his or her former life; a disciple is called to proclaim the gospel and a disciple is called to a life of humility and service.

The fact that Mark's audience was in doubt about Jesus's identity as the true Messiah, Mark had to address this problem in a Christological manner by emphasizing Jesus's power and superiority and divine ordination. On the other hand, Mark portrays a very critical image of the disciples who abandoned their faith in the face of suffering. Jesus's superiority and divine ordination are contrasted with the disciples' blindness and their inability to recognise Jesus as such. Mark's readers could certainly identify with this and therefore recognise their own failures in the characterisation of the disciples. The evangelist certainly hoped that this would lead to his readers experiencing a catharsis.[86]

Mark *distinctively* (my emphasis) stresses the importance for the disciples to remain faithful amidst the danger of suffering and persecution. This feature is intact with the historical situation of the Roman Christians, who were concerned about their safety. The persecution endured under Nero only six years prior and their association with Judaism in the light of the recent violent suppression of the Jewish revolt, made an appeal to their experience of safety and security. Therefore some left the movement, while others remained faithful. Mark seems to be very serious in addressing this issue, for he places the demands to remain faithful even in the face of suffering in the mouth of Jesus himself.[87]

Jesus in no uncertain terms instructs his disciples at Caesarea Philippi that following in the footsteps of Christ inevitably entails the denial of oneself and the experience of suffering (cf. Mark 8:34). Only those who are able to remain faithful in the face of danger, even until death, will be saved (Mark 13:13). Jesus is not promising that the faithful will be spared persecution, but that the disciples should remain faithful even through persecution. This can be understood as the evangelist's pastoral response to the situation of his

---

85. Ibid., 182–83.
86. Ibid., 194.
87. Ibid., 195.

addressees.[88] Furthermore the disciples are instructed to remain *watchful* (cf. 1 Pet 5) in the light of the *parousia* drawing near.[89]

The purpose of Mark's Gospel could thus be summarised as follows: Primarily the evangelist responds to the community's Christological crisis. Secondly, in the aftermath of the destruction of the temple and the outcome of the Jewish war, the church feared for its safety. The recent persecution the Christians endured under Nero's rule was also still fresh in their memories. Mark answers to these fears with undeniable evocation to remain faithful even until death. The ones that endured will be the ones that will be saved.[90] The Roman church further wanted to provide a strategic response to the situation they found themselves in and the society in which they lived.[91]

> This society was deeply disorganised by the impact of war, depression and the uprooting of membership in ancient structures... ages of perceived disorganisation and dislocation are almost invariably rich in efforts to achieve forms of community through religious, as well as political and social channels. Rome during the first century AD was fertile soil for the proliferation of religious movements which could offer their communicants not merely hope of a better world after this life but also some kind of communal release from alienation and insecurity in this life. Christianity, most especially its primitive first-century form, was almost ideally equipped to respond to such alienation and insecurity, for its message, its "good news" was precisely that of communal refuge.[92]

## The Attitude of the Christians in Rome's towards the Roman Empire

As far as the Markan community's attitude towards the state was concerned they did not regard head-on collisions to be constructive or to serve any purpose. It was not the task of Christianity to reform Roman political or social institutions. Rather they were to endure the same suffering as Christ

---

88. Ibid., 196.
89. Ibid., 198.
90. Ibid., 200.
91 Elliott, *A Home*, 286.
92. Nisbet, *Social Philosophers*, 177.

did without any resistance. Actions as those undertook by the Jewish rebels had to be avoided.⁹³

Kee also makes the point that there is no inclination in the Gospel of Mark that the audience should engage in revolutionary activity.⁹⁴ Mark's addressees were however at risk to be associated with such movements because of their messianic language, their apocalyptic expectation of the everlasting kingdom of God and the fact that they followed a man who was crucified in Jerusalem. Mark's author wants to emphasise that Jesus should not be understood in such a framework at all.

The picture Mark draws of Pilate seems to be in conflict with what we know about him from extra-biblical sources. According to Philo (*Legat.* 38) Pilate was "inflexible, merciless and obstinate." Mark, on the other hand, depicts Pilate as the puppet of the Jewish councils and the mob of Jerusalem. Pilate subjects to the demands of the crowd and therefore is characterised as being a weakling. It seems as if the author of Mark purposefully wants to portray Pilate in a negative way.⁹⁵

Through Mark's narration of the continuous questioning of Jesus by Pilate, Mark wants to make clear that Pilate could find no legal grounds for Jesus's execution. Rome is actually manipulated by the Jews. Whether this situation is historically true is not what is in focus here, but the rhetorical strategy of the author of the Gospel. What does he want to accomplish by depicting Pilate in this manner and how would he want his readers to response to his report?⁹⁶

Ὁ κεντυρίων ὁ παρεστηκὼς ἐξ ἐναντίας αὐτοῦ (Mark 15:39a) is distinctively Markan when compared to the parallels in Matthew (27:54) and Luke (23:47). Mark uses the word κεντυρίων three times, while it does not occur in Matthew or Luke at all. It seems that Mark wants to emphasise that it was indeed a *Roman* officer whose testimony confirms that of Peter and it is a *Roman* officer who recognised the kingship of Jesus whereas the Jewish leaders failed to do so. This testimony of the centurion forms the climax of the Gospel of Mark and the way Mark establishes a contrast between the Roman response and the Jewish response to Jesus could not be missed by his readers.⁹⁷

In Mark 12:13-17 we find the question about the paying of taxes to Caesar. An issue which as emphasised by Witherington threatened the very

---

93 Brent, *Political History*, 69.
94. Kee, *Community*, 93.
95. Wilde, *Social Description*, 172.
96. Ibid., 173.
97. Wilde, *Social Description*, 174.

existence of Galilean fishermen and peasants.[98] The evidence of Markan redaction is in the mentioning of the Pharisees first, who were probably sent by the Sanhedrin. Mark illuminates the irony in their address of him as διδάσκαλε because they did indeed not recognise his authority. The fact that Jesus answers with a rhetorical question: τί με πειράζετε serves as an emphasis on Jesus's authority that supersedes that of the Pharisees, for he knows their evil intensions and their hypocrisy.[99]

It seems as if Mark wants to depict the Jews to be the villains and not so much the Romans. Jesus and his followers should not be regarded as in opposition to Roman law and order. Instead it is the corrupt Jewish religious establishment which is in need of desperate reform. The Jews even went as far as to abuse the Roman law system in pursuit of their own unrighteous goals.

Perhaps Mark's moderate handling of the Romans could be better understood against the background of his imminent eschatological expectation. Roman rule and oppression, although a mighty force to be reckoned with, will soon be overpowered by the coming kingdom of God. It only needs to be tolerated for a little while. Therefore, followers of Jesus might as well pay their taxes to Caesar. There is no reason to provoke the anger of the Roman government, especially in the light of the fear that the Romans have for nationalistic revolts. There is no need to antagonise Roman authorities, for the end of their reign is at hand.

This approach of the evangelist is further substantiated by the fact that the Jews enjoyed religious freedom and the protection of Romans at least to a certain degree and the Christian community did not enjoy this privilege. Mark does not want the Christian movement to be associated with nationalistic and rebellious desires. The threat of persecution was already present. There was no need for the Christians to enlarge the threat posed by the recent happenings in Judea.[100]

It seems as if Mark wants to focus on the corrupt co-operation between Jewish leaders and the Romans. "Whatever Mark thinks of Rome, he thinks of the Pharisees, Scribes and priests." Their association with one another always involves betrayal (Mark 13:9; 15:1) or impure motives (Mark 12:13). Jesus's persecution is the result of the Pharisees's, Scribes's, and the priests's plotting and scheming against him. For Mark political power, religious power, governors and kings are synonymous with corruption, betrayal, trials and torture.

---

98. Witherington, *Gospel of Mark*, 30–34.
99. Wilde, *Social Description*, 175–76.
100. Ibid., 178.

When Mark talks about "bearing witness" or "to testify," he does not have a Roman trial in mind where a person is accused of a crime and could be incriminated by another's testimony. Mark rather stresses to bear witness to the good news of Christ and the coming kingdom which entails the reformation of all and the dawning of a new age. "Preaching the good news in such extremely trying moments is remaining steadfast in the faith (Mark 13:9) to the end (Mark 13:13), in the face of hatred (Mark 13:13), betrayal (Mark 13:9), moments of severe trial (Mark 13:11) and even murder (Mark 13:12)."[101]

Mark draws a parallel between Jesus's trial before Pilate and the oppression his community experienced. Yet amidst these trying times the good news about the coming of the Son of Man is preached from the beginning to the final climax placed in the mouth of the Roman centurion.

Mark's community, although in an extremely difficult political situation, had the example of Jesus and his attitude towards Roman authorities. The way Jesus endured his trial before Pilate is the way they should endure their persecution under Roman authorities by bearing witness to their faith. It is possible for Mark's community to endure this persecution in the light of the promise that the good news holds for them. This assures them of a glorious future to come.[102]

## The Importance of the Traditions, Reputation, and Kerygmatic Teachings Associated with Peter in both these Documents

### Did Mark Originate from Rome?

To ask the question whether Mark originated from Rome already suggests that there existed a tradition linking Mark with Rome. This tradition seems to be present since around AD 150 and enjoyed wide acceptance during the second century. There is however a huge difference between tradition and historicity. Tradition, lacking true historical information, believes everything and hopes everything and often acquires a vivid imagination. Tradition also displays a preference for the most widely accepted and popular perspective.[103] *The Acts of Peter and Paul* tells the story of Simon Magnus' flight to Rome after being expelled from Jerusalem by Peter. Consequently

---

101. Ibid., 180.
102. Ibid., 182.
103. Bacon, *Is Mark?*, 7.

Peter travels to Rome in pursuit of him. After an elaborate dual Peter defeats him and by doing so regains Rome for Christ.

Later church political and liturgical documentation give rise to the idea of co-operation between Peter and Paul in Rome. The earliest example comes from Dionysios, bishop of Corinth in AD 170.[104] The image of Peter as constructed by the writings of the New Testament is unfortunately contaminated with a later idealisation of his person and his authority within the early church. As in the case of historical Jesus research, there certainly exists historical activity behind the text, but the final text as we have it was already influenced by the *kerygma* of the early church.[105]

Since this study employs the methodology of social-scientific exegesis in connection with historical criticism, the rhetorical strategy of the author embedded within the social context of the audience he addressed deserves our attention. These pre-existing, early Christian traditions were used by New Testament writers in different ways to accomplish different goals. As Elliott, an exponent of social-scientific research notes:

> A sociological exegesis is not complete until it has explored the manner in which the 'comprehensive patterns of cognitive and moral beliefs about man, society and the universe in relation to man and society'[106] contained and advanced in a given document are intended to function in the social order, the collective needs and interests they present and the way they exemplify the intersection of ideas, ideals and social action.[107]

A religious movement is always embedded within a certain social context and the literature which originates within these movements therefore always has sociological interests which become clear when the rhetorical strategy of a document is examined. There is a universal need for human beings as well as religious movements to understand themselves in relation to the context they find themselves in and to justify their existence in order to secure their unique place in the world. The common answers all those belonging to a certain religious group give to these questions could be defined as their ideology. An ideology includes their worldview, their anthropology, their sociology and on what is possible and what not. As previously stated, an ideology is of a shared nature; in other words the members of the group's ideas and perspectives are shaped by shared interpretations, expectations

---

104. Böttrich, *Petrus*, 224.
105. Brown, Donfried, and Reumann, *Der Petrus der Bibel*, 142.
106. Haubeck and Bachmann, *Wort*, 250–67.
107. Elliott, *A Home*, 265.

and hopes. These motivate them to achieve common goals.[108] Ideologies create a common framework of consciousness within which social realities are interpreted. This framework provides the foundation to legitimise collective needs and interests.[109]

It is important to note that since Mark was the first Gospel, and as such the first New Testament writing of its kind. Therefore linking the Gospel with a particular author was not important until other similar documents appeared on the scene. Formerly, it could only exist as "The Gospel," but after the composition of the Gospels of Matthew and Luke and later John a need for differentiation occurred.[110]

Shortly after the first Gospel was assigned to Mark, the tradition of its origin in Rome developed, since the content of the Gospel originated from Peter, to whom Mark acted as a secretary and who allegedly died in Rome.

This tradition was preserved by Papias who claimed that because of the relation between Peter and Mark, Mark could be viewed as a reliable source.[111] It is often argued that the tradition was delivered from Peter to his secretary Mark, which Papias received from the Elder, John. Papias writes during the reign of Hadrian, which means that the Mark-tradition of the John the Elder must be at least two generations older. This tradition reaches further back than the letter of 1 Peter (ca. AD 100).

The Papias-tradition is not a defender of Mark's authority as an author, rather a criticism thereof. Mark was not an eyewitness nor did he record the tradition in the right sequence. His sole authority rests on being subjected to the oral preaching of Peter. What he remembers from Peter, that he recorded. According to Irenaeus (*Adv. Haer.* 3.1.1) the Roman congregation was left, after the death of Peter and Paul, with Mark who continued the preaching that he received from Peter.[112]

Papias did not claim that Mark originated from Rome simply based on tradition. He substantiated his believe by referring to 1 Pet 5:13. Papias regarded this text as proof of Mark's association with Peter in Rome.[113]

A further association between Peter and Mark could be derived from Acts 10–12. He seemed to have accompanied Peter to Antioch (Acts 15:38), since his ways with Paul departed.[114]

---

108. Ibid., 268.
109. Davis, *Problem of Slavery*, 14.
110. Bacon, *Is Mark?*, 11.
111. Ibid., 13; cf. Böttrich, *Petrus*, 223.
112. Hengel, *Der Unterschätze*, 75–76.
113. Bacon, *Is Mark?*, 15–16.
114. Ibid., 17.

Papias also commends Mark for not writing anything falsely and that he took great care in writing down what he heard from Peter.[115]

However, no other text in the New Testament, except 1 Pet 5:13, indicates a relation between Peter, Mark and Rome and as argued previously in this study, there exists no historical evidence to the fact that Peter ever set foot in Rome. The period covered by the Pauline epistles does not refer to Peter being present in Rome and we cannot be sure that he went to Rome after Paul's death nor if he aligned forces there with Paul's former co-workers, Mark and Silvanus.

The question that needs to be asked though is whether Papias grounds his statement solely in this text and whether he only appeals to Scripture. Is it not possible, as is the case in many other instances, that Scripture merely affirms a pre-existing belief?[116]

As indicated earlier, the author of 1 Peter used the name of Peter to lend authority to his writing, and this letter was by no means composed by the Apostle Peter himself or by a secretary of him. It is unclear whether this anonymous author believed in Peter's presence in Rome. What is clear is that he refers to Rome as the place from which he lets Peter, in whose name he writes, send his regards to the entire Christian brotherhood in Asia Minor.[117]

Papias certainly seemed to think that the Gospel of Mark also originated from Rome. It is difficult to determine whether there exists any historical evidence behind this belief that soon enjoyed wide acceptance.[118]

> Considering that this was an anonymous Gospel, a writing which most ardent champions did not venture to claim for it more than second-hand relation to one of the apostles, the degree of respect shown for it by Matthew and Luke at the very threshold of the second century is truly extraordinary. This is difficult to account for unless the Gospel had already attained wide currency and acceptation, implying that it was vouched for in high quarters. A document which on its face makes so little pretence of authority could hardly be expected to attain such standing if emanating from some obscure region, undistinguished as the seat of any "apostolic" church.[119]

---

115. Ibid., 19.
116. Ibid., 21–24.
117. Ibid., 27.
118. Ibid., 30.
119. Ibid., 34.

To reflect on the question of why the Gospel was then not written in the name of one of the Apostles, it needs to be considered that such a step would seriously challenge Jerusalem's unique claim as the preserver of the apostolic tradition of Jesus's words.

It is indeed remarkable that a writing of such humble origins exercised such incredible influence in the composition of the other Gospels. However, Mark's prominence was later overshadowed by Matthew which attained the status of "the Gospel" in the early church and which enjoyed higher claims to apostolic authority. Matthew's more comprehensive Gospel also met the demands of the age for a generally acknowledged authoritative report of the life and works of Jesus Christ. Mark's Gospel as mere notes reported from the memory of Peter could not compete with the status Matthew enjoyed.

Furthermore, Mark was outshined by the magnificent double work of Luke-Acts. This raises the question of how it is possible that Mark survived at all. It was only its initial influence that could save it.[120]

Stylistically and rhetorically Mark was also not regarded as in the same category as Matthew and Luke. Just as Mark could not compete with the other two synoptic Gospels on grounds of contents and authorship, the same was true regarding style and rhetoric. At least that is as far as the opinion of the apostolic church goes. Markan scholars today quite convincingly established Mark as a narrative and rhetorical genius in his own right, structuring his short narrative to suite his unique theological goals. The apostolic church, nevertheless, was of the opinion that Mark's unpolished and somewhat "barbaric" Greek was corrected by Matthew and Luke. So once again we are left with the question why Mark survived at all?[121] "Either, then, this primitive Gospel must have emanated from some centre of very great authority and importance, with or without the important sanction of an alleged derivation from Peter; or we are at a loss to account for the dominant position it acquired in every region of the early church to which our knowledge extends."[122]

It is possible that this place of "authority and importance" might be Rome, since it is not likely that it originated from Jerusalem or Antioch.

Since we do not have any historical evidence attesting to Peter ever being present in Rome, we need to consider Papias' claim of an association between Peter, Mark and Silvanus in "Babylon" solely based on 1 Pet 5:13. If we accept that Peter was never in Rome, and we regard "Babylon" and the mentioning of the names of Mark and Silvanus simply as part of the

---

120. Ibid., 37–38.
121. Ibid., 40.
122. Ibid., 40.

metaphorical devices employed by the author of 1 Peter to strengthen his pseudographical authority, we still need to answer the question why Papias' claim of a relationship existing between Peter and Mark was so widely and undisputedly accepted as far as the origin of the first Gospel is concerned. If any other place than Rome was suggested as the origin of Petrine teaching, Papias may not have been so successful. There existed a need for Papias to connect Peter with Rome and 1 Pet 5:13 met this need. Why was this so important for Papias? Simply because it seems to be the intention of the author of 1 Peter to let Peter (or at least the authority of Peter's name) speak from Rome. This would provide unequalled authority to the Roman church and to Papias as the bishop of Rome. Additionally, this would increase the value of the Gospel of Mark.[123] The unknown author of the pseudographic letter written in the name of Peter must have had an idea of Peter's presence or at least association with Rome. The First Letter of Clement also attests to this tradition. Ignatius, bishop of Antioch in AD 117, which is deported to Rome as a captive, compares himself to the apostles Peter and Paul.[124]

If the Gospel of Mark were to originate from Palestine, it would hardly have enjoyed any authority if ascribed to anyone else but one of the Apostles, especially those Apostles who enjoyed prominence in the Jerusalem church. Rome is the only place where a person by the name of John Mark was known. The Pauline Epistles refer to him as the faithful co-worker of Paul in Rome. It is therefore only the Roman church that could associate the name with a known person.[125]

Rome was however hesitant to claim that the Gospel derived directly from Peter himself. This hesitance needs to be explained on the grounds of the tension between Jewish and Gentile Christianity and Jerusalem's eventual loss of being the centre of the Christian faith to Rome. Within the Gentile Greek-speaking world a Gospel written in the name of the chief Apostle would enjoy unmatched glory. No other document would have been able to compete with it. Yet within Jewish circles a preference still existed for oral tradition. The reason for this was that written material could be the property of anyone, but the tradition of the forefathers handed down by word of mouth could exist within a confined and controlled space where true orthodoxy could be nurtured. The mother church in Jerusalem as the custodian of the life and words of Jesus and the very origin of the Christian faith still enjoyed a privileged position over written documents.

123. Ibid., 41.

124. Böttrich, *Petrus*, 222; cf. Brown, Donfried, and Reumann, *Der Petrus der Bibel*, 131–132.

125. Bacon, *Is Mark?*, 42–43.

The first circulated Gospel, therefore, was written in Greek, although based on Aramaic traditions. As this document became more and more influential because of the fact that it could be accessed by a larger community and as the amount of Gentile Christians increased, the Aramaic Fathers were necessitated to produce written Gospels as well. These were however based upon the Greek ones and only originated in the second century. The effects of the Jerusalem church's earlier conservatism could not be undone. This had the consequence that the early church did not turn to Jerusalem for its first written narrative of the life and words of Jesus Christ, but to Rome. Remarkably, this document could not claim Apostolic authorship, because this was the exclusive prerogative of the Jerusalem church and an author situated in Rome did not have direct access to the teachings preserved by the eye-witnesses of the earthly Jesus.

Yet as the amount of Gentile Christians increased the moment was seized by the Roman church, which was ministered by leaders from Paul's circle and which had access to the Pauline teaching, especially his comprehensive theological epistle written to them. Therefore the First Gospel was welcomed by the Gentile Christians, who would of course want to exercise greater influence within the broader Christian movement. Additionally, they would ardently defend the Gospel's claim to (although secondary) apostolic origin and the authority it exercised as such.[126]

Hengel boldly states that it is absurd to suppose that the revolutionary work of the first Gospel was written by a nameless Gentile Christian without any recognised authority. The fact that a brilliant theologian and skilled author like Luke used Mark and that the author of Matthew so abundantly used Mark, gives reason to believe that Mark originated from a trustworthy and acknowledged apostolic source.[127]

It could therefore be concluded that the only reason why a Gospel written in the name of a non-apostolic author could exercise such extensive influence within the early church was because it was written from Rome.

> By virtue of its claim to represent the teaching of Peter, whose spiritual "son" Mark had been, and no less by virtue of the refusal on the part of the "successors of the Apostles" at Jerusalem, who regarded themselves as the trustees and guardians of the "commandments delivered by the Lord," to publish their deposit of the faith in written form, this Gospel attained that pre-eminence

---

126. Ibid., 44–45.
127. Hengel, *Der Unterschätze*, 70.

in the field which produced the phenomenon known to modern criticism as the "Synoptic" tradition.[128]

This laid the foundation for the tradition of bringing Peter to Rome. Matthew and Luke still tried to maintain that Jerusalem was the centre of Petrine authority. Matthew attests to the fact that the church was built upon this Rock and that he held the keys to the heavens. However, the fact remains that Matthew's Gospel used Mark as a source and is therefore on a literary level depended on Mark. And the Roman church, from which it originated, claimed that Mark was directly influenced by the teaching of Peter, which would ultimately imply that the Apostle himself spoke from Rome. From this perspective, it could almost be said that Mark "relocated" Peter and so to speak moved him from the East to the West.[129]

It cannot be denied that it was Rome, and not Jerusalem, that provided the Christian church with its first written report of the life and words of Jesus Christ, based on the teachings of the Apostle Peter. As a result of this, Rome became the bearer of the keys to heaven.[130] In order for the Roman church to defend its authoritative and leading position, it had to establish itself as grounded in the legacy of two significant apostles, namely Peter and Paul. Since AD 258 the death of these apostles is annually commemorated on the 29th of June.[131]

It is important not to underestimate the importance of the role played by the Apostle Paul and his tremendous efforts to unify Jewish and Gentile Christians. In the last years of his activity he departed for Jerusalem in the hope to reconcile a Jewish Christianity, which still demanded circumcision, and a Gentile Christianity. Before this venture, he commends his co-workers in Rome, by personally addressing them and he requires them to pray for him and to remain strong for his sake.

Furthermore, Petrine and Pauline churches were influenced by the same theology and the same traditions and external hostility forced them to combine forces. It needs to be considered that the person of Mark acts as a bridge between Peter and Paul, being a co-worker of both. The Roman church, although not founded by Paul, was influenced by Pauline theology. Yet, when Mark writes his Gospel from Rome, the Roman church claims that the tradition on which he based his Gospel derived from Peter and not from Paul. Later, the First Epistle of Peter, also strongly influenced by Pauline theology, also originated from Rome, however not in the name of Paul, but in the

---

128. Bacon, *Is Mark?*, 46.
129. Ibid., 46.
130. Ibid., 47.
131. Böttrich, *Petrus*, 225.

name of Peter. Clement, bishop of Rome, in his letter to the Corinthians also wanted to establish the presence of both Apostles in Rome.[132]

It could almost be argued that Mark wrote a Petro-Pauline Gospel, drawing upon the legacy of both. At Rome, leaders associated with Paul, used the names of Peter and Mark to encourage the churches in Asia Minor, the area of Paul's prior missionary activity (cf. 1 Peter). Additionally, these same leaders used these same names in order to preserve the life and sayings of Jesus (the Gospel of Mark).[133]

The role Peter played in the tradition regarding Jesus's earthly existence proved to be so important that no gospel could be written without paying special attention to Peter. It is therefore also difficult to determine how much of the character of Peter as portrayed in the Gospels actually goes back to the historical Peter and how much is simply a projection of his later role in the church. The fact that Peter is the one to confess Jesus as the Christ, although with the Jewish Messianic expectation in mind, could also be a projection to the later role of Peter in the church, being the representative of the true apostolic faith.[134]

Since 1 Peter is a pseudographical letter and only written in the name of Peter, the indication of being a witness to the suffering of Christ is even more convincing, because the audience might have been familiar with Peter's alleged martyrdom in Rome (cf. 1 Pet 5:1). Furthermore, the command to the elders not to exercise their authority to their own advantage and not to govern violently, also finds its foundation in the example of Peter, who as the ultimate shepherd was still willing to suffer martyrdom. It is very possible that the author is here drawing upon the Johannine tradition (cf. John 21:15–19) where Peter is ordered to let the sheep graze, followed by what could be understood as an allusion to his martyrdom. Once again this is not an example of the author of 1 Peter being literary depended on John, but rather that both authors were familiar with the same tradition.[135]

## The Importance for the Roman Church to let Peter "Speak" from Rome

Luz rightfully asks the question why Peter becomes the foundation of the Apostolic tradition of the church?[136] The answer which he provides is simply

132. Bacon, *Is Mark?*, 104.
133. Ibid., 105.
134. Brown, Donfried, and Reumann, *Der Petrus der Bibel*, 139.
135. Ibid., 131–33; cf. Elliott, *A Home*, 273.
136. Luz, *Matthäus*, 469.

because of his relation to Jesus. Although this is correct, it is not sufficient. Why do the other eleven not enjoy the same prominence, especially the "beloved disciple" from the Gospel of John, which according to the author of John, shares a very unique and special relationship with Jesus? It is further not the "beloved disciple" but Peter who receives the command to look after the flock. Peter is the one who conquers the crisis in the midst of the disciples by his confession and according to John he will be the one martyred in his following of Christ.[137]

The question remains unanswered why Peter enjoys this prominence above the other disciples and why he is the one par excellence by the side of Jesus. The fact that the other apostles in Acts, the evangelists and the letters of Paul so often refer to Peter gives the impression of an extraordinary theological competence associated with his person, although he was not, as in the case of Paul, an educated man.[138]

Although the Markan community rejected the authority of James as the brother of Jesus in Jerusalem, they did acknowledge the authority of the twelve apostles. Unlike the community in Jerusalem, the Roman community, which was joined by many pagan converts, did not expect compliance with Jewish purity and dietary laws.[139]

If asked whom the Roman community did view as authoritative, the answer is given by the prominence that the Gospel of Mark gives to the twelve who were elected and especially to Peter, John and James (the sons of Zebedee). This inner disciple group receives instructions and insight into the coming kingdom of God in private apart from the crowds. This group is entrusted with the messianic secret of the passion that Christ must endure before his glorification.[140]

The Markan community's criticism of Jewish food and purity laws becomes evident in Jesus's statement that all food is pure. The openness to pagan converts is also conveyed by putting the confession of Jesus as the Son of God in the mouth of a Roman centurion. Although the community could be regarded as open and inclusive they viewed the teaching derived from the apostles to be authoritative and a nonnegotiable condition for entering the community.[141]

---

137. Hengel, *Der Unterschätze*, 48.
138. Ibid., 49.
139. Brent, *Political History*, 59.
140. Ibid., 61.
141. Ibid., 62.

From the content of Mark it becomes clear that he views the Twelve to be authoritative figures from the beginning and from the initial Judean tradition that came to Rome.

Mark's Jesus did not come to liberate only the persecuted Jewish Christians. His message is much more universal.[142]

The audience of 1 Peter was assumed to have known the biblical texts from the Septuagint, given the letter's many quotations of it and allusions to it. If the texts were known and the teaching of the Apostles was regarded as authoritative, the persons would also have been known.

The Roman community's own experience of suffering (cf. the persecutions under Nero) adds substance to their message of consolation and hope to the communities in Asia Minor. These three persons' own lives already bore witness to what the author(s) of the letter wished the addressees to resemble.

According to Luke in the Acts of the Apostles Peter is the leader of the mother church in Jerusalem at least until the persecution by Agrippa in AD 42–43. Thereafter, James, the brother of Jesus, becomes the main figure in Jerusalem. It is however noteworthy that in all four the Gospels it is Peter who acts as the leader and the depiction of the brother of Jesus is rather negative. This further gives rise to the question of why Peter becomes such an influential figure, not only in Jerusalem and among Jewish Christians in Diaspora, but especially among the Gentile Christians even in Rome and that his influence remain prominent at least until the second century.[143]

His influence is attested to by all four Gospels, The Acts of the Apostles, *1 Clement*, Ignatius and the pseudographical letter of First Peter, written in his name. The earliest Christian writer, Paul, also mentions and commends him.

As previously argued in this study the letter of 1 Peter most probably originated from Rome. The fact that a letter, written in the name of Peter and originating from Rome, mentions Mark is indicative of the assumption that Mark's person enjoyed a growing prominence in the area of Paul's former missionary activity. It further suggests an association between Peter and Mark.[144]

It is possible that some of the addressees of 1 Peter were present at the Pentecost and heard Peter speak (cf. Acts 2:9). They therefore had a personal encounter with Peter and could have informed the rest of the community about it. It cannot be concluded whether Peter himself actually ever visited

---

142. Ibid., 63.

143. Hengel, *Der Unterschätze*, 47.

144. Bacon, *Is Mark?*, 28.

these communities. What is however quite certain is the fact that Peter, as a prominent leading figure in the church in Jerusalem, was known, at least by reputation to these communities.[145]

The addressees of 1 Peter were confronted with slandering and hostility from their non-believing neighbours. Against this background the letter of 1 Peter was composed in order to convey the message to these suffering Christians that they are part of a universal brotherhood of faith. This message was intended to strengthen their collective identity and to enhance their perception of themselves. Furthermore, the letter stressed the necessity of internal unity within the Christian communities promoted by their shared commitment to the values and goals of Christianity.[146]

The majority of current New Testament scholars reached consensus that 1 Peter is a pseudonymous letter written in the name of the Apostle Peter, but they are not so certain about why exactly the name of Peter was chosen. Those in favour of the argument that 1 Peter is the product of a Pauline circle often confuse the distinction between common Christian tradition and literary dependency. They seek to maintain that the geographical residence of the addressees was an exclusive Pauline missionary area, ignoring the possibility that there could have been an independent Petrine mission. Probably the most convincing reason to invalidate this argument is its lack of realizing the distinctive theological and literal differences between 1 Peter and the Pauline writings.[147]

Those who claim that the letter was written by Silvanus or another individual ignore the possibility that there might have been a group behind the composition of the letter. Instead of maintaining that the letter was written by an individual, the possibility should be taken seriously that there existed a Petrine group in Rome of which Silvanus, Mark and the unnamed sister (cf. 1 Pet 5:12–13) were part. This group held fast to the teaching and memory of the Apostle Peter, which according to tradition (as indicated in this study), was associated with Rome. In this sense the letter could even be regarded as "authentically" Petrine since it attests to the ideas, theologies and worldview believed to be held by the Apostle himself, and which this group, as his followers wished to continue.

The letter does not only want to stress Peter's authority as an apostle and representative of the true faith, but especially as a leading figure who has compassion with the addressees of the letter (cf. 1 Pet 4:13; 5:1). The legacy of Peter was to serve as an example to the audience. Peter himself

---

145. Elliott, *A Home*, 274.
146. Ibid., 270.
147. Ibid., 271.

experienced suffering, but held steadfast to the faith. His solidarity with the Christian congregations is further illuminated by his referral to himself as "co-elder" and not superior to the elders in the community.

The reason why the letter was written in the name of Peter now becomes clear. It forms part of the whole strategy of the letter. Peter was the one on whose teachings, theology and memories the Roman church was founded; it attests to the fact that common Christian ideas and traditions were known to a wide and geographically scattered audience; a personal and supportive bond is established between the Petrine circle in Rome and the Christian communities in Asia Minor and it enforces the community's self-esteem and serves as an authenticated and authoritative encouragement.

The Petrine circle, who might have witnessed Peter's death, seeks to pay tribute to the visions and hope Peter had for the Christian movement and to realise these in honor of his memory.[148]

As far as the self-interests of the Petrine circle in Rome is concerned, they sought to enhance the position of the Roman church as a church which could speak with authority and that would have the ability to influence the rest of the Christian world.[149]

The position of the Roman church is further strengthened by their claim that both Apostles, Peter and Paul, were present in their midst and that they witnessed their martyrdom after having the privilege of receiving their teachings.

"It would be unlikely for a group at the political, economic and cultural hub of power and influence not to derive benefits from its location and not to take advantage of its position and capabilities in the furtherance of personal and movement-wide causes."[150]

Rome would have been the perfect place where the essence of the Christian faith and traditions were preserved and where traditions from all over the Mediterranean merged, again to be distributed throughout the Christian world.[151]

The Petrine Roman community would not in their lifetime witness the realisation of their dream that all Christian roads for centuries led to Rome.

In order to establish unity and to encourage the commitment of believers to the Christian movement a letter was composed in the name of the leading disciple, Peter, to be delivered by another person with a reputation of credibility, Silvanus. This letter contained an ecclesiology and ideology

---

148. Ibid., 275.
149. Ibid., 280.
150. Elliott, *A Home*, 281.
151. Ibid.

which the Roman church sought to extent to Christianity throughout the world. Their motive was not only to enhance the position of the Christian church in Rome, but the general position of the Christian movement throughout the world.

It would have made sense to consolidate different and divergent Christian traditions under the name of the leading Apostle, Peter, in Rome. To legitimise the teachings, ecclesiology and ideology derived from Peter as ultimately authoritative, the danger of divisions and heresy within the Christian movement could be successfully combated.[152]

The person of the Apostle Peter forms an important bridge between the memory of the historical Jesus in the Gospels and the mission of the Paul to the Gentiles as narrated in the Acts of the Apostles.[153]

### Elliott's Hypothesis of a Petrine Circle in Rome

Elliott makes the important point that the ideas and views of a particular individual can only be preserved and perpetuated if they are shared.[154] This statement substantiates the idea of a Petrine group. Although the New Testament does not give any account of house churches and communities founded by Peter as it does in the case of Paul, there is no reason to believe that it was entirely impossible for Peter to establish his own Christian communities. The same could be argued for the other apostles, e.g., James and John. All missions were conducted with the aid of co-workers and supporters, including local households that provided hospitality to travelling missionaries and offered their houses as a place where the congregation could assemble.

The suggestion of more than one person behind the Petrine letter is evident from the contents of the letter itself (cf. 1 Pet 5:12–13).

According to 1 Pet 1:1 the letter was written in the name of the Apostle Peter which indicates that the person and character of Peter was known to the author as well as to the audience.[155]

The fact that the associates of Peter are addressed in familial terms, e.g., Mark as "son," Silvanus as "faithful brother," and the "co-elect sister in Rome" is in accordance with the idea that the addressees of the letter form part of a larger Christian family. The close familial ties the text suggests to

---

152. Ibid., 282.
153. Hengel, *Der Unterschätze*, 129.
154. Elliott, *A Home*, 272.
155. Ibid., 273.

be between these individuals served as an example to the addressees of the solidarity that ought to be displayed by Christian communities.

The mentioning of the names also added a personal character to the letter, aiming at establishing a personal relation between senders and receivers. There is on the other hand no reason to regard the author's reference to the other co-workers, Mark and Silvanus, as fictional or metaphorical. Silvanus was probably the co-finder with Paul to most of the congregations the letter is addressed to and Mark is known from Acts to be a follower of Barnabas, Paul and Peter and features as an important link between Paul and Peter.[156] The fact that the letter mentions these persons' names and the reputations associated with them is part and parcel of the strategy of the letter to convey the senders's interest in universal unity and solidarity within the Christian movement. Through the mentioning of these names a common social and religious bond is established between the Christians in Rome and the addressees in Asia Minor. Not only does the letter refer to persons known by both communities, but the emphasis is also on the shared kerygma and traditions and the suffering and hostility experienced by Christians throughout the world. Not only do they have the suffering in common, but they also share in the hope of a future glorification which is their heritage through the resurrection of Christ. In other words the senders of the letter are advocating a distinctive Christian identity.

Silvanus, on the other hand, had a much more positive relationship with Paul. Silvanus' close collaboration with Paul does not mean that his thoughts and theologies were exclusively shaped by Paul, nor does the mentioning of his name in 1 Peter prove that 1 Peter is a Pauline writing. Neither could Gal 2:7–9 be interpreted as the absolute and final word on missionary activities. Peter was by no means prohibited to undertake a mission to the Gentiles and ordered to restrict his proclaiming of the gospel to Jewish audiences. Given the fact that most Christian communities were a mixture of Jewish and Gentile converts such a division would be impractical on geographical as well as ethnical grounds. Asia Minor can therefore not be understood to be exclusive Pauline territory.[157]

The crucial meeting that took place in Jerusalem, of which Acts 15 reports, where the main point on the agenda was the mission to the Gentiles, was attended by Silvanus, John Mark and Peter. It is of definite significance that these three figures met here and furthermore that they now seem to be re-united in Rome. Acts 15:22–23 and 1 Pet 5:12 both attribute the function of being the bearer of a letter to Silvanus in remarkably similar words.

---

156. Bacon, *Is Mark?*, 28.
157. Elliott, *A Home*, 277.

As indicated by the agenda of the meeting of the Jerusalem council, they were concerned with the universal nature of the Christian movement but at the same time sought its unification. These are also concerns aired in the letter of 1 Peter.

Even though the mentioning of the names in 1 Peter is part of the pseudographical nature of the letter as some scholars would maintain, the fact remains that these names were of significant meaning to the addressees of the letter. "The careers and reputations of the three persons mentioned are linked with the origins, crucial developments and decisions, and widest outreach of the worldwide Christian movement."[158]

It could not be certain whether Rome was the place where Mark and Silvanus were situated at the time of the composition of 1 Peter, but the fact that the author mentioned their names suggests that some authority was linked to their persons. The author purposefully refers to these persons and that seems to be an indication of their significance. It is therefore quite possible, that this Mark, as a former co-worker of both Paul and Peter, continued the work of the apostles within the capital of the Roman Empire.[159] If the Silvanus and Mark whom 1 Peter mentions are indeed the same Silas and John Mark to whom the rest of the New Testament refers (a view held by the majority of New Testament scholars), then the Petrine circle gains additional authoritative prominence. The mentioning of their names adds additional credibility to the message the letter wants to convey.

The first mentioning of John Mark is in Acts 12:1-17, and this narrative attest to his residence in Jerusalem and his association with Peter. After Peter's escape from prison he is said to have gone to the house of Mary, the mother of John, who was also known as Mark. It could therefore be concluded that a relationship between Mark and Peter existed.[160] Furthermore, Mark is perceived to have ties with the mother church in Jerusalem. It seemed that his ways with Paul parted, but he was still involved in missionary activity.[161]

## The Existence of a Petrine Tradition in Rome

Scholarship today needs to take the question seriously as to what extend the Gospel writers were simply redactors of tradition or creative theological composers. As far as the Gospel of Mark is concerned this question is

---

158. Ibid., 279.
159. Bacon, *Is Mark?*, 29.
160. Hengel, *Der Unterschätze*, 73–74.
161. Elliott, *A Home*, 276.

even more important, because we do not have access to any pre-Markan sources. If we were to opt for the prior position that the Gospel writers were merely redactors, we need to ask to what extend these traditions which they employed derived from actual eyewitness memory or did these memories undergo substantial alterations as they developed.

Vincent Taylor is an exponent of the first option, namely that the author of Mark was a conservative redactor of early Christian tradition which is linked with eyewitness testimony.[162] He therefore understands the episodes in the Gospel involving Peter as to go back to the historical Peter. Such a view would imply that Peter, as characterised in the Gospel of Mark, was already portrayed as such in pre-Markan tradition.[163]

In other words there existed within the pre-gospel tradition a distinctive and consistent picture of the person of Peter. This would lead to the conclusion that the traditions about Peter's character were also reflected in the other Gospels since they go back to the historical person.

On the other side of the spectrum stands William Kelber, who states that the Markan passion narrative was the author of Mark's own composition, which displays the author's skill as a narrator as well as his theology.[164] The author approached his task with creativity and decided on his own order. He changed traditional material for his own theological purposes. He therefore concludes that there is very little historical foundation for the characterisation of Peter within the Gospel.[165]

If it is taken into account that Kelber's focus is primarily on the passion narrative, the role Peter plays in the narrative and the connection to his prior actions and statements in the build up to the passion narrative must also be the author's own composition. As mentioned earlier, Mark's Gospel displays consistency and coherence in its portrayal of Peter, therefore it would make sense that the author linked Peter's objection to Jesus's suffering, his inability to stay awake in Gethsemane and his denial in his composed characterisation of Peter.[166] This study would argue for a compromise between these two diverse perspectives. Similar to the historical Jesus, a historical person is indeed behind the tradition and teachings derived from Peter as well as the narratives containing biographical information about his person. On these grounds this study agrees that the author of Mark used pre-existing traditions and narratives and edited them in order to serve his own theological interests. Having

---

162. Taylor, *Foundation*.
163. Wiarda, *Peter*, 207–8.
164. Kelber, "Conclusion," 153–80.
165. Wiarda, *Peter*, 209.
166. Ibid., 210.

said this, the author's own creativity in his composition of the Gospel is not denied. We are dealing with a theological document and not with a historical writing and in the ancient worldview tradition, mythology and history were often indiscernibly intertwined. To determine which content in the Gospel of Mark has an actual historical foundation and which was the product of his own creativity, would be extremely difficult. The only thing that remains certain is the fact that pre-gospel traditions about Peter's person did indeed exist and that the author of the first Gospel chose to employ these traditions to accomplish theological and ideological goals.

The ancient tradition that goes back to the second century AD, which was preserved by Eusebius, claims that Mark was the author of the first Gospel and that he was the secretary of Peter. According to this tradition it seems as though Mark was urged to preserve the tradition derived from Peter within the Roman community.

The New Testament seems to suggest an association between Peter and Rome, especially if one considers that 1 Peter was written from Rome in the name of Peter. This study is not arguing for a historical relation between the Apostle Peter and the author of the Gospel of Mark as the Papias tradition would like to claim. It is rather a matter of association and because Mark wrote from Rome, he is strongly influenced by the memory of the teachings of the Apostle Peter.

The situation of Rome during and in the aftermath of Nero's persecution of the Christians, as described by Tacitus and Josephus, seems to be reflected by the contents of the Gospel of Mark. Mark's contents attest to the imminent return of the Son of Man and the author lays his own apocalyptic thoughts and expectations in the mouth of Jesus (cf. Mark 13).[167]

## The Possibility (or not) of the Historical Presence of Peter in Rome

The critical question that should be asked by church historians is whether Peter was present in Rome at all.[168]

Contrary to Paul, Peter disappears from the scene in Acts. It is only a later tradition that holds that Peter journeyed to Rome and was martyred there. Ignatius of Antioch in his letter to the Romans dated around AD 107, states that Peter and Paul were apostles in Rome. Irenaeus of Lyons, who wrote around AD 170, claims that the Roman church was founded by Peter

---

167. Brent, *Political History*, 39–40.
168. Böttrich, *Petrus*, 220–21.

and Paul. This aided the Roman church in gaining bigger influence, since they could boast that both apostles were present in their midst.[169]

Christian tradition merely assumed the presence of Peter in Rome. Furthermore a tradition existed that Mark, written from the teachings of Peter, originated in Rome shortly after Peter's martyrdom. This puts Rome in the privileged position of being the place from which the first Gospel originated. This new genre, containing biographical material about the actual words and deeds of Jesus, is a powerful testimony to the rest of the Christian world of the strength of the church in Rome.[170]

The fact that Peter and Paul "bore witness" should not be understood as martyrdom. It is only during the cause of the second century AD that "baring witness" became to be understood as testifying by blood. This becomes unmistakably clear from 1 Clem. 5.4.7. Peter "departed to the place of glory" and Paul was "removed from this world" after baring witness. This euphemistic language reveals nothing of a violent death. On the contrary, the suffering they endured was the result of their strife for honor, which they eventually conquered and therefore they serve as such good examples for the congregation in Corinth.

Viewed historically, it is highly plausible that at least Paul found himself in Rome during Nero's persecution of the Christians in AD 64 and it is therefore probable that Paul met his death during this period when large numbers of Christians were killed in the arena as reported by Tacitus.[171]

There exists, however, no historical evidence that Peter ever functioned as an elder of a specific congregation also not in the church in Rome.[172]

Archaeological evidence as far as the burial of Peter underneath the Basilica is not yet conclusive.[173] No archaeological excavations underneath the St. Peter's Church lead to the discovery of a grave older that the second century AD. There is also no evidence to prove that this necropolis belonged exclusively to Christians. Neither is there any indication that the necropolis was established by Christians.[174] This necropolis at the earliest dates back to the second century AD, which makes it impossible that Peter could be buried there, unless he was buried there before the establishment of the necropolis.[175] We can, however, conclude from archaeological evidence that

169. Green, *Christianity*, 45.
170. Ibid., 46.
171. Böttrich, *Petrus*, 216–17.
172. Brown, Donfried, and Reumann, *Der Petrus der Bibel*, 134.
173. Böttrich, *Petrus*, 234.
174. Zwierlein, *Petrus in Rom*, 5.
175. Böttrich, *Petrus*, 230.

cultic activity in regard to honoring the bones of the apostles around the Via Appia existed since AD 260. But also in the surroundings of the Via Appia no existence of a grave could be proven.[176]

It is however quite possible that Peter was crucified, since it was a common form of execution for those who were viewed as threats to Roman authority. Therefore, although the story is possible, there exists no historical evidence to corroborate it. It is even possible that Peter was in Rome, since Paul wanted to depart for Spain and on the way visit Rome and died before he could realise his plans. In Paul's absence the church may have enjoyed the guidance of Peter. Furthermore both these apostles are understood to be executed during the reign of Nero.[177]

It is however highly unlikely that Peter was present in Rome before Paul's letter to the Romans, because even though Paul writes that he does not wish to build upon the foundation of someone else (cf. Rome 15:20), he would certainly have mentioned it if that someone was as significant as the Apostle Peter or if Peter was still present with them. Peter therefore could only have gone to Rome after Paul's arrest.

It is even possible that Peter went to Rome after the catastrophe of the fire in order to provide some comfort to the distressed Christian community. This would explain why Irenaeus viewed Peter as the founder of the church in Rome. According to *The Acts of Peter*, Peter went to Rome to resolve a crisis after Paul's arrest. This crisis could be the conflict between Jewish and Gentile Christians, already addressed by Paul's letter to the Romans.[178] If the relation between Jewish and Gentile Christians worsened after Paul's arrest, a visit by Peter would make sense.[179]

From the apocrypha yet another picture is drawn. In *The Acts of Peter and Paul* (ca. end of the second century) it is narrated that these apostles engaged in personal conflict with the house of Nero. When dealing with early Christian traditions and the memory of the first persons who acted as the vehicles of the faith, it is important to note that the best attempts to construct a historical report of their lives do not bring us any closer in discovering what their significance were for the early church.[180]

In the apocryphal work, *The Acts of Paul*, a detailed narration is given about the legendary martyrdom of Paul in Rome. As in the case of the martyrdom of Peter, this legend only originated by the end of the second

176. Zwierlein, *Petrus in Rom*, 6.
177. Green, *Christianity*, 48.
178. Ibid., 49.
179. Ibid., 50.
180. Brown, Donfried, and Reumann, *Der Petrus der Bibel*, 147.

century and is also not historically conclusive. Given the ancient context in which these legends originated the concern was not so much about historical truths, but rather about honoring those who were representatives of the gospel and who led exemplary lives. According to this elaborate narrative Paul was decapitated by Nero amidst wonders and conversions conducted by the apostles. However, there does seem to be some historical truth behind this romanticised tale. Paul was executed in Rome during the reign of Nero and his death was probably not part of Nero's execution of the Christians after the fire of AD 64.[181]

Similar to *The Acts of Paul*, *The Acts of Peter* also originated near the end of the second century. In this apocryphal writing Peter travels to Rome to counter Simon, the magician. Peter receives a direct command from God in a vision to travel to Rome. Peter enters into a "magical contest" with Simon, making a dog speak, bringing a fish to life and making an infant speak in the voice of a man. This contest reaches its climax when Peter raises a man from the dead in the Forum and Simon's emulation of him turns out to be a fraud. Then Simon flees and is hunted down by Peter. Peter further converts a woman by the name of Xanthippe, the wife of Albinus, a friend of the emperor. After her conversion she no longer wished to sleep with her husband and this evoked anger in him and he wanted to kill Peter. He was however warned by Xanthippe and left Rome. Upon the way the so-called *Quo Vadis* incident occurred and Peter was ordered by Christ to return to Rome and to face his martyrdom. Peter preferred to be crucified upside down, for he did not view himself worthy of dying in the same way as Christ did.[182]

During later traditions the martyrdom of Peter in Rome is accepted as factual without questioning. Many tourists visiting the city of Rome are captivated by the majestic St. Peter's Cathedral in the Vatican City, allegedly build upon the place where Peter was buried. The vivid imagery of his martyrdom was also engraved in the minds of people by the acclaimed film *Quo Vadis* by von Henryk Sienkiewicz.

It may be concluded that the literary testimonies regarding Peter's martyrdom or death are by no means unanimous. Neither are they free from church political agendas and legendary fantasies.[183]

---

181. Green, *Christianity*, 44.
182. Ibid., 47.
183. Böttrich, *Petrus*, 227.

# 3

# Christology as Foundation for Ethics

## Introduction

CHRISTOLOGY AND ETHICS ARE so implicitly bound together, for the freeing through the sinless Christ and his example once again strengthens the summons in 1 Pet 2:19 to doing good and avoidance of evil; but, above all, by means of following Jesus (1 Pet 2:23), who did not pay back abuse and blows with the same coin and thereby embodied the ethical goal of the whole paraenesis (cf. 1 Pet 3:9) and who is distinguished as an example of the renunciation of retaliation. This motif also reminds one of the song of God's servant (Isa 53:7), tangible above all in the Passion of Jesus in his silence towards the charges (Mark 14:61).

## Christology in Early Christianity

One of the greatest, if not the greatest, challenges of the early Christian movement was to move beyond the shame of the cross. It was an unreasonable demand to the human mind to discover in the cross of Calvary an act of divine salvation. In 1 Cor 1:23 Paul is challenging the intellectual criticism against the Christian faith. Paul argues that the idea of a crucified Saviour is not absurd but paradoxal. He recognises within the cross an act of God that turned human standards and value systems upside down. Divine wisdom is so great that it cannot be encompassed by human wisdom. According to Paul it is part of the mystery of God's wisdom that God gives particular preference to the weak and the foolish. This provocative act of God stuns the arrogant.

As far as the opponents of Jesus were concerned his death on the cross was merely the result of his scandalous and blasphemous behaviour.[1]

---

1. Erlemann, *Jesus der Christus*, 5.

He took the authority of God upon himself, however, whenever proof of his divine authority was demanded, he boldly refused especially during his temptation in the dessert. Therefore the miracles and the teachings of Jesus remain ambivalent—they do not necessarily succeed in convincing the sceptics, for some even viewed his authority as originating from the devil (cf. Matt 12:24). Furthermore, the idea of a suffering Messiah was unacceptable for the contemporaries of Jesus (cf. Mark 8:11). The Gethsemane narrative depicts Jesus as desperate and helpless and up until the last minute of the narrative he does not succumb to the temptation to save himself from the cross (cf. Mark 15:29–32). His divine identity therefore remains secretive until his death and in the eyes of his opponents it is thereby refuted.

Therefore, the question about the divinity, or at least the divine authority of Jesus was relevant since the very beginning of the Christian movement. His own claim to divine authority as well as the Messianic claims of his disciples provoked a demand for an objective, rational and conceivable piece of evidence. So the Christian faith remains a perpetual provocation of the human mind.[2]

By Jesus's death on the cross many human expectations and desires about a messianic saviour were shattered and for many of his contemporaries all hope was abandoned. This raises certain questions that remain relevant to this day: Why doesn't Jesus heal all people? Why did he not save himself from the cross? Why did Jesus not better his own world? Do we still believe in his return?

A crucified Messiah is an unreasonable demand in order to conceive an almighty, good and compassionate God. The fact that God forsook his Son on the cross, is inconceivable for many. How does one perceive that a loving God sacrifices his own Son? That does not sound like fatherly love, but rather despotism, or in the best scenario helplessness and total loss of control. People are certainly not pleased with a seemingly helpless and powerless God who just allows for his Son to be nailed to a cross. Can it be possible that the almighty God simply sacrifices his one and only Son? Why does He not intervene on behalf of his Son? Why does He allow for the worst to happen? Where was God when Jesus was crucified? According to the Christian tradition his last words were: "My God, my God, why have you forsaken me?" (cf. Mark 15:34; Matt 27:46; Ps 22:2).

At first glance the divinely ordained Messiah on the cross seems like a loud contradiction to the omnipotence of God.[3]

---

2. Ibid., 6.
3. Ibid., 7; cf. Wolff, *Neuer Wein*.

As far as the works of God is concerned, there is no tried and tested methodology. Yet, a narrative about Jesus of Nazareth within which God is not prominently mentioned as an actor is possible. This necessarily means that it could have been narrated in a different way as was the case with the other written Gospels. It also indicates that God could speak at any time and in any way.[4]

The hiddeness of the works of God does not mean that reality of God is invisible. Furthermore, it should be kept in mind that the way of Jesus is indeed mysterious. When we speak about the hiddeness of God, or as Luther coined the term "Deus absconditus," it does not mean that God does not become present or able to be experienced by humans.[5] What it means is that something that is not necessarily presentable could be observed none the less and this possibility is open to anyone.

Eventually, God is revealed in the crucified Jesus. Without the passion of Jesus God is not recognised. Ironically, the glorification of the Son of Man comes to the fore in his humiliation. Through the narrative of the passion it becomes possible for the reader or hearer to recognise and experience God. It is therefore something different than a mere theory about God or an abstract listing of his divine attributes. In the words of Sommer: "Die Passionsgeschichte verweist auf die Geschichte Jesu als den Ort, wo zu erfahren ist wer Gott ist."[6] Through Mark's account of the passion the hearer has the opportunity to rejoice in God, for the account also defines the identity of the hearers. It provides them with an orientation towards God and towards their own circumstances. The fact that Peter who became the biggest failure was able to restore his discipleship to the full (cf. Mark 16:7) gives the hearers a perspective on their own failures.

Through the passion narrative the hearers come to view themselves as humans in need of forgiveness and finding it. Because God becomes present in the event of Jesus's crucifixion the human in search of God has the experience of God being revealed. Significant is that God becomes present in the disgusting and barbaric circumstances of a crucifixion. This is the mystery of the gospel. The harsh reality of this world, Calvary, becomes the locus of God's revelation. This leads to the conclusion that it is not possible to speak of God without simultaneously speaking of reality.[7]

Intensive theological reflexion is required to recognise behind a seemingly helpless God, a God who is in control of how human history plays out.

---

4. Sommer, *Die Passionsgeschicte*, 240.
5. Luther, *De servo arbitrio*.
6. Sommer, *Die Passionsgeschicte*, 246.
7. Ibid., 247.

The first prerequisite is to get rid of the static understanding of omnipotence as if God has to proof Himself as omnipotent in all circumstances, for such a view cannot provide comfort. When God created humans in his image (cf. Gen 1:27), he did not create a puppet, but a strong minded counterpart. Similarly, God's history with his people was a constant battle for their loyalty and commitment. Over and over again Israel went their own way and left behind their created identity and their covenant because of their relationship with their Creator. And again God sent his prophets to lead his people back to Him. After God's judgement and wrath, a new beginning followed and a renewal of the covenant. With the sending of his own Son, God renews his covenant with his people in a special, never to be repeated way. In the parable of the tenants (Mark 12:1–12) God's own expectation is stated namely that his Son will experience a different kind of treatment: they will respect him (cf. Mark 12:6). The parable illustrates God's disappointment with the outcome of events, because the omnipotence of God is no instrument to disable the independent decisions of humans. God refrains from using force to publicly display his omnipotence. This he will do at the end of time. Biblical testimony to the omnipotence of God is furthermore dynamic; for God created humans as his counterparts and therefore he already refrained from enforcing his omnipotence. Jesus also refrained from public power displays (cf. Matt 4 and Luke 4). The powerful enforcement of His divine reign is expected for the end of the world. When we think about the crucifixion in this way, it does not contradict God's omnipotence. Yet, it provokes our thinking about God and his extraordinary way of being involved with humans.[8]

Secondly, Sommer makes the important point that in essence, faith is not rational.[9] Faith is no rational or philosophical abstraction. One cannot apply oneself to come to faith through thinking. We will not recognise God through rationality. Without experience of the world, experience of God will not be possible, or put differently: experience of God is necessarily experience of the reality of this world. The further dimension is that the passion narrative has significance for the everyday living situation of the faithful.

The "Heilsbeteutung" of the cross is not accessible through intellectual meticulousness, but is worked by the Holy Spirit of God. Therefore the theological significance of the crucifixion for the faith is not a logical construct and as such is not able to be proven. The theological significance of the crucifixion can only be confessed and that as a result of a God given

---

8. Erlemann, *Jesus der Christus*, 8.
9. Sommer, *Die Passionsgeschicte*, 249.

insight. That does not mean that the narrative is incomprehensible or without reason. However, what is narrated is strange and unique for it entails a different estimation of values for the negative barbaric and criminal symbol of the cross becomes a symbol of the presence of God and divine victory over the forces of evil.

Although it is not possible for the faith to be proven historically, faith is not impossible and it is not excluded that knowledge of history could have a positive impact on faith. However, faith is liberated from having to prove its inherent truth by historical reliability.

The New Testament text also generates truth when it creates hope among its hearers and readers. They perceive God and themselves in a different light after encountering what is narrated in these texts and this effect of the text cannot be researched historically.

God does not only become present through what is said about him, for the reality within which we perceive and experience God can also merely be narrated. After all the goal of Mark's narrative was to communicate the reality about God within the framework of the reality of the hearers' everyday lives. Through these texts God communicates to people within their lived reality. This communication only becomes possible through the composure of texts and that was and still remains the purpose of Mark's Gospel. The Gospel is not concerned with historical fact but with the proclamation of Jesus Christ. Furthermore, the Gospel of Mark makes the experience of God concrete and not abstract. The narrative genre makes the events present. The narrative links the present with the events narrated.[10]

Even when the omnipotence of God is not refuted by the crucifixion, the question still remains why a loving, good and compassionate God, could not spare His Son the martyrdom of the cross and achieve the salvation of humankind in a different manner. Or why did He not inaugurate His new heaven and earth before the horror of the crucifixion? Was it His plan all along to sacrifice His Son in this cruel way? Many early Christian texts attempt to address these incomprehensible questions: God is omnipotent and omniscient and therefore He had known in advance what was to happen. This is basic to the doctrine of Christian theology. However, to the modern mind, this seems somewhat sadistic and it makes the cross seem like a regression to an out-dated Old Testament sacrifice-theology.

When we take another look at the parable of the tenants (Mark 12:1–12), the idea that God planned the death of His Son becomes questionable. Instead of sadism, it seems here that God was disappointed and disillusioned with the behaviour of the tenants. The fate of the Son remained open and

---

10. Ibid., 262.

his death was not predestined. The later meaning of the death of Jesus as a reconciliation sacrifice or as the accomplishment of salvation seems contradictory. However, when one considers both options, one recognises a God that by sacrificing His Son, achieves the salvation of the entire humankind. One could think of God as a "Crisis Manager," who keeps his eye on his plan for the salvation of humankind in spite of human interference. Instead of resigning helplessly, or enforcing his will forcefully, God refrains from dictating human history. His ultimate goal remains the salvation of humanity and achieving reconciliation with them. He allows for countless detours caused by the independent decision making of humans. This God is neither sadistic, nor helpless. Rather he has the reconciliation with humans in mind and in achieving that he is incredibly patient and unwavering.

What Mark's passion narrative makes explicit is that the entire event was according to the will of God. Mark 14:21 states that it was the will of God that Jesus falls into the hands of sinners and the will of God clearly becomes a subject in Mark 14:36. From Jesus's prayer in Gethsemane we learn that everything is unfolding according to the will of God. So it becomes evident that the will of God ultimately determines what happens in reality. When the readers perceive that God is ultimately in control about what happens in the world, they are encouraged to take up their task to follow in the footsteps of Christ.

Furthermore, the presence of God on Cavalry is to be understood as an act of benevolence for all of humankind. God does not leave the world at its own mercy, put places it in relationship with Him.[11]

The passion narrative therefore aids the faith. What is confessed in faith took place in public, for all to observe, yet not everyone has insight into the meaning of these events for the faith. Without the passion event faith would not be possible. The public nature of these events has the consequence that what is confessed by faith is not an apocalyptic secrecy. Because of the public nature of these events faith is accessible and inclusive and not the privilege of a selected enlightened few. Through the passion narrative the Jesus of the *kerygma* is in principle accessible to all. This allowed for Christianity to become a public practice and not something doomed to the private sphere.[12]

Another question that the early church had to deal with was the possibility of a suffering God.[13] For ancient philosophers a suffering God was a

---

11. Ibid., 252.
12. Ibid., 253.
13. See Moltmann, *Der gekreuzigte Gott*; McGrath, *Luther's Theology*; McWilliams, *Passion of God*; Placher, *Narratives*; Ngien, *Suffering of God*; Bauckham, *God Crucified*.

ridiculous idea, but on the contrary, biblical discourse allowed a highly developed ability for God to endure suffering: God is a God who is perpetually disappointed by his created counterparts.[14]

The Gnostics tried to resolve this issue by arguing that it wasn't God that suffered and died on the cross, but merely a human.[15] However, in orthodox Christianity the biblical image of God prevailed who had always shown Himself to be on the side of the underdog. The fact that God displayed sympathy for the small and the weak actually literally means that he suffered with them. The cross of Jesus signifies this willingness of God to participate in the suffering of humanity even if this means death. This means that God does not succumb to the temptation to bypass suffering. He shows compassion and condolences with His creation and He does not use His omnipotence or divinity to establish a distance between Himself and his suffering creation. He makes the fallibility of his creation his own and he uses it as an opportunity to conquer death. The cross and the resurrection are the ultimate expressions thereof.

The God of the Bible created humans as counterparts whom He takes seriously, especially with their expected ability to think independently. Ever since then it is his unwavering goal to lead humans to their salvation, not with the crowbar of his power, but with gentle and perpetual appeals. Where his appeals are not met with acceptance or where he is disappointed, He does not react with wrath, yet He always opens new doors and new possibilities for renewed reconciliation. The ways of God are incomprehensible and unfathomable (cf. Rom 11:33), yet he reveals himself as unlimited in his love and patience, and committed to his goal of reconciliation with or without the co-operation of humans.[16]

A divine Saviour that was crucified by the Romans as a rebel contradicts the ancient understanding of the gods in a similar way as it did that of the contemporaries of Jesus. The confession formula "Jesus the Christ" does not allow itself to be proven. Jesus's public ministry was also somewhat contradictory and it did not answer to public expectation. Additionally, his message offered people a surprisingly new perspective on reality and turned the current value systems upside down. What was recognised by the faithful as the advent of salvation for the people of God, the sceptics and opponents of Jesus viewed to be a stumbling stone, for with the crucifixion of Jesus the Christian faith and confession were open for debate. The confession of Jesus

---

14. Erlemann, *Jesus der Christus*, 8.
15. Cf. Ritter, *Alte Kirche*, 59.
16. Erlemann, *Jesus der Christus*, 10.

of Nazareth as the Son of God demands an earnest revision of the perception of the divine.

The God of the Bible is a dynamic and personal Counterpart of humans; He displays emotions and always acts surprisingly good. As far as the gods of the ancient philosophers were concerned, they were an abstract concept, impersonal and an ontologically static principle. These gods are without needs and feelings and incapable of suffering and not susceptible to change. As far as Aristotle was concerned the divine was the highest good, *summa bona,* the unmovable Mover and he is transcendent.[17]

The post-Easter reflexion about the meaning of Jesus Christ leads to the re-evaluation of many of the traditional expectations about the Messiah of Israel. No theological tradition remained unaffected. The conviction that in Jesus of Nazareth God sent His beloved Son as the long expected anointed and resurrected him after the Easter events, profoundly changed the Messianic hope. Simultaneously, the new conviction was also a return to the central theological insights of the Old Testament.[18]

The evaluation of the Easter events led to a radical theological re-interpretation. This re-interpretation does not mean a change in the perception from a righteous judge God to a loving Father God, but the turning away from the idea that the omnipotent God will somehow enforce his reign with power and might. Contrary to this idea God announces his reign by coming into this world as a humble human being who avoids the use of power and might at all costs. Christ became the incarnation of God not only in his divinity, but especially in his abstinence of divine power display. God becomes human in the most humble way in order to liberate humans from their captivity.

The understanding of the *Heilsgeschichte* of Israel was also changed by the Christ-event: Israel's Liberator did not bring political freedom, but liberated the entire human race from the bondage of sin. With the crucifixion on Calvary the expectation of a Davidic "King of the Jews" was shattered, but after Easter the conviction was born that the crucifixion actually achieved much more namely the once and for all salvation of the entire world. The coming of Jesus of Nazareth also had profound social implications for the Son of God did not associate himself with the higher social strata of the Jewish population, but with the socially marginalised: the impure, the sick and the sinful, the lost and the forgotten. Ever since then election was not merely the exclusive privilege of the religious elite, but a gift from God.

---

17. Aristotle, *Metaph.* XII 1:1069a30–1069b2, see Erlemann, *Jesus der Christus,* 11.
18. Erlemann, *Jesus der Christus,* 133.

Consequently, the traditional criteria for election became outdated. Instead of ethnic purity and religious correctness, faith in Jesus as the Christ and allegiance to the will of God became the determinative factors. While Jesus became a stumbling stone to the Jewish religious leadership, he became the cornerstone and hope of a new people of God consisting of Jews and Gentiles alike.[19]

The new theological reflexion also has ethical implications. Jesus of Nazareth's interpretation of the Torah became the paramount interpretation that became authoritative for the Christian church: man is not made for the law, but the law is made for man (cf. Mark 2:27) and the love commandment became key to the interpretation of the Torah.

This Christology turned many traditions upside down. The expectation of the God of Israel, who will enforce His reign through is Messiah with power and might, is replaced by a God who humbles Himself. The issue of the cross as the final accomplishment of God's salvation history is paradoxal if not absurd. Yet his compassion for outsiders makes him the Messiah of others. Jesus becomes the image of God *par excellence*. Jesus is ethically advanced, obedient until his death on the cross and thereby fulfils the goal of creation and salvation of the lost.[20]

## First Peter's Christology

In support of the argument proposed by this study, Richard states that the author of 1 Peter "employs a well-defined and particular Christology" in order to cultivate perseverance among the believers in Asia Minor.[21]

The author of 1 Peter is interested in the theology of suffering, but as indicated earlier in this study, not suffering as a result of official Roman persecution, but suffering as a result of social ostracism, hostility and harassment by the general public.[22]

Suffering plays a key role in the author's Christology. Πάσχω is used twelve times in connection with Jesus Christ and those who follow him. The author emphasises the suffering of Christ exactly because of the believers' situation of perpetual suffering because of their allegiance to Christ. The suffering Christ is also central to their author's soteriology and provides the foundation for his paraenetic comments. However, the author never talks

---

19. Ibid., 134.
20. Ritter, *Alte Kirche*, 144–5; cf. Erlemann, *Unfassbar?*, 6–23.
21. Richard, "Functional Christology," 121.
22. Ibid., 126–77; cf. Lohse, "Parenesis," 73–85; Elliott, *A Home*, 84–87; Balch, *Let Wives*, 10–15; Brox, "Situation und Sprache," 1–13.

about the suffering and death of Christ without simultaneously mentioning the resurrection and the implication thereof for Christ as well as his followers. The resurrection is key to providing the basis for hope and eternal life and the believers' faith is firmly grounded within the event of the resurrection.[23]

Therefore, for the author of 1 Peter Jesus is the image of suffering and glory. The author interprets the Christ-event in terms of his believers' situation and therefore he does not focus on the life of Christ, or the miracles that he performed or the parables that he told, but specifically on his suffering. The author is also not interested so much in the event of the resurrection as in the implication thereof for Christ, namely his glorification.[24]

The theme of suffering and glorification forms the contours of the author's Christological frame. Suffering and glorification create a parallel with the believers' current situation and serve a soteriological purpose by insisting on the consequences of Jesus's death for humanity.[25]

Furthermore, Jesus becomes the author's model for suffering and glory and between these two polls lies the interim period that concerns his audience. It is during this period that the author urges his audience to endure their suffering patiently, for that is pleasing to God and in accordance with their vocation (cf. 1 Pet 2:21).[26]

This framework also constitutes the believers's vision of their reality, in other words their suffering is "teleologically conditioned by glory or salvation."[27] For this purpose the author favours the term "suffering" rather than "death" to refer the complete event of Christ's passion and death. The use of "suffering" also serves the author's rhetorical strategy. He is mindful of his audience's pain, abuse and the social ostracism that his audience was enduring within a pagan society. The suffering of the audience becomes part of the author's Christological model, for the imitation of Christ means to be obedient to God and God's plan. Furthermore, this pattern of suffering and glory frames the faithful Christian's concerns. Christ suffered innocently, but as a result of his complete trust in the righteous judgement of God, he is now glorified. Similarly the believers now endure innocent suffering, but because of the Christological pattern they are assured that they too will be glorified if they live their lives in accordance to the will of God.[28]

---

23. Richard, "Functional Christology," 132.
24. Ibid., 133; cf. Lohse, "Parenesis," 70.
25. Ibid., 134; cf. Calloud and Genuyt, *La Première*, 152.
26. Ibid., 135.
27. Ibid., 136; cf. Calloud and Genuyt, *La Première*, 152–63.
28. Richard, "Functional Christology," 136; cf. Osborne, "Guide Lines," 406–8.

The author also encourages good conduct for missiological purposes. The author hopes that husbands will be converted (1 Pet 3:1); hostile neighbours might by silenced (1 Pet 2:15); that unbelieving neighbours might come to glorify God in the end (1 Pet 2:12). They ought to live in accordance with God's will and not in accordance with their fleshly desires.

According to Michaels, 1 Peter repetitively makes the point that it is easier to endure the wrath of humans in this age than the wrath of God in the next and that it is better to suffer for doing what is good than to endure suffering because of doing evil.[29] Peter is concerned with the age old biblical problem of the suffering righteous (cf. 1 Pet 2:23).

According to Green, Jesus's death on a Roman cross was not a denial but rather an affirmation of his status before God.[30] His death was purposeful and meaningful for it overcame the powers of death and evil. He demonstrated that his suffering was for righteousness and not for sin.

As far as the author of 1 Peter is concerned all paths lead to and through Christ, firstly the suffering Christ and then the vindicated Christ. The character of God is known through Christ, the end-time is inaugurated by Christ and Christ is active as the mediator of God's benevolence in the present. Within the person of Christ, the Christian community finds its basis and its model and Christ is the one to whom allegiance and loyalty are due.

The letter's key Christological declarations can be summarised as follows: Christ's death was liberating, Christ's death was paradigmatic and Christ journeyed through suffering into glory.[31] According to Green, Peter's Christology recognises the supremacy of God the Father but Christ forms "the centre of the letter's rhetoric."[32] Green further explores the particular understanding of Christ in 1 Peter:

1. "Christ" functions as a second name for Jesus with special reference to the sufferings of Christ (cf. 1 Pet 4:13; 3:15; 1:11) which alludes to Isa 8:31.

2. Christ is the Lord, worthy of praise (cf. 1 Pet 1:3, 25; 2:3; 3:15) and the one with the authority to send Peter as his representative (cf. 1 Pet 1:1).

3. Christ is innocent and righteous and completely obedient to the will of God (cf. 1 Pet 1:2, 3).

4. Christ's death was exemplary and effective (cf. 1 Pet 1:2, 19; 2:21–25; 3:18–24; 4:1; 5:1)

29. Michaels, "Eschatology," 401.
30. Green, *1 Peter*, 4.
31. Ibid., 210; cf. Goppelt, *Der erste Petrusbrief*, 176–78.
32. Green, *1 Peter*, 210.

5. Christ was vindicated by God and therefore his resurrection has salvific implications (cf. 1 Pet 1:3, 11; 2:4; 3:18–22; 5:1).

6. Christ is the mediator (cf. 1 Pet 2:5; 3:16; 4:11; 5:10, 14).

Despite its origin as a negative scolding label given to the followers of Christ, the crucified rebel, by outsiders, the name "Christian" came to be embraced in an honorable way by those who identified with Christ.[33]

Therefore, the author's message of the suffering Christ was crucial to an audience whose suffering in the world was the direct result of their allegiance to Christ. Consequently the author develops his Christology of the suffering Christ on three levels: Firstly, Christ becomes the "model of innocent suffering."[34] Although righteous, Christ suffered at the hands of those whose disbelief placed them in direct opposition to the will of God. Christ's faithfulness and obedience become evident both in his refusal to retaliate and by the fact that his suffering was undeserved. Secondly, Christ becomes the model of "effective suffering,"[35] for Christ's suffering forms the basis of his liberation. His suffering in itself has a missionary effect for it turned the hearts of the unfaithful to God. The suffering of the followers of Christ is participation in the suffering of Christ making the followers of Christ co-active in bringing about the age of salvation. Thirdly, Christ is the "model of the vindication of the suffering righteous."[36] The passion of Christ illustrates that suffering as a result of faithfulness to God is not the end or the final word. Suffering is rather a precursor, however a necessity to be glorified and vindicated. Nor is vindication a liberation or rescue from suffering. Suffering is the necessary path to vindication.

First Peter's Christology therefore constructs the "metanarrative" by which the audience ought to perceive their reality. His Christological narrative reaches from before the creation of the world (1 Pet 1:20) to the last time (1 Pet 1:5). Therefore, a careful reading of 1 Peter's Christology calls for a re-evaluation of human systems of judgement and valuation (see *Christology in Early Christianity* above).

As far as the suffering of the followers of Christ is concerned the author of 1 Peter displays a well-developed registry of terms pertaining to the experience of suffering including: πειρασμός, οῦm "period or process of testing, trial, test" (1 Pet 1:6), δοκίμιον, ουn "testing, act of testing; genuineness" (1 Pet 1:7; 4:12); πάθημα, τος n "suffering; passion, desire" (1 Pet 1:11; 2:19,

---

33. Cf. Tacitus, *Ann.* 15.44; Hengel, *Studies*, 8.
34. Green, *1 Peter*, 213.
35. Ibid.
36. Ibid.

21, 23; 3:14, 17; 4:1, 13, 15–16, 19; 5:1, 9, 10), κολαφίζω "beat, strike; harass, trouble," the tree as instrument of execution (1 Pet 2:24), ταράσσω "trouble, disturb, upset; terrify, frighten; stir up (of water)" (1 Pet 3:14), καταλαλέω "speak evil of, say bad things against, slander," πύρωσις, εως f "burning; fiery ordeal, painful test," ὀνειδίζω "reproach, denounce, insult" and κρίμα, τος n "judgment; decision, verdict; condemnation, punishment; lawsuit; power or authority to judge." According to Green from this terminology three brief observations can be made:[37] In the first instance the author does not envision a situation of formal persecution. Secondly, the suffering and persecution the author has in mind is mainly verbal shaming which was an effective way to accomplish social ostracism. Luke Timothy Johnson makes the following very important point:

> Persecution and martyrdom, after all, have a certain clarity and comfort. Lines of allegiance are obvious. However painful the choice, it need be made only once. But scorn and content are slow-working acids that corrode individual and communal identity. Social alienation is not a trivial form of suffering. Persecution may bring death, but with meaning. Societal scorn can threaten meaning itself, which is a more subtle form of death."[38]

And thirdly, the author ties the experiences of his audience into the experience of Christ's suffering and death in order to establish a parallel and to give meaning to their suffering by illustrating their solidarity with Christ.

According to Green the author provides the following perspectives on suffering:[39]

1. Suffering has a purgatory effect by which the faith of believers is perfected (cf. 1 Pet 1:6–7; 4:1–2, 12).[40]

2. Suffering may be the hostile outsiders's way to inflict humiliation and shame on the followers of Christ, but the author turns this interpretation upside down. Instead of seeing suffering as a sign of being damned or rejected by God, suffering becomes a sign of the purity and sincerity of one's faith. Suffering becomes an opportunity to receive blessing and to experience the power of the Holy Spirit (e.g., 1 Pet 2:4–8, 15, 19–21; 3:17; 4:14, 19).[41]

---

37. Ibid., 227.
38. Johnson, *Writings*, 435.
39. Green, *1 Peter*, 227.
40. Cf. Talbert, "Educational Value," 42–57.
41. Cf. Berger, *Historical Psychology*, 180, 184.

3. For those who have adopted the new way of thinking proposed by our author not to retaliate but to trust God in suffering, a conversion of their perception of their reality occurred (cf. 1 Pet 1:17; 2:23; 3:5; 4:15–19). "Suffering without retaliation is a refusal to tear away from God his role of determining the standards of and carrying out justice."[42]

4. Through innocent suffering believers imitate Christ and express their solidarity with Christ and with believers throughout the world who experience similar circumstances (cf. 1 Pet 2:21–25; 4:1; 5:1, 9).[43]

5. The author emphasises the temporary nature of suffering (cf. 1 Pet 1:6, 17; 4:2; 5:10) in contrast with the eternal nature of their glory and divine vindication (cf. 1 Pet 1:4; 5:10). The suffering that believers are experiencing in the present is the result of their allegiance with Christ which cuts against the grain of the larger society.[44]

6. The same liberating effect the suffering of Christ brought about (cf. 1 Pet 1:2, 18–19; 2:21–25) is possible through the suffering of believers for it becomes a catalyst for the conversion of non-believers (cf. 1 Pet 2:12).

7. It is almost inconceivable that the author never vilifies the outsiders and unbelievers who are responsible for the suffering that the believers have to endure. He does not allow for a negative view of pagans or an evaluation of them as evil because of the way they treat believers. Furthermore the author does not encourage withdrawal from society or advocate a sectarian existence. On the contrary the experience of suffering provides the occasion to display solidarity with Christ and vigilance, to imitate Christ, to display mutual love within the Christian family and courage.[45]

8. Suffering becomes part of the journey that started with the believers' rebirth and will end in vindication and glory. Meaning is generated from the pattern of the Suffering Righteous that runs like a golden thread through the Scriptures of the Old Testament.

The author aims to view the experience and threat of suffering within the larger context of Gods salvation and his involvement with people, as not determined by the Roman struggle over power and the status one enjoys

---

42. Green, *1 Peter*, 226.
43. Cf. Berger, *Historical Psychology*, 182.
44. Cf. Ibid., 183.
45. Cf. Berger, *Historical Psychology*, 181, 184.

within Roman society. Although social ostracism is not trivialised, the author offers a greater perspective.

According to Green, the much debated πύρωσις "fiery ordeal, painful test" mentioned in 1 Pet 4:12 refers to the danger for those who experienced social ostracism because of their conversion to Christianity to re-enter into their previous state of living and to assimilate back into their pagan existence.[46] This temptation is described as diabolical (cf.1 Pet 5:8) and this places the suffering of the believers within the cosmic realm. The believers are not merely confronted with hostile human beings. The temptation to return to their previous ways is evil incarnate. Therefore they are urged to respond to evil by doing good. Concretely, that means to practice mutual love within the family of believers, to refuse to retaliate and to courageously insist on doing good and maintaining impeccable behaviour. These acts, attitudes and dispositions have a definite missionary dimension, for the ever present adversaries witness that and will be thereby influenced towards conversion. In other words, love within the community and conviction, in terms of engagement with the outside world, are the weapons to be employed in order to combat evil forces. As direction, believers ought to orientate their behaviour around the will of God.

For the author of 1 Peter the will of God is the umbrella term under which all ethics is constructed. Christians are enslaved to God and not to humans and human institutions. Therefore the honor owed to the emperor is no different than the honor owed to any other human being regardless his or her social status (cf. 1 Pet 2:15–17).

For long scholarship on First Peter has been dominated by the debate between Balch and Elliott, with Balch claiming that the author encourages his audience on pragmatic and apologetic grounds to integrate into the Roman society, and Elliott arguing that the author wrote to a sectarian audience and that their separation from the world served the author's purpose for a unified identity.[47] Miroslav Volf introduces a third possibility, namely the category of "soft difference"—not weak, but soft, not hard but strong.[48] Although the author does not envision the changing of social structures, the believers' new birth into a living hope does not isolate them from society and hope in the living God, the Creator and Saviour, knows no boundaries.

Seland coined the nuanced social scientific terms "acculturation" and "assimilation" to argue that the author's main concern was not the relation of the believers to the outside world, but to cultivate a distinctive

---

46. Green, *1 Peter*, 228.
47. Balch, *Let Wives*; and Elliott, *A Home*.
48. Volf, "Soft Difference," 24.

Christian ethos within the Christian faith where obedience to Christ is the primary value.[49]

Like Christ suffered undeservedly, the believers experience undeserved suffering. From 1 Pet 4:12–14 one may conclude that the author is almost exclaiming to his audience that the suffering was inevitable for it happened to Christ and it would be naïve to expect that his followers would somehow be spared. It is therefore unimaginable that the author would urge his audience to fit in in order to avoid further suffering.[50]

Language, rhetoric and words are the author's most power weapons in order to equip his audience to offer resistance. Since the suffering that believers have to endure is predominantly verbal, the author is well aware of the fact that language creates reality and aids in the experience of reality. In other words: *words do things*.[51] For example the author uses κύριος to refer to Jesus Christ and not to the emperor, he uses φοβέομαι in order to refer to reverent awe and not as intimidation, terror or anxious dread. The author aims to establish that one's relationship with God determines everything else in life. Κρίνω is not the prerogative of Rome and not concerned with one's social standing in the community or based on human evaluations and furthermore it does not serve as motivation for faithful living. God has the monopoly on judgement and he is not affected by human concerns about honor and shame. Ὑποφέρω does not pertain to long-suffering or passivity, but rather "unyielding perseverance" or "courageous steadfastness in the face of opposition."[52] The author wanted his audience to resist in an active manner, but without apocalyptic violence.

The first century Mediterranean social values of honor and shame dominated the social context of the addressees. The author constantly exhorts his audience to "do good" ἀγαθοποιέω but one must ask by whose standards? Ἀγαθοποιέω does not carry within itself the standard by which good is determined. The same could be said about "honor." Within the Roman world these terms were clear and became synonymous with public benefaction.[53] On the same level were matters such as how to behave towards one's superiors and inferiors, therefore knowing one's place in the hierarchy of status stratification. Within the Roman world these matters were socially conditioned since birth, as the Romans engineered a society towards behavioural and attitudinal conformity. This is obviously not what our author

---

49. Seland, "Assimilation and Acculturation," 188–89.
50. Green, *1 Peter*, 284.
51. Green's italics; see ibid., 287.
52. Ibid., 287.
53. Cf. Winter, "Public Honouring," 87–103.

has in mind with "doing good" and "honor." For the author of 1 Peter "doing good" is synonymous with doing nothing other than the will of God. As far as "honor" is concerned, God has the monopoly to bestow honor as an expression of his grace and in pursuit of following in the footsteps of Christ should become evident in one's evaluation of other people and things. This view is grounded within the conviction that God makes no distinction as far as a person's status is concerned. God is not influenced by matters such as prestige, gender, age, ancestry, wealth or one's social circle.

The author expects his audience to be somewhat "amphibious." They do not become a third race, nor do they cease to be Jew or Greek or Roman. They remain part of their own culture, yet because of their conversion they became outsiders to their own culture.[54] In effect they became "bicultural," living between two worlds which were in tension with one another.

> How they choose to live in that tension and whether they chose to resolve it by fully withdrawing from the one in favour of the other is the issue to which Peter devotes himself. For this reason it is impossible to imagine that Peter's theological strategy could be reduced to a concern either for internal cohesion or for external separation"[55]

To follow the crucified Christ was to determine both internal and external relations—internal as far as intramural hospitality and the unity established by the sanctifying Spirit were concerned and external as a political and missiological act. The addressees of 1 Peter were therefore a house of God whose vocation was to mediate the presence of God. They were to write the next chapter in the history of God's people, the new Israel, *id est* the Christian church. The Holy Spirit empowered them in order to maintain their allegiance to Christ and each other by undertaking the journey through suffering in the hope of eschatological honor. And in doing so they bore witness to the coming of a new age.

## Mark's Christology

Christology is the driving force behind the Markan narrative. Although the gospel pays attention to discipleship, eschatology and ecclesiology it is Christological concerns that caused the Gospel to come into existence.

---

54. Green, *1 Peter*, 287; cf. Meeks, *Origins*, 50.
55. Green, *1 Peter*, 288.

Discipleship, eschatology and ecclesiology are not to be separated from Christology or the person of Jesus.[56]

Mark uses diverse Christological titles and designations in order to communicate the significance of Jesus. All are derived from tradition and were influenced by previous biblical, religious and cultural contexts. No Christological title is a Markan creation. Mark's Christology could be called narrative Christology.[57]

## Suffering Servant

"Servant" (Hebrew עֶבֶד) occurs in the Old Testament and Jewish tradition as an eschatological saviour figure sent by God often explicitly associated with the Messiah (cf. Ezek 34:23–24; 37:24–25; Zech 3:8).

However, the Jewish tradition of the Suffering Servant found in Isaiah 53 is never portrayed in Messianic terms, and the expected Messiah is not identified with Isaiah's Suffering Servant. The explicit Christological appeal to Isaiah's suffering servant seems to be a later development in New Testament Theology (cf. 1 Pet 2:22–25). Δοῦλος and διάκονος, Mark's terms for "servant" occur seven times but is never explicitly applied to Jesus. However, in Mark 10:45 Mark uses the verb διακονέω "serve, wait on; care for, see after, provide for; serve as a deacon" as central to Jesus identity and ministry: "the one who serves and gives his life as ransom for many" is a definite allusion to Isaiah 53. The fact that Isaiah is central to Mark and the role of the Isaiah servant-hymns in Mark and the way in which the entire narrative alludes to the Isaiah-imagery support the possibility that Isaiah's suffering servant is at the back of Mark's Christological mind.[58]

## Narrative Christology

Crossan is of the opinion that the Gospels are neither histories nor biographies.[59] Rather they consist of "original, developmental, and compositional layers." According to Crossan, "Jesus left behind thinkers, not memorizers, disciples, not reciters, people, not parrots."

---

56. Boring, *Mark*, 248.

57. Ibid., 249; cf. Porkorny, *Gottessohn*, 2–17; Kertelge, *Die Wunder Jesu*, 190; Kingsbury, *Christology*; Boring, "Christology of Mark"; Broadhead, *Naming Jesus*, 27, 90; Malbon, "Christology," 33–48; and Tannehill, "Gospel of Mark," 57–96

58. Boring, *Mark*, 253; see Lohse, *Märtyr*.

59. Crossan, *In Parables*, xxx.

Because of Mark's choice for a narrative genre, he is allowed to juxtapose radical contradicting Christologies. Some of the Markan images and language portray Jesus as the truly divine agent of God's salvation, acting in God's place and doing what only God is capable of. Mark's *"epiphany Christology"*[60] portrays Jesus as the powerful divine son of God which is difficult to reconcile with a suffering Messiah who dies on the cross. Mark's other images of a truly human Jesus, who identifies with human weakness and suffering, are difficult to reconcile with the powerful divine figure who heals and performs miracles and exorcisms. One could label this suffering human Christology as *"kenosis Christology."*[61]

"Kenosis Christology" portrays the power of God coming to its full disclosure in a truly human weak, crucified man from Nazareth.

In the situation where Marks writes his gospel, advocates of each view held the position that the one necessarily excludes the other. Mark realised the necessity for reconciling these two views: "Miracle stories and passion narrative, the divine man and the crucified, need relating in a new way."[62]

Mark actually does the inconceivable by trying to combine these two Christologies without compromising one of them or both. Because conceptually, the once excludes the other: a Jesus who can walk on water is able to come down from the cross and then the crucifixion does not make sense. A Jesus who cannot come down from the cross cannot walk on water and then the miracle stories cannot really be miracles. How can a truly human Jesus be a truly divine Jesus or a truly divine Jesus be a truly human Jesus? Skillfully and masterly Mark is able to affirm both Christologies and within the narrative framework he chooses he is able to claim and explicate both.

However, one should not consider Mark as offering a "synthesis" or "integration" of two opposing views. The narrative is able to include both perspectives without adjusting the other.

Wrede's view still holds firm, with one important qualification.[63] Wrede's argument was that the evangelist has two contrasting motifs, but in his consciousness they do not clash. He simply presents them as standing next to one another. On this essential point this study agrees. Having said that however, this study does not agree with Wrede's statement that the juxtaposition is only possible if the narrator was not aware of the conclusions drawn from the historical picture form each of the two ideas by those who reflected on them.

---

60. Boring, *Mark*, 258. Boring's emphasis.

61. Ibid. Boring's emphasis of Lee-Pollard, "Powerlessness as Power," 173–88, see Placher, *Narratives*.

62. Luz, "Secrecy Motif," 75.

63. Wrede, *Messianic Secret*, 38.

If one were to argue that point, one must hold that Mark stumbled blindly into the insight and that he presented his Christology without giving it much thought. This study would rather argue that Mark's Christology is indeed a product of careful reflection. The author was not unaware that his reflection upon these two conflicting views would present problems to conventional logic. It was precisely his reflection upon these two conflicting views that influenced his decision for the narrative form which offered the possibility for holding these two traditional Christological views together.[64]

Regarded from a narratological perspective, the Markan Jesus is a character and the presumed analogy of the character Jesus with the historical Jesus is a category mistake, for narrative criticism recognises the character Jesus as the creation of the implied author. Kermode writes: "The advantage of third person narration is that it is the mode which best produces the illusion of pure reference. But it *is* an illusion, the effect of a rhetorical device."[65] Therefore, as far as narrative Christology is concerned, one cannot simply assign the view of the Markan Jesus to the historical Jesus as if the first century author shared the twenty first century's concern with historical accuracy.[66] It is therefore safer to conclude that the Markan Christology derives from the early church rather than from the historical Jesus.

Elizabeth Struthers Malbon writes:

> My study of the characterization of Jesus as Markan narrative Christology draws attention to the enigmatic nature of a story told in such a way that the narrator's commendation of a central character is tempered by that character's commitment to a character who, even though minimally present in the action, is more central to it—God. Despite the tension between the Markan Jesus and the narrator, God confirms the narrator's application of "Son of God" to the Markan Jesus and also confirms that what the Markan Jesus does and says is pleasing to God, serving almost as a mediating character between them, confirming them both in different ways.[67]

The Gospel of Mark's view is neither the view of the Markan narrator nor the view of the Markan Jesus. It is the point of view of the implied author as received by the implied audience. Therefore, the gap between the narrator and Jesus is not a gap to be filled or a problem to be solved. Rather

---

64. Davis, "Mark's Christological," 3–18.
65. Kermode, *Genesis of Secrecy*, 117.
66. Malbon, *Mark's Jesus*, 254.
67. Ibid., 257.

the Christological confession offered by the implied author to the implied audience should be embraced as a challenge and a mystery.[68]

The narrative genre also allows the hearer to become acquainted with the person of Jesus Christ. It is because of Jesus that the hearer is interested in the narrative. For the faith community the focus is not on the events narrated, but about what the events convey about the person of Jesus Christ.

Furthermore, the narrative provides the faith with a firm foundation and prevents the content of the faith to be reduced to philosophical speculation.

What is believed about Jesus Christ cannot be separated from the events narrated in the passion narrative. In the words of Sommer: "Wir glauben weil Jesus gekreuzigt wurde, nicht obwohl er gekreuzigt wurde."[69] The confession of the words is grounded in the passion event and the consequent experience of God. This results in God being acknowledged as Lord of history and guards against the misconception that God is simply another actor within world history. Above all the conspiring of the Jewish religious leaders and the Roman world rulers, the will of God prevails.

Through the passion narrative new meaning is generated as far as God's relationship to humanity is concerned. God is recognised in a brand new way and a new covenant between God and his people is established. By narrating the events of the passion of Jesus the author speaks about God.[70]

What the author of Mark aimed for was to make the confession of God's unconditional love for all humanity accessible and visible to everyone:

> Der Unterschied der Passiongeschichte zu einer Auflistung von Fakten zeigt sich darin das sie das Erzählte versteht. Sie kann es dabei nur von Gott her betrachten. Ihre Absicht beschränkt sich nicht darauf Informationen über Vergangenes zu vermitteln, sodern aufgrund der verstandenen Geschichte Jesu die Liebe Gottes zu 'allen' sichtbar und glaubbar zu machen.[71]

The narrative also succeeds in drawing attention to commonalities between the events narrated and the present. So for example Ps 22 offers comfort to those reading it in the present. Similarly, the Christian community receiving the Gospel of Mark identifies with the scenes of mockery and slander that Jesus had to endure as well as the scenes of public trials. The addressees also experienced that they were at the mercy of evil forces over which they had no control, but in identifying with the way the power of God

---

68. Ibid., 258.
69. Sommer, *Die Passionsgeschicte*, 256.
70. Ibid., 259; cf. Weder, *Neutestamentliches*, 361, 382.
71. Sommer, *Die Passionsgeschicte*, 260.

became evident through these events they found hope and courage to face their own circumstances.[72]

In the narrative the proclamation of Jesus Christ takes place. The narrative familiarises the audience with the persons and the events narrated. Something unknown is being told and in the process the audience is called upon to reflect upon what is being narrated. The narrative does not allow for any dogmatisation around Jesus Christ. It is left to the audience to conduct their own theological reflexion. The audience must become active in the creation of meaning. This is implicit to the narrative, for the audience is never specifically addressed as is the case with a New Testament letter. Yet the narrative has an effect on the audience.[73]

The narrative is selective in the sense that it only includes or excludes what was of theological significance for the understanding of Jesus. The narrator evaluates his source material in a certain way, for the tradition about Jesus had a profound effect upon him. He himself had the experience of God becoming present within the passion of Jesus and therefore he is able to narrate with personal conviction. He testifies to his own experience of God. The author of Mark passed on what he had heard about Jesus.[74] In the centre of Mark's narrative is the narrative of the uniqueness of Jesus's suffering and death.

It is not possible for the witness to the events of the passion narrative to prove that his testimony is historically true. The onus is upon the hearer or the reader to acknowledge the truth within what is being narrated to them. The witness needs to understand that faith is not a human achievement or the by-product of human reflection, but a gift bestowed by God. Therefore, the witness has to accept the great possibility that what he narrates will be rejected by his audience. Faith cannot bring any concrete evidence to the table, but it can and it must tell the story of Jesus from Nazareth.

This has an ethical implication for the passion narrative becomes a "code of conduct" desired from the followers of Jesus Christ, especially for those who find themselves in a situation of persecution.[75]

The passion of Jesus, although unique, becomes a model for disciples to follow. In the words of Sommer: "Jesu einmalige Geschichte wird dabei in eine höhere, allgemeine moralische Wahrheit aufgelöst."[76]

72. Ibid., 263.
73. Ibid., 273.
74. Ibid., 275.
75. Ibid., 280.
76. Ibid., 281.

The Gospel of Mark makes a moral appeal to its readers: they are being told what they ought to do. The audience is being addressed as people touched and moved by the love of God and liberated to become disciples of Christ.

## Mark and 1 Peter's Use of Isaiah's Suffering Servant

In Isaiah 53's suffering servant Christian theology finds the salvation meaning of the death of Jesus Christ within the Old Testament.

In its original context, Deutero-Isaiah (Isaiah 44–55) offers the proclamation of hope and consolation to the people of God in the Babylonian exile that the period of divine punishment has come to an end and that God is coming to gather his people (cf. Isa 40:1–11). The humiliated and impoverished people who lamented that YHWH's way became obscured to them, that they no longer receive his righteousness, that YHWH has forgotten them now receive the revelation of God's unfathomable ways: it was not the gods of Babylon who delivered Israel into exile, but YHWH himself because his people grew weary of him and worshipped lifeless foreign idols. And it is YHWH, who now by the means of king Kyros of Persia, becomes their Saviour and the judge of the Babylonian people. Therefore the people of God should prepare his way in the desert, for YHWH is about to start with the recreation of his people.[77]

In the four texts regarding YHWH's servant the servant is also addressed as YHWH's elect (cf. Isa 41:8; 44:1, 21; 45:4; and 48:20) and by this it is clear that God's people, Israel, is implied. With this collective address it becomes clear that God did not forget them and still chooses them as his own. He will still reveal his righteousness and keep them safe against their enemies as their Saviour. God will bestow his Spirit on his people and he will erase their sins of the past. Through the message of the prophets God is making an appeal to his servant (cf. Isa 41:10; 44:22).

YHWH's suffering servant as God's elect has the mission to reveal God's righteousness to the nations (cf. Isa 42:10). This mission is not merely the result of the servant's silent suffering, but is a direct consequence of Gods salvation plan. It is the oracle of the ultimate victory of YHWH's servant.

God's planned act of compensation also becomes clear in Isa 53:10 with the use of the Hebrew word אשם 'asam but here not in the Levitical cultic sense as in Lev 5:14–26 or Lev 16:10. The Isaiah text is free from cultic terminology and it does not have the meaning of the elimination of sin, but the endurance thereof on behalf of others, to suffer on behalf of others and

---

77. Woyke, "Der leidende Gottesknecht," 200.

to offer compensation for their guilt. This plan for the salvation of many was to unfold through the suffering of the servant.[78]

The original meaning of the "many" in Isa 53:11 should be understood in terms of Israel's surrounding nations and their kings because they were to be moved by the sacrifice of the suffering servant. The suffering servant of Isaiah 53 is therefore better understood as an individual and not as the people of God as a collective. The suffering individual compensates for the sins of the people of God and therefore their sins are forgiven.

> Als Repräsentant des Jhwh-Dieners Israel, durch dessen Leiden, Tod und Erhöhung Jhwh seeinem Volk Vergebung und eine Zukunft verheißt und gewährt und sie zu sich zurück- und aus der Verbannung führt, richtet dieser einzelne Jhwh-Diener nun auch unter den Völkern Gottes Recht und Weisung auf und wird gemäß seinem Auftrag zum Licht für Völker, damit Gottes Heil bis ans Ende der Erde reicht (Jes 49,1ff).[79]

As far as the *Wirkungsgeschichte* of Isaiah 53 is concerned one cannot asume that in Jewish or in early Christian circles Isa 52:13—53:12 was read as a closed unit.

As far as the New Testament's use of Isaiah 53 is concerned different modi are used: a direct citation or an allusion.

Direct citations are found in the relatively late New Testament writings of Matthew, Acts and 1 Peter. For this study the citations in 1 Peter are of importance. Similar to 2 Macc 7, the author indicates that the unjust suffering was to be understood in terms of the gospel and in terms of the future glory of God's eschatological righteousness. Unjust suffering is founded in the suffering of Christ on behalf of the addressees—he suffered on their behalf and by doing so it became possible for them to follow in the footsteps of Christ (cf. 1 Pet 2:21).

Consequently a table of the direct citations from Isaiah 53 in 1 Peter:[80]

| | |
|---|---|
| 1 Pet 2:22 ὃς ἁμαρτίαν οὐκ ἐποίησεν οὐδὲ εὑρέθη δόλος ἐν τῷ στόματι αὐτοῦ | Isa 53:9 ὅτι ἀνομίαν οὐκ ἐποίησεν οὐδὲ εὑρέθη δόλος ἐν τῷ στόματι αὐτοῦ |
| 1 Pet 2:24 ὃς τὰς ἁμαρτίας ἡμῶν αὐτὸς ἀνήνεγκεν ἐν τῷ σώματι αὐτοῦ ἐπὶ τὸ ξύλον, ἵνα ταῖς ἁμαρτίαις ἀπογενόμενοι τῇ δικαιοσύνῃ ζήσωμεν, οὗ τῷ μώλωπι ἰάθητε. | Isa 53:4–5 οὗτος τὰς ἁμαρτίας ἡμῶν φέρει ἐπ' αὐτόν τῷ μώλωπι αὐτοῦ ἡμεῖς ἰάθημεν |

---

78. Ibid., 207.
79. Ibid., 208.
80. Ibid., 217.

1 Pet 2:25 ἦτε γὰρ ὡς πρόβατα πλανώμενοι	Isa 53:6 πάντες ὡς πρόβατα ἐπλανήθημεν

As far as allusions in the New Testament to Isaiah 53 are concerned it is important for this study to pay attention to Mark 10:45: καὶ γὰρ ὁ υἱὸς τοῦ ἀνθρώπου οὐκ ἦλθεν διακονηθῆναι ἀλλὰ διακονῆσαι καὶ δοῦναι τὴν ψυχὴν αὐτοῦ λύτρον ἀντὶ πολλῶν which seems to be a combination of Isa 43:3, ὅτι ἐγὼ κύριος ὁ θεός σου ὁ ἅγιος Ισραηλ ὁ σῴζων σε ἐποίησά σου ἄλλαγμα Αἴγυπτον καὶ Αἰθιοπίαν καὶ Σοήνην ὑπὲρ σοῦ, and Isa 53:6 καὶ κύριος παρέδωκεν αὐτὸν ταῖς ἁμαρτίαις ἡμῶν.

Woyke writes:

> Faziniert von demjenigen, der landauf, landab als Herold der nahenden Königsherrschaft Gottes auftrat und sie in seinem Handelen in geheimnisvoller, autoritativer Weise gerade zu vergegenwärtigte, ja verkörperte; schockiert von seinem vermeintliche Scheitern und irritiert fragend, ob dieses Ende wie ein Verbrecher nicht doch Rücksclusse auf seine Gottesferne zulieẞ, sodann überwältigt durch rie Erfahrung der Wirklichkeit der Auferweckung Jesu von den Toten, bot sich Jes 53 als Teil der Trostbotschaft des Jesajabuchs auf eigenartige Weise an, dies alles als Gottes Ratschluss staunend zu begreifen und zu artikulieren.[81]

What follows is a closer examination of selected pericopes from the Gospel of Mark and 1 Peter in order to illustrate how the re-interpretation and evaluation of Isaiah's Suffering Servant was employed by both authors to substantiate their Christology of suffering. This study hopes to indicate that a similar Christological thought is present in both New Testament texts.

### First Peter 2:18–25

> *Servants, be subject to your masters with all fear; not only to the good and gentle, but also to the crooked. For this is thankworthy, if a man for conscience toward God endures grief and suffers wrongfully. For what glory is it if you suffer when you sin and be harmed because of it? If you suffer when you do well, that is grace with God. For even hereunto were you called: because Christ also suffered for us, leaving us an example, so that you my imitate him, who did no sin, neither was guile found in his mouth, who, did not insult again when he was insulted, he threatened not; when*

---

[81] Ibid., 225.

> *he suffered, but committed himself to him, that judges righteously, who his own self bare our sins in his own body on the tree, by whose wounds you were healed, that we, should live unto righteousness: being dead to sins. For you were like sheep going astray; but are now returned unto the Shepherd and Bishop of your souls.*

### Literary and Discourse Analysis

Achtemeier understands οἰκέται in its widest interpretation as referring to slaves in general.[82] However, many scholars understand οἰκέται in a narrower sense, referring specifically to household slaves including house stewards, librarians, secretaries, physicians etc.[83] Achtemeier further argues that this word was chosen by the author because of his general employment of household language and his considering of the Christian community as the household of God.[84]

Achtemeier views ὑποτασσόμενοι not to have imperative force as is the case in (1 Pet 2:13), but understands it as an adverbial principle of means, being descriptive of *how* the slaves are to carry out the imperatives given in verse 17.[85] The subordination of the slaves is to be carried out ἐν παντὶ φόβῳ ("with all reverence"), which does not refer to their attitude towards their owners, but towards God.[86] This meaning is coherent with how the word is employed throughout the letter (see, e.g., 1 Pet 2:17: τὸν θεὸν φοβεῖσθε, τὸν βασιλέα τιμᾶτε). "Reverence" is an imperative reserved exclusively for the attitude towards God. The author does recognise that slaves should be aware of their subordination in terms of their social rank and therefore act accordingly, but in continuation with the previous verse, φόβος, ου "fear," "terror"; "fear," "reverence (for God)"; is only owed to God. Caesar and all other people merely receive τιμάω "honor," "regard," "acknowledge the status of" (1 Pet 2:17). The difference is clearly indicated by verse 17 and therefore it is highly unlikely that φόβος which is not even owed to Caesar should be given to a master.[87]

---

82. Achtemeier, *1 Peter*, 194; cf. Elliott, *1 Peter: New Translation*, 517;cf. Philipps, *Kirche*, 36; see Aristotle, *[Mag. mor.]* 1.33.15–17 for the use of οἰκέται in contrast to δεσπότος.

83. E.g., Michaels, *1 Peter*, 138; cf. Moffatt, 1918, 126.

84. Cf. Elliott, *A Home*.

85. Achtemeier, *1 Peter*, 194.

86. Cf. Elliott, *1 Peter: New Translation*, 517.

87. Feldmeier, *First Letter*, 170.

## CHRISTOLOGY AS FOUNDATION FOR ETHICS    163

Achtemeier pays attention to the author's use of δεσπόταις for the masters of the slaves, although the word κύριος was commonly used to refer to one's master.[88] This is no coincidence, but the author's intended reservation of the latter for Christ.[89] However, Feldmeier states that in contradiction to Eph 6:5, the slaves' obedience to their masters is not paralleled to their obedience to Christ, but the parallel lies in the suffering of Christ and the suffering of the slaves—both innocently.[90]

For Elliott γὰρ provides motivation for the previous imperative in verse 18.[91] Achtemeier notes the chiasmic pattern in verses 19-20:

A τοῦτο γὰρ χάρις

   B πάσχων ἀδίκως

   B ἀγαθοποιοῦντες καὶ πάσχοντες

A τοῦτο χάρις παρὰ θεῷ.[92]

This is not only a chiasm, but an inclusio, which again underscores the author's excellent rhetorical and literary talent. In both verses the suffering of the addressees is viewed from God's perspective. Achtemeier further notes that χάρις, ιτος f "grace," "kindness," "mercy," "goodwill" (ἔχω χ. πρός "have the goodwill of," Acts 2:47); "a special manifestation of the divine presence, activity, power or glory"; "a favour, expression of kindness," "gift," "blessing" (κατὰ χ. as a gift Rom 4:4, 16; ἵνα δευτέραν χ. σχῆτε, "in order that you might be blessed twice," 2 Cor 1:15); "thanks," "gratitude"; "graciousness" (ὁ λόγος ὑμῶν πάντοτε ἐν χ, "your speech should always be pleasant" Col 4:6) here has the meaning of something that is pleasing to God, respecting to God's will or "credible" in God's sight.[93] Bigg emphasises that the use of χάρις here should not be read as a synonym of its use in Pauline literature and therefore agrees with the scholars mentioned above for a meaning of "pleasing" or "praiseworthy" to God.[94]

This argument is further supported by the use of κλέος in verse 20. Διά "prep. with: (1) gen. through, by means of, with; during, throughout

---

88. Achtemeier, *1 Peter*, 195.

89. Cf. Michaels, *1 Peter*, 138; Goppelt, *Der erste Petrusbrief*, 192.

90. Feldmeier, *First Letter*, 170.

91. Elliott, *1 Peter: New Translation*, 518.

92. Achtemeier, *1 Peter*, 196; cf. Elliott, *1 Peter: New Translation*, 518.

93. Cf. Elliott, *1 Peter: New Translation*, 518; Selwyn, *First Epistle*, 89; Michaels, *1 Peter*, 135, 139 and Gundry, "Recent Investigations," 97-114; cf. The use of χάρις in Luke 6:32-34; *Did.* 1:3-5; Ign. *Pol.* 2:1; 2 *Clem.* 13:4.

94. Bigg, *Critical and Exegetical*, 143-44.

(διὰ παντός continually); through, among, throughout; (2) acc. because of, on account of, for the sake of; through, by (rarely); διὰ τοῦτο therefore, for this reason; διὰ (τό)with inf. because; διὰ τί why?" modifies the verb that immediately follows it. διὰ συνείδησιν θεοῦ also functions as a qualification of the verb. The verse is concerned with the slave's suffering because of his identity as a Christian and not because of laziness or inability to perform his work. Διὰ συνείδησιν θεοῦ is a phrase that occurs nowhere else in the New Testament. Since συνείδησιν is defined by θεοῦ, its normal meaning of "conscience" is rejected in favour of "awareness," "consciousness."[95] Συνείδησις, εως f does not merely mean knowledge of God's will, but a sensitivity towards God's will in terms of conduct that is pleasing to God. This understanding once again emphasises that the author is concerned with suffering that is caused by behaviour according to God's will and not because of the immoral or unfair actions of the slave owner.

Ὑποφέρει third person singular present indicative active of ὑποφέρω "endure, bear up under" according to Elliott often has the metaphoric meaning "to endure danger, affliction or injustice."[96]

By the employment of τίς, τί gen. τινός dat.τινί acc. τινά, τί enclitic pro. and adj. "anyone," "anything"; "someone" it is clear that the author does not merely have slaves in mind but a more general application of the command.

Λύπη, ης f "grief, sorrow, pain"; resonates λυπέω"pain, grieve, injure; pass. be sad, sorrowful or distressed; grieve, weep" in 1 Pet 1:6 which describes the general condition of all the believers.

Achtemeier understands πάσχων ἀδίκως as "an adverbial participle of attendant circumstance" to be translated as "when you suffer unjustly," emphasizing that suffering should be endured with patience even if this suffering is caused unjustly.[97] Elliott translates the clause as "while suffering unjustly," indicating a continuous state of events.[98] In Hellenistic thought the owner's relation to his slaves need not be just,[99] while this was distinctively different in Jewish and later Christian thought, which regarded slaves as human and therefore deserving of humane and just treatment.[100]

It is argued in this study that πάσχων ἀδίκως by subjecting to the will of God and following in the footsteps of Christ forms the central theme of

---

95. Cf. Acts 24:16; Rom 9:1; 1 Tim 1:18–19; cf. Brox, *Petrusbrief* (2nd ed.), 127; Windisch, *Katolishe Briefe*, 64; Best, *1 Peter*, 119; Kelly, *Peter and Jude*, 117.

96. Elliott, *1 Peter: New Translation*, 519; cf. 2 Macc 7:36; 1 Clem. 5:4, 14:1.

97. Achtemeier, *1 Peter*, 196.

98. Elliott, *1 Peter: New Translation*, 520.

99. Cf. Aristotle, *Eth. nic* 5.10.8.

100. Cf. Philo, *Spec.* 3.136–143.

the letter of 1 Peter (cf. 1 Pet 1:11; 2:21, 23; 3:18; 4:1, 13; 5:1) because this was the experience of all the addressees of the letter (cf. 1 Pet 3:14, 17; 4:19; 5:9–10) and precisely this theme is what constitutes a legitimate comparison between 1 Peter and the Gospel of Mark. Of further significant importance is the employing of "slaves" as the "paradigmatic of the entire community."[101]

Verse 20 aims to explain why only undeserved suffering, for being a believer in Christ is laudable.[102] The word κλέος, ους n "credit," "honor" only occurs here in the New Testament, but twice in the LXX in Job 28:22; 30:8 and in the Hellenistic world it belongs to the semantic category of "honor" and its synonyms including "good report," "praise," "fame."[103] As in the case of χάρις it should be understood from God's perspective. The two participals, ἁμαρτάνοντες participle present active nominative masculine plural of ἁμαρτάνω "do wrong," and κολαφιζόμενοι participle present passive nominative masculine plural of κολαφίζω "beat," "strike"; "harass," "trouble" has the general meaning of doing wrong and being punished accordingly.

Εἰ ἁμαρτάνοντες "when you do wrong" is understood by Elliott to be a rhetorical question, expecting a negative answer; id est: "you cannot expect honor with God by committing wrongdoings and then receiving punishment accordingly."[104] Furthermore, Elliott understands ἁμαρτάνοντες not as committing a sin against God, but as being disobedient to one's owner, as explicitly expressed by the previous verse, regardless of the owner's behaviour or character. κολαφίζω "beat, strike"; constitutes the appropriate punishment for disobedience to one's master. However, the cruelty of slave-owners was often frowned upon by Greco-Roman moralists, e.g., in Seneca's *On Anger* he writes: "You may take (a slave) in chains and at your pleasure expose him to every test of endurance; but too great violence in the striker has often dislocated a joint, or left a sinew fastened in the very teeth it has broken. Anger has left many a man crippled, many disabled, even when it found its victim submissive" (*Ira* 3.27.3).[105] For this study it is significant to note that κολαφίζω is the same word that is used by Mark in Mark 14:65 when reporting the passion of Jesus.

Ἀλλ' εἰ ἀγαθοποιοῦντες καὶ πάσχοντες ὑπομενεῖτε,τοῦτο χάρις παρὰ θεῷ echoes a well-known Hellenistic wisdom, namely that it is better to suffer injustice than to cause injustice and therefore inflict suffering on another. ἀγαθοποιέω "do good," "help"; "live uprightly," "do what is right or good"

---

101. Elliott, *1 Peter: New Translation*, 520.
102. Feldmeier, *First Letter*, 172.
103. Cf. Plato, *Leg.* 633A.
104. Elliott, *1 Peter: New Translation*, 521.
105. Translation in ibid., 521; see also Seneca, *Ep.* 47.

therefore is not a Christian invention, but a general Hellenistic principle of being ardent for the welfare of one's fellow citizen. However, to do good is also a recurring theme in the letter of 1 Peter (1 Pet 2:14, 15; 3:6, 11, 17; 4:19). Furthermore, suffering when doing good equals "unjust" suffering which is argued in this study to be the crux of the letter.

Ὑπομένω "endure, hold out, stand firm; bear, put up with" is synonymous with ὑποφέρω in verse 19. This is indicative of the fact that the suffering which is endured by the addressees is continuous and that the suffering endured by the slaves is representative of the suffering endured by the entire community (cf. 1 Pet 3:14, 17; 4:1, 19; 5:10). Ὑπομένω once again was used in Mark's report describing Jesus's patient endurance of suffering (cf. Mark 13:13). τοῦτο χάρις παρὰ θεῷ once again emphasises God's approval of their endurance of suffering in order to align themselves with his will.

It is the conclusion of the verse, which frames the inclusio with verse 19, the verse is given its distinctive Christian character: παρὰ θεῷ. The patient endurance of unjust suffering is further placed in a Christological frame by the following verses. This study views Achtemeier to be correct in his evaluation of the verse as "the point of this section and indeed one of the major thrusts of the letter as a whole; its repetition throughout the letter shows it to be paradigmatic of the vocation of all Christians."[106]

Elliott argues that verses 21–25 are linked with verses 18–20 syntactically as well as thematically (e.g., innocent suffering, wrongdoing, just vs. unjust, commitment to God, God's approval, servants and slaves and Christ as the obedient servant of God) and produces the second Christological motivation for their desired conduct.[107] The pericope contains various examples of early Christian traditions, e.g., kerugmatic formulas of the suffering and death of Christ and on the theme of discipleship) especially with reference to Isaiah, the author's most cited prophetic writing, which is supportive of the argument for Mark and 1 Peter's reliance upon the same theological tradition.

Ἐκλήθητε 2nd person plural aorist indicative passive of καλέω "call," "name," "address"; "invite"; "summon," "call in" has the meaning in 1 Peter of being called into the salvation present in the sphere of God (cf. 1 Pet 1:15; 2:9; 3:9; and 5:10). The use of the passive implies God as the subject. It is possible that the divine calling could refer to the recent conversion of the addressees and their consequent baptism.

ὅτι καὶ Χριστὸς emphasises the Christological nature of the divine vocation and the Christological foundation of the paraenetic content in 1 Pet

---

106. Achtemeier, *1 Peter*, 198.
107. Elliott, *1 Peter: New Translation*, 522.

2:18. ἔπαθεν ὑπὲρ ἡμῶν: the reason why slaves can endure their suffering at all is because Christ suffered on their behalf. The phrase "Christ suffered on your behalf" is unique to the New Testament. Elliott explains the author's preference for "suffer" instead of "died" in terms of the connection he wants to establish between Christ's suffering and the suffering of the addressees as well as the letter's central focus on suffering—πάσχω is used 12 times in the letter, more than any other New Testament writing. Furthermore, the concept of suffering is more comprehensive than death, since the former includes the latter.[108]

Εἰς τοῦτο also connects with the preceding verse in order to supply an answer for the question implied. Suffering for doing good was also the fate of the one in whose footsteps they follow, namely Christ. ἔπαθεν does not only refer to the suffering of Christ, but also to his death.[109] Ὑπὲρ ὑμῶν further establishes the personal nature of Christ's suffering in his relation with the believers and echoes the early Christian creedal formula.[110]

The reference to Christ's suffering in this particular pericope is to describe the example to be followed by believers, cf. ὑπογραμμός m "example." This word occurs only here in the New Testament and has the literal meaning of a pattern of the letters of the alphabet by which children learns to write by tracing over the letters.[111] The term also occurs three times in *1 Clement* twice referring to Christ (16:7 and 33:8) and once to Paul (5:7). Polycarp in *Phil* 8:2 clearly echoes 1 Pet 2:21–24. The "pattern" or "example" to be followed is that of Christ described by the purpose clause introduced by ἵνα ἐπακολουθήσητε τοῖς ἴχνεσιν αὐτοῦ, literally: "so that you may follow in his footsteps."

Ἐπακολουθέω "follow" only occurs in Mark 16:20 and 1 Tim 5:10, 24 in the New Testament and in Josh 14:9; Lev 19:4; and Isa 55:3 in the Old Testament and ἴχνος, ους, ους n "footstep, step" only occurs in Rom 14:12 and 2 Cor 12:18 in the New Testament and in Prov 5:5 and 30:19 in the Old Testament. Ἴχνος is understood as a mode of behaviour in Sir 21:6. Ἴχνος also occurs in a martyr context.[112] This interpretation of the phrase ἐπακολου θήσητε τοῖς ἴχνεσιν αὐτοῦ however increasingly received an emphasis on physical endurance and suffering.[113] The phrase also inspired

---

108. Ibid., 525; cf. Richard, "Functional Christology."
109. Cf. Goppelt, *Der erste Petrusbrief*, 200.
110. Cf. Kelly, *Peter and Jude*, 119, cf. Elliott, *1 Peter: New Translation*, 526.
111. See Clement, *Strom.* 5.8.49; cf. Elliott, *1 Peter: New Translation*, 526.
112. Cf. Ign. *Eph*.12:2 and *Mart. Pol.* 22:1.
113. Cf. *Barn.* 5:1, 5, 6, 12; Ign. *Pol.* 3.2; Pol. *Phil* 1:2; 8:1; Justin, *1 Apol.* 50:1; 63:10; 16; *Dial.* 68.1; 121.2.

centuries of Christian piety, of which the *Imitatio Christi* of Thomas a Kempis (1379-1471) was probably the most renowned. This understanding also manifested in the theology of Dietrich Bonhoeffer, who emphasised not only the Christological but especially the ethical implications of following Christ which does not merely entail mimicking Christ, but the actual experience of the personal "cost of discipleship" resulting in innocent suffering because of obedience to the will of God.[114]

The combination of the two words ἐπακολουθέω and ἴχνος is unique to 1 Peter. It is not to be understood in a literal manner or in a manner referring to martyrdom. Rather, it has a figurative meaning. Christ should be followed in his selfless behaviour, his innocence and obedience to the will of God. It therefore establishes a pattern of behaviour to be followed. The idea communicated by the author is similar to the idea communicated in the Synoptic Gospels when Jesus called his disciples.

The content of this example is provided by verses 22-24. This sentence has often been misunderstood as having an *Imitatio Christi* meaning, but as Goppelt correctly indicates, this verb is a technical term for being a follower of Christ, in other words "to follow" and not "to imitate" and therefore a call for discipleship based on the paradigm of the acquired behaviour of the slaves within the Christian community.[115] Interpreting the Passion of Christ paraenetically, the uniqueness of the salvation within suffering is highlighted. Our author already coupled the Passion of Christ with hermeneutics of prophetic texts (cf. 1 Pet 1:10) viewing the prophets as proclaiming the suffering and glorification of Christ.[116] This study opts, in agreement with Elliott, that verses 21-24 link with verses 18-21 on the grounds that as Christ subordinated himself to the will of God, the addressees should follow Christ's example in doing the same.[117]

Ὅς ἁμαρτίαν οὐκ ἐποίησεν is the first of four parallel phrases all starting with ὅς, in this case a relative pronoun: "he who." Verse 22 starts with an explanation of the content of this example, namely the behaviour of Christ in a similar situation of unjust suffering. The emphasis is on Christ's innocent suffering and therefore the slaves, which here serves as a *pars pro toto* for all believers, will only find favour with God if their suffering is a result of their devotion to Christ.

Οὐδὲ εὑρέθη δόλος ἐν τῷ στόματι αὐτοῦ: here reference is being made to the anatomical part of the body from where speech, whether honest or

---

114. Bonhoeffer, *Cost*; cf. Yoder, *Politics of Jesus*, 115-34.
115. Goppelt, *Der erste Petrusbrief*, 202.
116. Feldmeier, *First Letter*, 173.
117. Elliott, *1 Peter: New Translation*, 526.

deceitful, originate. Christ's innocence therefore was not only in his behaviour but also in his speech.

Because Christ refused to retaliate, recognizing that such behaviour would by futile anyhow, this decision expressed his freedom to choose to do good instead. Such behaviour in the Greco-Roman context would have been considered weak and not worthy for a god. However, for our author Christ is the ultimate example of moral strength.[118] From Jesus's perspective, his behaviour is not that of moral superiority, but rather of complete trust in God, who will ultimately judge with righteousness. Neither is Jesus trying to convey a moral exhortation to his enemies by acting in this manner. Rather, he is expressing comfort to those, who like him, became victims. They are to be encouraged by the righteousness of God. This righteous God will vindicate those who now suffer unjustly and they can look forward to justice at the *parousia*. This perspective should encourage them to disregard efforts to obtain their own justice (cf. Rom 12:17–20).

Λοιδορούμενος participle present passive nominative masculine singular of λοιδορέω "curse, speak evil of, insult" in the present participle indicates that it was repetitive verbal abuse. The same insults and slandering which the suffering servant had to endure, was also endured by Jesus during his passion, where he was mocked and humiliated (cf. Mark 15:16–20). This is now also the experience of the addressees of the letter (cf. 1 Pet 2:12; 3:16; 4:4, 14).

Οὐκ ἀντελοιδόρει: ἀντελοιδόρει third person singular imperfect indicative active of ἀντιλοιδορέω "reply with a curse": the preposition ἀντι combined with λοιδορέω indicates a reciprocal action, meaning that Christ did not insult in return. The combined verb occurs only here and in Acts 23:4.

This statement is however not based on actual eye-witness accounts of historical events but rather on oral traditions about the trail of Jesus known to the author.[119] The emphasis is not so much on Jesus's silence but rather on his refusal to retaliate the abuse he suffered in any manner. This attitude of Jesus did not only define his trail but his entire earthly activity (cf. Matt 5:43–48). This argument is supported by the author's use of the imperfect, a tense which describes habitual and repeated actions.[120]

Elliott argues that πάσχων present participle active nominative masculine singular of πάσχω "suffer" and ἠπείλει third person singular imperfect indicative active of ἀπειλέω "threaten; warn" both in grammatical form and content parallels with verse 23a, with the imperfect tense indicating

---

118. Feldmeier, *First Letter*, 174; cf. Origen, *Cels*. 2.3.5.
119. Cf. Schelkle, *Die Petrusbriefe*, 84.
120. Cf. Elliott, *1 Peter: New Translation*, 529.

continuous and repetitive action.[121] Ἀπειλέω "threaten; warn" only occurs here and in Acts 4:17 indicating that Jesus did not return suffering with suffering. Πάσχω "suffer" links the entire verse to the central motif of the letter. Although the word is not explicitly used by the Isaian author, the experience of the servant is that of suffering (cf. Isa 53:3, 4, 5, 7, 8, 10, 12). In Isaiah, the narrative of Jesus's crucifixion in Mark and in the letter of 1 Peter, suffering is the central theme, making that the mark of comparison between these writings. It also provides evidence for the thesis that the authors of Mark and Peter display affinities for the same Old Testament sources. As Elliott states: "Christ's innocent suffering in subordination and obedience to the Father's will links his experience with that of the suffering servant of Isaiah, the suffering servants/slaves of 1 Pet 2:18–20 and the suffering addressees of 1 Peter as a whole."[122]

Δέ "but, to the contrary, rather; and; now, then, so" constitutes the actual response of Christ to the abuse he suffered. He did not defend himself, but trusted in God for his vindication and the final establishment of his innocence. Παραδίδωμι "hand or give over, deliver up (pass.) often be deliver, entrust, commit, give; hand down, pass on; commend" is a verb that prominently features in the passion tradition (cf. Mark 14:10; Luke 22:4–6; John 19:12). The verb also occurs in Isa 53:6 and 12, although it has no specific object in 1 Pet 2:23. Τῷ κρίνοντι δικαίως implies God as the righteous judge as is the case in 1 Pet 1:17; 4:5, 6; 17–19.

Elliott sees a parallel between πάσχων ἀδίκως (1 Pet 2:19) and κρίνοντι δικαίως (verse 23) comparing the unjust human judge, Pontius Pilate, with God as the righteous judge who will have the final say in the ultimate vindication of Christ.[123] Therefore Jesus's "deliverance" or "commitment" to the will of God should be imitated by the slaves in this pericope and ultimately by the entire Christian community.

Achtemeier views verse 23 as a commentary on verse 22, providing an example for how Jesus remaind sinless throughout his life.[124] By lack of explicit quotation of Isaiah 53, it could be concluded that verse 23 was composed by the author himself.

Verse 24: ὃς τὰς ἁμαρτίας ἡμῶν αὐτὸς ἀνήνεγκενἐν τῷ σώματι αὐτοῦ ἐπὶ τὸ ξύλον, ἵνα ταῖς ἁμαρτίαις ἀπογενόμενοι τῇ δικαιοσύνῃ ζήσωμεν, οὗτω μώλωπι ἰάθητε shows strong parallels with Isa 53:4: οὗτο ϛτὰϛἁμαρτίας ἡμῶν φέρεικαὶ περὶἡμῶν ὀδυνᾶταικαὶ ἡμεῖς ἐλογισάμεθα αὐτὸν εἶναι ἐν

---

121. Elliott, *1 Peter: New Translation*, 530.
122. Ibid.
123. Ibid., 532.
124. Achtemeier, *1 Peter*, 201.

πόνῳκαὶ ἐν πληγῇκαὶ ἐν κακώσει, Isa 53:11 ἀπὸτοῦ πόνου τῆς ψυχῆς αὐτοῦ δεῖξαι αὐτῷ φῶς καὶ πλάσαι τῇ συνέσει δικαιῶσαι δίκαιον εὖ δουλεύοντα πολλοῖς καὶ τὰςἁμαρτίαςαὐτῶν αὐτὸς ἀνοίσει, and Isa 53:12: διὰ τοῦτο αὐτὸς κληρονομήσει πολλοὺςκαὶ τῶν ἰσχυρῶν μεριεῖ σκῦλα ἀνθ᾽ ὧν παρεδόθηεἰς θάνατον ἡ ψυχὴαὐτοῦκαὶ ἐν τοῖς ἀνόμοις ἐλογίσθη καὶ αὐτὸςἁμαρτίας πολλῶν ἀνήνεγκενκαὶ διὰ τὰςἁμαρτίας αὐτῶν παρεδόθη. The author is not citing one of these verses specifically, but rather combines them in the composition of his argument.

Ἀναφέρω "offer (of sacrifice) (cf. Lev 17:5; Isa 57:6; Jas 2:21; Heb 7:27); lead or take up; bear the burden of; take away." Elliott rejects Schelkle's suggestion that ἀναφέρωin 1 Pet 2:24 should be understood as Christ offering himself as a sacrifice on the "altar" of the cross, on the grounds that 1 Peter never refers to the suffering of Christ as a sacrifice.[125] Additionally the cross does not have the meaning of an "altar" anywhere in the New Testament. There also exists an interpretation of Christ's "bearing the sins of many" should be paralleled with the scapegoat ritual on the Day of Atonement.[126] However, this ritual involves two scapegoats: the one being slain as a ritual offering and the other being chased into the desert. A close reading of Isaiah 53 does not display any explicit parallels with this ritual and Isaiah serves as a source for 1 Peter. Rather the central idea is that just as the suffering servant's "bearing of sins" was vicarious, so was the action of Christ.

Ξύλον, ου n "wood," "tree"; "club"; "cross" refers to Christ's crucifixion. The word "wood" was often used by early Christian authors to refer to the cross, cf. John 1:29; Heb 9:28. A further reference to the crucifixion is made by ἐν τῷσώματι. The author's employment of Isaiah 53 describes the redemptive nature of Christ death on the cross. Furthermore τῇ δικαιοσύνῃ ζήσωμεν refers to the Faithfull's response to this sacrificial death by living a life of righteousness in accordance with God's will. Οὗτῷ μώλω πιἰάθητε is a direct citation of Isa 53:5: τῷ μώλω πιαὐτοῦ ἡμεῖς ἰάθημεν with two changes: the author opts for οὗ instead of Isaiah's αὐτοῦ with no particular change to the meaning; and the change of ἰάθημεν (first person plural) to ἰάθητε (second person plural) in order to address his addressees personally and to emphasise the personal nature of the salvation acquired for them on the cross. The author also changes the αὐτοῦ (second person plural) that was used throughout the passage to ἡμῶν (first person plural) which according to Elliott has the function of making the statement inclusive of all believers.[127] It emphasises

---

125. Elliott, *1 Peter: New Translation*, 532, rejects Schelkle, *Die Petrusbriefe*, 85.
126. Cf. Lev 16:1–34; Goldstein, "Die Kirche," 43–44.
127. Elliott, *1 Peter: New Translation*, 533.

that the same convictions are shared by the senders as well as the addressees of the letter. It is the same faith that binds them together.

Ἁμαρτίαις ἀπογενόμενοι: "so that we may die to sin" is understood by Feldmeier within the context of forgiveness.[128] Sin is not mentioned in order to discredit a person, but that the "sinner" is re-established into a relationship with the forgiving God." Exactly this opened up the τῇ δικαιοσύνῃ ζήσωμεν: the ability to live a new life orientated by the ultimate goal of righteousness.

Ἀπογενόμενοι aorist participle nominative middle nominative masculine plural of ἀπογίνομαι "die," i.e. "have no part in" could be understood as "dying in sinful ways" in order to indicate a radical separation from ἁμαρτία, αςf "sin" and in order to parallel with ζήσωμεν first person plural aorist subjunctive active of ζάω "live," "be alive"; "remain alive"; "come back to life." The paralleling datives, ἁμαρτίαις dative plural feminine and δικαιοσύνῃ, feminine singular dative of δικαιοσύνη, ης f "what God requires"; "what is right," should be taken as datives of respect and therefore indicating—"died with respect to sin" and "made alive or live with respect to what is right." Elliott also links ζήσωμεν with the motifs of new life and rebirth stressed in 1 Pet 1:3; 2:2, 4, 5; 3:7.[129] This possibility was opened up by the redeeming death of Christ and is grounded in the Christological model of Christ who died on the cross, but who was resurrected and made alive by God.

Δικαιοσύνη feminine singular dative of δικαιοσύνη, ης f "what God requires"; "what is right," "righteousness," "uprightness," "justice"; "(man) in a right relationship (with Himself)"; "religious duties or acts of charity" (Matt 6.1). In Israelite and early Christian circles δικαιοσύνη indicated the human fulfilment of the will of the divine (cf. Job 27:6; 29:14; Ps 44[45]:7; Matt 3:15; 5:6, 10, 12) and doing what is right in God's sight (Acts 10:35; 1 John 2:29; 3:7, 10; Rev 22:11). For the Petrine author, just as is the case in Isaiah, the servant establishes righteousness. He employs δικαιοσύνη in order to indicate "upright conduct" or a synonym for "doing what is right." This is a distinctively different use of the word than which is found in Paul, for Paul uses the term in order to indicated the "righteousness of God" or the "righteousness bestowed by God." This along with the unique reference to the suffering servant which is also not present in Pauline literature indicates the letter's independence from Pauline literature.[130]

Οὗτῷ μώλω πιλάθητε: Once again Christ's saving work is expressed by reference to the suffering servant imagery in Isa 53:5 with αὐτοῦἡμεῖς

---

128. Feldmeier, *First Letter*, 175; cf. Elliott, *1 Peter: New Translation*, 535.
129. Ibid., 535.
130. Cf. ibid., 536.

changed to οὗ and ἰάθημεν first person plural aorist indicative passive changed to ἰάθητε second person plural aorist indicative passive.

Μώλωψ, ωπος m "wound" only occurs here in the New Testament and could also have the meaning of a wound or bruise caused by being whipped (cf. Sir 28:17). Since the Petrine author previously referred to the reality of slaves often suffering under a cruel master, it is possible that he used this reference to Isaiah with them in mind. The focus, however, is that Christ's entire suffering is meant here and that his suffering had the effect of healing. Once again Christ is not only the example, but the enabler—his bruises brought about the healings of others and this healing restored the relationship with God.[131]

The author therefore sees Christ's suffering to be on behalf of the addressees, a theology present in the suffering servant imagery of Isaiah 53. The author's usage of this imagery will be further discussed in this chapter. "Because Christ's innocent suffering bears away the sin that separates Jesus's followers from God, they are free to endure similarly innocent suffering, because they know that such suffering, far from being evidence of their rejection by God, is in fact proof that they have been called by him (1 Pet 2:2)."[132]

In verse 25: ἦτε γὰρ ὡς πρόβατα πλανώμενοι, ἀλλὰ ἐπεστράφητε νῦν ἐπὶ τὸν ποιμένα καὶ ἐπίσκοπον τῶν ψυχῶν ὑμῶν the author once again employs imagery from Isaiah 53 and this time from verse 6: πάντες ὡς πρόβατα ἐπλανήθημεν ἄνθρωπος τῇ ὁδῷ αὐτοῦ ἐπλανήθη καὶ κύριος παρέδωκεν αὐτὸν ταῖς ἁμαρτίαις ἡμῶν.

By starting with γὰρ it is clear that the author sees verse 25 as a continuation of verse 24, providing a further explanation.[133] The sheep's healing in this case means their return to their true shepherd, an idea also found in Isa 6:10: καὶ ἐπιστρέψωσιν καὶ ἰάσομαι αὐτούς. The image of Israel as lost, scattered sheep is a recurring theme in the literature of the Old Testament (cf. Jer 27:6; Isa 13:14; Ezek 34). Israel is also often depicted as sheep without a shepherd (cf. Num 27:17; 1 Sam 22:17; 2 Chron 18:16). This image was transferred into the New Testament tradition (cf. Mark 6:34; Matt 9:36, etc.). Linked with the passion of Christ, Jesus is portrayed as citing Zech 13:7: ῥομφαία ἐξεγέρθητι ἐπὶ τοὺς ποιμένας μου καὶ ἐπ' ἄνδρα πολίτην μου λέγει κύριος παντοκράτωρ πατάξατε τοὺς ποιμένας καὶ ἐκσπάσατε τὰ πρόβατα καὶ ἐπάξω τὴν χεῖρά μου ἐπὶ τοὺς ποιμένας, in his anticipation of the scattering of the disciples during and after his crucifixion (cf. Mark 14:27). The

---

131. Ibid., 537.
132. Achtemeier, *1 Peter*, 203.
133. Cf. Elliott, *1 Peter: New Translation*, 537.

image of the Christian community as God's flock is also a recurring theme in 1 Peter (cf. 1 Pet 5:2–4) along with Christ being the chief Shepherd.[134]

According to Achtemeier this turning refers to the predominantly Gentile audience's recent conversion to the Christian faith.[135] For Feldmeier the imagery is clearly ecclesiological.[136] Elliott elaborates on this theme in stating that the metaphor of the scattering and re-gathering of God's sheep became one of the primary images in describing God's final gathering of his scattered people and God's final salvation.[137] For our author πλανώμενοι nominative masculine plural present participle passive of πλανάω "lead astray," "mislead," "deceive"; pass. "stray away," "go astray"; "be mistaken"; "be deceived or misled"; "wander about" refers to the state of his audience prior to their conversion. This parallels with the use of νῦν adv. "now," "at the present" indicating the present state of those under the care and mercy of God. Their ἐπεστράφητε, second person plural aorist indicative passive of ἐπιστρέφω "turn back," "return"; "turn to"; is indicative of their collective re-unification with Christ with God being the implied subject. First Peter's words, τὸν ποιμένα καὶ ἐπίσκοπον τῶν ψυχῶν ἡμῶν, only occurs here in the Bible and is therefore a creation by the author.

### Traditions– and Theological "Wirkungsgeschichtliches" Background

The text strongly relies on language drawn from Isaiah's portrait of the suffering servant (Isa 52:13—53:12) which the author interprets Christologically as referring to Christ's innocent suffering in obedience to God, now expected from the addressees. According to Elliott the Christological unit is framed by verses 21 and 25.[138] With the single exception of ἁμαρτίαν instead of ἀνομίαν verse 22 cites the LXX version of Isa 53:9b verbatim: αὐτοῦ ὅτι ἀνομίαν οὐκ ἐποίησεν οὐδὲ εὑρέθη δόλος ἐν τῷ στόματι αὐτοῦ. The author's clear reliance upon Isa 52:13—53:12 affirms the author's affinity for Isaiah and especially for the suffering servant-imagery. Isaiah's portrait of the suffering servant of God, παῖς (Isa 52:13) and παιδίον (Isa 53:2) provides the ideal framework for his description of Christ as the innocent suffering servant of God, which in turn serves as an example to be followed by the entire Christian community. The servant imagery links perfectly with the

---

134. Ibid.
135. Achtemeier, *1 Peter*, 204.
136. Feldmeier, *First Letter*, 176.
137. Elliott, *1 Peter: New Translation*, 538.
138. Ibid., 523.

slaves in this pericope who become the ultimate example of how suffering should be endured by the entire Christian community.

Verse 23 is also inspired by the suffering servant imagery of Isa 53:7, cf. ὡς πρόβατον ἐπὶ σφαγὴν ἤχθη καὶ ὡς ἀμνὸς ἐναντίον τοῦ κείροντος αὐτὸν ἄφωνος οὕτως οὐκ ἀνοίγει τὸ στόμα αὐτοῦ, however creatively employed by the author in his memory of the silence Jesus maintained in the face of the violence and abuse he endured during his trial and crucifixion (cf. Mark 16:41).

Furthermore, although the Shepherd in the Old Testament refers to YHWH the identity of the shepherd in the New Testament is taken over by Jesus (e.g., John 10:11-13; 21:15-17) as well as the particular use in 1 Pet 5:10.[139] Two aspects of the character of Christ are highlighted by the comparison of Christ with the Shepherd: Firstly, Christ plays the role of overseer and should therefore be obeyed as an authoritative figure. Secondly, the Shepherd's care for his flock is expressed by the metaphor. Christ is the caretaker of the believers, looking out for their wellbeing. This care was perfected by his life giving sacrifice (cf. 1 Pet 2:21; 3:18).[140] This verse is concerned with expressing the contrast between once and now in terms of the lives of the addressees, a dominant theme in the theology of the letter as a whole. The "now" of the readers is defined by their current status as members of the Christian community within which they become the heirs of the glorious future that is made possible by Christ's resurrection.

The focus on Isa 52:13—53:12, the suffering Servant-imagery, is of extreme importance for this study. Apart from Acts 8:12 this pericope forms the largest allusion to Isa 52:13—53:12 in the New Testament. The instruction to the slaves is entirely founded upon 1 Peter's Christological interpretation of Isaiah's suffering servant. First Peter's Christology forms the substantiation for his instruction to the slaves. Therefore it is safe to conclude form this pericope that the author's ethics are founded upon his Christology. First Peter's allusion to Isa 52–53 represents his understanding of Christ as the suffering servant of God who suffered on behalf others. It illustrates the author's theology and his knowledge and employment of Septuagint material from which he argues.

This tradition is firmly grounded in the concept of the "suffering righteous one" well known to Israel. The tradition initially developed from the concept of Israel's king as the righteous one (cf. Ps 18:21, 25; 2 Sam 22), and subsequently the righteous one who prays for God's justification (cf. Ps 5; 7; 17; 25; 31; 71; 119; 143) and especially Isa 52:13—53:12. The concept of

---

139. Cf. Feldmeier, *First Letter*, 176; and Elliott, *1 Peter: New Translation*, 538; contra Brox, *Petrusbrief* (1st ed), 139.

140. Feldmeier, *First Letter*, 176.

the suffering righteous one and martyrdom was first combined in 4 Macc 18:6–19 in the description of the martyrdom of the seven brothers under the cruel regime of the Antiochus Epiphanes. This theological theme became of such importance to Israel that it became the motivation behind the Maccabean revolt as well as the Judean-Roman conflicts in AD 66–73. Israel understood the suffering righteous one as the one who will ultimately be vindicated by God.[141] For the followers of Jesus this theological tradition became a prominent divine and Scriptual sanction for Jesus's suffering and death. Kerygmatic and creedal formulations originated through the use of this theme as well as that of the suffering servants.[142]

As this tradition progressively influenced the early Christian tradition, the passion and ultimate glorification of Christ were understood as the fulfilment of Scripture (cf. Acts 8). At the stage of the pre-Markan tradition the suffering, resurrection and glorification of the Son of Man or Messiah came to be understood as the fulfilment of God's will as expressed within Scripture. The fact that Christ had to suffer at the hands of humans (cf. Mark 9:31; 14:41) was also seen as the fulfilment of God's will. During the formation and development of the early Christian passion tradition, the passion was understood as the fulfilment of God's will but did not contain any soteriological meaning yet. The only allusion to Scripture was the sanctioning of the suffering righteous one. The first traces thereof manifested in the pre-Markan and pre-Pauline tradition found in Mark 14:24; 10:45 and 1 Cor 15:3b–5 concerning the cup within the Last Supper tradition. These are the first traces of the tradition of the vicarious suffering of Christ and Jesus's suffering and death as a self giving act on behalf of others (cf. Mark 14:22—25) and 1 Cor 11: 22–25).[143]

What is found in 1 Peter is the most extensive use of Isa 52:13—53:12 in the entire NT, in "elaborating the details, significance and soteriological effect of Jesus's suffering and death and in presenting him as a model to be emulated." The author's Christology involves a connection between household servants, the suffering servant and Christ as servant.[144]

---

141. See Ruppert, *Jesus als der leidende Gerechte?*; Ruppert, *Eine Motivgeschichtliches Untersuchung*; Ruppert, *Der Leidende Gerechte und seine Feinde*.

142. Elliott, *1 Peter: New Translation*, 544.

143. Ibid., 546.

144. Ibid., 547.

| 1 Peter | Isaiah 53 |
|---|---|
| 2:21–22 | 53:9 (Christ is without sin) |
| 2:23a | 53:7 (silence) |
| 2:23b | 53:3–5, 7, 8, 11, 12 (suffering and death) |
| 2:23c | 53:6, 12 |
| 2:24a | 53:4, 11, 12 |
| 2:24b, c | 53:5, 11 (righteous one) |
| 2:24d | 53:5 |
| 2:25a | 53:6a |

### Social and Historical Context

Social historian Moses Finley comments as follows:

> In principle the slave is an outsider, a "barbarian" and that sets him apart from all the other forms of involuntary labour known to history—from the Egyptian peasants who were conscripted to build the pyramids, from the *clientes* of early Rome, from debt-bondsmen, serfs or peons. The slave is brought into a new society violently and traumatically, uprooted not only from his homeland, but from everything which under normal circumstances provides human beings with social and psychological support. He is torn from his kin, from his fellows, from his religious institutions, and in their place he is given no new focus of relations other than his master, and in every unreliable way, his fellow slaves. Nor can he expect support from other depressed groups within the new society to which he has been transported. He has lost control not only over his labour but also over his person and his personality.[145]

This is also true of the slaves described in 1 Peter which becomes a description of the situation of the entire Christian community across Asia Minor who was experiencing a social and psychological predicament not comparable to any other group in antiquity. They were also often uprooted from their homes and no longer experienced the support of their kin and were subjected to the abuse and oppression of their superiors. They were a vulnerable community within a hostile society.

---

145. Finley, *Slaves*, 165–66.

Social scientific studies illuminated the dramatic change in social status by the conversion of slaves to the Christian faith. Within the Christian communities all members enjoyed the same status, and this presented a problem for the defined social order of slaves and masters respectively in the Greco-Roman world. Within the Christian community slaves enjoyed the same status as their masters, but within the normal daily activities the differences in social roles remained and this had a huge impact on the self-understanding of the slaves.[146] Within the Christian community slaves are no longer only objects at the mercy of their masters, but beloved by God as his possession. Therefore, it is Christ's evaluation of slaves which is the most important.[147] However, slavery *per se* was a unanimously accepted phenomenon in the first century Mediterranean world.[148] No biblical text criticises this institution, nor does it advocate the abolishment thereof. Slaves are not urged to rebel against their masters or to engage in revolutionary activities in order to accomplish their freedom. New Testament authors were explicitly aware of the horrible consequences of such actions which would result in persecution by Roman authorities and the death penalty.[149] Slaves who joined the "corrupting superstition"[150] of Christians against the will of their masters, could run into serious trouble. Therefore the best advice early Christian writers could give the slaves among their addressees was to remain obedient to their owners, regardless of how they were treated. Slave owners should have no mistrust in their slaves or reasons for accusing them of unacceptable behaviour. Christians have to behave in such a way that they will not be reprimanded.[151]

With regards to Jesus's silence, within the ancient Mediterranean context silence could be understood as an inability to respond and therefore a weakness and a cause of shame. This was however not always the case, for silence could also be regarded as an indication of honor and courage. It was a mark of dignity for a noble man to keep calm when reviled by an enemy. Pilch also indicated in his social-scientific study of the New Testament that to courageously endure pain in silence was viewed as honorable.[152] Therefore the honor for the silence of the suffering servant is underscored (Isa 53:7) and emphasised in the narrative of the passion of Christ (cf. Mark

---

146. Cf. Schelkle, *Die Petrusbriefe*, 79; Philipps, *Kirche*, 40.
147. Feldmeier, *First Letter*, 170.
148. Cf. Ibid., 168.
149. Achtemeier, *1 Peter*, 195; see *Did.* 4.10; *Barn.* 19.7; Pol. *Phil* 4.3.
150. Tacitus, *Ann.* 15.44.2.
151. Feldmeier, *First Letter*, 169.
152. Pilch, *Introducing the Cultural Context*, 71–94.

14:61; 15:5). Furthermore, a Hellenistic idiom existed that it was through suffering that one achieved knowledge.¹⁵³ In 1 Peter the suffering of Christ is presented as an example to be followed by the believers.

When one takes into consideration the passage in Deut 21:23, οὐκ ἐπικοιμηθήσεται τὸ σῶμα αὐτοῦ ἐπὶτοῦ ξύλουἀλλὰ ταφῇ θάψετε αὐτὸνἐν τῇ ἡμέρᾳ ἐκείνῃὅτι κεκατηραμένος ὑπὸ θεοῦ πᾶς κρεμάμενος ἐπὶξύλου καὶ οὐμιανεῖτετὴν γῆν ἣνκύριος ὁ θεός σου δίδωσίν σοιἐν κλήρῳ, the Christian movement faced a serious problem (see discussion above in *Christology in early Christianity*). The cross and the crucifixion presented a scandal and whoever was crucified, was cursed by God.¹⁵⁴ This problem is addressed by our author. He interprets the crucifixion as a vicarious action—because of this act it became possible for followers of Christ to abandon their sinful ways and live a life pleasing to God.¹⁵⁵

Ξύλον, ου n "wood," "tree"; "club"; "cross" further refers to the punishment used by the Romans, especially in the provinces, to deal with rebels against Roman law and order. It was used as a deterrent for anyone who planned a revolt. Therefore it was particularly employed for the punishment of violent criminals, rebellious slaves and those who committed subversive deeds.¹⁵⁶ Thousands of Jews were crucified in Judea in order to calm down the revolts in the province.¹⁵⁷ Apart from the torture that accompanied crucifixions, the crucified was completely degraded and humiliated in public. Cicero (*Rab.* 4) describes the cross as *arbor infelix* "a tree of shame." After the description of the crucifixion as exactly that, degrading and humiliating, by the passion narratives found in the Gospels,¹⁵⁸ our author tries to make sense of this scandalous event, by emphasizing its soteriological and life-givig effects.¹⁵⁹ This also opened the way for later Christian authors to put a positive spin on the crucifixion event.¹⁶⁰

---

153. Cf. Herodotus, *Hist.* 1.207.
154. Cf. Wilcox, "Deut 21:22–23"; Sänger, *Die Verkündigung*.
155. Elliott, *1 Peter: New Translation*, 534.
156. Cf. *Servile supplicium* Valerius. Maximus. 2.7.; Plautus, *Mil. glor.* 372–73.
157. Cf. Josephus, *B.J.* 2.75, 241, 253, etc.
158. Cf. Malina and Neyrey, *Calling Jesus Names*, 88–91; Malina and Rohrbaugh, *Synoptic Gospels*, 158–65.
159. Cf. Elliott, *1 Peter: New Translation*, 354.
160. Cf. Justin, *Dial*, 86.1–6.

## Theological Implications

According to Elliott this passage addressed to the slaves was skilfully composed to speak not only to the slaves but also to the entire suffering community.[161] By employing biblical themes and motifs as well as the extensive use of Isa 52–53 suffering servant-imagery the author clearly distinguishes himself from the typical Pauline style, and creates something that is unique in the entire New Testament. The author acknowledges the slaves as active moral agents capable of rational argumentation, moral responsibility and commitment to the Christian movement. For Elliott it is important to note the household imagery in employing οἰκέται and thereby emphasizing the household as the sphere of their activity and significance.[162] The slaves as a collective become an exalted group in the sense that they are placed on the same level as the Christ. On the other hand it creates the problem of to what extent the slaves were still able to obey their cruel masters.

This pericope has the implication that slaves are merely to subordinate themselves to the commands of their owners in as much as these commands are not in conflict with their obedience to God.[163] All commands, including idolatry, the renunciation of Christ etc., are to be disregarded even if this behaviour results in suffering.[164] The slaves' possibility to be more loyal to Christ than towards their slave owners is precisely an expression of their freedom in Christ.[165] The slaves here form a prototype for the entire Christian community which ought to accept suffering as far as it is a result of their alliance with Christ. The submission to their owners required from the slaves is a command regardless of the type of master they serve, whether fair or cruel. Σκολιός, ά, όν "crooked," "perverse," "dishonest" (of people); "crooked" (of roads)[166] indicates that the behaviour of the slaves is not to be defined in terms of the moral character of the slave owners. Rather their behaviour is defined by their submission to the will of God. It is important to note that this command is in continuation with the author's insistence on his audience's participation in the secular sphere. Their conversion to the Christian faith does not require total withdrawal from society nor the abandoning of their occupational duties.[167] Elliott underscores that the idea

---

161. Elliott, *1 Peter: New Translation*, 540.
162. Elliott, *A Home*; Elliott, *1 Peter: New Translation*, 542.
163. Cf. Feldmeier, *First Letter*, 170.
164. Cf. Goppelt, *Der erste Petrusbrief*, 291.
165. Feldmeier, *First Letter*, 170.
166. Cf. Deut 32:5; cf. Acts 2:40; Phil 2:15.
167. Cf. Goppelt, *Der erste Petrusbrief*, 16.

of suffering under an unjust slave owner links with the central idea of unjust suffering because of obedience to God within the letter.[168]

By implication the Christians were not only not in a position to change their social circumstances, but they were in serious danger if they attempted to do so and such an action would confirm the general mistrust and suspicion of their neighbours. Because the author has understanding for this predicament he stresses that his addressees should not engage in revolutionary activities, although their alliance with Christ causes them to suffer. The slaves, because of being part of the lowest social rank, are the most vulnerable, therefore the author emphasises that precisely here God offers his grace. The grace to be received is connected with the suffering endured because of being a follower of Christ. As Feldmeier confirms:

> When participation in this salvation is explicitly granted here and in the following verse to those who as the weakest members are most defencelessly exposed to the arbitrariness and hostility of the world around them, when these then in verse 21 are even placed in an immediate relationship to the suffering Christ, then socially underprivileged slaves are revalued upward in the context of the Christian community.[169]

The starting of verse 21 with γὰρ answers the implied question of the previous verse, namely why slaves suffering unjustly finds favour with God. The answer is that such suffering is in continuation with their divine call received in the gospel proclaimed to them (cf. 1 Pet 1:12; 22-25). Christ's innocent suffering illustrates the example to be followed by believers. This paraenetic clause is in continuation with the Christians' following in the footsteps of Christ, up until his crucifixion as a model for Christian life. εἰςτοῦτο according to Elliott refers to verses 18-20 in terms of behaviour in accordance to God's will.[170]

Suffering in terms of 1 Peter is not a result of wrongdoing and being punished accordingly. The following verses emphasises how Christ suffered although he was absolutely innocent. Christ's suffering, however, differs from his followers in the sense that it was a vicarious deed on behalf of others. Elliott notes that dying on behalf of others was a foreign concept to the Greeks and Romans, but, writes Elliott "the emphasis here on the vicarious character of Christ's suffering and death reflects a broad current of early Christological and soteriological Christian tradition that has its nearest roots in antecedent Israelite thought concerning the atoning power

---

168. Elliott, *1 Peter: New Translation*, 517.
169. Feldmeier, *First Letter*, 172.
170. Elliott, *1 Peter: New Translation*, 523, cf. Selwyn, *The First Epistle*, 178-179.

of virtuous conduct, suffering and death,"[171] Although the concept of a suffering Messiah was foreign to Israel, they were familiar with the atoning power of vicarious suffering which significantly influenced early Christian tradition. This influence was used by early Christianity in order to positively redefine the scandalous death of Christ on cross to have a soteriological significance. Here we see a clear example of the author of 1 Peter's creative re-interpretation of the suffering servant-imagery in Isaiah 53 to have Christological meaning. Our author underscores that the suffering of Christ was not merely vicarious, but also exemplary. Therefore, Christ becomes both the enabler and the example. In his classic study on lordship and discipleship Schweitzer explains this idea by sketching a scenario of a child following his father through a valley of deep snow.[172] The snow is too deep for the child to find his own way, but by following step by step in the footsteps of his father he could find his way. This is what 1 Peter wants to communicate: Christ in his innocent and patient response to suffering provided the "footsteps" in which those who choose to follow him may tread. The footsteps of Christ therefore have kerugmatic and paraenetic meaning.[173]

Salvation is granted by the suffering of Christ in obedience to God. Because Christ entrusted himself to the will of God, he was able to endure suffering. This is the same pattern of behaviour that should be followed by the believers.[174]

The expression of this relationship between Christ and the believers draws the parallel between Christ's suffering for the sake of the believers and their suffering because of their commitment to obeying his will.[175] Their suffering is therefore an inevitable consequence of their call to follow Christ. This provides an excellent example of ethics being implicitly interwoven into Christology. Christ obtained salvation for the sake of the believers through suffering on their behalf and giving his life for them. As the other part of the same coin Christians endure suffering because they became heirs to the salvation given by Christ. In the words of Feldmeier: "This interleaving of the soteriological singularity and ethical exemplarity is characteristic of 1 Peter."[176]

---

171. Elliott, *1 Peter: New Translation*, 525; cf. Statius, *Thebais* 10.768–769; Livy 8.10.7.

172. Schweitzer, "Son of Man," 11.

173. Elliott, *1 Peter: New Translation*, 258.

174. Feldmeier, *First Letter*, 173.

175. Achtemeier, *1 Peter*, 199.

176. Feldmeier, *First Letter*, 174.

The paraenetic part of the pericope did not merely exhort the slaves to subject to their masters' authority, but they should do what is right and endure the unjust suffering to which they were exposed.[177]

The author is pleading for mindfulness of the will of God, in their obedience in suffering as illustrated by Christ. Elliott notes that this is the only example in the New Testament where the instruction to slaves contains so much Christological information (cf. vv 21–25).[178] This is also the most extensive Christological statement in the entire epistle. It is of special significance for the hypothesis of this study to note this parallel between the suffering condition of slaves and that of Christ during his passion. Christ further becomes a model to be imitated by the slaves especially in terms of their underserved and innocent suffering. It is remarkable that the author recognizes slaves not only as autonomous moral agents, but also models for the entire Christian community. Once could argue that this pericope becomes the panicle of 1 Peter's theology and the culmination of various themes, e.g., ideas of subordination in reverence of God; the avoidance of wrongdoing; doing what is right in accordance to the will of God; enduring unjust suffering: being called by God; Christ's suffering on behalf of the believes; their healing and Christ as the enabler to do good; Christ leaving an example for all servants to follow; Christ's resistance of retaliation and his entrusting of his cause to God.

This conflux of themes is indicative thereof that the exhortation was not merely addressed to the slaves but to the entire community. The slaves are presented as paradigmatic of the vocation of the entire brotherhood. Our author's Christology is illuminated through his portrayal of the atoning work of Jesus Christ—his innocence, his suffering on behalf of others, his submission to and trust in God, his wounding through which others are healed—and the saving effect of Christ's suffering sheds positive light on the shame of the cross. Christ is portrayed as the one who liberates form wrongdoing and enables believers to do good—this is in continuation with the kerugma first preached to the recipients. This once again unites them with the community in Rome from where the letter was sent. First Christ becomes the model to be imitated by the slaves and then the slaves forms the paradigm to be imitated by the entire community. The slave, with his/her up-rootedness from home, lack of social support and exposure to the cruelty of their masters, becomes the perfect prototype for the Christian community's vulnerability within a hostile environment. Furthermore they become exemplary for the conduct of the entire Christian community

---

177. Elliott, *1 Peter: New Translation*, 540.
178. Ibid., 541.

which ought to be in accordance with the will of God, and their vocation to follow in the footsteps of Christ.

The author exalts slaves, as the lowest social ranking, to become an example to the entire Christian community. This clearly affirms the author's understanding of God as opposing to the proud and generously giving grace to the humble (cf. 1 Pet 5:5). This rings true to the essence of the gospel (cf. Mark 10:31; 10:43–35).[179]

## Mark 14:26–31

*And when they had sung a hymn, they went out into the Mount of Olives. And Jesus said to them, "You will all become apostate, for it is written, 'I will strike the shepherd, and the sheep will be scattered.' But after I am raised, I will go before you to Galilee." Peter said to him, "Even though they all become apostle, I will not." And Jesus said to him, "Truly, I say unto you, this very night, before the rooster crows twice, you will deny me three times." But he said emphatically, "If I must die with you, I will not deny you." And they all said the same.*

### Literary and Narratological Analysis

This unit prepares the reader for what is to be expected in the passion narrative. Jesus predicts that all disciples would take offence and be scattered (verse 27) and this is fulfilled in the account of his arrest in verse 50. Jesus promised his disciples that after he had been raised, he would go before his disciples to Galilee (verse 28) and these exact words will be repeated by the young man in white awaiting the women at the tomb in Mark 16:7. Jesus further predicts that Peter will deny him in verse 30 and this is reported in verses 54 and 66–72. These connections could be indicative thereof that this unit originally formed part of a passion narrative which the author used as a source.[180]

Bultmann described this unit as an historical account with legendary traits. He further defined it as a "faith legend" because of the apologetic motifs. Because the Gethsemane-story is linked to the following arrest-story as was the case in the original source used by Mark, it is likely that verses 26

---

179. Elliott, *1 Peter: New Translation*, 543.
180. Collins, *Mark*, 667.

to 31 are Markan redaction.¹⁸¹ The passage continues the theme of Jesus's rejection.

Ὑμνήσαντες, aorist participle active nominative masculine plural of ὑμνέω intrans. "sing a hymn; trans. sing praises to": This participle was composed by Mark to conclude the account of the last supper of Jesus and his disciples.¹⁸² This alludes to the general practice of singing hymns, most likely the Psalms, during the Passover meal and it picks up the story of the preparation for the celebration of the *Pascha*.¹⁸³ According to the Mishna the Levites sang the *Hallel* (Psalms 113–118) in the temple court while the people were slaughtering and preparing the Passover offering.¹⁸⁴ In the Mishna it is also stated that four cups of wine must be drunk during the Passover meal.¹⁸⁵

On the Mount of Olives Jesus says to the disciples: πάντες σκανδαλισθήσεσθε."You will all become apostate," σκανδαλισθήσεσθε second person plural future indicative passive of σκανδαλίχω "cause (someone) to sin, cause (someone) to give up his faith (pass. give up one's faith, be led into sin, fall into sin; pass. With ἐν reject, desert, have doubts about; anger, shock." This word is commonly used in the New Testament to refer to stumbling. It is found eight times in Mark (Mark 4:17; 6:3; 9:42, 43, 45, 47; 14:27, 29), twenty-six times.

He then elaborates on this prediction with an explicit citation of Scripture, Zech 13:7b: λέγει κύριος παντοκράτωρ πατάξατε τοὺς ποιμένας καὶ ἐκσπάσατε τὰ πρόβατα"The Lord said: 'Strike the shepherd!' and the sheep will be scattered." Zechariah 13:7b is highly ambiguous within its original context. It is not clear whether the image represents a prophet or a ruler, although the latter is preferred by Meyers and Meyers.¹⁸⁶ It is however probable that Mark approached this text with a hermeneutic of prophecy being fulfilled, since the true meaning becomes apparent only when it is fulfilled within the Passion narrative.¹⁸⁷

The words of Jesus in verse 28 are a further prediction: ἀλλὰμετὰ τὸ ἐγερθῆναί με προάξω ὑμᾶςεἰςτὴν Γαλιλαίαν. "After I am raised, I will go before you to Galilee" and this adds a further detail namely that the disciples are instructed to go to Galilee to meet Jesus after his resurrection. This

---

181. Bultmann, *History*, 267.
182. Collins, *Mark*, 668; cf. Schenke, *Passionsgeschichte des Markus*, 349.
183. Cf. Evans, *Mark 8:27—16:20*, 399; Donahue and Harrington, *Mark*, 401.
184. Cf. Danby, *Mishnah*, 142.
185. Cf. *m. Pesaḥ.*10.1.
186. Meyers and Meyers, *Zechariah*, 384–89.
187. Collins, *Mark*, 669; cf. Suhl, *Die Funktion*, 65.

saying is echoed in the words of the man clothed in white who meets the women at the grave on the morning of the resurrection (cf. Mark 16:7). Ἀλλὰ is an indication that the promised meeting in Galilee has the potential to restore the relationship between Jesus and his disciples. A relationship they do not even realise at this point is going to be broken. However, this verse suggests that the crucifixion of Jesus and the scattering of the disciples will not be the end. The same God who strikes the shepherd and scatters the disciples will also raise Jesus from the dead and re-gathers the community. Although Mark does not explicitly narrate the resurrection or the reunion of Jesus with his disciples both are presupposed in his narrative (cf. Mark 16:7). The imagery of the shepherd is continued: "Jesus will go before his frightened and dismayed disciples, but this is to be visualised as the resurrected Lord preceding his disciples to Galilee and encountering them there not as though Jesus will rejoin his disciples in Jerusalem and lead them to Galilee."[188] Yet, Mark does leave his Gospel open-ended. The point the evangelist is making is that the possibility remain to be a follower of Jesus and to belong to his community even after their denial of him and their flight from the horror of the crucifixion. The scattering could be seen as divine judgment and the re-gathering as divine grace.

Van Iersel views the phrase εἰςτὴν Γαλιλαίαν in 14:28 and 16:7 to be translated as "in Galilee" instead of "into Galilee" since Mark often uses εἰς instead of ἐν (1:21, 39; 2:1).[189] This translation will have the implication that instead of Jesus just going before his disciples to Galilee,[190] he will already be in Galilee when his disciples arrive, and he will give them leadership there. The military usage of προάξω,first person singular future indicative active of προάγω intrans. "go before or ahead of; come or go before," (2 Macc 10:1) supports this interpretation.

Ὁδὲ Πέτρος ἔφηαὐτῷ\εἰκαὶ πάντες σκανδαλισθήσονται, ἀλλ'οὐκ ἐγώ. Peter disagrees with Jesus's prediction, but Jesus is not persuaded, because Scripture says otherwise. Furthermore, it is not the first time in the Gospel of Mark that Peter is mistaken (Mark 8:31-33, 9:5-7). Mark is not trying to humiliate Peter nor is Peter's incomprehension part of the Markan Messianic secret.[191] Mark rather wants to make a point that Jesus is superior in power, insight and faith. That, which ordinary people fail to comprehend and even fears it with dignity and complete submission to the will of God.

---

188. Boring, *Mark*, 394.
189. Van Iersel, "Mark 14,28," 365-70.
190. Evans, *Mark 8:27—16:20*, 402; cf. Gundry, *Mark*, 845.
191. Evans, *Mark 8:27—16:20*, 402; cf. Wrede, *Messianic Secret*, 105.

Here at least is seems as if Peter is grasping that Jesus will die and that he is calling his disciples to follow him even if it means that they could also die. Peter is adamant that he will never deny Jesus even if he must die with him. He uses the same form of the verb δει ("be necessary, must; should, ought; be proper; had to, should have") that Jesus used earlier to express his own death as part of God's divine plan (cf. Mark 8:31, 9:11-12). Here is a classic example of dramatic irony since the readers of the Gospel already know that despite Peter's protest he is indeed going to deny Christ.[192]

The fact that Peter will deny Jesus three times is linked with Mark's recurring theme of using threefold, once in this context it is understood to indicate completion.[193] Peter continues to protest, pledging his loyalty to Christ until death even if he is the only one. Mark eludes the Maccabean martyrs who would rather die than compromise their commitment to the faith (cf. 2 Macc 6-7). It is most probable that Peter's intentions were sincere, but he is completely unaware of what awaits him. Mark's audience will soon find out that Jesus predictions did indeed come true first in his disciples abandoning of him during his arrest and finally in peters denial. Because these predictions were fulfilled he followers of Jesus may trust that his resurrection and glories return will also come to pass.

Furthermore, Peter's protest recalls his earlier misunderstanding in 8:32-33 and his claim that he will remain faithful and then follows Jesus shocking reply that Peter will indeed deny Jesus three times. The prediction of Peter's denial (Mark 14:30; Matt 26:34; Luke 22:34; John 13:38) and the actual event of his denial (Mark 16:66-72; Matt 26:69-75; Luke 22:56-62; John 18:25-27) were considered so important in early Christian tradition that it is among the few incidents recorded in all four canonical Gospels. Being an incident that puts the conduct of the early Christian community in a bad light, its inclusion in all the Gospels attests to its solid historical foundation.

Καὶ λέγει αὐτῷ ὁ Ἰησοῦς ἀμὴν λέγω σοι ὅτι σὺ σήμερον ταύτῃ τῇ νυκτὶ πρὶν ἢ δὶς ἀλέκτορα φωνῆσαι τρίςμε ἀπαρνήσῃ: Jesus responds directly to Peter and adds a further prediction. The introductory ἀμὴν adds emphasis and gravity to the words of Jesus which is about to follow. The pronoun "you" σὺ the subject of the verb ἀπαρνέομαι is emphatic here after σοι.[194]

The temporal expressions move from specific σήμερον ("today"), to more specific ταύτῃτῇνυκτὶ ("this very night") to most specific πρὶνἢ δὶς ἀλέκτορα φωνῆσαιτρίς ("before the cock crows twice"). These emphatic and

192. Boring, *Mark*, 394.
193. Evans, *Mark 8:27—16:20*, 403; cf. Derret, "The Reason," 142-44.
194. Donahue and Harrington, *Mark*, 403.

almost superfluous references to Peter and the exact moment of his denial are ironic in relation to the bold and self-confident statement of Peter that even if everyone else becomes apostate and leaves Jesus, he will not do so.

According to Mark Peter will deny Jesus three times before the cock crows twice, whereas Matthew and Luke retain the triple denial, but mention only one cock crow (cf. Matt 26:34 and Luke 22:34). This is probably due to the fact that Mark's formulation was too complicated and was therefore simplified by the later evangelists. Mark's formulation is however vivid and adds verisimilitude to the prediction. The fact that Peter ignores the first cock crow heightens the impression of his weakness and his over-estimation of his own abilities. The prediction of Peter's denial is quite detailed with regards to when, but the interest of the audience is kept as to when, where and how the denial will take place. In verse 31 Peter's response becomes even more vehement (cf.ἐκπερισσῶς). Peter is adamant that even if he has to die with Jesus he will not forsake or deny him. The other disciples respond in exactly the same way. This passage becomes extremely important in Mark's portrayal of the misunderstanding of the disciples.[195]

### Traditions–and Theological "Wirkungsgeschichtliches" Background

The passage contains multiple intertextual references to the Old Testament, including references to the *Hallel* Psalms which commemorates the Exodus, an allusion to David's flight from Jerusalem after being betrayed by a confidant and explicit citation of Zech 13:7. This underscores the notion of the early Christian church to refer to the scriptures in order to substantiate that Jesus death was "according to the Scriptures."[196] In this passage the motif of the suffering righteous person who is abandoned by his friends during his moment of trial becomes evident (cf. Job 19:13–22). The quotation from Zech 13:7 stands central in the passage and provides another passion prediction by Jesus that also looks forward to the resurrection. It also contains a reference to the failure of Jesus own followers instead of referring to the hostile actions of his antagonists.[197]

The context of Zechariah which is cited in verse 27 begins with a disaster which is introduced with a decree by YHWH (cf. Zech 13:7–9a) and concludes with the reaffirmation of the relationship of the remnant with their God (cf. Zech 13:9b).

---

195. Collins, *Mark*, 672.
196. Cf. Brown, *Death of the Messiah*.
197. Donahue and Harrington, *Mark*, 404.

## CHRISTOLOGY AS FOUNDATION FOR ETHICS 189

Jesus is able to make this prediction because it is written in Scripture and this gives authority to the statement of Jesus which is probably authentic since it would be unlikely that early Christianity including the author of Mark would view Zech 13:7, ῥομφαία ἐξεγέρθητι ἐπὶτοὺς ποιμένας μου καὶἐπ' ἄνδρα πολίτην μου λέγει κύριος παντοκράτωρ πατάξατε τοὺς ποιμένας καὶ ἐκσπάσατε τὰ πρόβατα καὶ ἐπάξω τὴν χεῖρά μου ἐπὶτοὺς ποιμένας, as a prophetic reference to Jesus. This application of Jesus is similar to one found in the Qumran literature: a passage cited in the *Damascus Document* where it is understood that the "sheep" are the members of the Qumran-community while the "shepherd" is probably their Teacher.[198]

Jesus's reference to Zechariah is further significant because of their being on the Mount of Olives; cf. Zech 14:4: καὶ στήσονται οἱ πόδες αὐτοῦ ἐν τῇ ἡμέρᾳ ἐκείνῃ ἐπὶ τὸ ὄρος τῶν ἐλαιῶντὸ κατέναντι Ἱερουσαλημ ἐξ ἀνατολῶν καὶ σχισθήσεται τὸ ὄρος τῶν ἐλαιῶν τὸ ἥμισυ αὐτοῦ πρὸς ἀνατολὰς καὶ τὸ ἥμισυ αὐτοῦ πρὸς θάλασσαν χάος μέγα σφόδρα καὶ κλινεῖ τὸἥμισυ τοῦ ὄρους πρὸς βορρᾶν καὶ τὸ ἥμισυ αὐτοῦ πρὸς νότον.

Mark reverses the word order of the LXX in order to draw attention to the sheep which will be lost and scattered without their leader. The scattering of the sheep is a temporary setback to the Messianic Mission which is the gathering of the sheep, the lost and exiles.[199] It is possible that this saying forms part of the tradition that predicts Jesus resurrection. Marcus views the reference to the resurrection as further evidence of the influence of an eschatological tradition associated with Zechariah.[200] He is of the opinion that the resurrection reading of Zech 14:1–5 was known by Mark. The promise that the shepherd will "go before you" anticipates that the sheep will be gathered once again.[201]

Two thirds of the people will not survive, but one third, after severe testing, will survive. The image of "testing" is fitting to the context of the disciples, whose loyalty to Jesus will be severely tested during his arrest and crucifixion. The image of the scattering of the sheep fits with the flight of the disciples as narrated in verse 50. In the Masoretic Text, as well as in the LXX, God instructs his agent(s) to strike the shepherd, whereas in Mark God says: "I will strike the shepherd." This illuminates that the Markan author understood the crucifixion as God's will.[202]

198. Cf. Rabin, "Historical Background," 1.
199. Num 27:17; 1 Kgs 22:17; 2 Chr 18:16; Ezek 34:8; Zech 10:20.
200. Marcus, *Way of the Lord*, 155–57.
201. Evans, *Mark 8:27—16:20*, 401.
202. Collins, *Mark*, 670; cf. Guttenberger, *Die Gottesvorstellung*, 54, 116; Flesseman-Van Leer, "Prinzipien der Sammlung," 407; Donahue and Harrington, *Mark*, 401.

When David is betrayed by a trusted friend he goes to the Mount of Olives where he weeps and prays to God (cf. 2 Sam 15:16–30). It is just another example of how Mark's passion narrative is deeply influenced by biblical imagery.[203] Mark's text does not agree with the Masoretic Text or the LXX reading of Zech 13:7, because his concern is not the literal or historical context of Zecharia. Rather he reads the text Christologically as an expression of his own theology.[204]

Marcus argues that the Zechariah text probably played a role in the nationalist or military theology of the zealots during the 66–70 revolt and that when Mark cites it here he alters the understanding to that the promise of God's faithfulness will not be fulfilled by a military Messiah but one who voluntary suffers and dies.[205] To be a disciple of such a Messiah is not to take up arms against Rome but to follow him all the way the cross.

"The idea that the events of the passion narrative took place in accordance with the Scriptures may be at work here as a way for the author and the audience to make sense of the death of Jesus and to understand him as a willing subject in the events rather than a humiliated and disgraced object of forces beyond his control."[206] This is extremely important for the argument of this study. This prediction of Jesus looks ahead to the events that will follow in the narrative, in the rest of chapter 14: the flight of the disciples and the denial of Peter and chapter 15: the death of Jesus. It functions in a similar manner as the divine oracle in some ancient novels in order to catch the attention of the audience and to arouse their interest in the events to follow in the narrative.[207] To those, familiar with the events to follow, this saying of Jesus adds irony to the protest of Peter and the disciples in verses 29 and 31. Jesus's introductory statement interprets the flight of the disciples and the denial of Peter as "becoming apostate" (σκανδαλίζω). This also refers back to the parable of the sower, for the disciples become like the seed sown on rocky ground (cf. Mark 4:17). The disciples also become like the people of Nazareth in Mark 6:3, for their becoming apostate belongs to a theme of misunderstanding and lack of understanding on the part of the disciples.[208] In Mark 4:17 Jesus is explaining the meaning of parable of the sower and he describes the shallow-rooted as those who fall away at the first sign of persecution or tribulation. In Mark 6:3 the people of Nazareth are scandalized

---

203. Cf. Brown, *Death of the Messiah*, 145–67.
204. Boring, *Mark*, 393.
205. Marcus, 1993, 161–63.
206. Collins, *Mark*, 670.
207. Cf. Tolbert, *Sowing the Gospel*, 67.
208 Schenke, *Passionsgeschichte des Markus*, 428.

at Jesus. In 9:42–45 σκανδαλίζω probably means "to sin." It is possible that the shallow rooted in Mark 4:17 could apply to disciples, for because of their lack of depth they also fall away as soon as they have to endure suffering. It will not be until the resurrection that the disciples will be rooted enough to take up their apostolic responsibilities.

In Mark's interpretation, the shepherd is Jesus and he applies biblical imagery for God to Jesus. The sheep are Jesus's disciples and they will be scattered because they are overwhelmed by the events to happen. The passive voice indicate that they will not be their cause of their scattering but their scattering is brought about by the fact that the shepherd was struck by God and therefore their being scattered is also an act of God. What God does, does not only affect Jesus but it affects the disciples too.[209]

### Social and Historical Context

Mark nowhere else mentions that Jesus or his disciples where singing hymns, so it is possible that the author or the tradition from which he draws was influenced by the Christian practice of signing at Eucharistic meals. Psalm 118 already played an important role in the shaping of Mark's narrative (cf. Ps 118:22, Mark 8:31; Ps118:22–23, Mark 12:10–11; Ps 118:25–26, Mark 11:9–10). Similarly the Mount of Olives is always present in the prediction of eschatological events (cf. Zechariah 13–14). As is stipulated in the Passover regulations, Jesus and his disciples do not return to Bethany where they had been staying (cf. Mark 11:11–12; 14:3) but they remain in the city. Passover participants were to stay in Jerusalem for the entire night and in order to accommodate the additional guests staying in the city the rabbis declared part of the Mount of Olives as belonging to the city.[210]

Although historically rooted the passage is also rooted in the Old Testament as already mentioned. It may also have conveyed a powerful message to Mark's Roman audience who experienced apostasy among its members in the face of persecution. Mark probably wanted to comfort his readers that Jesus experienced the same betrayal that they now experienced by their fellow-believers who renounce their faith because of Nero's persecution.

According to the Roman historian Tacitus many Christians were arrested because of testimony provided by other Christians.[211] A community that had to reconcile with those believers who submitted under the pressure of persecution could find consolation and encouragement in Mark's

---

209. Boring, *Mark*, 394.
210. Ibid., 393.
211. Tacitus, *Ann.* 15.44.

portrayal of Peter, since Peter who became the rock where upon the church was built himself once failed Jesus.

## Theological Implications

Peter attempts to argue with Jesus, at least as far as his personal capacity is concerned. In the same way Peter rejected Jesus's revelation of the mystery that the Son of Man has indeed come to suffer. Here, Peter is not concerned so much that the Shepherd will be struck, but he disputes Jesus's prediction that the disciples will scatter. This is indicative thereof that Peter still lacks understanding in the events that are about to happen as well as his own role and the severe testing that is awaiting him and his fellow disciples. However, the events narrated reveal that Jesus's prediction was indeed exactly correct. The instruction echoed in the words of the young man in Mark 16:7 implies that the disciples and especially Peter will have a second chance. The failures of Peter and the other disciples at the time of Jesus's arrest and crucifixion are not absolute. During the narrative of the arrest and the crucifixion the disciples still serve as negative examples to the audience, for they fail to deny themselves, to take up their crosses and to follow Jesus. Instead, they seek to save their own lives rather than losing it for the sake of Jesus and the good news.[212]

Peter categorically distinguishes himself from the other disciples: The fact the sentence ends with οὐκ ἐγώ places the emphasis on ἐγώ over and against the others. The scattering of the disciples is already starting since Peter is separating himself from the others. Each individual responds to the events of the passion differently and this causes the community to disintegrate.

A major Christological theme in Mark's gospel becomes evident here namely the suffering righteous servant of Isa 52:13—53:12. This imagery becomes a reality in what is about to happen to Christ: the shepherd will be struck; the sheep will scatter; Peter will deny Jesus three times and Jesus will be resurrected and he will meet his disciples in Galilee and gather them once again. This is ultimately a message of reassurance and hope.[213]

---

212. Collins, *Mark*, 671.
213. Donahue and Harrington, *Mark*, 405.

## Mark 15:1–5

*And as soon as it was morning, the chief priests held a consultation with the elders and scribes and the whole Sanhedrin. And they bound Jesus and led him away and delivered him over to Pilate. And Pilate asked him, "Are you the King of the Jews?" And he answered him, "You have said so." And the chief priests accused him of many things. And Pilate again asked him, "Do you not answer? See how many charges they bring against you." But Jesus gave no further answer, so that Pilate was stunned.*

### Literary and Narratological Analysis

The narrative follows the exact same pattern as Jesus's trial before the Sanhedrin in Mark 14:60–62:

| Mark 14:60–62 | Mark 15:4–5 |
|---|---|
| ὁ ἀρχιερεὺς εἰς μέσον ἐπηρώτησεν τὸν Ἰησοῦν λέγων | ὁ δὲ Πιλᾶτος πάλιν ἐπηρώτα αὐτὸν λέγων |
| οὐκ ἀποκρίνῃ οὐδὲν τί οὗτοί σου κατα μαρτυροῦσιν | οὐκ ἀποκρίνῃ οὐδέν; ἴδε πόσα σου κατηγοροῦσιν |
| ὁ δὲ ἐσιώπα καὶ οὐκ ἀπεκρίνατο οὐδέν | ὁ δὲ Ἰησοῦς οὐκέτι οὐδὲν ἀπεκρίθη |
| πάλιν ὁ ἀρχιερεὺς ἐπηρώτα αὐτὸν καὶ λέγει αὐτῷ σὺ εἶ ὁ Χριστὸς ὁ υἱὸς τοῦ εὐλογητοῦ | Καὶ ἐπηρώτησεν αὐτὸν ὁ Πιλᾶτος σὺ εἶ ὁ βασιλεὺς τῶν Ἰουδαίων |
| ὁ δὲ Ἰησοῦς εἶπεν ἐγώ εἰμι | ὁ δὲ ἀποκριθεὶς αὐτῷ λέγει σὺ λέγεις |

Of course within the original Greek text there are not any chapter breaks and therefore the text from chapter 14 to chapter 15 continues seamlessly. The author resumes the scene he left at Mark 14:65.

Καὶ εὐθὺς πρωΐ "as soon as it was morning" is one of Mark's favourite introductory phrases. The term is especially prominent earlier in the gospel (See Mark 1:3, 10, 12, 18, 20, 21, 23 etc.).

Πρωΐ adv. "early morning, in the morning, morning" could be used in general to mean "early" or specifically to refer to the fourth night watch (3 am to 6 am). In either case it was not unusual that proceedings like these took place very early in the morning.[214] Roman courts normally commenced

---

214. Donahue and Harrington, *Mark*, 430.

at sunrise.²¹⁵ The Sanhedrin was therefore eager to bring Jesus in front of the governor at the scheduled hour.²¹⁶

Pilate decided the matter in a *cognitio extra ordinem*,²¹⁷ i.e. an informal legal procedure often used by Roman governors when ordinary provincials were involved. The only accusation that could have been deserving of the death penalty would be a verdict of *seditio* (stirring up revolt).

Ἀπήωεγκαν καὶ παρέδωκαν Πιλάτῳ: This phrase has significance on two levels: firstly the fact that Jesus needed to be handed over to Pilate, for Pilate is the only person with jurisdiction over capital cases, and secondly it takes up the term that was used earlier in the Gethsemane narrative where Jesus is "handed over into the hands of sinners" (ἰδοὺ παραδίδοται ὁ υἱὸς τοῦ ἀνθρώπου εἰς τὰς χεῖρας τῶν ἁμαρτωλῶν, Mark 14:41). Παραδίδωμι "hand or give over, deliver up (pass. often be arrested); betray, deliver (to death); deliver, entrust, commit, give; hand down, pass on; commend." It also alludes to Isa 53:12: ὧν παρεδόθη εἰς θάνατον ἡ ψυχὴ αὐτοῦ καὶ ἐν τοῖς ἀνόμοις ἐλογίσθη καὶ αὐτὸς ἁμαρτίας πολλῶν ἀνήνεγκεν καὶ διὰ τὰς ἁμαρτίας αὐτῶν παρεδόθη.²¹⁸

Jesus is immediately questioned by Pilate: σὺ εἶ ὁ βασιλεὺς τῶν Ἰουδαίων "Are you the king of the Jews?" Bultmann argued that this question as well as Jesus's answer was a Markan addition.²¹⁹ As noted above, the focus of this account is not so much the historicity thereof, but the events narrated are shaped by apologetic motives. The apologetic perspective here is that Jesus is executed because he admitted that he was the "Messiah," which in Pilate's view was the same as "king of the Jews" and therefore that he did indeed pose a threat to the Roman authorities. The question posed by Pilate presupposes that the Jewish council informed Pilate of the charges against Jesus. Jesus answers with: σὺ λέγεις "you say so," which is an ambiguous answer. It is neither a denial, nor an affirmation.

Σὺ εἶ ὁ βασιλεὺς τῶν Ἰουδαίων: This is the first reference to Jesus as the "King of the Jews." This is a Roman designation, for Josephus describes how Mark Antony made Herod "King of the Jews."²²⁰ "Messiah," "Son of David," and "King of Israel" were Jewish designations. Pilate's address of Jesus as such suggested that he had someone more impressive in mind and was sur-

---

215. Cf. Seneca, *Ira* 2.7.3; and Sherwin-White, *Ancient Cos*, 45.

216. Boring, *Mark*, 418.

217. Collins, *Mark*, 700; cf. Evans, *Mark 8:27—16:20*, 443; see Berger, *Encyclopaedic Dictionary*; cf. Bauman, *Crime and Punishment*, 12-23.

218. Evans, *Mark 8:27—16:20*, 476.

219. Bultmann, *History*, 272.

220. Josephus, *B.J.* 1.144 §282.

prised to see someone of Jesus's calibre claiming this title. Jesus replies to Pilate's sarcasm with σὺλέγεις—it was Pilate who chose to address him as such and not Jesus. However, Jesus does not deny the title, but he does not prefer it, nor is it the evangelist's preferred Christology.[221] It is important to note that the title, ὁ βασιλεὺςτῶν Ἰουδαίων, is of Gentile origin.[222] The Jews themselves would have said: ὁ βασιλεὺςτῶν Ἰσραὴλ (cf. Mark 15:32). In Pilate's view Jesus is just another nationalist revolutionary who is rebelling against Roman law and order. Many similar figures featured in the troublesome years prior to and during the Jewish revolt of AD 66–70. Some Zealot leaders even claimed the title "king."[223] It is important to note that there is a transfer of the charge made against Jesus: the Sanhedrin accused Jesus of blasphemy, because of his claim to be the Christ, whereas "king of the Jews" is the Roman translation of this charge into political terms.[224] The Markan audience knows that Jesus is the Christ, the anointed, the eschatological king of the kingdom of God. They also understand that in Pilate's view Jesus did not claim to be the king of the Jews in a Davidic sense, since the Markan author was critical of such a title from the very beginning, whereas Jesus's response to the Sanhedrin whether he was the Christ was affirmative in no uncertain terms: ἐγώεἰμι. His response to Pilate, on the other hand, is somewhat evasive: σὺλέγεις. Jesus's answer could be interpreted in various ways: 1) the emphatic affirmative somewhat like the colloquial "you said it"; 2) as a denial "you say I am a king, I do not"; 3) as intended ambiguity in order to put the ball back in Pilate's court; 4) as non-committal, evasive and suggestive "you might put it that way"; 5) as corrective "king is your word, not mine, for what I claim and who I am" and 6) as a question "are you saying so?"[225] It seems that the same Jesus who commanded forthrightness from his followers when they were to appear in front of Roman courts (cf. Mark 13:9–13; 8:38) is now being coy. Yet the correct way to understand this is to say that Jesus cannot answer affirmatively to a question wrongly conceived. What is important for the narrative is the fact that Pilate does not comprehend Jesus's answer as being a clear "yes" and therefore finds no guilt in him. Pilate does not seem to be offended by Jesus's lack of courtesy and respect that governors would expect from provincials brought before

221. Evans, Mark 8:27—16:20, 478.

222. Boring, Mark, 419.

223. E.g., Simon, Athronges and Judas; cf. Josephus, A.J. 17.271–278; B.J. 2.4.3. 60–62.

224. Even though Herod Antipas wanted to claim the title "king of the Jews," he was hesitant to do so out of fear of Roman reprisals. When his wife finally persuaded him to petition Rome for the title, he was immediately banished to Gaul (Josephus, A.J. 18.8.2).

225. Collins, Mark, 715; cf. Catchpole, "Answer of Jesus."

them. Pilate states that others might have made claims that Jesus is the king of the Jews (Mark 5:12), but that Jesus himself did not. The narrative is not reporting history, nor is he making a psychological analysis, but he is simply arguing Christologically. The chief priests continued to make the charge against Jesus, even though he did not affirm it as was the case in Mark 14:62–64. This will be Jesus's last words before his crucifixion. Pilate, who is not familiar with the understanding of Jesus as the Suffering Servant, who is unjustly accused (cf. Isa 53:7) would have been amazed that Jesus did not even attempt to defend himself.

The statement κατηγόρουν αὐτοῦ οἱ ἀρχιερεῖς πολλά "the high priest accused him of many things" introduces a theme that will be developed extensively throughout the account namely that as far as Pilate was concerned, Jesus was innocent. Despite his innocence, Jesus was in the end condemned to death because of the pressure of the Jewish council and the crowds in Jerusalem.

Verses 4–5 depict Pilate's responsibility as a Roman court official in a legal proceeding to determine the facts and to give the accused an opportunity to respond to the charges made against him and to give a proper defence.[226] Normally the accused would make the most of this opportunity to defend himself. This is why Jesus's silence came as a surprise to Pilate. The narrator does not attempt to explain Jesus's lack of response, but in the light of the allusion to the Suffering Servant in Isa 53:7 (καὶ αὐτὸς διὰ τὸ κεκακῶσθαι οὐκ ἀνοίγει τὸστόμα ὡς πρόβατον ἐπὶσφαγὴν ἤχθη καὶ ὡς ἀμνὸς ἐναντίον τοῦ κείροντος ἄφωνος οὕτως οὐκ ἀνοίγει τὸ στόμα αὐτοῦ) the theological reasoning of the author becomes clear.

### Traditions–and Theological "Wirkungsgeschichtliches" Background

It is possible that the pre-Markan passion narrative already interpreted Isaiah's Suffering Servant in Messianic terms. It is however, just as probable that this is a Markan insight.[227]

Pilate's amazement could be an allusion to Isa 52:15 (οὕτως θαυμάσονται ἔθνη πολλὰ ἐπ' αὐτῷκαὶ συνέξουσιν βασιλεῖς τὸστόμα αὐτῶν ὅτι οἷς οὐκ ἀνηγγέλη περὶ αὐτοῦ ὄψονται καὶ οἳ οὐκ ἀκηκόασιν συνήσουσιν). The argument of this study is that the suffering servant-imagery forms the background of Marks Christological account. Pilate was amazed at Jesus refusal to defend himself for Roman law demanded a defence in order to prove innocence.

---

226. Collins, *Mark*, 716; cf. Sherwin-White, 1969, 25–26; no Sherwin-White entry for 1963.

227. Collins, *Mark*, 717; cf. Collins, *Beginning*, 494.

The account of Jesus silence was aimed at impressing Mark's audience for he displayed tranquillity and courage in the face of danger. Jesus is portrayed as a just man who faces death with nobility and stoic calm.[228]

Jesus's silence is also in contrast with Jewish and Christian martyrs, who used the occasion of their unjust deaths to make elaborate apologetic speeches (cf. 2–4 Macc; Acts 7). This poses the question of why Jesus did not speak a powerful and transforming word as, e.g., in Mark 1:16–29. The question could be answered that the narrator's concern here is not the powerful Son of God who acts divinely, but the truly human Jesus who accepts his suffering as the divine will. Jesus's silence therefore becomes an expression of Markan soteriology.[229]

### Social and Historical Context

This is the first reference to Pontius Pilate in the New Testament. He was the Roman governor of Judea during AD 26–37. Pilate's normal residence was in Caesarea Maritima, but for special fests and holidays he resided in Herod's palace in Jerusalem.[230]

One could engage in endless speculation about the picture the author of Mark draws of Pilate, especially because it radically differs from what is known from extra-biblical sources. Philo, e.g., calls him "merciless and obstinate."[231] Mark makes Pilate the helpless and almost pathetic pawn of the Jewish religious leaders. He is portrayed as yielding and decidedly weak.[232]

Jewish writers portray Pilate in a very negative light. Philo of Alexandria describes him as "a man of an inflexible, stubborn and cruel disposition" and wrote that this administration was marked by "briberies, insults robberies, outrages, wanton injuries, executions without trial and endless and supremely grievous cruelty."[233] Philo's remarks should be read against the backdrop of the incident of the golden shields that Pilate had placed in Herod's palace in Jerusalem. His remarks are politically motivated and most probably exaggerate the faults of Pilate transferred military standards bearing the image of the Roman emperor from Caesarea Maritima to Jerusalem.

---

228. Evans, *Mark 8:27—16:20*, 479.

229. Boring, *Mark*, 420.

230. Cf. Josephus *B.J.* 2.14.8 [301].

231. Extra-biblical sources portray Pilate as cruel and insensitive, hateful of the Jews and did not take the trouble to understand his Jewish subjects (cf. Josephus, *A.J.* XVIII 35 [ii.2]; 55–62 [iii.12]; 177–78 [vi.5]; *War II* 169–77 [ix.2-4]; Philo, *Legat.* 38).

232. Wilde, *Social Description*, 172.

233. Philo, *Embassy* 38§§301–2.

A large group of Jews went to Caesarea Maritima and protested that the standards should be removed. Because they were prepared to die for this cause, Pilate was completed to have the standards returned.[234] Josephus also accounted another incident where Pilate stole from the temple treasuring in order to fund a municipal project.[235]

Again the Jewish people offered resistance and protested. Pilate responded by sending in soldiers, dressed as civilians, who began to beat people with clubs which resulted in the killing of some and the injuring of many. However, Caiaphas, the high priest, and Pilate enjoyed each other's support.[236]

Mark highlights that Pilate, the official Roman governor of Palestine, the one with the actual power to inflict the death penalty on Jesus, finds no legal grounds for Jesus's execution. In Mark's narrative, Rome merely becomes an instrument in the hands of the Jewish religious leaders. Once again, it should be kept in mind that Mark is not concerned with historicity—he wants his audience to perceive his narrative in a certain way.

The Roman historian, Tacitus, affirms that Jesus was sentenced to death under the government of procurator Pontius Pilate.[237] However, to be called procurator was incorrect, because prior to AD 41 the Roman governors of Judea were prefects.

The author does not convey anything about the person or office of Pontius Pilate. We are to conclude that his audience was familiar with first century judicial procedures and might have heard something about the person of Pilate within the Christian tradition.[238]

In the Gospels, Pilate is called ἡγεμών ("governor; ruler, prince") cf. Matt 27:2; Luke 3:1) which generally designate "leader" or "governor" and could be the Greek equivalent of either procurator or prefect. A prefect was a military rank while a procurator was a civil office whose main concern was to protect the financial interests of the empire.

### Theological Implications

Allen argued that Jesus did claim to be the Messiah, but in a sense different from any current meaning attached to the title.[239] Jesus answers evasively, in

---

234  Josephus, *B.J.*2.9.2–3§§ 171–74; *Ant.* 18.3.1§§55–59.
235. Evans, *Mark 8:27—16:20*, 477; cf. Donahue and Harrington, *Mark*, 431.
236. Evans, *Mark 8:27—16:20*, 478.
237. Tacitus, *Ann.* 15.44.
238. Cf. Hengel, "Entstehungszeit," 13.
239. Allen, *St. Mark*, 182.

a similar way as to the question posed to him about paying taxes to Caesar (cf. Mark 12:16–17). Jesus avoids saying anything that would provide substantiation for a proper charge before the Roman governor. This portrayal of Jesus by Mark is probably within the framework of the author's recognition of the social reality that provincials needed to be very careful when appearing in front of representative of the Roman Empire.[240]

When Pilate uses this title "King of the Jews" the religious significance thereof is not the focus, but rather the political implication. This is necessary in order for Pilate to have solid grounds to find Jesus guilty of a crime deserving capital punishment. A mere religious quarrel among the Jews would not be worthy of such a punishment and the Roman authorities would not even bother to get involved. That which necessitated Roman intervention was the claim that Jesus did not recognise the authority of the Emperor and ultimately wished to become the ruler of the Jews. This interprets the Messianic claim in political terms. However, as clearly illustrated throughout the Gospel of Mark, such a claim could not be further from the truth. Jesus was never interested in establishing an earthly kingdom. On the contrary, he strongly opposed it. This is made abundantly clear by the entire passion narrative. God is not revealed in the demonstration of power and might, but in a seemingly helpless and weak crucifix. God's power comes to completion in human weakness.

But in order for the Jews to manipulate the Roman authorities into imposing the death penalty it had to be presented as if the kingdom of God, which Jesus is proclaiming, presented a direct threat to the Roman Emperor and was aimed at removing him from his seat of power. Such a claim would immediately enjoy the attention of the Roman authorities for it proposes a danger and a threat to law and order. It is even more dangerous when such a rebel claims that his mission is divinely ordained.[241]

The world rulers are able to put Jesus to death, divine power is able to resurrect him. The world rules do not have the final say about the outcome of the Easter events. In this way human power becomes relativised: God's sovereignty is absolute. Mark's portrayal of Pilate, as representative of the almighty Rome, is actually quite weak and powerless, for Pilate fails to prove Jesus's guilt. Yet he becomes the helpless pawn in the hands of the Jewish religious leaders. The violence he imposes on Jesus is injust. Pilate defies the essence of Roman law, because he is afraid of a Jewish unrest. Consequently, he convicts Jesus without any solid testimony. Pilate does nothing in order to prevent this injustice from happening.

240. Collins, *Mark*, 716.
241. Sommer, *Die Passionsgeschichte*, 164.

Jesus himself never accepts the title "king of the Jews." He responds to Pilate with σὺλέγεις, a highly evasive answer at best and far from Jesus's confession in Mark 14:62. The political expectation of the Messiah was that he would liberate the people from Roman oppression and lead them into a new era of independence. The episode in the passion narrative where Jesus appears before Pilate makes abundantly clear that this was not Jesus's intent. Jesus is not gathering an army around him and he is not protesting against the injustices his people have to endure. Instead, he remains quiet. His divine mission was not to fight but to suffer. His stance against the injustice of his time became evident in the fact that he calmly and patiently endured it. Jesus did not fight evil with evil, leading to greater injustice, but he took the evil of the entire world upon himself and conquered it. His mission was never to urge his people into fighting for their own salvation. Rather he was focussed upon taking the evil of the world upon himself. Once again Jesus illustrates that salvation is not a human accomplishment. Salvation is an act of God, a divine gift. The salvation that the Messiah brings did not constitute the political independence of Israel under a new Davidic king. It rather reveals the paradoxical mystery of the gospel namely a suffering Messiah. God is revealed in the suffering Jesus on the cross. The cross is no longer a symbol of godforsakeness, but God becomes vividly perceptible on the cross. In the words of Sommer: "Die Nähe Gottes zu dieser Welt zeigt sich am klarsten in der Passion Jesu."[242] Consequently, suffering in this world loses its meaning and becomes something preliminary.

## Christology as Foundation for Ethics

### First Peter 3:13–18

*Then, who will harm you, if you are followers of that which is good? But and if you suffer for righteousness' sake, you are indeed honored. And be not afraid of their terror, neither be troubled; But sanctify the Lord God in your hearts: and be ready always to answer to every man, who asks you a reason for the hope that is in you. But with gentleness and fear, have a good conscience so that they may be ashamed; They who speak evil of you, who slander your good behaviour in Christ. For it is better, that you suffer if the will of God wants it so, because you do good than you do evil. For Christ also has once suffered for sins, the just for the unjust, that he might bring us into the presence of God, being put to death in the flesh, brought to life by the Spirit.*

242. Sommer, *Die Passionsgeschicte*, 165.

## Literary and Discourse Analysis

Achtemeier opts for an understanding of the καὶ with which verse 13 opens not to be a copulative "and" but rather as "then."[243] The verse does not aim to make a statement about the absence of social rejection or even persecution, but the absence of a much worse circumstance, namely to be separated from God.[244]

According to Feldmeier the τίς that introduces the verse indicates a rhetorical question.[245] According to Elliott,[246] καὶ τίςὁ κακώσων ὑμᾶς constitutes a rhetorical question expecting a positive answer in terms of Gods favour which is bestowed upon those whose conduct is in accordance with God's will. Καὶ serves the function of linking the verse with the foregoing meaning: "in the light of what was said." Now, the evil which is done to believers by others/outsiders is in focus. Once again imagery from Isaiah's suffering servant song (cf. Isa 53:7 καὶ αὐτὸςδιὰ τὸκεκακῶσ θαιοὐκ ἀνοίγει τὸστόμα ὡς πρόβατον ἐπὶσφαγὴν ἤχθη καὶ ὡς ἀμνὸς ἐναντίον τοῦκείροντος αὐτὸνἄφωνος οὕτως οὐκ ἀνοίγει τὸστόμα αὐτοῦ) is employed.

Κακώσων nominative masculine singular future participle active ofκακόω"treat badly," "harm"; "be cruel and force (someone to do something") (Acts 7:19) occurs often in Acts in order to express the persecution of Christians, but its meaning here is probably a more general social hostility. The phrase τοῦ ἀγαθοῦ ζηλωταὶ γένησθε uses the word ζηλωτής, ου m "one who is zealous or eager" which in the LXX has the meaning of describing God as "jealous."[247] However, in Hellenistic Greek it is a fairly common term for describing to be ardent for moral ideals.[248] In our author's thought it probably has the meaning of being devoted to the good in order to live in accordance to God's will.'Ἐὰνwhich introduces the conditional clause makes clear that the promise is only applicable for those who became "zealots" for what is good—emphasizing zeal for behaving according to God's will. Being part of the Christian community has the condition of a certain "lifestyle" which is fitting for followers of Christ.[249]

Elliott is of the opinion that it is not possible that our author is referring to these revolutionists, the Zealots, as Reicke suggests.[250] It is rather the idea

243 Achtemeier, *1 Peter*, 229.
244. See Kelly, *Peter and Jude*, 140; Schelkle, *Die Petrusbriefe*, 11.
245 Feldmeier, *First Letter*, 193.
246 Elliott, *1 Peter: New Translation*, 619.
247. E.g., Exod 20:5; 34:14; Deut 4:24; 6:15.
248. Cf. Philo, *Somn*. 1.124.8.
249. Cf. Feldmeier, *First Letter*, 194.
250. Elliott, *1 Peter: New Translation*, 621, see Reicke, *New Testament*, 107.

of having zeal for the Law that our author has in mind. In fact revolutionary behaviour is the exact opposite of what the author wishes to encourage. Any kind of wrongdoing is not compatible with what is in accordance with the will of God.[251] However, doing what is right in accordance with the will of God could lead to unjust suffering.[252]

Verse 14 forms a chiasm with verse 13:

  **A** Καὶ τίς ὁ κακώσων ὑμᾶς

   **B** ἐὰν τοῦ ἀγαθοῦ ζηλωταὶ γένησθε

   **B** ἀλλ' εἰ καὶ πάσχοιτε διὰ δικαιοσύνην

  **A** μακάριοι

The author now addresses the predicaments which ultimately lead to the composition of the letter, namely the innocent suffering of Christians in spite of doing what is right.

Achtemeier also makes clear that although the author is not denying the possibility of persecution or even of violent persecution, which he views not only to be a possibility but in fact a reality (cf. 1 Pet 4:12–19),[253] in this verse he wants to emphasise that regardless of what form the harm being done to them my take, it cannot separate them from the divine grace they received in Jesus Christ. Feldmeier reads this verse in connection with 1 Pet 3:4: ὁ κρυπτὸς τῆς καρδίας ἄνθρωπος, indicating that in harmony with the rest of the letter, the "inner person of the heart" cannot be hurt, because that is the sphere protected by God and is precious to God.[254] The author makes this statement in order to encourage and console them to remain steadfast in the faith in the midst of the hostility they experience from those who did not accept the gospel.

Many exegetical questions are raised by the use of πάσχοιτε, second person plural present optative active, in verse 14 for it is possible that the optative disregards the possibility of suffering in this verse. According to Elliott, πάσχοιτε and εἰδέον (1 Pet 1:6) are optatives communicating what is desirable, namely good conduct even though it may lead to unjust suffering because suffering and abuse are already a reality of the recipients.[255] Their good conduct is not the result of their own achievement but because of the

---

 251. Cf. 1 Pet 2:15–16, 19–20; 3:11.

 252. 1 Pet 2:14.

 253 Achtemeier, *1 Peter*, 230.

 254. Feldmeier, *First Letter*, 193;cf. Kelly, *Peter and Jude*, 139; Schenke, *Passionsgeschichte des Markus*, 100; Beare, *First Epistle*, 162; Brox, *Petrusbrief* (1st ed.), 157.

 255. Elliott, *1 Peter: New Translation*, 622, cf. Danker, "1 Peter 1:24," 100.

vicarious death of Christ Elliott once again states that the suffering of the addressees is the result of "sporadic, local and unorganized" ostracism and abuse of their unbelieving neighbours.

Achtemeier explains it that, while suffering always remains a real possibility in the lives of his addressees, the author does not have insight in whether they undergo suffering at the time that he writes, or by the time that they will receive the letter. In order to express this sporadic reality, the author opted for the use of the optative.[256]

Διὰ δικαιοσύνην reinforces the theme of the letter of the suffering inflicted upon Christians because of their identity as Christians and because of their behaving accordingly, and not because of malevolent actions. Van Unnik associates δικαιοσύνη with the Christians's final break with evil. When suffering for the sake of righteousness, they are blessed, μακάριοι.[257] Feldmeier links this verse with a tradition also manifested in Matthew in the eight Beatitude of the Sermon on the Mount.[258]

Elliot states that in an eschatological context μακάριος has the meaning of the ultimate vindication of the upright.[259] Since the ancient Mediterranean societies were defined by the values of honor and shame. Μακάριος has the meaning of the group's judgement of an individual or group as honorable (cf. Ps 126:5). In the New Testament μακάριος occurs forty times to express the value judgement of an individual or group as honorable. Often in the New Testament as an expression by Jesus or early Christianity it often designates a challenge of conventional values. Jesus and early Christianity challenge the conventional idea that honor belongs to the wealthy and elite, and attribute honor to the poor and the socially marginalised. Once again this use of μακάριος echoes the Old Testament tradition of the suffering righteous (cf. Ps. 33 and Isa 52–53). Μακάριος is often translated as "blessed" or "happy," however as a confirmation of honor it should rather be translated as "honorable." A social scientific reading of the text would also suggest such a translation since honoring by God is contrasted with shame by the hostile neighbours.[260] Since the believers were elected by God they received a new status.[261]

What follows is a list of commands of how the Christians are to react to the innocent suffering that they are called to endure. Firstly the double

---

256. Achtemeier, *1 Peter*, 231.
257. Van Unnik, "Christianity," 83.
258 Feldmeier, *First Letter*, 194.
259. Elliott, *1 Peter: New Translation*, 623.
260. Cf. 1 Pet 2:4; 1 Pet 4:2.
261. Cf. 1 Pet 1:3—2:10.

prohibition of fear: μὴ φοβηθῆτε μηδὲ ταραχθῆτε "do not fear and do not be distressed." The second command is ἁγιάσατε, ἁγιάζω "set apart as sacred to God"; "make holy," "consecrate"; in order to express their fidelity to Christ. Then follows the explanation of how this fidelity is to be realised: ἕτοιμοι ἀεὶ πρὸς ἀπολογίαν παντὶ τῷ αἰτοῦντι ὑμᾶς λόγον περὶ τῆς ἐν ὑμῖν ἐλπίδος.

The Christian traditions that one should fear none but God and be willing to give witness to their faith under any circumstance could be traced back to the words of Jesus, but our author here relies on Isa 8:12–13:[262]

Isa 8:12b: τὸν δὲ φόβον αὐτοῦ οὐ μὴ φοβηθῆτε οὐδὲ μὴ ταραχθῆτε

1 Pet 3:14b: τὸν δὲ φόβον αὐτῶν μὴ φοβηθῆτε μηδὲ ταραχθῆτε

Isa 8:13: κύριον αὐτὸν ἁγιάσατε καὶ αὐτὸς ἔσται σου φόβος

1 Pet 3:15a: κύριον δὲ τὸν Χριστὸν ἁγιάσατε ἐν ταῖς καρδίαις ἡμῶν

The word φόβος, ουμ "fear," "terror"; "fear," "reverence (for God)"; "respect (for persons)" in this context refers to the addressees not having to fear the terrorisation of their unbelieving neighbours. However, this meaning is coherent with the use of the word in the rest of the letter to indicate "reverence" towards God. God is the only one that should be "feared" or "revered." If the Christian believer fears only God, no other should be feared. Verse 15 once again provides the positive interpretation of the preceding description of the reality of the addressees. Fear for anyone else is unnecessary, since Christ will be the one to decide their final fate. Feldmeier sees the author's dependence on Isa 8:12–13 as a Christological interpretation of Christ as "Lord."[263]

Ἁγιάσατε second person plural aorist imperative active of ἁγιάζω "set apart as sacred to God"; "make holy," "consecrate"; "regard as sacred"; "purify," "cleanse" as quoted from Isa 8:13 should be understood as living a life which is orientated by the will of God.

The phrase ἐν ταῖς καρδίαις ὑμῶν deepens the command, because for our author καρδίαι is the innermost centre of the human being (cf. 1 Pet 3:4) and also the source of Christian love for each other and this emphasises the sincerity and intensity of the command.[264] However, as the following part of the verse indicates, this is not a command to turn inward and to seclude themselves.

Λόγος, ου,m, of course has a broad range of meanings depending on the context: "word," "statement," "speech," "reason," etc. Elliott suggests that

---

262. Cf. Feldmeier, *First Letter*, 194; Elliott, *1 Peter: New Translation*, 624.

263. Feldmeier, *First Letter*, 195.

264. Feldmeier, *First Letter*, 195.

with the accompanying words περὶ τῆς ἐν ὑμῖν ἐλπίδος, a translation of "account" seems to fit best.[265] This fits with the same use of the word in 1 Pet 4:5. When these two texts are read in juxtaposition with one another it indicates the elevation of the believes and humiliation of the unbelievers: those who now require an account from the believers will ultimately be called to give and account before God: "of the hope that fills you": Christians are to give account of the ἐλπίς, ίδος f "hope" (that is the content of λόγον) that lives in them and not about their "faith." The author prefers "hope" because that is in his concern central to the Christian life. Their new life is orientated by the fate of Christ, which is in strong contrast to the futile ending of those who do not believe.[266] Achtemeier interprets the phrase ἐν ὑμῖν not to mean "within you" but "among you," because it is exactly this hope that binds the members of the Christian communities to one another.[267]

The author emphasises that it is the hope that live in the believers that ultimately distinguishes them from their unbelieving neighbours. The theme of the hopelessness of the unbelievers reoccurs in the New Testament (cf. 1 Thess 4:13; Eph 2:12). It is possible that this condition urged the unbelievers to inquire about the hope that defines the life of the believers. Hope seems to be the distinguishing characteristic which defines a believer's life on earth. This hope is grounded in the person of Jesus Christ (cf. Col 1:27; 1 Tim 1:1; Titus 2:13; 3:7). Hope is a prominent theme in 1 Peter as well.

Ἀπολογία, ας f "verbal defence," "defence" in combination with αἰτοῦντι ὑμᾶς λόγον "ask," "request," "require" or "demand" "an account" could present the idea that what the author has in mind here is the Christians's legal response when they are interrogated in front of a Roman magistrate. It is however also possible that the context that the author has in mind is that of a private dispute. Achtemeier prefers the latter interpretation because of the word πᾶς, πᾶσα, πᾶν without the article "each," "every (pl. all)"; πᾶς ὁ with ptc. "everyone who" which indicates a general application.[268] Any member of society could request from the believer why he or she does not confirm to the norms of society and why they do not participate in normal cultural and religious activities. Feldmeier sees a strong missionary intention here—the believers are required to bear witness to anyone and at any time.[269] For Feldmeier, ἀπολογία is an affirmation of the command not to live a life in separation, but to actively engage with

265. Elliott, *1 Peter: New Translation*, 628.
266 Feldmeier, *First Letter*, 196.
267. Achtemeier, *1 Peter*, 233.
268 Achtemeier, *1 Peter*, 233.
269 Feldmeier, *First Letter*, 195.

the unbelievers.[270] In the words of Goppelt: "This linguistic clothing shows an openness for the Hellenistic world."[271]

Verse 16 starts with an explanation of *how* this command is to be given. Christians are not to give account of their faith in an arrogant or aggressive manner. Rather, these accounts ought to remain in the same spirit as how Christians should respond to all other forms of suffering, namely free of any form of retaliation. Their account should be characterised by πραΰτης, ητος f "gentleness," "humility" and φόβος, ουm "reverence (for God)"; "respect."[272] Christian conduct *par excellence* is to be defined by "gentleness," as described by the teachings of Jesus (e.g., Matt 11:20). This is described in the words of Brox "the signature of Christian ethos."[273] Φόβος here does not mean "fear" but "reverence for God," also in the sense of being accountable before God; and "respect" for one's fellow human being. Gentleness and respect describe the way Christians should react to those who slander them.

The phrase συνείδησιν ἔχοντες ἀγαθήν provides further clarification. Ἔχοντες nominative masculine plural present participle active of ἔχω "have, hold, possess; keep" here has an adverbial meaning in order to describe and attribute that should be held by the Christians. Συνείδησιν ἀγαθήν "good conscience" describe the believers alliance to God which should determine all their other attributes. Nothing in their response should be of such a nature that it compromises their good conscience before God. They are not to be guilty of any words unworthy of their belonging to God even if they are provoked by cruel interrogators. The purpose of this attitude is explained by the rest of verse 16, following the ἵνα: ἐν ᾧ καταλαλεῖσθε κατα ισχυν θῶσιν οἱἐπηρεάζ οντες ὑμῶν τὴν ἀγαθὴν ἐν Χριστῷ ἀναστροφήν. Achtemeier understands ἐν ᾧ to mean "when" or "whenever."[274] The passive καταλαλεῖσθε has as subject those who speak evil of the believers because they insult their conduct: οἱ ἐπηρεάζοντες. Achtemeier further argues that καταλαλεῖσθε and ἐπηρεάζοντες indicate that what evil that the author has in mind here is not as severe and life-threatening, but mere social hostility although the cruelty thereof should not be underestimated.[275] The social hostility is caused by what the author describes as ἀγαθὴνἐν Χριστῷ "good in Christ." Although much of Christian behaviour could be considered to be good in terms of Greco-Roman morality, the phrase ἐν Χριστῷ qualifies the particular

270 Ibid.
271 Goppelt, *Der erste Petrusbrief*, 236.
272 Cf. Feldmeier, *First Letter*, 196.
273 Brox, *Petrusbrief* (1st ed), 161.
274 Achtemeier, *1 Peter*, 237.
275 Ibid., 236.

behaviour of Christians grounded in their identity. Achtemeier interprets ἐν Χριστῷ as a dative of sphere, namely to act and think within the sphere of Christ's influence.[276]

It can safely be concluded that what is in focus in these verses is an "informal vilification"[277] and not a proper legal proceeding, which can be disregarded as soon as the proper content of the Christian faith is illuminated.

Verse 17 opens with γὰρ in order to indicate that what follows is related to the previous verses. The purpose is to assure the addressees that the behaviour which is insulted by their non-believing neighbours is indeed good and not evil, because it flows from their conviction in the Christian faith and cannot by the ethical standards of the Greco-Roman world be ruled out as evil. Indeed, the idea that it is better to suffer evil that to cause evil was well-known among Greco-Roman moralists.[278] Feldmeier shows how this wisdom was adapted by Justin in his apology in order to state that the social rejection, discrediting and persecution of Christians are indeed rejections of righteousness.[279] As far as our author is concerned the adaption of this wisdom could have to implications: firstly, that it is a Christian reflection and therefore reinterpretation of a well-known wisdom within the Greco-Roman philosophy, and secondly, as having eschatological implications namely that it is better to suffer now at the hands of human beings than to suffer at God's hands because of their denial of their faith.[280] The command given to the slaves in 1 Pet 2:20 is now given to the entire Christian community.

The verse is however elevated beyond a mere confirmation of a well-known Greco-Roman wisdom, because "good" in the Christian, and especially in our author's sense, is acting in accordance to God's will and not simply to follow socially accepted norms and morals.[281] In accordance with 1 Pet 4:15–16, the addressees are not to provide their opponents with reasons for hostile response by committing evil of any kind. They can testify to their hope only when their hope is consistent with their behaviour. Christians are able to endure suffering precisely because of the possibilities their hope offers them through Christ's resurrection, because it provides them with new perspectives far beyond their current realities.

276. Ibid.
277. Ibid.
278. E.g., Plato, Gorg.474B; Cicero, Tusc. 5.56: "*accipere quam facere praestat iniuriam,*" "It is preferable to accept rather to inflict injustice." Translation by Achtemeier, 1 Peter, 237.
279. Feldmeier, First Letter, 197; cf. Justin, Apol. 5.3f.
280. Cf. Michaels, 1 Peter.
281. Cf. Vanhoye, "1 Pierre," 123.

Εἰ θέλοι τὸ θέλημα τοῦ θεοῦ: forms a conditional clause and involves an optative—θέλοι third person singular present optative active of θέλω "wish, desire, want; will; like." Here once again the author's literary genius is at work. Furthermore Christian suffering is linked to the will of God. Often suffering serves as a divine testing of the purity of faith.

In agreement with Achtemeier this study opts for the former because of the author's familiarity with such ethical reasoning (cf. 1 Pet 2:20; 4:15–16); the absence of a polarity between the judgement of humans and of God within the preceding verses and the fact that γὰρ links this verse with the preceding two verses.[282] An eschatological undertone throughout the letter cannot be denied, but that is not the primary focus in this verse. Rather Achtemeier understands verse 17 to form an inclusio with verse 14a, namely that those who suffer for doing good are blessed and in verse 17 that it is better to suffer for doing good than to be the cause of evil.[283] It should be noted that in both cases it is God's evaluation that carries the greater weight and not that of humans.

The ὅτι with which verse 18 opens is causal in order to provide a reason for what is stated in the preceding four verses.[284] Ἅπαξ adv. "once," "one time"; "once for all time" here has the latter meaning of "once and for all" in order to refer to the uniqueness of Christ's redemption and the significance of his passion.[285] This is confirmed by the rest of the verse: περὶ ἁμαρτιῶν ἔπαθεν, δίκαιος ὑπὲρ ἀδίκων. Whether the phrase communicates an absolute and final break with sin accomplished by Jesus's passion that does not need to be repeated in future, or refer to the contrast between the custom of sacrifice in the Old Testament literature which needed constant repetition and Christ's sacrifice which was a complete sacrifice pleasing to God[286] is not of importance because in both cases the emphasis is on the uniqueness of Christ's passion.[287] The reference to the suffering of Christ also includes his death as is highlighted by the use of θανατωθεὶς.

The point of Christ's innocent suffering is further explained by the ἵνα-clause that follows: ἵνα ὑμᾶς προσαγάγῃ τῷ θεῷ. The purpose of Christ suffering was in order to lead the unrighteous to God. Προσάγω trans. "bring to or before"; intrans. "come near" also describes access to God.[288] Christ's

---

282. Achtemeier, *1 Peter*, 237.
283. Ibid., 238.
284. Cf. Vogels, *Christi Abstieg*, 19.
285. Cf. Feldmeier, *First Letter*, 201.
286. E.g., Heb 7:27; 9:12, 26, 28; 10:10, cf. Bigg, *St. Peter and St. Jude*, 159.
287. Achtemeier, *1 Peter*, 247.
288. Cf. Rom 5:2; Eph 2:17.

redemption made access to God, which was denied by sin, possible. The two participia θανατωθεὶς and ζῳοποιηθεὶς presents a contrast.

Θανατωθεὶςμὲν σαρκὶ is clear to explain: it confirms that Christ has indeed died in the flesh on the cross. The second clause ζῳοποιηθεὶς δὲπνεύματι is less clear. This lead to much discussion about how and in what form Christ was actually made alive. Normally the word ζῳοποιέω "give life to," "make alive" is associated in the New Testament with Christ's resurrection.[289] It is also used in the Hellenistic-Jewish sphere in order to indicate the creative power of God. And the contrast between Christ's death and his being made alive is usually associated with the death on the cross and the resurrection.[290] There is a second contrast present in σαρκι and πνεύματι. This contrast is commonly used in the New Testament to refer to two modes of living: the one sinful, the other after effected by the righteousness made possible by God's salvation.[291] The biblical understanding of the contrast between σαρκι and πνεύματι, is however not reconcilable with the Hellenistic understanding of "body" and "spirit" to be to opposing and excluding aspects. Rather it describes to forms of behaviour: the one driven by the desire of the flesh and the second driven by the sanctification made possible by the Holy Spirit.

The description of the dative used in σαρκι and πνεύματι presents another problem. Many scholars are convinced of a dative of sphere in order to express to spheres of life: the one the human existence and the other made possible by the Spirit.[292] It could however also be an adverbial dative, i.e. a dative describing Christ's death as within the flesh and his being made alive within the Spirit.[293] Achtemeier however opts for a dative of instrument indicating that Christ was risen by the Spirit of God as is often stated in the New Testament.[294] This would have the implication that Christ was put to death by humans, but made alive by the divine Spirit. This is consisted with the author's emphasis on God's evaluation contra the evaluation of humans. Just as Christ was disregarded and rejected by humans, the same will happen to his followers. But as Christ was made alive by the Spirit of God, so his followers will receive eternal life. Such an interpretation also allows for

289. E.g., John 5:21; Rom 4:17; 8:11; 1 Cor 15:22; Eph 2:5; Col 2:13.

290. Cf. Feldmeier, *First Letter*, 201.

291. E.g., Matt 26:41; Mark 14:38; Luke 24:39; John 3:6; Rom 1:4; 8:4, 5, 6, 9, 13; Gal 3:3; 4:29; 5:16–19 etc.

292. Cf. Kelly, *Peter and Jude*, 151; Best, *1 Peter*, 139; Brox, *Petrusbrief* (1st ed.), 170; Goppelt, *Der erste Petrusbrief*, 246.

293. Cf. Selwyn, *The First Epistle*, 196.

294. Achtemeier, *1 Peter*, 250; e.g., Acts 3:15; 4:10; Rom 10:9; 1 Cor 6:14; Gal 1:1; 1 Thess 1:10.

the possibility of a bodily resurrection, because the resurrection is described in terms of the way that it has been brought about and not in terms of the sphere within which it occurred.[295]

Verse 18 wants to communicate a ground of basis for the addressees' confidence that although their current circumstance indicates a different reality, Christ conquered all opposing powers and faithful Christians will share in this glory. The verse is concerned with the uniqueness of Christ's passion and not so much with the ethical implications that this has for the followers of Christ.

Ότι καὶ Χριστὸς ἅπαξ περὶ μαρτιῶν ἔπαθεν: The Christological foundation introduces the unit starting with ὅτι. Verse 18-22 provides the Christological basis for the foregoing exhortation in 3:13-17. Jesus Christ is the ultimate model to be followed. It should further be noted that the vicarious nature of Christ's death as well as the atonement established because of his death is highlighted. Ἵνα ὑμᾶς προσαγάγῃ τῷ θεῷ θανατω θεὶς μὲν σαρκὶ ζῳοποιηθεὶς δὲ πνεύματι forms a purpose clause in order to express the result of Christ's suffering, as well as its savings consequences which forms the basis for Christian conduct.

Ἅπαξ underscores the singular, comprehensive and conclusive aspect of the suffering of Christ.[296] Δίκαιος ὑπὲρ ἀδίκων: Once again the vicarious nature of Christ's death is emphasized. δίκαιος meaning the one obedient to the will of God (cf. 2:21-25) once again recalls the suffering servant imagery of Isaiah 53. Christ is therefore portrait as "righteous," "innocent" and "obedient" to the will of God. These attributes ought to be imitated by believers.[297]

Ὑπὲρ ἀδίκων: This contrasts the innocence of Christ with the unrighteousness of those he suffered for. Ἀδίκων adjective genitive masculine plural no degree of ἄδικος, ον "evil, sinful; dishonest, unjust" equals all human activity which is not consisted with the will of God. Although the phrase only occurs here in the Bible it echoes Isaiah's suffering servant who was righteous and faithful to the will of God. Here we also find traces of Israel's martyr theology claiming that the martyrs who give their lives for the sins of many will please God in such a manner that He will not judge them according to their sins.[298] Ἵνα ὑμᾶς προσ αγάγῃ τῷ θεῶ expresses the result or consequence of Christ's vicarious death, namely to unite believers with God.

---

295. Achtemeier, *1 Peter*, 250.
296. Cf. Heb 3:26, 28; 9:12; 10:10; Rom 6:9-10.
297. Elliott, *1 Peter: New Translation*, 641.
298. Cf. Lohse, *Märtyr*, 67-68.

The personal nature of this act of God is highlighted—it was precisely for the sake of the addressees.[299]

Προσαγάγῃ third person singular aorist subjunctive active of προσάγω trans. "bring to or before"; intrans. "come near" occurs rarely in the New Testament[300] and in the LXX.[301] In this sense it should be understood as providing "access" to God. Christ's suffering was therefore aimed at uniting believers with God. This was the ultimate goal of the suffering and resurrection of God according to 1 Peter.

### Traditions–and Theological "Wirkungsgeschichtliches" Background

The phrase περὶ ἁμαρτιῶν is familiar to the Septuagint's description of an offering provided to reconcile the sin of the people.[302] The same use is also familiar to other New Testament writings.[303] The phrase περὶ ἁμαρτιῶν is familiar to New Testament tradition and also descriptive of Christ as the "Righteous one."[304] This explains why Christ's passion was unique because as the "Righteous One" he did not have to repent his own sin.[305] This is consistent with the Old Testament idea of sacrifice. The death of a righteous person has atoning value for others and could be referred back to the Jewish martyr-theology present in 4 Macc 6:28 and 2 Macc 7:37. This verse also echoes the "impeccability" of the sacrificial lamb, descriptive of the inheritance reserved for believers.[306] The ἀδίκων in this case refers to the addressees which recently converted to the Christian faith. For them, who were previously unrighteous, Christ died as the Righteous One. The emphasis on righteousness by presenting it in contrast with unrighteousness reinforces the intention of the author that the promise is only valid for those who suffer for the sake of righteousness.

---

299. Elliott, *1 Peter: New Translation*, 642.
300. Cf. Matt 18:24; Luke 9:41; Acts 12:6; 16:20; 27:27.
301. Exod 29; 10; Lev 1:2.
302. E.g., Lev 5:6–7; 6:23; Ezek 43:21.
303. E.g., Rom 8:3; Heb 10:26; 1 John 2:2.
304. E.g., Matt 5:45; Acts 24:15.
305. Cf. Goldstein, "Die Kirche," 48.
306. Cf. 1 Pet 1:19.

## Social and Historical Context

Achtemeier notes that the command to give account of their faith is in strong contrast to other esoteric religious groups in the Greco-Roman world.[307] Such a disclosure of the content of their practices would have been considered to be betrayal to their communities and their gods. Christians, on the contrary, had to remain open for such discussion. This conversation and dialogue is encouraged by the author as in continuation of what it means to do good. Isolation is not desired by our author. Rather Christians should not be ashamed of their new identity, but actively engage with their hostile neighbours and remain performing their daily duties.

As noted earlier, the explanation described in verses 15 to 16 could fit a general dispute or an interrogation by a Roman court. From Pliny's correspondence with Trajan it is clear that he as governor did question, convict and punish Christians even with death.[308] Pliny does not mention anything about the content of the Christians' faith, but rather he punished them because of their stubbornness. As far as the content of the faith is concerned, Pliny only views Christianity to be a perverse superstition that spread like wild fire throughout the Empire, including cities and rural villages and that people's conversion to this belief caused them to refrain from attending Roman temples and Roman festivals. They also did not purchase meat at the markets any longer. It is difficult to determine whether it was the way that the Christians answered the questions that determined their fate or whether it was their refusal to renounce their faith. Achtemeier regards the matter as follows: "Given the total context of Pliny's letter, and his expressed view of the Christian's faith as an obnoxious superstition that threatened the Roman way of life and hence its hegemony in Asia Minor, it is not likely that a less obnoxious defence by the Christians of their persistence in holding the faith and refusing to recant would have spared them the death sentence."[309] This is confirmed by Trajan's response: those Christians who refused to recant and to worship the Roman gods were to be punished, regardless of the way in which they answered the questions.

## Theological Implications

The author is not responding to suffering for the sake of righteousness in general, but actual suffering and he wants to convey God's grace in this

---

307. Achtemeier, *1 Peter*, 234.
308. Cf. Sherwin-White, *Fifty Letters*.
309. Achtemeier, *1 Peter*, 235.

particular situation. This is repeated in a slightly different form in 1 Pet 4:14. Therefore, verse 14 does not contradict verse 13, but explains it. The statement that nothing can harm those who are zealous for performing the will of God, is confirmed by the statement that they will be blessed indeed when they suffer in being faithful to God's will. They are therefore ultimately blessed and not harmed. The sharp contrast between God's evaluation and the evaluation of their hostile neighbours should be noted. Ultimately what is of significance is how God sees them.

Here we find a clear example of the author's ethics at work. Christological substantiation serves as foundation for the author's moral exhortation. The narrative of Christ is placed in the centre namely his innocent suffering on behalf of others but especially his vindication by God, his resurrection, ascension, exaltation to the right hand of God. Therefore it is possible for believers to be placed in relationship with God. Within this pericope Israelite and early Christian traditions merge, in a manner unparalleled in the New Testament.[310]

## Mark 14:32–42

*And they went to a place called Gethsemane. And he said to his disciples, "Sit here while I pray." And he took Peter and James and John with him, and began to be greatly distressed and troubled. And he said to them, "My soul is very sorrowful, even to death. Remain here and keep watch." And going a little farther, he fell on the ground and prayed that, if it were possible, the hour might pass him by. And he said, "Abba, Father, all things are possible for you. Take this cup away from me. Yet do not what I will, but what you will." And he came and found them sleeping, and he said to Peter, "Simon, are you asleep? Could you not keep watch for one hour? Watch and pray that you may not enter into temptation. The spirit indeed is willing, but the flesh is weak." And again he went away and prayed, saying the same words. And again he came and found them sleeping, for their eyes were very heavy, and they did not know what to answer him. And he came the third time and said to them, "Are you still sleeping and resting? It is enough; the hour has come. The Son of Man is delivered into the hands of sinners. Rise, let us go; Behold, my betrayer is near."*

---

310. Elliott, *1 Peter: New Translation*, 638.

### Literal and Narratological Analysis

The Gethsemane-episode functions as a bridge between his arrival at the Mount of Olives (Mark 14:26-31) after the Last Supper and his betrayal by Judas and his consequent arrest. The whole pericope emphasises Jesus humanity as well as the weakness of his disciples. Jesus goes to Gethsemane to pray and then we learn about the content of his prayer. Mark firstly offers the content of the prayer in indirect speech and then in direct speech. Mark emphasises Jesus personal distress and emotional agony by employing ἐκθαμβεῖσθαι present infinitive passive of ἐκθαμβέομαι "be greatly surprised or alarmed; be greatly distressed" and ἀδημονεῖν present infinitive active of ἀδημονέω "be distressed or troubled" and then with an echo of an Old Testament lament Psalm (Ps 42:5, 11; 43:5). The second sequence concerns Jesus's struggle to accept what is about to happen to him, first by praying that the hour might pass away for him and then by delivering himself into the hands of his father.

In Mark 14:35-42 Jesus parts with his disciples three times to go pray and every time he returns, he finds his disciples asleep. Mark singles Peter out for criticism (Mark 14:37), because Peter was the one who claimed moments earlier that he would never betray Jesus even if the other disciples did. He, who boasted that he would never become apostate, could not even stay awake for one hour. The threefold proof of Peter's weakness prepares us for his following threefold denial (Mark 14:66-72). Despite his disciples' weakness and the fact that they indeed entered into temptation (Mark 14:38), he still asks them in Mark 14:42 to accompany him on his way to Cavalry.

Mark's fondness of triades becomes evident in the links he establishes between the Gethsemane-episode and the three predictions of Jesus passion.[311] In contrast to the transfiguration episode which highlights the divine aspects of Jesus's character, the Gethsemane-episode shows the fragile, human aspects of his character.[312]

The Gethsemane narrative was most probably the first chapter in the pre-Markan passion narrative, but in its current form was heavily edited by the author.[313] It is the first time in the Gospel that Jesus is portrayed as having distress or anxiety in the face of his impending suffering and death. Here the humanity of Jesus and his human weakness are explicitly expressed.

In contrast to Jesus's miracle working power and confidence in the power of faith expressed earlier in the Gospel, here Jesus's human weakness

---

311. Mark 8:31; 9:31; 10:33-34.

312. Donahue and Harrington, *Mark*, 411; cf. Boring, *Mark*, 397.

313. Collins, *Mark*, 673; cf. Schenke, *Passionsgeschichte des Markus*, 353, 360-62, 562; Collins, *Beginning of the Gospel*, 106-7; Feldmeier, *Der Krisis*, 111-12, 126-27.

is emphasised. According to Dibelius the scene does not "bear witness to disillusionment, for then it would not have been accepted into the Gospel at all, but to a certain understanding of revelation. Like the entire Markan Passion it is orientated not psychologically, but soteriologically."[314] Dibelius concluded that the Gethsemane narrative is unhistorical, because there are no witnesses to "the essential part of the scene, since the witnesses are asleep."[315] Contrary to Bultmann,[316] Dibelius is convinced that the story never circulated independently, but that it was found in a passion source used by Mark.[317]

The Gethsemane narrative serves as an introduction to Mark's extensive account of the Passion of Jesus which is about to take place. This was probably already the case in its pre-Markan form.[318] On the other hand Werner Kelber argued that Mark was the "sole creator and composer of the Gethsemane story, relying at best upon a minimal core of tradition."[319] Kelber based his argument on the grounds that the "kerygmatic force" of the passage is a matter of "discipleship theology" and this theology is defined as the "incorrigible blindness of the disciples."[320] In a later article Kelber argued that with the Gethsemane story Mark makes two important theological points:[321] 1) "Jesus's plea for release from the Passion" which "raises the question whether he will live out the truth of the Gospel of the Kingdom which is contingent upon his suffering and death"[322] and 2) "The disciples' continuing lack of understanding," which marks "a pivotal point on their collision course with Jesus."[323]

The author was compelled to force Jesus "to the brink of recanting his passion identity because the Evangelist deals with Christians who are indifferent or hostile towards a suffering Messiah."[324]

---

314. Dibelius, *From Tradition*, 211.

315. Ibid., 211.

316. Bultmann, *History*, 267.

317. Collins, *Mark*, 674; cf. Dibelius, *From Tradition*, 212.

318. Cf. Collins, *Beginning of the Gospel*, 107; Schenke, *Passionsgeschichte des Markus*, 551–52.

319. Kelber, "Conclusion," 166.

320. Ibid., 176, 180.

321. Ibid., 160.

322. Ibid., 46.

323. Ibid., 53.

324. Ibid., 59.

The name Γεθσημανὶ probably means "oil press."[325] The Mount of Olives was traditionally associated with prayer[326] and it was the place where God would appear in judgement (Zech 14:4). The name is derived from the Aramaic meaning "oil press."[327]

Καὶ λέγει τοῖς μαθηταῖς αὐτοῦ καθίσατε ὧδε ἕως προσεύξωμαι: The Gospel of Mark narrates that Jesus often prayed or gave instruction on prayer (cf. Mark 1:35; 6:46; 9:29; 11:17; 11:24–25; 12:46; 13:18).

Καθίσατεῶ δε ἕως προσεύξωμαι "Sit here while I pray" is probably a Markan insertion which prepares the reader for the remark that he took Peter, James and John with him. This addition is probably Markan because of Mark's fondness of separating these three disciples from the rest of the twelve.

Καὶ παραλαμβάνει τὸν Πέτρον καὶ[τὸν] Ἰάκωβον καὶ[τὸν] Ἰωάννην μετ' αὐτοῦ: It happened three times before that Jesus took these three disciples, Peter, James and John with him in separation: in Mark 5:37–43 where they witnessed the healing of the daughter of Jaïrus, in Mark 9:2–8 where they witnessed the transfiguration of Jesus and heard the voice of God and in Mark 13:37 where they were instructed about the end times. Jesus wishes these three to accompany him because he wants to instruct them until the end. It is also possible that Jesus wanted to have witnesses with him because of what lies ahead.[328]

The emotional state of Jesus is described with the words: ἐκθαμβεῖσθαικαὶ ἀδημονεῖν "greatly distressed and troubled."Καὶ ἤρξατο ἐκθαμβεῖσθαικαὶ ἀδημονεῖν: This is the only time in the New Testament where ἐκθαμβεῖσθαι, present infinitive passive of ἐκθαμβέομαι "be greatly surprised or alarmed; be greatly distressed," is used with Jesus as its subject.[329]

Περίλυπός ἐστιν ἡ ψυχή μου ἕως θανάτου. The word περίλυπος, ον "very sad, deeply distressed" appears only here and in Mark 6:26 in the Gospel. In 6:26 it describes the emotion of Herod Antipas when he realised that his stepdaughter's request will result in the death of John the Baptist.

Μείνατε second person plural aorist imperative active of μένω "remain, stay, abide; live, dwell; last, endure, continue; trans. await, wait for" and γρηγορεῖτε second person plural aorist imperative active of γρηγορέω "be or keep awake; watch, be alert; be alive": The fact that the present tense

---

325. Cf. Thorsen, "Gethsemane," 997–98.
326. Cf. Ezek 11:23; 2 Sam 15:32.
327. Cf. Donahue and Harrington, *Mark*, 407.
328. Cf. Deut 17:6; 19:15; Evans, *Mark 8:27—16:20*, 405.
329. Evans, *Mark 8:27—16:20*, 406.

is used adds weight to the command. γρηγορέω is used three times in the eschatological discourse in 13:34, 35, 37.

Gundry is of the opinion that the meaning here is that Jesus wanted his disciples to act as vigilantes in order to provide him with a warning in advance when his enemies approach.[330] This is in sharp contrast with the accounts of the martyrdoms and deaths of the Maccabean heroes, or famous Greeks and Romans, who amidst danger and suffering displayed great composure and courage.[331]

After the narrator's description of Jesus's anguished state, Jesus now speaks directly: περίλυπός ἐστινή ψυχή μου ἕως θανάτου μείνατε ὧδεκαὶ γρηγορεῖτε. "My soul is exceedingly sorrowful, until death." This statement of Jesus recalls the refrain of an individual lament found in Pss 41:6, 12; 42:5.[332] This phrase also occurs in Jonah 4:9. The effect of the citation of the Psalms is that Jesus becomes the speaker of the traditional lament, which is very important for the passion theology of Mark.[333]

After Jesus's personal lament, the typical Markan separation of Peter, James and John occurs as Jesus asks them to stay awake with him. Kelber draws attention to the fact that γρηγορέω "be or keep awake; watch, be alert; be alive" occurs in Mark only in the parable of the doorkeeper and here in the Gethsemane-scene.[334] Kelber's conclusion was that the disciples's falling asleep and their failure to stay awake and remain watchful had eschatological repercussions. The use of γρηγορέω in the two passages are quite different. The first in Mark 13:33-37 is indeed an eschatological context, for it refers to a time when Jesus is absent and the disciples must stay alert in order to be prepared for the glorious return of the Son of Man. In the Gethsemane narrative Jesus is present in all his humanity; he is distressed and anxious. It is a much more existential appeal to the disciples and especially his leading disciples to stay awake in order to provide comfort and support. Although the nearness of these three disciples are important to the suffering Jesus, he leaves them at a distance to pray alone. It is therefore only the omniscient narrator who is able to report what Jesus is saying in his prayer.

The narrator states that Jesus fell on his face unto the ground; a gesture that indicates a highly emotional state.[335] Jesus hopes that he might escape

---

330. Gundry, 1993, 845.
331. Collins, *Mark*, 675; cf. Cullmann, *Christology*, 9-53.
332. Collins, *Mark*, 676; cf. Gerstenberger, *Psalms 1*, 9-10, 11-14, 174.
333. Cf. Hays, "Christ Prays," 125-26.
334. Kelber, "Conclusion," 48-49; see Mark 13:33-37.
335. Collins, *Mark*, 677.

this severe experience and what it will pass him by παρέλθῃ third person singular aorist subjunctive active of παρέρχομαι "pass, pass by."[336]

The narrator now reports the prayer of Jesus. Προσηύχετο ἵνα εἰ δυνατόν ἐστινπαρέλθῃ ἀπ'αὐτοῦἡ ὥρα, "he prayed that if it was possible that the hour might pass away from him." In his prayer to be spared the "hour" Jesus seeks to avoid the suffering and death that he has announced to his disciples earlier. The "hour" refers to the time when the Son of Man is to be delivered into the hands of sinners.[337] The meaning of this is twofold: On the surface the deliverance refers to Jesus's arrest and his being taken into custody. On a deeper theological level the "hour" becomes symbolic of the entire passion of Jesus and the realisation of the eschatological moment when Jesus dies on the cross and he is acknowledged as the true son of God. "Hour" is the fulfilment of the prophecies of Jesus in Mark 8:31; 9:31; 10:33–34.

The summary of the prayer in indirect speech in verse 35 εἰδυνατόνἐστιν contrasts with the direct speech in verse 36: πάντα δυνατά σοι. Now the prayer is reported in direct speech: Αββαό πατήρ, πάντα δυνατάσοι παρένεγκε τὸ ποτήριον τοῦτο ἀπ' ἐμοῦ ἀλλ' οὐ τί ἐγὼ θέλωἀλλὰ τί σύ. "Abba, Father, all things are possible for you: take away this cup from me, nevertheless not what I want, but what you want."

Καὶ ἔλεγεν: It was common in antiquity that prayers were said aloud. Silent prayers were frowned upon (1 Sam 1:12–16 where the priest Eli mistakes Hannah's silent prayer for drunkenness.)

Αββα is the Greek transliteration of the Aramaic vocative form of אב "father." Joachim Jeremias argued that the use of αββα was unique to Jesus, since the term does not occur in contemporary Jewish texts or prayers.[338] Jeremias argued that the word was central to Jesus's teaching and that it was an expression of the intimacy Jesus shared with God the Father, because of the origin of the word in a young child's address of his father. It is the only occurrence of αββα in the Gospels. The only other occurrences in the entire New Testament are Gal 4:6 and Rom 8:15. Both these forms occur here in the vocative. Jesus's manner of speaking and his address of God as his father in prayer have been the cause of great debate among scholars often with reference to the work of Jeremias. In a series of studies, Jeremias claimed that Jesus was first to address God in this way.[339] Jeremias also became famous for his claim that αββα is the word used by children to address their fathers

---

336. Evans, *Mark 8:27—16:20*, 411.

337. Collins, *Mark*, 678; cf. Kelber, "Conclusion," 44; Collins, *Beginning of the Gospel*, 106–7.

338. Jeremias, "Abba," 15–67.

339. Jeremias, "Prayers of Jesus," 96.

and could therefore be legitimately translated as "daddy."[340] However, this view was recently challenged.[341] Jesus's use of αββα was not unique and it did not imply a unique sense of divine Sonship. It was however distinctive and somewhat unconventional. This distinctiveness is one of the reasons why it could be regarded as authentic.[342] The problem is that Jeremias relied on Rabbinic and Targumic material which originated after the New Testament and does therefore not reflect the language and conventions of first century Palestine. Presedence should however be given to earlier sources and references to God being addressed as Father found in Scripture itself.[343] Furthermore, Jesus distinctive usage is reflected not only in the Gospels but also in the Pauline literature. From this we may conclude that this style of addressing made a deep impression on the early Christians. Grassi suggests that Paul's use of this form emphasised Christian kinship and obedience to God and this may be useful in our interpretation of Jesus prayer in Gethsemane.[344] Viewed in this manner Jesus's address indicates filial obedience. Jesus is faced with a severe test of his commitment to the will of God. When Jesus then cries out: "Abba! Father," and moments later verbalises his willingness to submit to the will of God, it is indicative of this filial obedience. Furthermore the echo of Gen 22:1–19 is heard in Isaac's similar willingness to obey the will of his father even if it meant death.

It could be that Jesus used the term, but it is impossible to say for certain whether this address of God does indeed go back to the historical Jesus, because, as noted above, Jesus's prayer in direct speech took place in private. Therefore at most, the term is a representation of what the author of the pre-Markan passion narrative, or, if redactional, Mark himself, imagined the prayer to be.

Πάντα δυνατάσοι: This statement is both a request and a confession: a request that Jesus may be spared this terrible suffering and a confession of faith in God's omnipotence and that everything is possible for him; παρένεγκε second person singular aorist imperative active of παραφέρω "take away, remove; carry or lead away; drive along."[345]

When Jesus addresses Peter Σίμων, καθεύδεις; "Simon, are you sleeping?" it is a further indication of Jesus's anguish and the audience becomes

---

340. Cf. Jeremias, *CentralMessage*, 19–20.

341. Fitzmyer, "*Abba* and Jesus' Relation," 47–63; Barr, "Daddy," 23–47; Charlesworth, "A Caveat," 9; and Davies and Allison, *Saint Matthew*, 601–2.

342. Cf. Gnilka, *Markus*, 262.

343. Evans, *Mark 8:27—16:20*, 412; cf. Boring, *Mark*, 399–400.

344. Grassi, "Another Approach," 449–58; and Grassi, "Abba Father," 320–24.

345. Cf. Isa 51:17 LXX and Isa 51:22.

aware of Jesus's disappointment in his close friends, because they failed to support him during a time of need. It is possible that Jesus's address of Peter as "Simon" is an indication that he did not live up to the expectations of his new name "the Rock." This idea is reinforced by the second question Jesus poses to him: οὐκ ἴσχυσας μίαν ὥραν γρηγορῆσαι; "Were you not strong enough to stay awake for one hour?" The verb ἴσχυσας second person singular aorist indicative active of ἰσχύω "be able, can, have resources, be strong, grow strong" introduces the proverbial saying in verse 38b: τὸ μὲν πνεῦμα πρόθυμον ἡδὲ σάρξ ἀσθενής. "The spirit is willing but the flesh is weak." The verbs in the questions addressed to Peter in verse 37 are in the second person singular. The exhortation of verse 38 γρηγορεῖτεκαὶ προσεύχεσθε, ἵνα μὴ ἔλθητε εἰς πειρασμόν "Stay awake and pray that you will not fall into temptation" occurs again in the second person plural.

The one possibility is that Jesus here addresses James and John with Peter and the other possibility is that Jesus addresses the twelve. Either way, it is easy for the Markan audience to identify with this exhortation. The disciples as well as the Markan audience should hear these admonitions: γρηγορεῖτε second person plural present imperative active of γρηγορέω "be or keep awake; watch, be alert; be alive" and προσεύχεσθε second person plural present imperative middle of προσεύχομαι "pray." This prayer is echoed in the Lord's Prayer in Matt 6:13 and Luke 11:4. Jesus here becomes the example of faithful prayer. In the immediate context it could mean that the disciples should pray that they will not be arrested and interrogated in the same way as is about to happen to Jesus.

Previously Jesus only ordered them to watch now they have to watch and pray just as he has been praying. The conjunction ἵνα suggests the content of the prayers of the disciples. The purpose of their prayers is so that they may not enter into temptation. In the New Testament the noun πειρασμός, οῦ m "period or process of testing, trial, test, temptation, enticement" refers to the temptation to sin or to yield to the desire of the flesh.[346] This is not what is implied here. Jesus warning rather is to avoid the temptation of abandoning the cause to which Jesus has called his disciples, in other words to do the same as Judas—to betray Jesus and the kingdom of God.

Jesus is worried that his closest friends do not comprehend the severity of the dangers that he is about to face. Because they fail to keep watch and pray, but fall asleep they are vulnerable.

Τὸ μὲν πνεῦμα πρόθυμονἡ δὲ σάρξἀσθενής occurs only here and in the Mathean parallel. The only other occurrence in the New Testament is Rom

---

346. Cf. Acts 20:19; Gal 4:4; Jas 1:2.

1:15 where Paul talks about his eagerness to preach the gospel to those who are in Rome.

The point Jesus is making is that humans are often eager to follow Jesus and to take up their responsibility in the advancement of the kingdom of God, but like seed that were casted upon the shallow soil they sprout up quickly but when withers away under the hot sun (cf. Mark 4:16–17) and they abandon the cause of the kingdom at first sign of persecution.

The tension between the spirit and the flesh in verse 38 becomes apparent in Peter's vehement claim that he will not forsake Jesus, and if necessary, will die with him, rather than to deny him. Jesus's prediction and the narrative fulfilment thereof provide the manifestation of the proverb that indeed the spirit was willing but the flesh was weak. Within this narrative context one could conclude that πειρασμός is directly linked to the suffering consequence of discipleship. The instruction to pray not to be put to the test implies that the audience should not seek out opportunities to become martyrs, in other words they should not attempt heroism. Nevertheless, for some this opportunity will be inevitable as the Markan Jesus predicts in Mark 13:9, 12–13a.[347]

Ἀπέχει third person singular present indicative active of ἀπέχω "receive in full; perhaps = it is enough or the account is settled" usually has a commercial or financial meaning. Brown translates it as "the money is paid"[348] and thereby ἀπέχω maintains its usual financial or commercial meaning and implies Judas as the subject with reference to the promise by the chief priests to give money to Judas in return for his betrayal of Jesus (cf. Mark 14:11).

Ἦλθεν ἡ ὥρα "The hour has come": In light of Mark 14:35 and Mark 13:32 ὥρα refers to the historical moment of Jesus's death and has eschatological implications. First Jesus prayed προσηύχετο ἵνα εἰ δυνατόν ἐστιν παρέλθῃ ἀπ' αὐτοῦ ἡ ὥρα that "the hour might pass away from him." Now he announces that his hour has come: ἰδοὺ παραδίδοται ὁ υἱὸς τοῦ ἀνθρώπου εἰς τὰς χεῖρας τῶν ἁμαρτωλῶν, "The Son of man is being handed over into the hands of sinners."

Παραδίδοται third person singular present indicative passive of παραδίδωμι "hand or give over, deliver up (pass. often be arrested); betray, deliver (to death); deliver, entrust, commit, give; hand down, pass on; commend" recalls the language of Jesus's predication of his Passion. Mark introduces the element of "sinners": ἁμαρτωλῶν adjective genitive masculine

---

347. Collins, *Mark*, 681.
348. Brown, *Death of the Messiah*, 1379–83.

plural no degree of ἁμαρτωλός, όν "sinful; sinner" as the people to whom Jesus will be delivered.

Ἄγωμεν first person plural present subjunctive active of ἄγω "lead, bring; go": This same command appears in Jesus's farewell discourse according to John 14:31. "Despite the disciples' persistent weakness and failures Jesus invites them to accompany him as he moves forward to the cross."[349] Ἰδοὺ ὁ παραδιδούς με ἤγγικεν: "The one who hands me over has come near." Judas is described as ὁ παραδιδούς and thus alludes back to the plot between Judas and the chief priests in Mark 14:10:11.

### Traditions–and Theological "Wirkungsgeschichtliches" Background

The Old Testament laments that form the background of the Gethsemane-episode explain Jesus expressions of genuine distress and his simultaneous expressions of trust in God. The laments provide Mark with imagery and language to describe Jesus's Passion within the Old Testaments frame of the suffering servant. This imagery is essential to the understanding of Mark's Christology and theological significance. Mark also establishes a contrast between Jesus's noble and heroic character and the weak and cowardly disciples.[350]

David was considered to be the author of these lament Psalms by the Jews of the late second Temple period. Therefore it could well be that Mark and his audience understood verse 34 in terms of Jesus as the suffering Messiah speaking in the voice of David, the lamenting prototypical king of Israel. Jonah shows one particularly different aspect to the Markan citation for as in Jonah it is God who initiates the dialogue and both parties speak. In the Markan context Jesus initiates the dialogue, but God remains quiet. It is possible that the Markan author is implying that divine activity, as far as Jesus is concerned, is pre-determined.[351]

The request addressed to God, παρένεγκετὸ ποτήριον τοῦτο ἀπ' ἐμοῦ "take away this cup from me," recalls the question the Jesus posed to the sons of Zebedee in Mark 10:38, δύνας θεπιεῖντὸ ποτήριον ὃ ἐγὼ πίνω "can you drink from the cup I drink of?" It is not absolutely clear whether the author of the pre-Markan narrative or Mark himself drew upon a symbol from the Old Testament, i.e. "the cup of wrath," or whether Mark 10:38 and 14:36 reflect upon the emerging of a new symbol, namely "the cup of suffering." Leonard

---

349. Donahue and Harrington, *Mark*, 410.
350. Ibid., 413.
351. Cf. Collins, *The Beginning*, 491.

## CHRISTOLOGY AS FOUNDATION FOR ETHICS 223

Goppelt was in favour of the latter.³⁵² It is likely that the foundation of Mark's usage is the Old Testament's "cup of wrath."³⁵³ The symbol is associated with the theme of the judgement of the nations, for the experience of divine judgement is compared to extreme intoxication. If this is the case verse 36 suggests that Jesus, although innocent, will take upon himself the "wrath of God" that others deserve. It is the idea of the innocent righteous one suffering on behalf of many. In the Old Testament the "cup" image is often used by the prophets describing the suffering that God will bring on the enemies of his people or our the wicked.³⁵⁴ Jesus's prayer also echoes the challenge to James and John to drink the cup that Jesus drinks (cf. Mark 10:38–39), as well as the words of Jesus at the Last Supper (cf. Mark 14:24).

### Social and Historical Context

Καὶ προελθὼν μικρὸν ἔπιπτεν ἐπὶ τῆς γῆς intensifies the distress that overtook Jesus. Matthew 26:39 καὶ προελθὼν μικρὸν ἔπεσεν ἐπὶ πρόσωπον αὐτοῦ προς ευχόμενος sheds some light on how Mark would have been interpreted. It was common for Jews to stand while praying with their eyes looking towards the heavens.³⁵⁵ The famous Jewish prayer the *Amida* does mean "standing." Falling to the ground on one's face was typical of the ancient Middle Eastern custom prior to the origin of the Bible.³⁵⁶

When these people fell on their faces it is either indicative of great distress or fear in the presence of God. Προσηύχετο ἵνα εἰ δυνατόν ἐστιν παρέλθῃ ἀπ' αὐτοῦ ἡ ὥρα: Jesus's use of εἰ δυνατόν reminds the Markan audience of Jesus teaching in 9:23, τὸ εἰ δύνῃ, πάντα δυνατὰ τῷ πιστεύοντι, or even more pertinent 10:27, ἐμβλέψας αὐτοῖς ὁ Ἰησοῦς λέγει παρὰ ἀνθρώποις ἀδύνατον, ἀλλ' οὐ παρὰ θεῷ πάντα γὰρ δυνατὰ παρὰ τῷ θεῷ. In a moment Jesus will say exactly this to God. In this moment Jesus is facing a severe testing of this own faith in God whose kingdom he has been proclaiming Jesus prayer is that the hour ἐστιν παρέλθῃ ἀπ' αὐτοῦ. The hour will soon be defined as the time when the "Son of man" will be delivered into the hands of sinners (v. 41), and these sinners will abuse and execute him just as he had predicted (cf. Mark 8:31; 9:31; 10:33–34). The intensity of Jesus fear strongly contrasts with the equanimity displayed by the Maccabean martyrs.

---

352. Goppelt, "Der Staat," 144, 152–53.
353. Collins, *Mark*, 680; cf. Best, *Temptation*, 156.
354. Cf. Isa 51:17; Jer 25:15–16; 51:7; Ezek 23:33; Ps 75:8.
355. Cf. Mark 6:41; Luke 18:11.
356. Cf. Gen 17:1–3; cf. Boring, *Mark*, 397.

## Theological Implications

Jesus is praying to the God for whom everything is possible and whose sovereignty is not limited by a preordained plan even if it was his own plan. There are three levels intertwined in this pericope:

1. The historic man of Nazareth is a human being who despite his trust in God trembles at the prospect of death. He is neither a Stoic, serene in his transcendent philosophy and left cold by what might happen to him physically nor is he a triumphant martyr. The Jesus portrayed by Mark in Gethsemane is not at all a hero.

2. For Mark the Gethsemane scene is not merely an account of a person suffering because of human sin and injustice. It is a Christological scene as and stated earlier Mark's Christology does accommodate and affirm the reality of a human Jesus including his weakness and his suffering. Mark needs to present Jesus as truly human and truly divine. In the present scene it is Jesus's humanity that is underscored, however ultimately he submits his will to God's redemptive plan. Jesus's death has a purpose—it is not the tragedy of the death of a righteous man, it is God's ultimate saving act. However, Mark does not entertain the theology of atonement. For Mark Jesus is not the scapegoat for the sins of humanity. He is certainly not a third person involved in the reconciliation-process between God and humanity. Mark is rather appreciative of God's savings act in the weakness and death of a truly human Jesus and he values the mystery of God being the saving agent behind the acts of those who deny, betray, condemn and crucify him.

3. Mark merely provides raw material for later developments in Christian Christological doctrine.[357]

Brown states that Jesus struggled with the following problem: Was it not possible for the Father to bring about the kingdom in some other way that did not involve this horrendous suffering and dying on the cross.[358] However, the words that Jesus utters are also echoed in Matthew's version of the Lord's Prayer (cf. Matt 6:10). This expresses the idea that the cross was the perfect subordination to the will of God.[359]

---

357. Boring, *Mark*, 398.
358. Brown, *Death of the Messiah*, 177–78.
359. Cf. Donahue and Harrington, *Mark*, 408; Boring, *Mark*, 397.

## The Significance of the Gethsemane Narrative for Mark's Christology of the Suffering Christ

The whole Gethsemane narrative is influenced by the shock and anxiety of Jesus. The extreme circumstances within which Jesus finds himself are highlighted from the perspective of the narrator and from the perspective of Jesus himself. In his prayer Jesus alludes to Ps 42 in his expression of his extreme sadness and his plight for the intervention of God the Father. The sadness of Jesus should be interpreted in connection with a much deeper suffering which goes beyond mere physical suffering and death, namely the experience of being abandoned by God (cf. Ps 42:4, 11). These questions can be addressed only to God, like the question in Mark 15:34 (a citation from Ps 22:2), and bears witness to a negative and bitter evaluation of the divine and it qualifies the suffering as not only the absence of God but as the active rejection by God. It qualifies death as an evil death, a death as total termination of relationships and a death without God.[360]

With the description of Jesus being afraid and deeply sorrowful the narrator ponders upon Jesus's experience of being overwhelmed by this kind of death and the feeling that God as become foreign and distant.

The depth of his suffering only becomes evident once it is actualised that the absence of God is here experienced by the person whose entire life up until now was a revelation of God's presence within this world and it seems, in the light of the current circumstances, to be untrue. The people, on whose side the Son of Man appeared in order to lead them back to their heavenly Father, now triumph over him as his enemies and God allows for this to happen. However, Jesus already predicted, recognised and accepted this state of affairs as the will of God, although this is not at all an example of the common ideal of *per aspera ad adstra*. It is rather the introduction to a paradox that could not be. In the words of Feldmeier:

> der Widerstand des Menschen gegen (den ihm in Jesus nahegekommenen) Gott, der Widerstand, der den "Menschensohn," welcher nicht ohne die Menschen bei Gott sein will, nun vom Vater trennt. Weil er aus einger einzigartigen Einheit mit dem Vater kommt, erfährt der "Sohn" hier am fruchtbarsten die Verborgenheit Gottes in einer von ihrem Schöpfer losgerissen Welt.[361]

Yet, it should be kept in mind that every Psalm alluded to in the lamenting prayer of Jesus is the expression of the faith that the now seemingly

---

360. Feldmeier, *Der Krisis*, 238.
361. Feldmeier, *Der Krisis*, 239.

absent God will not remain absent and that the person praying may be assured of the faithfulness of God amidst his suffering.

Jesus does not merely trust in the nearness of God amidst an experience of being abandoned by God, but he unconditionally trusts God as his Father. Similar to "Abba" as employed uniquely to address God, is the closing of the prayer: ἀλλ' οὐ τί ἐγὼ θέλω ἀλλὰ τί σύ.

This could express the will of Jesus to subject his will to the will of the Father. However, according to Feldmeier,[362] such a reading is incorrect, for there is no μή in the sentence but the objective negation οὐ which means that Jesus is expressing a fact and not a request, for that the will of God will be done is inevitable—it will happen regardless of human requests. Jesus's request is rather that God, for whom everything is possible, might find another way which his will could be done and avoid the passion. In the words of Lohmeyer: "Es scheint, als sole hier nicht menschliche Willkür den göttlichen Willen entgegengesetzt werden, sondern als spräche einer der auch Gott gegenüber das besondere Recht hat, von ‚Sienen Willen' zu sprechen und gerade deswegen sich dem höheren Willen Gottes beugt."[363]

Therefore, Jesus preserves the sovereignty of his Father, meaning that God will in all circumstances remain his Father and not only in the case of God giving in to the request of Jesus. It is furthermore an expression of Jesus's believe that everything that happens to him is the will of the Father. It is however strange to understand the passion of his Son as the will of God the Father.

According to Feldmeier,[364] this mystery can only be clarified by understanding Jesus from his relationship with the Father as existing only for the benefit of the world. This is perhaps best explained with reference to two biblical narratives. The first is found in Exodus 32:32 when the people of God created the golden calf and God became so angry that He wanted to eradicate his entire people and only continue his salvation history with Moses and his offspring, Moses pleaded with Him to forgive them and if not to remove his name from the book of life as well. Moses identified with the fate of the people of Israel to such an extent, that it does not make sense to him to continue his own life without them. A similar example is found in Rom 9:3 with regards to the people of Israel when Paul states that he would rather be cursed and separated from Christ if it would be to the benefit of his fellow Israelites. Both Paul and Moses confess that as far as they are concerned there is something more important than themselves and more

---

362. Ibid., 243.
363. Lohmeyer, *Markus*, 316.
364. Feldmeier, *Der Krisis*, 243.

important than their own salvation and that is the salvation of their people who became separated from God. It is this exact attitude that is found in the conduct of Jesus as well as in his self-sacrificing dedication and utterances as in Mark 10:45: καὶ γὰρ ὁ υἱὸς τοῦ ἀνθρώπου οὐκ ἦλθεν διακονηθῆναι ἀλλὰ διακονῆσαι καὶ δοῦναι τὴν ψυχὴν αὐτοῦ λύτρον ἀντὶ πολλῶν.

It speaks of the incredible love of the Son of Man, who does not want anything for himself, but who completely took upon him the fate of sinners, in order to guide them back to God. Cranfield formulated the relation between the Gethsemane-prayer and the crucifixion on Calvary as follows: "The burden of the world's sin, his complete self-identification with the sinners, involved not merely a felt, but a real, abandonment by his Father. It is in the cry of dereliction that the full horror of man's sin stands revealed."[365] Jesus is suffering alone, while the stubborn people do not know what they are doing and because they do not comprehend that their rejection of Jesus is their own damnation. That is the *cup* or *chalice* that Jesus prays will pass him by and this clarifies why Jesus is making an appeal to the omnipotence of God. When Jesus was merely looking for a way to avoid the way of suffering, he could have committed suicide in the garden and his enemies would have gone home empty handed.

Rather when Jesus is praying that the cup might pass him by, because with God everything is possible, he is turning to a Father who has the power to bring about the conversion of these people and that is a power which is stronger than everything humanly possible. And it is with this conviction that Jesus prays. He remains steadfast in his trust that the will of God the Father is a good will which can turn a seemingly triumph of evil into something ultimately good. By doing so Jesus perfectly preserves his identity as the Son of God in his most helpless hour. This challenges the early Christian belief, which is still very popular today, that the Gethsemane episode displays the humanity of Jesus Christ in its purest form, for it is questionable whether such a standpoint is influenced by a concept of God which is defined by power and might, while the self-sacrificing unconditional love for humanity which allows for humiliation is overlooked.[366]

Jesus never received an answer. We are only told that Jesus returned from praying to find his disciples asleep. The fact that Jesus did not receive an answer is answer enough, for as far as God's unique relationship to this human is concerned (cf. Mark 1:11; 9:6) it now seems like a calculated silence and a negation of his unique election. Three times Jesus prayed without receiving an answer and all three times he returns to find his disciples

---

365. Ibid., 244.
366. Cranfield, *St. Mark*, 458.

asleep. Jesus was especially disappointed in Peter (cf. Mark 14:37). This further intensifies Jesus's feeling of abandonment. When Jesus returns for the third time, he announces that his hour has come.[367]

When even those who were the first to become followers of Jesus (Mark 1:16–20), who witnessed one of his greatest miracles (Mark 5:37), who so his heavenly glory (Mark 9:2), who received his authority (Mark 13:3), when even they fall asleep in this deciding moment, who would still be open to words and works of Jesus? In this unfaithful refusal to take part in the suffering of Jesus there is a parallel to the reticence of the entire world. For Jesus this sleep, despite his lamenting, his pleading, his admonishing, is an expression of his complete loss of all relationships. However, according to Lohmeyer the sleep of the disciples is not only a sign of the disciples lack of faith, it is also a mysteriously concealed answer of God to Jesus's prayer. "Darum kann Gott schweigen, weil Er durch das Geschehen der Stunde um so klarer redet."[368]

Within the context of the narrative, the admonishment should be read in relation to the consequence. According to the narrator the spirit of the disciples is willing, but the flesh is weak which alludes to the disciples being willing to take part in the suffering of Christ. However this willingness does not have the slightest consequence. The failure of the disciples in general and especially that of Peter involuntarily reminds of the preceding insistence of the disciples and especially Peter that they will not abandon Jesus. However, without staying watchful and praying, solidarity with Jesus Christ is not possible. In other words without continuously re-affirming one's alliance with Christ and renewal of one's faith in Christ, the mere willingness is actually a form of deceiving oneself and an overestimation of one's own human ability. There is therefore a warning in this episode that trust in one's own willing spirit is ultimately destined for failure, for only God has the power to guard against falling into temptation. It should also be noted that this was the last admonishment Jesus addressed to his disciples.[369]

For the disciples this final failure of Jesus separates them from him for what follows is their flight and their denial and their total absence during his suffering which is the result of their sleeping which is almost metaphorical for their falling into the ways of the world and the destruction of their relationship with their Lord. Furthermore, it becomes clear that the disciples were not in the least an eschatological community who, by their own vigilantism, inaugurated the new Messianic age, for they

---

367. Feldmeier, *Der Krisis*, 245.
368. Ibid., 246.
369. Lohmeyer, *Markus*, 320.

much rather conformed to the current state of affairs. Jesus is alone in the eschatological struggle.

The reader of Mark's Gospel becomes aware of how the prior predictions of Jesus are now realised. The people who are failing Jesus here are his *disciples*, i.e. the people who chose to follow him. They were familiar with what the consequence of this decision was in no uncertain terms (cf. Mark 8:34).

Ironically, although the disciples were painfully aware of the implication of their discipleship they have done the exact opposite. They have not denied themselves and taken up their cross, but they allowed their Master to undertake the journey of suffering alone. They wanted to save their own lives and they fled. In his personal capacity the leading disciple, Peter, denies Jesus in the court of the high priest. Therefore, by falling asleep, which becomes symbolic of the disciples apostasy, they failed Jesus in everything which he expected from his disciples.

However, the hearers of the Gospel know that this damnation is not the last word about the disciples, for on the Sunday morning the women were commanded to proclaim to his disciples and especially Peter that they will meet the resurrected in Galilee as he promised (cf. Mark 16:7), not as a judge, but as a master who calls them to renewed loyalty. As a consequence the disciples became the founders of a new community of salvation. In the words of Feldmeier: "Jenseit ihres in Jesu Tod besiegelten und nach weltlichen Maßstäben nicht mehr gutzumachenden Versagens wird ihnen so durch Gottes Eingreifen die Möglichkeit neuen Lebens eröffnet, ja mehr als das: Sie warden zu Gottes Boten, gerade in diesen Schwachen wird Gottes Kraft mächtig."[370] Jesus therefore does not allow for the relationship to remain broken, but he seeks reconciliation.

Ἄγωμεν first person plural subjunctive present active of ἄγω "lead, bring; go;" was also used in Mark 1:38 when Jesus summoned his disciples to follow him and to become part of his circle of disciples. In light of the Easter events Jesus does not abandon his solidarity with his people and his expression of grace is renewed. It is grounded in the fact that the Son of Man has endured everything that will befall the disciples and all future followers of Jesus.

The pericope concludes with the words: ἦλθεν ἡ ὥρα, which highlights the situation of God who became absent and that the heavens which opened with God the Father's announcement that Jesus is his beloved Son were now closed and that the hour that Jesus prayed might pass him by, has now arrived. Jesus highlights his rejection with the words of a formula

---

370. Feldmeier, *Der Krisis*, 248.

of excommunication: ἰδοὺ παραδίδοται ὁ υἱὸς τοῦ ἀνθρώπου εἰς τὰς χεῖρας τῶν ἁμαρτωλῶν.

With this statement the prerequisite of Jesus's entire existence is once again highlighted: that not only in everything what happens through him, but also in everything that happens to him and with him, God's will will be done and because it is the will of the Father it is necessarily benevolent. Jesus can say this only from the conviction that even though he surrendered his status as the Son of Man, he still speaks as the one to whom God has entrusted the inauguration of the new age. For this reason Jesus can respond to the mocking questions of Pilate and the Sanhedrin whether he really is the Son of God.[371]

Jesus is convinced that God remains his Father up until the very end (cf. Mark 15:34) even if the circumstances seem to indicate that God has indeed abandoned his Son. Jesus unconditionally surrenders to the will of the Father even where it seems that his experience contradicts his belief. In the words of Feldmeier: "In dieser Hingabe an den Vater selbst dort, wo dieser sich selbst zu widersprechen scheint, in Jesu bedingungslosem Ja zu Gottes Willen auch dann, wenn dieser nach dem Urteil des 'schwachen' Fleisches mit dem Widerstand des Bösen identisch wird, leuchtet eine Einheit von Vater und Sohn auf, deren Kraft und Gewißheit starker ist als die scheinbar eindeutige Sprache der Tatsachen."[372]

Finally the Gethsemane episode points to God's answer to the passion of the Son: he does not abandon the way of suffering, yet he re-affirms and re-qualifies it. The absent God in the passion event is not God's recanting of his becoming present in his Son, but rather the realisation thereof. "Das Unheilsgeschehen selbst muß—wenn es nach dem guten Willen des Vaters geschehen ist—Heilsgeschehen für diese Welt sein." With these words of Jesus the episode in Gethsemane is concluded and Jesus meets his traitor heads on and his real passion commences.

### First Peter 4:1–6

> *Christ then suffered for us in the flesh. You must be of the same mind, for he that suffered in the flesh ceases to sin, so that he no longer lives according to human desires, but according to the will of God in his remaining time in the flesh. For it is enough that the past time has been completed according to the desire of the Gentiles; wandering in lasciviousness, lusts, and excess of wine,*

---

371. Ibid., 250.
372. Ibid., 251.

> *revellings, banquetings, and abominable idolatries: Wherein they think it strange that you run not with them to the same excess of recklessness, speaking evil. Who shall give account to him that is ready to judge the living and the dead? For this cause was the gospel preached also to the dead, that they might be judged according to men in the flesh, but live according to God in the spirit.*

### Literary and Discourse Analysis

Once again the theme of innocent suffering is resumed, and a hortatory thought is introduced by οὖν "therefore" introducing the moral implication of 1 Pet 3:18-22.

Χριστοῦ οὖν παθόντος σαρκὶ: Christ should become a model for the believers to interpret their own suffering.

Παθόντος aorist participle active genitive masculine singular of πάσχω "suffer, endure, undergo; experience" echoes ἔπαθεν (1 Pet 3:18) but it is not the expiatory nature of Christ's suffering but the paradigmatic character thereof which is stressed.[373]

The οὖν with which the pericope opens connects with 3:18, although the genitive absolute construction connects with the entire 3:19-22.[374] Σαρκὶ emphasises Christ's human suffering and therefore forms a parallel with what is experienced by the believers as well as an example that they should follow. Feldmeier is also of the opinion that with the keywords πάσχω "suffer," "endure," and σάρξ, σαρκός f "flesh," "physical body"; "human nature," "earthly" the verse is connected with 1 Pet 3:18.[375]

The phrase, a genitive absolute construction combines suffering with flesh, σαρκὶ dative feminine singular common of σάρξ, σαρκός f "flesh, physical body; human nature, earthly descent." This places Christ's suffering in a human frame. This once again establishes that a connection exists between the suffering of Christ and the suffering of his followers.

Καὶ ὑμεῖς: the experience of Christ serves as the motivation for the behaviour of the believers (cf. 2:4-5; 2:18-25; 3:13-22; 4:12-16). Καὶ and αὐτὴν make the correlation between the suffering of Christ and the suffering of the believers explicit.

Ὁπλίσασθε second person plural aorist imperative middle of ὁπλίζομαι "arm oneself with" occurs only here in the New Testament and is

---

373. Ibid., 252.

374. Cf. Elliott, *1 Peter: New Translation*, 711.

375. Cf. Reicke, *Disobedient Spirits*, 202; Michaels, *1 Peter*, 225; Schelkle, "Das Leiden," 14; Feldmeier, *First Letter*, 212.

employed metaphorically in order to describe the struggle of the moral life. The use of military language within a moral context was common practice among the Greek and Roman philosophers.[376]

The preceding verses, 3:18–22, were concerned with the description of Christ's ultimate victory and therefore also imply Christ's victory over human suffering. This insight was aimed to encourage the believers to remain steadfast in the faith and therefore also continue behaving in a way which is pleasing to God. The parallel between Christ and the believers is confirmed by καὶ ὑμεῖς. The New Testament often employs military metaphors like ὁπλίσασθε and here it is use to describe the dangerous conditions within which the believers find themselves.[377] The armour with which the believers are to arm themselves is ἔννοια, ας f "attitude," "thought"; "intention," "purpose" which refers back to Christ's human suffering as is supported by αὐτὴν "the same" and provides the content of ἔννοιαν. Ἔννοια is mentioned only twice in the New Testament, namely here and in Heb 4:12. It also occurs in the LXX, most often in Proverbs in order to describe mental activity, particularly with regard to moral activity. The implication is that what the suffering Christ endured was in accordance with God's will and the same should be true of the suffering that the followers of Christ have to endure.[378] In continuation with the general emphasis of the letter, the author replaces Christ's death with his suffering, because the believers' experience of enduring the same suffering as Christ did, is a central theme in the letter.[379] This leads to the believers having solidarity with Christ and as Christ suffered in accordance to God's will, they should also live their lives in accordance with God's will. This is the greatest effort expected from believers. The salvation which Christ suffering brought about cannot simply be transferred to believers, but it has to affect the believer's life (cf. Gal 5:6). This connects with the *imitatio Christi*-idea which was expressed in 1 Pet 2:21 which is now emphasised by the use of ὁπλίσασθε second person plural aorist imperative middle of ὁπλίζομαι "arm oneself with."[380] War-metaphors are common in New Testament writings for it describes the everyday experience of Christian existence in a hostile world.[381] However, as Feldmeier emphasises the

---

376. Feldmeier, *First Letter*, 212.
377. Cf. Plato, *Apol.* 28d.5—29a.1; Seneca, *Ep.* 59: 7–8; 96:5.
378. Cf. Rom 6:13; 13:12; 2 Cor 6:7; 10:4; Eph 6:11–17; 1 Thess 5:8.
379. Cf. Michaels, *1 Peter*, 225.
380. Cf. 1 Pet 2:19; 3:13; 4:13; 5:1.
381. Feldmeier, *First Letter*, 212.

metaphor does not indicate retaliation against hostile people, but against evil in general (cf. 1 Pet 5:8).[382]

Achtemeier understands ὅτι to have an explanatory meaning in connection with ἔννοιαν and therefore gives the content of the "thought" or "intent" with which the Christians' were to be armed. Our author also used it in this sense and it also implied mental activity (1 Pet 1:12, 18; 2:3).[383]

Ὁ παθών is understood by Achtemeier to refer to the baptised Christian.[384] The baptised Christian, who shares in Christ's human suffering in the flesh, acts according to God's will. This implies that the flesh no longer governs their desires. Their suffering, similar to Christ's suffering, is caused because they align themselves with the will of God. This kind of suffering is understood by the author of the epistle as the believers' vocation (1 Pet 2:20–21) because of their command to follow in the footsteps of Christ (1 Pet 2:21b–23).[385] Because Christians endure suffering by aligning themselves to the will of God, they ceased to conduct themselves in a way that is not pleasing to God.[386] Therefore the Christian ceased to sin, πέπαυται ἁμαρτίας.

The syntactical function of the clause is to provide a reason for the imperative to follow.

Ὁπαθώνσαρκι in this case does not particularly refer to Christ but is applicable to anyone who suffers innocently. Within the context of the letter the author by παθόντοςaorist participle active genitive masculine singular of πάσχω "suffer, endure, undergo; experience" most probably means innocent suffering and not death.[387]

Σαρκὶ dative feminine singular common of σάρξ, σαρκός f "flesh, physical body; human nature, earthly descent" is a dative of respect and as elsewhere in the letter refer to the physical or mortal frame within which this suffering may occur.

Εἰς τὸ μηκέτι ἀνθρώπων ἐπιθυμίαις ἀλλὰ θελήματι θεοῦ τὸν ἐπίλοιπον ἐν σαρκὶ βιῶσαι χρόνον provides the purpose of why Christians should arm themselves. Μηκέτι underscores the contrast between the "now" after their conversion and the "then" before their conversion—a theme our author is fond of. The contrast is expressed by the opposition between ἀνθρώπων ἐπιθυμίαις and θελήματι θεου. Ἀνθρώπων ἐπιθυμίαις is descriptive of the

---

382. Cf. Rom 13:12; Eph 6:11–17.
383. Feldmeier, *First Letter*, 212.
384. Achtemeier, *1 Peter*, 278.
385. Ibid., 278.
386. Cf. Brox, *Petrusbrief* (1st ed), 192.
387. Cf. Michaels, *1 Peter*, 228.

addressees' former existence in harmony with Greco-Roman culture and paganism. Their previous lives and the remainder of their lives in the flesh are placed within the framework of God's eternity because they are released from sin.[388]

The implied subject of the verb βιῶσαι aorist infinitive active of βιόω "live" is most probably the "you" in verse 1b.[389] This is argued because of the link of this verse with the previous exhortation to the addressees. εἰς τὸ βιῶσαι is a purpose clause and the verb βιόω "live" occurs only here in the New Testament and in combination with χρόνον has the implication to live to the fullest.[390]

Μηκέτι ἀνθρώπων ἐπι θυμίαις ἀλλὰ θελήματι θεοῦ: The argument of the author here is that suffering with respect to the flesh entails control over one's physical desires and therefore over the compulsion to sin. Therefore the addressees have the choice to conduct their lives according to the will of God and no longer according to their fleshy desires.[391]

Ἀνθρώπων ἐπι θυμίαις and θελήματι θεοῦ are placed directly opposed to each other in order to indicate the opposing standards of living, previous to their conversion and after their becoming Christians. The thought re-emphasises the theme of transformation. Their physical suffering aids in this transformation.

Ἐπίλοιπον adjective accusative masculine singular no degree of ἐπίλοιπος, ον "remaining" also unique in the New Testament refers to the believers' remaining mortal existence.

Ἐπιθυμία, ας f "desire," "longing"; "lust," "passion"; "covetousness" is the all encompassing concept the author uses to describe the addressees' existence prior to their conversion. Allegiance to God's will stands in opposition to this culture as also mentioned in 1 Pet 3:17 and 4:4. Christians were to live in accordance to God's will despite the suffering this entails.[392]

Βούλημα τῶν ἐθνῶν is a further explanation of what is meant by ἀνθρώπων ἐπιθυμίαις. Γὰρ introduces the justification of verses 1–2.

Παρεληλυθὼς χρόνος refers to the time when they were at home within their Greco-Roman environment and behaved accordingly ἀρκετὸς, "sufficient."

---

388. Elliott, *1 Peter: New Translation*, 713; contra Goppelt, *Der erste Petrusbrief*, 282; and Martin, *Metaphor*, 230.

389. Feldmeier, *First Letter*, 213.

390. Elliott, *1 Peter: New Translation*, 718; cf. Kelly, *Peter and Jude*, 169; Goppelt, *Der erste Petrusbrief*, 275.

391. Cf. Job 29:18.

392. Elliott, *1 Peter: New Translation*, 719.

Ἀρκετὸς γὰρ ὁ παρεληλυθὼς χρόνος τὸ βούλημα τῶν ἐθνῶν κατειργάσθαι probably answers a typical question of recently converted believers: were they to break completely with their former lifestyles, or did there exist certain exceptions. The author's reply is unambiguous: ἀρκετός, ή, όν "enough"; "it is enough." Their participation in pagan activities irrevocably belongs to the past, prior to their conversion. Feldmeier describes this reorientation as a "psychological counteracting force" which now manifests in the cultural and societal contexts.[393] The subject of the infinitive κατειργάσθαι is probably the addressees: they were to refrain from "doing" in accordance with the will of the Gentiles. Then follows the condemnation of a list of vices all rejected by the Christian authors, although some of these vices were also rejected by secular moralists, especially from the Stoic tradition.[394] In such a context Christians could present themselves as morally above criticism and even practicing moral excellence. Thereby our author wants to emphasise, that although motivated by a different religion, there exists no reason for moral criticism against Christians. On the contrary, being different or foreign, they actually receive an elite status, which once again promotes a positive self-understanding. Furthermore the emphasis is on doing good and avoiding evil—a motivation for a better lifestyle.[395] However, the vices listed all refer to the believers' previous existence and the language underscores the futility (cf. 1 Pet 1:18) and the darkness (1 Pet 2:9) which dominated their previous lives.

Κῶμος, ου m "carousing," "orgy," "revelry" and πότοις noun dative masculine plural common of πότος, ου m "drunken orgy" describing the activities that commonly took place during pagan worship. Ἀσελγείαις noun dative feminine plural common of ἀσέλγεια, ας f "sensuality," "indecency," "vice" is intended as a general introduction of the vices to follow. Therefore, it may be concluded that our author considers Greco-Roman culture as generally immoral and emphasises the radically different behaviour expected of followers of Christ.

Ἀνθρώπων genitive masculine plural common of ἄνθρωπος, "man, human being, person" denotes all that are in direct opposition to God. In this sense "Gentiles" denote not merely non-Israelites but all that rejected Christ including Israelites. It is therefore indicative of all that do not belong to the household of Christ and is synonymous with "disobedient."[396]

---

393. Cf. Feldmeier, *First Letter*, 213.
394. Ibid., 213.
395. Cf. Seneca, *Ep.* 83.17; Plato, *Eryx.* 405E; Philo, *Ios.* 2.185.
396. Feldmeier, *First Letter*, 214.

The list of vices to follow in verse 3 is typical of the behaviour associated with Gentiles especially "lawless idolatries." These vices also serve as evidence that the addressees are mostly of non-Israelite origin. This is further underscored by the words (former ignorance" (1 Pet 1:14) and "futile conduct inherited from your ancestors" (1 Pet 1:18). However, this is not so clear cut since the same criticism could be applied to Israel for they are often reprimanded in the Old Testament for their relapse into idolatric practices.

Πεπορευμένους announces various vices which characterised the addressees's previous existence. Here it is used in the sense of an embarkment on a moral journey or a behavioural way.[397]

First Peter 4:3 seems to be an allusion to Ps 1:1: μακάριος ἀνήρ ὃς οὐκ ἐπορ ἐπορεύθηἐν βουλῇ ἀσεβῶν καὶ ἐν ὁδῷ ἁμαρτωλῶν οὐκ ἔστη καὶ ἐπὶ καθέδραν λοιμῶν οὐκ ἐκάθισεν.

Its perfect tense links with κατεργάζομαι and παρέρχομαι. Lists of vices were often used by New Testament writers for hortatory purposes. Vice lists are often balanced with virtue lists in order to explicitly mention required Christian behaviour.[398] These vices occurring in the plural were also discouraged by Greek and Roman moralists.[399]

Ἐν ᾧ with which verse 4 opens anticipates the following genitive absolute: μὴ συντρεχόντων ὑμῶν: συντρεχόντων masculine plural genitive participle present active ofσυντρέχω "run together"; "join with," "plunge with" (1 Pet 4:4) is another clear indication of the addressees final break with their previous existence. In Feldmeier's words: "Christians do not swim of depravity."[400] Ξενίζονται third person plural present passive indicative of ξενίζω"surprise," "astonish" should not be interpreted as such in this case. The pagans are not "amazed" or "astonished" by the deviant social behaviour of the Christians but rather "upset" or "offended." Their behaviour estrange them from their social environment, for it was precisely this conduct of the Christians that caused the hostility of their Gentile contemporaries.[401] As described by the preceding genitive absolute the pagans are irritated by the Christians refusal to participate in cultural and religious activities and therefore understood as hatred towards humanity.[402] Συντρέχω therefore should not be understood literally, but figuratively meaning that they no

---

397. Cf. 1 Pet 2:7; 3:2.
398. Elliott, *1 Peter: New Translation*, 721.
399. Cf. e.g., Gal 5:19–21; Eph 4:25–31; Col 3:5–9.
400. Elliott, *1 Peter: New Translation*, 722.
401. Feldmeier, *First Letter*, 215.
402. Cf. Tacitus, *Ann.* 15.44; and Minucius Felix, *Oct.*, 12.

longer attend these activities.⁴⁰³ Their commitment and orientation towards God's will finds expression in a new ethical orientation.⁴⁰⁴

Μὴ συντρεχόν των ὑμῶν is a genitive absolute construction describing the cause of the Gentiles' being surprised and a reason for their hostility against the addressees.

Συντρεχόντων present participle active genitive masculine plural of συντρέχω "run together; join with, plunge with" involves the verb τρέχω "run; exert oneself, make an effort," which is used elsewhere in the New Testament in conjunction with believers's morality (cf. Heb 12:1; 1 Cor 9:24; Gal 2:2; 5:7; Phil 2:16). The participle used here has the meaning of joining others in immoral activities (cf. Ps 49 [50]:18). A continuous disassociation is therefore implied. The believer's conversion caused them to break with such immorality.

Εἰς τὴν αὐτὴν τῆς ἀσωτίας ἀνάχυσιν forms the summarizing description of the vices mentioned in verse 3. These vices were also conventionally condemned by Israel, as well as early Christianity. However, their occurance here is expressed in a manner unique to 1 Peter. The author uses a graphic negative image in order to describe the wild dissipation which characterised these gatherings.

Ἀνάχυσις, εως f "flood" is also unique to the New Testament and is a term associated with rock pools which is filled up by the waves of the sea during high tide.⁴⁰⁵ Here it is used figuratively to describe the wild "outpouring" of immorality.

Ἀσωτία, ας f "dissipation, reckless living" is associated with that which ruins good health. In Eph 5:18 it is used to refer to drunkenness in particular but here it is the universal term to describe all the manifestations of immoral living. Here we also find a fine example of the author's use of alliteration αὐτὴν ἀσωτίας ἀνάχυσιν (cf. 1 Pet 1:4, 6, 19; 2:12, 15, 16, 18–20, 21; 3:17).

Βλασφημοῦντες: The response of the Gentiles to the believers' estrangement is maligning. Because they no longer engage with Gentiles they provoke hostility. Βλασφημέω "speak against God, blaspheme; speak against, slander, insult" is the opposite of "honor" or "praise" and means to insult either God or humans or both.⁴⁰⁶ When God or the gods is the object it has the meaning of "blaspheme" i.e. "to speak profanely and disparagingly

---

403. Cf. Tacitus, *Ann.*15.44.
404. Cf. Chrysostom, *Ordin.* 4.119.
405. Feldmeier, *First Letter*, 215; cf. Elliott, *1 Peter: New Translation*, 725.
406. Cf. Strabo, *Geogr.* 3.1.9; 2.5.24.

of something sacred."⁴⁰⁷ When humans are the object it has the meaning of "to insult" or "to malign."⁴⁰⁸

Because our author so often speaks of the verbal abuse the addressees had to endure, it is quite possible that they could be an implied object here. The verb is used by Josephus in this sense to refer to the malignment of Israel by Gentiles.⁴⁰⁹

The maligning of believers because of their dissociation from former alliances is coherent with other forms of verbal abuse mentioned in the letter which the believers had to endure. It is characteristic of the constant efforts of the Gentiles to dishonor Christians.

Ἀσωτίας noun feminine singular common genitive of ἀσωτία, ας f "dissipation," "reckless living" is understood to mean the opposite of σωζω "to save" in order to indicate that the pagan lifestyle does not lead to salvation.⁴¹⁰ Our author's final qualification of the Gentile's reaction is βλασφημοῦντες verb nominative masculine plural present active participle of βλασφημέω "speak against God," "blaspheme"; "speak against," "slander," "insult." This seems to be the author's reaction to the Christians' unbelieving neighbours. The participle presents a causal introduction to the next verse expressing a link between their blasphemy and God's reaction. Although the unbelievers did not explicitly slander against the Christians' God, they slandered his followers which is an insult to God.⁴¹¹

Verse 5 is a continuation of verse 4 and links with the βλασφημοῦντες with which the previous verse ended. Such blasphemy cannot remain unpunished by God: οἳ ἀποδώσουσιν λόγον τῷ ἑτοίμως ἔχοντι κρῖναι ζῶντας καὶ νεκρούς.

Ἀπο δώσουσιν λόγον is a legal phrase and indicates a response to a question posed in a court of law. Ἀπο δώσουσιν λόγον is translated by Achtemeier as giving an account and is linked to the same legal context by the following τῷ ἑτοίμως ἔχοντι κρῖναι.⁴¹² The object of the judgement ζῶντας καὶ νεκρούς indicates that it is the final judgement at the *parousia* that is meant. This was intended to give the audience a sense of comfort, knowing that God will not forget the injustices that his followers had to endure.⁴¹³

---

407. Cf. Josephus, *A.J.* 8.358–359.

408. Cf. Isa 52:5; Acts 19:37; 26:11; Rom 2:24; 1 Tim 6:1 etc.

409. Cf. Mark 15:29; Acts 13:45; 18:6; Rom 3:8; 1 Cor 10:30.

410. Josephus, *C. Ap.* 1:223, 2:32.

411. Cf. Luke 15:13; Titus 1:6.

412. Cf. Senior, *1 & 2 Peter*, 75: "they unwittingly attack God's own people, his living temple."

413. Achtemeier, *1 Peter*, 286.

## CHRISTOLOGY AS FOUNDATION FOR ETHICS

The problem presented by the text is rather the subject of τῷ ἑτοίμως ἔχοντι: does this refer to God or to Christ? Christ is often understood in the New Testament to be the one who judges "the living and the dead."[414] On the other hand, God is also considered to be the eschatological judge in early Christian tradition (e.g., Matt 10:32-33; Rom 2:6; 3:6; 14:10; Luke 12:8-9, etc.). In the light of the other references to the final judgement in 1 Peter (1:17; 2:23; 4:19) Achtemeier opts for the latter.[415]

Verse 6 begins with γάρ which clearly indicates a causal phrase and εἰς τοῦτο points forward to the following ἵνα—clause.[416] The verse presents a number of difficulties: who preached what (εὐηγγελίσθη); the identity of the νεκροῖς and the relation of this verse to 1 Pet 3:19. The verse is certainly a reference back to 3:19. Feldmeier states that a relation between this verse and 3:19 explains the text in an unforced manner.[417]

Ζῶντας καὶ νεκρούς: The expression refers to all humanity and the totality of physically alive and physically dead humans (cf. Acts 10: 42; 2 Tim 4: 1; Rom 14: 9). This expresses the universal nature of God's judgement from which no one will be exempted. Verse 6 is the conclusion of this pericope but is not without its exegetical problems:

a. the subject of εὐηγγελίσθη

b. the identity of νεκροῖς

c. the relation of 1 Pet 4: 6 and 1 Pet 3: 19

d. the antithesis of verse 6b

Ἐκήρυξεν (3:19) and εὐηγγελίσθη (4:6) are often used in conjunction in the New Testament but are not intrinsically synonymous. They have different meanings and are used in the active and the passive voice respectively. Furthermore, the indirect objects of the two verbs "spirits" πνεύμασιν (3:19) and "dead" νεκροῖς (4:6) are not synonymous either. The "spirits" in 3:19 are not deceased humans but evil angelic spirits whose disobedience and rebellion against God caused the destructive Flood (cf. Gen 6-8).

Νεκροῖς in 4:6 has the same meaning as in verse 5 and here deceased humans are implied. Furthermore, in general νεκρός, ά, όν "dead, lifeless, a dead person, corpse" refers to humans.

---

414. Feldmeier, *First Letter*, 215.

415. Cf. Acts 10:42; Rom 14:9; 2 Tim 4:1.

416. Achtemeier, *1 Peter*, 286; cf. Goppelt, *Der erste Petrusbrief*, 275; Michaels, *1 Peter*, 235.

417. Cf. Best, *1 Peter*, 155; Selwyn, *The First Epistle*, 214; Kelly, *Peter and Jude*, 175 and Michaels, *1 Peter*, 238.

Εὐηγγελίσθη third person singular aorist indicative passive of εὐαγγελίζω act. and midd. "bring the good news," "preach the good news" "proclaim"; pass. "hear the good news (of persons)"; "be preached (of things)" with the implied subject "Christ." Therefore, the good news was preached by Christ as supported by the next verb:

Κριθῶσι third person plural aorist subjunctive passive of κρίνω "judge," "pass judgement."

Εὐηγγελίσθη third person singular aorist indicative passive of εὐαγγελίζω "bring the good news, preach the good news" is a rare impersonal passive. In the words of J. N. D. Kelly, "Almost invariably 'preaching the gospel' is an activity carried out by Christian evangelists always in this world,"[418] as is the case with earlier uses of the verb in 1 Peter (cf. 1 Pet 1:12, 25). These verses refer to the work of Christian missionaries and therefore it is likely that they are implied here as well.

The μὲνδὲ structure in the ἵνα-clause presents a difficulty in reading. Achtemeier understand the μὲν-clause to be subordinate to the δὲ-clause in order to formulate a concessive meaning: "although they were judged, they might live."[419] The complete ἵνα-clause then reads: "so that they, although they were judged, might live." The verse also presents interestingly constructed opposites: κριθῶσι/ζῶσι.

Κατὰ ἀνθρώπους / κατὰ θεόν, σαρκί/πνεύματι. In this case κρίνω ("judge," "pass judgement") cannot refer to a condemnation to death. Within these contrasts one sees a connection with 1 Pet 3:18.[420] This would have the implication that Christ's salvation is also offered to the once disobedient generation of the flood.

Νεκροῖς adjective normal masculine plural dative no degree of νεκρός, ά, όν "dead, lifeless" presents a problem if it is to be understood as those who physically died. If that were the case, who did the preaching? And whoever did the preaching therefore had to descend into the realm of the dead or the "disembodied souls" in Hades. Such a concept is not familiar to the writings of the New Testament.[421] This problem is solved by understanding the dead to be "spiritually dead," i.e. the human condition prior to their conversion to Christianity and their acceptance of the gospel.[422] Such an understanding is also found in the New Testament.[423] The implication would be that those

---

418. Feldmeier, *First Letter*, 216.
419. Kelly, *Peter and Jude*, 174.
420. Achtemeier, *1 Peter*, 287.
421. Feldmeier, *First Letter*, 216.
422. Achtemeier, *1 Peter*, 289.
423. Cf. Jones, "Christian Behaviour," 64; Bieder, *Die Vorstellung*, 125; Senior, *1 & 2*

who were spiritually dead prior to their acceptance of the gospel, and after their conversion mistreated by the unconverted, could experience eternal life through the Spirit of God. Such an interpretation here seems to be out of context.[424] This verse is concerned with the final judgement of God occurring at the *parousia*. The implication of the verse is rather that those who accepted the gospel and were therefore mistreated by their contemporaries according to their human criteria, have the prospect of final vindication and glorification at the *parousia*. The meaning of the verse seems to be that even death as a result of persecution, suffered by many Christians in the audience of the letter, which seems to indicate that their self-denial in order to obey God's will had been in vain, will be encouraged. Feldmeier however differs.[425] He understands the judgement as that which occurred in a human way and could refer to the unrighteous who died during the Deluge. Feldmeier supports his argument by the use of the aoristos in κριθῶσι linking it with the aoristos used in 3:19: ἐκήρυξεν.

As far as νεκροῖς is concerned takes the term to refer to "all who are physically dead and who are in this state when they hear the Gospel" and therefore it is implied that the gospel is now proclaimed to those who did not have the opportunity of hearing it while still alive.[426] This does however not imply that a "second chance" is offered to the deceased[427] and this would be no encouragement for the addressees to remain faithful in the present. Therefore it is saver to conclude that verse 6 is to be read in connection with verse 5 with the deceased among the addressees in mind.

This reading is coherent with the statement of the letter that the addressees were the recipients of the good news (cf. 1 Pet 1:12, 25) and therefore 4:6 refers to those among the believers who died after hearing and accepting the gospel while being alive. The consequence for the believers is therefore that they may look forward to their final vindication by God. It is in continuous coherence with the contrast between Gentiles and believers and humans and God. The author assures the addressees of their own resurrection based on the resurrection of Christ (cf. 1 Pet 3:21–22). The vindication of the believers by the justice of God is underscored by the rest of the verse. This is consistent with the letter's aim to console. Even the deceased among the believers will receive eternal life. Therefore the believers are

---

*Peter*, 76; Luther, *Luthers Epistel*, 233.

424. Cf., e.g., Luke 9:60; John 5:25; Eph 2:1, 5.

425. Cf. Dalton, *Christ's Proclamation*, 232; Selwyn, *The First Epistle*, 316; Reicke, *Disobedient Spirits*, 205.

426. Feldmeier, *First Letter*, 216.

427. Best, *1 Peter*, 156–157.

encouraged to endure their innocent suffering for they may look forward to their final vindication.

Ἵνα κριθῶσιμὲν κατὰ ἀνθρώπους σαρκὶ ζῶσι δὲ κατὰ θεὸν πνεύματι states the purpose of the proclamation of the good news and brings the unit to a conclusion.[428]

Κατὰ θεὸν has the meaning of acting in accordance to God's will (cf. 1 Pet 5:2; Rom 8:27) and κατὰ ἀνθρώπους to act according to human standards.[429] Achtemeier in agreement with Selwyn understand the comparison to be behaviour according to human standards against behaviour according to divine standards.[430] At the back of the mind of the author (in the light of verse 4) is probably the emphasis on God's judgement of the believers against the judgement of their pagan neighbours. Consequently, the abuse that the Christians currently endure will have to be endured by the unbelievers. Σαρκι/πνεύματι presents a comparison of two datives which lay on the same level as the previous between human and divine. Achtemeier understands both datives to be datives of sphere, i.e. that judgement will take place in the realm of the flesh (i.e. in the human sphere) and the divine sphere is the life-giving sphere.[431] Goppelt opts for a dative of respect with no significant change to the meaning.[432]

There exists no structural relation between 3:19 and 4:6. The two verses belong to different thought units all together. Additionally 3:19 refers to the condemnation of the disobedient spirits and the fact that they will be subordinated to the risen Christ. First Peter 4:6 on the other hand has the hope of the believers in mind contrasting judgement with eternal life.

In the letter the emphasis is consistently on behaviour according to the will of God and the fact that all humans will be judged according to their present lives. In the words of Selwyn: "The question at issue was not one of eschatological theory but of personal and practical importance namely the vindication of God's justice through the punishment of the wicked and the oppressors and the deliverance of the faithful and persecuted whether or not they had died before Christ's coming."[433]

Εἰς τοῦτο γάρ: the phrase also occurs in 2:21a and introduces support for a preceding statement. Here in conjunction with the ἵνα-clause to follow it has the content of the purpose clause in mind meaning: "for this reason."

---

428. Cf. 1 Pet 1:3–4; 3:10; 4:5, 18 and 5:8.
429. Elliott, *1 Peter: New Translation*, 734.
430. Rom 3:5; 1 Cor 15:32; Gal 3:15; 1 Cor 3:3; 9:8; Gal 1:11.
431. Achtemeier, *1 Peter*, 288; Selwyn, *The First Epistle*, 215.
432. Achtemeier, *1 Peter*, 288; cf. Best, *1 Peter*, 158.
433. Goppelt, *Der erste Petrusbrief*, 277.

Now the focus is no longer on the dead in general but those to whom the good news was proclaimed. In verse 6 the agent of judgement is not God as in verse 5 but humans and judgement according to human standards is contrasted with God's standards.[434]

Κριθῶσι third person plural aorist subjunctive passive of κρίνω "judge, pass judgment on (midd. and pass. often stand trial, go to law); condemn; decide, determine; consider, regard, think; prefer" and ζῶσι third person plural present subjunctive active of ζάω "live, be alive; remain alive; come back to life" are both in the subjunctive introduced by ἵνα to form a purpose clause. The subject of both verbs is the deceased believers and their fate at human hands and their future before God are contrasted against one another. The parallelism looks as follows: κριθῶσιμὲνκατὰ ἀνθρώπους σαρκὶ / ζῶσιδὲ κατὰ θεὸν πνεύματι. Three contrasts may be discerned: κριθῶσι/ζῶσικατὰ ἀνθρώπους / κατὰ θεὸν; σαρκὶ/πνεύματι.

Because of the aorist form the judgement of the believers refers to an event of the past and is contrasted with a present-tense verb with future meaning. Although κρίνω elsewhere in the letter refers to God's judgement[435] and although verse 5 speaks of God as the universal eschatological judge, here the inclusion of κατὰ ἀνθρώπους indicates that human judgement is in view. Σαρκὶ and its counterpart πνεύματι are both datives of respect and modify their preceding verbs.

As elsewhere in the letter σάρξ does not have sinful flesh in mind but the physical existence during which the believers are subjected to abuse and suffering. As in 3:18 the mortal existence is contrasted with eternal life in the spirit.

The emphasis on the present lives of the believers has the in view how believers, in the light of Christ's suffering, should behave during the remainder of their mortal lives.

Κατὰ in both formulations according to Selwyn express conformity to some form of standard, model or will.[436] The phrase qualifies the verb κριθῶσι while ἀνθρώπους identifies the norm according to which they will be judged. Here it is not humans in general which are meant but the believers' hostile neighbours. As in 2:4 the term is used to refer to nonbelievers who rejected Christ and slandered the believers (cf. 2:12). Additionally, human standards are contrasted with God's standards. The believers who

---

434. Selwyn, *St. Peter: Greek Text*, 337.
435. Elliott, *1 Peter: New Translation*, 731.
436. Cf. 1:17; 2:23 and 4:17.

were judged negatively by Gentiles according to their standards will be vindicated in the eyes of God.[437]

Ζῶσιδὲ κατὰ θεὸν πνεύματι states the goal of the proclamation of the good news and shifts the focus from being judged to the prospect of eternal life with God.

Κατὰ θεὸν contrasts with κατὰ ἀνθρώπους placing God's standards opposite human standards. The will of God is upheld as the standard by which Christians should conduct themselves.[438] Here, however, the emphasis is a little different, since it is the resurrected believers who are in view. Ζῶσιδὲ κατὰ θεὸν does not mean that the believers should live in accordance to the will of God but that it is God's will that the believers will live. Elliott argues that here conformity to God's intention is implied.[439] This is in continuation with 1 Pet 1:3 where the author argues that the rebirth of the addressees through the resurrection of Jesus Christ occurred in accordance with God's superfluous mercy κατὰ τὸ πολὺ αὐτοῦ ἔλεος. See also ἐνώπιον τοῦ θεοῦ (1 Pet 3:4) and παρὰ δὲ θεῷ (1 Pet 2:4, 20).[440] The point being made is that God's impartial judgement, his will, his intention and especially his divine disposition of mercy will "reverse all erroneous and malicious human criticism."

Ζῶσι third person plural subjunctive present active of ζάω "live, be alive" has the deceased Christians as subject and in conjunction with ἵνα which describes the intended result of the proclamation of the gospel.

Βιόω in verse 2 refers to the present mortal existence of the believers whereas ζάω as elsewhere in the letter refers to the life of resurrection offered by God in Christ. Christ was made alive (ζωοποιέω, 3:18) and became a living stone (λίθον ζῶντα, 2:4). The believers' shares in this life through their being reborn to a living hope.[441] The final realisation of their hope is in view. This life is synonymous with the believers' salvation (1 Pet 1:5, 9, 10; 2:2; 4:18); exaltation (5:66) and glorification (1:7; 5:10). This thought is found in the Maccabean literature as well: "It is good being put to death by humans to look for hope from God of being raised up again by Him" (2 Macc 7: 14). Πνεύματι is paralleled with the kerygmatic expression in 3:18 concerning Christ and Christ's resurrection serves as the basis of hope for all Christians.

---

437. Selwyn, *St. Peter: Greek Text*, 215.

438. Cf. Dalton, *Christ's Proclamation*, 50.

439. Cf. 1 Pet 2:15; 3:18; 4:2; 4:19; 5:4.

440. Elliott, *1 Peter: New Translation*, 239; contra Selwyn, *St. Peter: Greek Text*, 216, and Vogels, *Christi Abstieg*, 167–68.

441. Elliott, *1 Peter: New Translation*, 739;cf. Dalton, *Christ's Proclamation*, 236, 238–39.

## Christology as Foundation for Ethics   245

### Social and Historical Context

The author is not concerned with activities that were considered immoral or illegal by Roman authorities. That these activities are to be avoided by the audience goes without saying. Our author is concerned with ἀθεμίτοις adjective normal dative feminine plural no degree of ἀθέμιτος, ον "forbidden; disgusting (of idolatry)"εἰδωλολατρίαις noun "dative feminine plural common" of εἰδωλολατρία, ας f "idolatry."[442] Idolatry seems to be the panicle of all vices, which could possibly be an inheritance of the Jews's Diaspora existence in the Greco-Roman world. Their highest priority was their monotheistic belief in YHWH and their understanding of the catastrophe of the exile as a direct result of the kings's practices of idolatry. The idolatrous drinking parties often took place during the meetings of the well-known associations, clubs, and guilds which were typical of Greco-Roman society form the fourth century BCE onwards. These clubs were voluntary associations which provided occasions for socializing, occupational networking, business opportunities, religious groups, common interests and mutual aid. It could be assumed that the author had these associations in mind because it was highly probable that many of the addressees belonged to them.[443]

It is especially with these activities that the audience need to break. This cannot be reconciled with their conversion to Christianity. This lifestyle is not in accordance to the will of God. Τὸ βούλημα τῶν ἐθνῶν is also unique in the New Testament and is aimed in opposition to θελήματι θεοῦ. In the words of Goppelt: "The will of the Gentiles manifests itself especially in the forms of social and religious custom that become requirements through the power of habit and pressure for conformity."[444]

Verse 4 in a certain sense summarised the entire conflict which the Christians had to endure, since religion in antiquity was not separated from other cultural activities. It in fact included all human activities, e.g., the domestic sphere,[445] agriculture,[446] city life[447] and religious assemblies and

---

442. Cf. 1 Pet 1:3; 3:21; 2:5; 25:24.

443. Idolatry is foreign to secular Greco-Roman literature and is not used to describe their own religions. It is a unique term grounded in the Judo-Christian literature (cf. Goppelt, *Der erste Petrusbrief*, 273). This is a post-exilic emphasis on monotheism and a criticism of the idolatry practiced by the kings of Israel which caused the horror of the destruction of Israel and the following exile.

444. Elliott, *1 Peter: New Translation*, 725; cf. Reicke, *The Epistles*, 117–19.

445. Goppelt, *Commentary*, 284.

446. E.g., the gods of the household or "lares," cf. Juvenal, *Sat.* 11.37–40; 12.89–92.

447. E.g., the gods of the fields, cf. Martial, *Epig.* 10.92.

festivals.[448] As Price notes public festivals often included processions and sacrifices offered on public altars.[449] Therefore the Christians faced the problem of social withdrawal because their conversion no longer allowed them to take part in public religious activities which was expected from everyone residing in the Roman Empire. It may be assumed that Christians did participate in these activities prior to their conversion. After their conversion it was impossible for them to attend these activities for they all involved some sort of idolatry and in order to avoid that the Christians could no longer participate in the culture of their day. Additionally, Emperor veneration emerged all over the Roman Empire, especially in Asia Minor[450] which was of course impossible for Christians to acknowledge. Christians' avoidance of participation in state religious activities was regarded as disloyalty towards the Empire and even treason.[451] This verse could therefore also be understood in connection with 1 Pet 2:11: Christians became "aliens" and "strangers" within their own social context. They were not hated because they posed a political threat, but rather because they were socially deviant and therefore dangerous and obscure.[452] Living in this society social ostracism was an inevitable reality. As Seneca notes those who are wise will not upset the customs of the general population and will not engage in new and unfamiliar ways of living.[453] This suspicious behaviour could result in persecution, because it was considered disloyal to the Empire and provoked the anger of the gods which could cause catastrophes.

Behind this hostile behaviour lies the fear that Christians no longer honored expected modes of conduct. Christianity, like the people of Israel, faced the challenge of demonstrating to their neighbours that their break with former alliances and practices by no means implied their abandonment of honorable civil behaviour especially as far as law and order was concerned.[454]

---

448. E.g., marketplaces, city halls, the city council chambers cf. Chrysostom, *Ordin.* 50.1, because of the presence of shrines and statues of the gods.

449. Cf. Tertullian, *Apol.* 35.

450. Price, *Rituals and Power*, 111–113.

451. Ibid., 78, and Magie, *Roman Rule*, 452, note the following examples: Caligula claimed divinity (Suetonius, *Vit.* 4.22.2; cf. his accusation of the Jews for their refusal to acknowledge him as a god (Philo, *Legat.* 353); Vespasian's declaration that he became a god (cf. Suetonius, *Vit.* 8.23.4) and Domitian who wanted to be addressed as "our lord and god" (cf. Suetonius, *Vit.* 8.13.2).

452. Cf. Tacitus, *Ann.* 1.78, 4.37; Pliny, *Ep.*10.52, 82.

453. Achtemeier, *1 Peter*, 285; cf. Price, 1984, 125.

454. Seneca, *Ep.* 14.15.

## Theological Implications

As Achtemeier summarises: "Thus the situation the readers face provides ample evidence that, precisely because they suffer as did Christ for following God's will and not the (sinful) activities of their unbelieving contemporaries, they have in fact ceased from sin, that is, activities counter God's will."[455]

Our author has a different view of sin than Paul.[456] The Petrine author does not view sin as an external power as Paul does but as deliberate wrongdoing against the divine will.[457] Therefore the innocent suffering which the author refers to means the suffering caused by obedience and loyalty to Christ. It is not Christ that has ceased to sin for he has already been declared righteous (cf. 1 Pet 3:18) and free from sin (1 Pet 2: 22–23). Furthermore, if Christ's suffering caused all believers to stop sinning there would be no point in urging believers to do so. Rather the statement refers to a general human condition which enables the believers to conduct different from the sinful behaviour of the Gentiles. Elliott is of the opinion that the statement does not refer the "substitutionary and atoning power of the suffering and death" of the believers similar to what could be gathered from Israel's martyrdomical tradition.[458] According to this tradition the suffering and death of the righteous had atoning value for Israel.[459] Such atonement was achieved not merely by the suffering of the righteous but by the *death* (Elliot's emphasis) of the righteous. According to the Petrine author in continuation with the Christian tradition only the suffering and death of Christ alone has atoning power, and not that of humans.

Furthermore, in this case our author speaks of actual physical suffering and not of suffering in a metaphorical way. Additionally sinning, ἁμαρτία, ας f "sin" denotes concrete and deliberate disobedience to the will of God. Therefore it is not the deliverance of the controlling power of sin as in the Pauline sense but a concrete stance against sinful behaviour.[460] Neither is there any reference to the purifying power of suffering.[461] The texts cited to support this thought are also referring to deserved suffering rather than innocent suffering.[462] Elliott argues that in this case reference to suffering

---

455. Elliott, *1 Peter: New Translation*, 728.

456. Achtemeier, *1 Peter*, 280.

457. Cf. Rom 5:12–13, 20–21; 6:1, 10, 12–14; 13:14.

458. Cf. 1 Pet 2:22, 24; 3:8; 4:8:4:18.

459. Elliott, *1 Peter: New Translation*, 715.

460. Cf. 2 Macc 7:37–38; 4 Macc 1:11; 6:28–29.

461. Cf. Best, *1 Peter*, 151–152; Millauer, *Leiden als Gnade*, 122–130.

462. Contra Selwyn, *St. Peter: Greek Text*, 209; Best, *1 Peter*, 151; Millauer, *Leiden als Gnade*, 114–130; Vogels, *Christi Abstieg*, 142–159.

rather has a "disciplining function and refers" to the control of the desires of the flesh.[463] This idea figurates prominently in conventional Israelite wisdom, as well as Greco-Roman wisdom.[464]

Sirach writes: "He who loves his son will whip him often in order that he may rejoice at the way he turns out" (*Sir* 30: 1). According to Israelite wisdom this principle was applied to the divine Father's disciplining of his children (cf. Prov 3:11–12). This proverb is cited by the author of Hebrews in Heb 12:5–6 to interpret the suffering of the believers in a positive light. Christ as the Son of God "learned obedience through what he suffered" (Heb 5:8). Although Christ did not sin, as affirmed by both Peter and Hebrews, the general pedagogical principle still applies.

According to Elliott this statement by the author is neither baptismal nor reminiscent of Israel's martyr theology.[465] Rather innocent physical suffering disciplines the body by which sin is carried out and disciplines them to remain from further sinning. Through Christ's vicarious suffering believers were enabled to live uprightly and now their own suffering enables them to persevere on this new road taken.

In the same way God raised, honored and vindicate the "living stone" that was rejected by humans, so God wants the marginalised and judged believers to have life in abundancein the spirit.

Two aspects of divine reversal are highlighted: firstly those who judged the believers will be held accountable by God and secondly the suffering and rejected believers will be raised from the dead.

Verse 6 is grounded Christologically in God's raising of Christ but the theological idea of God's vindication of the suffering righteous one has a more ancient origin.

This idea of the divine vindication of the righteous is highlighted in 1 Peter by the author's portrayal of Christ as well as in the consolation he offers to suffer believers. Verse 6 concludes with the thought that believers should be confident in their eternal life and strengthened by their union with Christ especially in their solidarity with his suffering. This should encourage them to finally break with their behaviour prior to their conversion and to devote their lives to conduct which is in accordance with the will of God.[466]

God's exaltation and vindication of the suffering Christ forms the foundation of the motivation for believers to persevere and to continue to

---

463. Cf. *1 En* 67:9; *2 Bar* 13:10; 78:6.
464. Elliott, *1 Peter: New Translation*, 716.
465. Plutarch, *[Lib. ed.]* 12.16 (*Mor.* 12 A–D); cf. Pilch, "A Window."
466. Elliott, *1 Peter: New Translation*, 717.

do what is right despite innocent suffering. The suffering Christ is the ultimate example for the suffering believers.

The emphasis is also on the disciplining effect of suffering which enables believers to break with their ungodly ways. Their conduct should finalise the break that was initiated with their conversion and baptism. Once again our author is attempting to highlight the positive aspects of the suffering that the believers are enduring.

Pre-conversional and post-conversional behaviour are further contrasted as conduct in accordance with human cravings and conduct in accordance with God's will. To convert to the Christian faith means a life of nonconformity with the unbelieving society. This means disassociation, however not withdrawal from society. Believers still need to interact with pagan society and in such a manner that non-believers will come to respect and honor their laudable conduct. Disassociation, however, does cause resentment which could result in malicious marginalisation and even periodic persecution. The temptation to avoid this discrimination and to resume alliances with unbelievers was very prominent and an ever present reality for believers. Therefore they were urged to resist this temptation by being completely devoted to Christ even if this commitment entailed suffering. Furthermore, such conformity would undermine the very existence of the Christian community. The author's final word of consolation and motivation is that God will ultimately turn the tables and the current state of affairs will be radically reversed. Those who currently marginalise, shame and persecute Christians will be held accountable before God. Believers on the other hand will be exalted and glorified by God just as Christ was, and they will receive eternal life.[467]

## Christology as Paraenetic Strategy in 1 Peter

The standard paraenetic strategy employed by the author of 1 Peter is to use Christ as an example to be admired and followed. The Greco-Roman moralists often thought of moral exemplars to mediate instructions.[468]

Often there is alluded to elements of an individual's biography in order to present the individual's virtue or vice as an example to be followed or avoided. This individual could be either fictional or historical, although the latter was preferred for that would make the example a *realised* virtue. The individual could be alive or dead, known personally or only by legend. It must however be someone whose biography is to a certain extend known to

467. Ibid., 740.
468. Ibid., 741.

the reader. In the words of Seneca: "Nothing is more successful in bringing honorable influences to bear upon the mind, or in straightening out the wavering spirit that is prone to evil, than associating with good men. For the frequent seeing, the frequent hearing of them little by little sinks into the heart and acquires the force of precepts."[469][470]

In order to become virtuous one needs to practise virtuous deeds and in this process precepts play an important part for they define certain duties, but even more importantly, the cultivation of principle command certain duties. Therefore precepts require action as well as contemplation.

Virtuous examples become embodied laws or realised instructions. One adheres to an instruction, but one follows an example. Exemplars make instructions come alive for these individuals have lived in accordance with the principle that they embodied. Exemplars apply virtuous actions to practical situations, whereas instructions are the application of reason to certain circumstances of life.[471] Yet both imply contemplation and application. However, because exemplars are personal, they present a certain element of reality, which is missing from mere instructions. An instruction remains an unrealised theory, whereas exemplars by definition, represent the virtuous action within the sphere of human experience. Instructions only pertain to human potential.[472]

Exemplars also function on an emotional level, because they foster an admiration and love for themselves as well as for the principles that they embody. Examples establish a personal relationship between the exemplar and the follower. An exemplary individual must therefore be worthy of respect, because the relationship is defined be reverence because of the individual's virtuous life. The individual himself is exemplary, not his actions. The beauty of the virtuous deeds of the virtuous person leads to admiration and moves the follower to imitation. The virtuous person therefore needs to be worthy of the deepest respect and affection. According to Plutarch affection for virtuous men is absolutely essential in order to progress in moral life.[473]

Plutarch encourages his readers to "love good men" to the point of being "cemented" to them. Important for the argument of this study is that Plutarch admonished his readers not to shy away from following virtuous men even into tragic circumstances. In this manner virtuous men become guides through difficulties and temptations, for they do not merely present

---

469. Dryden, *Theology and Ethics*, 163; cf. Fiore, *Personal Example*, 93–94.
470. Dryden's translation.
471. Seneca, *Ep* 94.4 ; Dryden, 2006, 164.
472. Spohn, *Go and Do*, 33.
473. Dryden, *Theology and Ethics*, 165.

## CHRISTOLOGY AS FOUNDATION FOR ETHICS

behavioural patterns to be imitated, the individual himself ought to be revered and loved and it is from this emotional connection that the follower's commitment to a virtuous way of living is fuelled. For the follower does not merely follow ideas or doctrines, he is following in the footsteps of a real person. It further has the implication that to fail a person is must worse than simply to fail an idea and to succeed means to share in the honor of the virtuous example.[474]

Seneca writes:

> Cherish some man of high character, and keep him ever before your eyes, living as if he were watching you, and ordering all your actions as if he beheld them . . . The soul should have someone whom it can respect . . . Choose therefore a Cato; or, if Cato seems too severe a model, choose some Laelius, a gentler spirit. Choose a master whose life, conversation, and soul-expressing face have satisfied you, picture him always to yourself as your protector or your pattern. For we must indeed have someone according to whom we may regulate our own characters; you can never straighten that which is crooked unless you have a ruler."[475]

Therefore, one's virtuous exemplar becomes something of a trusted companion, a protector and a witness to one's actions and to shame one from dishonorable actions. Exemplars become intimate friends and function as moral guides.

Plutarch focuses his readers' attention on the characteristics of the person he wished his readers to follow. He does that by citing specific deeds in order to reveal the inner disposition of the exemplar for it is the virtuous character that ought to be imitated and not a specific deed. In doing so the virtue is applied more universally.

In 1 Peter Christ becomes the exemplar of virtue. Similar to the Greco-Roman moralists, it is not the deeds as such that should be imitated but the virtue that was revealed by the deeds. In the words of Spohn: "The story of Jesus is a *paradigm* (cf. ὑπογραμμός, 1 Pet 2:21; see discussion above), a normative pattern or exemplar that can be creatively applied in different circumstances. Disciples do not clone their master's life; they follow the master through discerning imaginations, graced emotions, and faithful community."[476]

---

474. Ibid., 167; cf. Plutarch, *De Prof. In Virt.* 84B–85C.

475. Dryden, *Theology and Ethics*, 168.

476. Seneca, *Ep*, 11.8–10. Dryden's translation, see Dryden, *Theology and Ethics*, 169.

Within the Greco-Roman paraenesis the authors always specifically indicate those aspects of the individual's biography that ought to be imitated. Therefore, the authors place constraints on the situation wherein the virtue can be applied. The principle is therefore flexible enough to be applied universally, but the application is guided by the author's selective portrayal of the individual. Often virtuous men embody a lot of different characteristics worthy of imitation and their virtues are therefore applicable to various different situations.[477]

As far as 1 Peter is concerned Christ serves as the example of those virtues needed to be imitated in the church. "The 'biography' of Christ is retold in such a way as to reveal a particular character trait that the author seeks to instill in his audience."[478]

According to Dreyden the bulk of 1 Peter's Christological material consists of *imitatio Christi* passages.[479] The three passages in focus, 1 Pet 2:21–25; 3:18, and 4:1, are seen as essential to the understanding of the thrust of the entire epistle.[480]

First Peter 2:21–25 appear at the end of the *Haustafel* directed at servants/slaves: οἰκέτης, ουm "house servant, servant." As Achtemeier notes that although there is no question that the slaves are indeed addressed in these verses, it is clear from the language that the author uses that it is applicable to the larger Christian audience.[481] Although the slaves are the primary addressees in this case, the verses function paradigmatically for all Christians suffering for their faith. This unit is introduced by ὑποτάσσω "put in subjection, subject, subordinate; pass. be subject, submit to, obey, be under the authority of; take a subordinate place" which is part of the epistle's overall call to do good in relation to their reverence for Christ.[482] Within this context the author urges the slaves to remain subordinate to their masters not only when they are kind and gentle but also if they are cruel.

The institution of slavery in the ancient world was, although socially acceptable, still an unjust system of power play, for the slave was the property of his or her master and possessed no legal or human rights. Often, this pericope has been read wrongly within the context of the absence of emancipation as if the author commands slaves simply to submit to their fate in whatever cruelty they are subjected to and therefore it has been

---

477. Spohn, *Go and Do*, 10–11.
478. Dryden, *Theology and Ethics*, 172.
479. Fowl, *Story of Christ*, 202–3.
480. Dryden, *Theology and Ethics*, 174; cf. Elliott, "Backward and Forward," 201–3.
481. Cf. Brox, *Petrusbrief* (1st ed), 128.
482. Achtemeier, *1 Peter*, 194.

wrongly assumed that the author condoned the cruel and unjust system of suffering.[483] In reality, the question at stake is slaves who have to endure cruelty for the sake of their faith, or as the author states: ἀγαθοποιέω "do good, help; live uprightly, do what is right or good." The author wants the slave to persevere in doing good and not to stop doing good in order to avoid unjust suffering. In the words of Neugebauer:

> In der Tat ist der Gafahr derer, die Unrecht leiden, daß sie aufhören, das Gute weiter zu tun, daß sie entweder gar nichts machen order das Falsche. Der Unrecht Leidende soll sich nicht auf sein Leiden zurückziehen, gerade nicht in Passivität versinken, soll schön gar nicht mit gleicher Müntze zurückzahlen (cf. 1 Pet 2:23; 3:9), sondern unbeirrt das Tun des Guten und Rechten fortsetzen. Leiden versetzt den Christen weder in die Regunglosigkeit noch ins bloße Reagieren, sondern gegenuber dem Unrecht und unter dem Leiden behält das Gute die Aktivität und die Initiative.[484]

The author therefore sees no merit in the endurance of suffering as such. As Jones-Haldeman notes: "The Christian slave, therefore, is not called to suffering; rather he is called, as a member of God's people, to doing good."[485] Similarly Filson writes: "The repeated exhortation to do the right hints that under persecution, to avoid suffering, the Christian may shirk his duty, shrink from steady expression of his faith in life, and so take the easy way."[486] He adds: "The Christian must not respond in opposition to ill-treatment with hate and retaliation. The example of Christ should teach them that."[487] Christ becomes the ultimate example in unjust suffering, because he never retaliated nor neglected to do the will of God.

Cervantes-Gabarron argues that 1 Peter like Luke-Acts and Hebrews uses πάσχω to speak of the suffering and death of Christ as a whole, as a single event.[488] Therefore, when our author states that Christ suffered, he has the entire passion narrative in mind which includes his death. His suffering and death are therefore inseparable.

Christ suffers for doing good, yet he continues to do good. What is in the author's focus is the fundamental principle of doing the will of God even if it entails unjust suffering. It is Christ's commitment to the will of God that

483. Cf. 1 Pet 2:15-17.
484. Dryden, *Theology and Ethics*, 176.
485. Neugebauer, "Zur Deutung," 80.
486. Jones-Haldeman, *The Function*, 192.
487. Filson, "Peter," 409.
488. Ibid., 406.

motivates his choice to endure suffering and to continue to do good. The statement: παθόντος σαρκὶ with reference to the actual physical suffering of Christ underscores his commitment to do so out of reverence for God. The idea which is emphasised is not that physical suffering has cleansing or purifying agencies *per se*, but that in choosing to endure physical suffering and to continue to do good amidst suffering is in fact a denial of the flesh, which naturally would be willing to compromise in order to alleviate suffering or which would be seeking an opportunity to satisfy the desire to retaliate. As far as the suffering of Christ is concerned, total obedience to the will of God is in focus and to choose to do what is right in the midst of suffering. The point therefore is that obedience to the will of God is a virtue that is cultivated by constantly choosing to do the will of God. If a person is able to do the will of God under difficult circumstances, where the temptation to abandon what is good is very strong, then the forming of the virtue takes place on a stronger level.[489]

In 1 Pet 2:23 it becomes clear that during his suffering Christ did not return evil with evil, but placed his trust completely in God. Similarly, the slaves ought to endure unjust suffering and should not pay their masters back in kind, but instead they should place their trust in the Lord, for he will vindicate them in the end. These verses are meant to highlight the actions of Jesus in order to provide a model for the slaves to be imitated. Jesus's actions also reveal his righteousness for he continues to do good amidst his suffering. Therefore he becomes both an exemplar and a saviour.[490]

The vicarious nature of Jesus's suffering does not come into play before 1 Pet 2:24, but because his suffering was an inevitable part of his sin bearing, his suffering is redemptive as such. Furthermore, Christ did not merely endure passive suffering, but he made an active choice in order to do so for he remained steadfast in his commitment to the will of God. The work Christ did on the cross was therefore redemptive and exemplary.

Christ becomes the model of the one who conquered sin and evil and fostered obedience to the will of God by actively choosing to remain loyal to the will of God. The act of Christ is exemplary as an act of obedience in the face of suffering. His suffering is only exemplary for its display of obedience and righteous behaviour and not for its vicarious nature for that is a once off event in God's history with humankind.[491]

Ὑπογραμμός, οὖm "example" as used in 1 Peter 2:21 does not refer to a specific action to be undertaken by slaves but rather to important

---

489. Cervantes-Gabarron, *La pasión*, 167.
490. Dryden, *Theology and Ethics*, 183.
491. Ibid., 185; cf. Elliott, *1 Peter: New Translation*, 529.

characteristics of Christ's sufferings which are to become universal guidelines.[492] When our author therefore states that Christ did not threaten, ἀπειλέω, it refers to the universal principle of Christ's commitment to do good even in the face of gross unjust suffering. His absolute devotion to the will of God is exemplary to the slaves who are called to obedience and commitment to the will of Christ.

Verses 24 and 25 of 1 Pet 2 remind the readers of God's love and care for them and this reinforces the affective force of Christ as an example to be followed. The slaves are the beneficiaries of Christ's redemptive work and the author aims to appeal to their gratitude which will strengthen their connection with him. They will follow Christ not because his example is worthy of following, but because he is their personal saviour and shepherd. Similar to the Greco-Roman paraenetic the emotional connection with the exemplar and their commitment to him is important for it counteracts the emotional appeal of a previous comfortable life.[493]

These *imitatio Christi* passages provides a window to the nature of the entire epistle. The author's theology furthers his paraenetic agenda. It provides the context for his ethical reflection as well as the motivational structures in order to encourage character formation. This is how the author of 1 Peter employs Christology as foundation for his ethics.

## Mark 8:34–38

> *And he called the crowd with his disciples to him and said to them, "If anyone would come after me, let him renounce himself and take up his cross and follow me. For whoever would save his life will lose it, but whoever loses his life for my sake and the sake of the gospel will save it. For what does it profit a man to gain the whole world and forfeit his life? For what can a man give in return for his life? For whoever is ashamed of me and of my words in this adulterous and sinful generation, of him will the Son of Man also be ashamed when he comes in the glory of his Father with the holy angels."*

---

492. Dryden, *Theology and Ethics*, 188–89; cf. Michaels, *1 Peter*, 148; Achtemeier, "Suffering Servant," 177.

493. Cf. Osborne, "Guide Lines," 392. No entry for 1995.

## Literary and Narratological Analysis

Mark here turns his own typical structure upside down. Normally Jesus first addresses to crowd and then speaks to his disciples privately, but in this instance Jesus first speaks to Peter, then to the disciples and then he calls the crowd to whom the following sayings are addressed. Often, the crowd is a creation of Mark's literary technique because they appear and dissolve as required by the narrator. It serves as a means to make Jesus's appeal universal. All, including insiders and outsiders are called to understand what it means to be a disciple of Christ.[494]

Crossan is of the opinion that this saying of Jesus about the cross is authentic.[495] He substantiates this view because of its proverbial nature and because it is found in a cynic context: "if you want to be crucified, just wait. The cross will come. If it seems reasonable to comply and the circumstances are right, then it is to be carried through and your integrity Maintained."[496] In the case of Jesus, however the cross does not come because of his commitment to the kingdom of God, and the fact that this commitment will ultimately clash with the Jewish religious leaders.

Jesus's words in verse 34 εἴ τις θέλει ὀπίσω μου "if anyone wants to come after me" recalls his command to Simon and Andrew in Mark 1:17 (δεῦτε ὀπίσω μου "come after me") as well as the narrator's comment to the sons of Zebedee in Mark 1:20 (ἀπῆλθον ὀπίσω αὐτοῦ "and they went after him"). This is an explicit articulation of the commitment required for being a disciple of Jesus. Within the context there is also an implied criticism of Peter.

Ἀπαρνησάσθω ἑαυτόν: ἀπαρνησάσθω third person singular aorist imperative aorist middle of ἀπαρνέομαι "disown, renounce claim to" is the direct opposite of the denial of Jesus as Peter does in Mark 14:68. Consequently, Peter is here described as a negative example to the audience. The follower of Jesus must also take up his cross, καὶ ἀράτω τὸν σταυρὸν αὐτοῦ, which means, when translated literally, to carry the cross beam to be used in a crucifixion.[497]

When Jesus tells his disciples to deny themselves, he does not mean that they need to renounce certain luxuries as if doing so or even enduring suffering would make them holy.[498]

---

494. Dryden, *Theology and Ethics*, 190–1; cf. Achtemeier, *1 Peter*, 204.
495. Boring, *Mark*, 243.
496. Crossan, *The Birth*, 353.
497. Epictetus, *Diatr.* 2:2–10.
498. Collins, *Mark*, 408; cf. Dewey, "Feminist Reading," 23–26.

CHRISTOLOGY AS FOUNDATION FOR ETHICS                257

The word translated with "deny" ἀπαρνέομαι "disown, renounce claim to" is found elsewhere in Mark only with reference to Peter's denial of Jesus.[499] "Deny" is therefore the opposite of "confess" or "acknowledge."

This is the first occurrence of the word σταυρός, οῦ m "cross" in the Gospel of Mark. This is intended to prepare the reader for the fate that will meet Jesus. The language here would have had a strong impact because execution by crucifixion was well-known within the Roman world as well as in the history of Judea.

Ὅς γὰρ ἐὰν θέλῃ τὴν ψυχὴν αὐτοῦ σῶσαι ἀπολέσει αὐτήν ὃς δ' ἂν ἀπο λέσει τὴν ψυχὴν αὐτοῦ ἕν εκενέμοῦ καὶ τοῦ εὐαγγελίου σώσει αὐτήν: Originally the saying in this verse was probably independent.[500]

It was probably a proverbial wisdom which Jesus expressed in personal terms and which came to belong to the general category of sayings of Jesus. There is a certain ambiguity to the use of ψυχή which could be interpreted in this context to mean either "life" or "soul." If "life" is meant to be understood as one's physical life, then the saying would be paradoxical. The Old Testament or Jewish thought understood ψυχή differently from the Greek thought. In the Greek understanding ψυχή is the immortal part of the self which is trapped with a mortal body. The Old Testament or Jewish understanding was that the human self was a unity and therefore ψυχή represented the entire person. Mark 8:34–38 reflects upon the actual reality facing the audience of Mark's Gospel. Their loyalty to Christ and his message could really cost them their whole life.[501]

Within the oral stage of the Gospel the significance of this proverb would have been clear from its application or its rhetorical force within a specific context. At some point the proverb received Christological significance by the addition of the words ἕνεκεν ἐμοῦ "for my sake."[502] The addition of ἕνεκεν ἐμοῦ evokes a context of persecution and this lead to the possible understanding of the saying by the audience as: "Whoever wants to save his *physical life* will lose *eternal life*, but whoever loses his *physical life* for my sake will save his *eternal life*." And this was further developed by the addition of καὶ τοῦ εὐαγγελίου "and the good news" either by the Markan author or at pre-Markan stage. Losing one's life for the sake of Jesus and the good news is equivalent to taking up one's cross and following Jesus. Verses 34–35 and verses 36–37 probably were independent sayings at its original stage,

499. Boring, *Mark*, 244; cf. Dewey, "Feminist Reading."

500. Cf. Mark 14:30, 31, 72.

501. Collins, *Mark*, 408; cf. Bultmann, *The History*, 83, 105 who concluded that the saying without the Christological elaboration goes back to the historical Jesus.

502. Boring, *Mark*, 24.

for both are proverbial and attributed to Jesus. There is nothing particularly Christian about verse 36. It is the universal questioning of the human strive for wealth and power which becomes exposed and robbed of its significance in the face of persecution and death. One could conclude therefore that physical life is less important than following Jesus.

It is not sane to exchange one's life for any amount of wealth, for life is precious and its value beyond measure. According to the philosopher Menander "nothing is more valuable than (one's) life."[503]

Yet people often trade away their lives in order to pursue fleeting pleasures and possessions. Jesus attempts to answer the question that might arise after Jesus warning that suffering and persecution lie ahead for his followers namely: "why should one follow Jesus?" Jesus followers acquire a rationale: why is following Jesus, proclaiming the arrival of the kingdom, suffering and even death prudent and wise? Because the kingdom of God which entails salvation of mankind has really dawned, and that Jesus does indeed enjoy God's favour and his authority.

To follow Jesus is not only wise for general reasons, but wise in terms of the coming judgement. Jesus may have to endure suffering in the near future, but he will return as the "son of man." The "Son of Man" will deny those who denied him and his word. This retribution is an example of *Uis Talions* (justice of equal terms). Which is common among the sayings of Jesus as well as in rabbinic literature.[504]

Some scholars, including Bultmann,[505] view Jesus referral to the "Son of Man" in the third person as referring to another eschatological figure. However, if this is the case the reasoning of Jesus would not make sense. Why would an eschatological figure other than Jesus be ashamed of those who were ashamed of Jesus? Jesus does indeed speak of his own suffering and shameful treatment and as the coming as the Father he will reverse the current state of affairs which entails compensation for the suffering and shame that he had to endure. The same applies to the disciples who have to endure the same suffering but will enjoy vindication by the coming "Son of man." The coming kingdom of God will be completed with the return of the "Son of man." As the suffering "Son of man" Jesus will appear before Caiaphas and the Jewish council and thereafter before Pilate and the Roman soldiers, but as the returning "Son of man" Jesus will enter

---

503. Collins, *Mark*, 409; cf. Bultmann, *The History*, 93, 151.

504. Menander, Fragments in Stobaeus, *Anthology* 843; cf. Evans, *Mark* 8:27—16:20, 26–27; Donahue and Harrington, *Mark*, 245.

505. Mark 4:24, 7:2;

as a conquering warrior this is aimed at arousing hope and anticipation among the disciples of Jesus.

Ὃς γὰρ ἐὰν ἐπαισχυνθῇ με καὶ τοὺς ἐμοὺς λόγους ἐν τῇ γενεᾷ ταύτῃ τῇ μοιχαλίδι καὶ ἁμαρτωλῷ, καὶ ὁ υἱὸς τοῦ ἀνθρώπου ἐπαισχυνθήσεται αὐτόν, ὅταν ἔλθῃ ἐν τῇ δόξῃ τοῦ πατρὸς αὐτοῦ μετὰ τῶν ἀγγέλων τῶν ἁγίων. This prophetic saying warns those who are afraid of Jesus's words because when the Son of Man returns in glory he will likewise be ashamed of these people. Already the idea of divine vindication is foresighted, for those who acknowledge Jesus before human being will be acknowledged by him.[506]

The shame (ἐπαισχυνθῇ third person singular aorist subjunctive passive of ἐπαισχύνομαι "be ashamed") Jesus is talking about here is the failure to proclaim the gospel as well as the denial of Jesus when interrogated. Ernst Käsemann coined this correspondence between humans being ashamed of Jesus and the Son of Man being ashamed of them from-critically as sentences of "holy law."[507] To be ashamed of Jesus is the exact opposite of denying oneself. Those who wanted to save their own lives will find that the Son of Man is ashamed of them when he returns. Those who were ashamed of the words of Jesus are those who refrained from proclaiming the gospel in the face of persecution. The literary context offers a negative view of the historical-political context within which the audience of Mark finds themselves, for the world rejects Jesus and his words as well as persecutes his followers. It is therefore inevitable that the followers of Jesus will collide with the rulers of their time. The audience were to expect tension and persecution until the return of the Son of Man.[508]

## Social and Historical Context

The call to deny oneself and to take up ones cross is not restricted to the apostles alone, but to all of the followers of Jesus. Within the context of the first century Roman Empire, to "take up one's cross" would be associated with carrying of a cross to the place of execution.[509] According to Josephus crucifixion in Palestine was common enough that no doubt should exist that the saying did not originate with Jesus himself.[510] However in a Jewish context the saying is strange. The Jewish idea was that a disciple was urged

506. Bultmann, *The History*, 112, 122, 128, 151–52.

507. Collins, *Mark*, 410.

508. Käsemann, "Das Problem," 248–60.

509. Collins, *Mark*, 411; cf. Lövestam, *Jesus*, 19.

510. Evans, *Mark 8:27—16:20*, 25; cf. Hengel, *Crucifixion*, 62: "People were all too aware of what it meant to bear the cross through the city and then be nailed to it."

to take up the yoke of the Torah or of the commandments but never a cross.[511] Therefore, Jesus's words would have sounded rather sombre to his audience. On the other hand its Christological significance implies that Jesus knows exactly what lies ahead of him and his followers. This implies divine omniscience, as well as Jesus's complete willingness to submit to the will of God.

There could be little historical doubt that Jesus did indeed call his disciples to radical action. However, the language used in this verse rather reflects the post-Easter vocabulary of the early church.[512] This ideal is substantiated by the test itself: it is the first reference to "cross" or "crucifixion" in Mark, yet the Greek definite article is antiphonic i.e. referring to a known object from previous reference. Neither the crowd nor the disciples, at this point in time in the narrative, would have such a point of reference. The post-Easter audience of Mark, however does have this frame of reference. When they hear "cross" or "crucifixion" the cross of Jesus comes to mind as well as the recent crucifixion of Christians by Nero.[513] There might also have been many Christians among the Jews crucified by Titus and Vespasian during the recent Jewish revolt.

## Theological Implications

Within the greater context the readers are called to rather deny themselves than to deny Jesus. In essence it means that one's priorities should change and that the self and its human desires should no longer come first. It is the reversal of the decision made by Adam who wanted to be like God, i.e. to be his own god and a return to the order God intended: Let God be God and the humans should be subject to his will.

Similarly, the command to take up one's cross does not refer to the inconveniences of sufferings that form part of everyday human life as in the familiar saying "the cross I have to bear." The Markan Jesus does not command the endurance of the inevitable pains and sufferings of life, what he commands is the *voluntary*[514] taking up of the cross in the sense of sharing the suffering involved in discipleship and the flowing of Christ and his mission. When Mark's original readers hear Jesus's command of willingness to take up one's own cross, they did not understand it metaphorically, for crucifixion was very real to them. It was not a matter of private or personal

---

511. Josephus, *A.J.* 17.10.10 [295].
512. *m. 'Abot* 3:5; *Ber.* 2:2.
513. Cf. Pesch, *Markusevangelium* 2.
514. Cf. Tacitus, *Ann.* 15.44.4.

devotion. Crucifixion was not merely a slow and agonizing death it was also a public sharing spectacle.

Mark 8:34 initiates the shocking Markan theology that the Son of Man will be crucified and killed.

## Christology as Paraenetic Strategy in Mark: Does Mark Glorify Suffering?

In Mark 8:34 Jesus invites everyone to follow him: εἴτις θέλει ὀπίσω μου ἀκολουθεῖν, ἀπαρνησάσθω ἑαυτὸν καὶ ἀράτω τὸν σταυρὸν αὐτοῦ καὶ ἀκολουθείτω μοι.

When read out of context and through the lens of the modern Western world, the verse could be misunderstood as a glorification of suffering and an encouragement to become a victim: "one is to deny oneself, sacrifice oneself, wipe out any sense of self, and to embrace the cross, that is, suffering in general." The verse portrays discipleship as to suffer now with the expectation of a reward to come at a later age. "Many a woman has failed to develop her own identity and strengths and has embraced or endured suffering that could be alleviated because she has come to believe that such a way of life is pleasing to God and an imitation of Christ. This is a fundamental misreading of the Gospel of Mark. Mark does not glorify either self-sacrifice or suffering."[515] On the contrary, the Markan Jesus inaugurates the coming of the kingdom of God, he alleviates suffering and empower others to do the same. What the Gospel of Mark does communicate is that a particular cause of suffering, that is, persecution by the powers that are in control, is inevitably part of discipleship. The self-denial talked about by the Gospel of Mark does not mean self-sacrifice as we understand it today.

Elisabeth Schüssler Fiorenza writes:

> It is true that Christian theology *overtly* condemns oppressive forms of exploitation and victimization of women . . . Nevertheless, the Christian proclamation of the kyriarchal politics of submission and its attendant virtues of self-sacrifice, docility, subservience, obedience, suffering, unconditional forgiveness, male authority, and unquestioning surrender to God's will covertly promotes in the name of God and love, such patriarchal-kyriarchal practices of victimization as Christian virtues.
>
> For women, insofar as they submit to the narrative world created by a Gospel, absorb not only the world's ideas about the proper role of women, but also its values. And if what Christian

---

515. My emphasis.

women readers absorb from reading Mark is a glorification of victimage, then no matter how powerful positive female role models in Mark may be, the Gospel is indeed harmful to women as they strive to lead Christian lives today.[516]

The argument that the Gospel of Mark does not encourage suffering and victimage requires a literary and socio-logical analysis of the Gospel. The people of the first century AD had a different view of suffering than we have in the modern Western world. In the modern Western world suffering is rejected as a normal part of everyday life. Pain should go away, preferably immediately. Suffering is an exception or disruption of normal life. It is something to be changed or overcome as soon as possible.[517]

On the other hand the ancients viewed suffering as a normal, although unpleasant part of life. Suffering was not an interruption of the normal human existence.[518] The ancients understood themselves to have very little control over what happens to them and therefore they could not exercise the power to make the suffering end. Therefore they cultivated ways to be able to endure suffering. This was furthermore a result of the fact that ninety per cent of the people in antiquity lived at substance level or below, making famine, disease and discomfort part of their everyday experience. The situation was worsened by the high taxation levied by the Romans which caused families to live in the constant danger of losing their land in order to cover their debt.[519] Therefore, in various degrees suffering was an ever-present reality in antiquity and parents raised their children with the skill to be able to endure suffering.[520]

The Gospel of Mark makes a clear distinction between human suffering in general, which is cured and alleviated with Jesus who inaugurated the kingdom of God (Mark 1:14–15) and suffering caused by persecution which is the fate of those who remain faithful to Christ. The inauguration of the kingdom of God entailed Jesus's power over nature and sickness. In Mark 1–8 the arrival of the kingdom of God is portrayed in Jesus's alleviation of suffering, his performance of exorcisms, his healing of the sick, his feeding of the multitude, his walking on the sea and his calming of the storm. The power Jesus has is also transferred to his disciples, for he sends out his disciples to preach, to heal and to perform exorcisms. Jesus expected his disciples to trust God's power. The inauguration of the kingdom of God

---

516. Dewey, "Feminist Reading," 23.
517. Schüssler Fiorenza, *Critical Issues*, 147.
518. Dewey, "Feminist Reading," 29.
519. Ibid., 30; cf. Pilch, "Understanding Healing," 26–33.
520. Cf. Herzog, *Parables as Subversive Speech*, 53–73.

does not give the power, however, to dominate or control other human beings or to exercise force against them. Yet, those in possession of power during the old age perceive the arrival of God's kingdom as a threat and will do everything in their power to destroy it. The powers of the old age are not fully defeated yet and Mark expects an imminent eschatology where God's rule will be perfected.[521]

Those who oppose the coming of the kingdom of God on the other hand do not hesitate to use force. We read in Mark 3:6 that the Pharisees plot with the Herodians to destroy Jesus. Jesus furthermore predicts that his disciples will suffer persecution and even execution (Mark 13:9–13).

In Mark 8:34 it is clear that to follow Jesus is both a blessing, as it marks the end of much human suffering, but it also marks the beginning of a different kind of suffering at the hands of those who were seeking to destroy the followers of Jesus. Mark puts the danger to the followers of Jesus in very strong terms: the followers need to take up their cross. The cross was the instrument used by the Romans for their executions. Crucifixion was cruel, shameful and the prerogative of the Roman authorities to use against rebels, slaves and instigators. Anyone who challenged Roman authority was viewed as a potential threat and the Romans believed in acting pre-emptively. Therefore, to take up one's cross, literary meant to pick up the cross beam and to carry it to the place of execution where one will be nailed and tied to it and hoisted in an upright position. The reference to execution must have been crystal clear to any ancient hearer and the cross would not have been confused with general human suffering. It is as if one would say in an American context: "Take up your electric chair." But, different from human suffering in general, to take up one's cross could be avoided easily. All one had to do was to renounce Jesus and his kingdom. It would only have become one's fate if one insisted upon following Jesus.[522]

In Mark 8:34 the author prepares the audience for the consequences of their following of Jesus and simultaneously encourage them to remain faithful amidst suffering. The inevitability of persecution in no way negates the blessings of God. To renounce oneself could sound to modern ears as a call to deny the individual self and to give up the individual's will. This is not what was heard by the original audience, first and foremost because they had no sense of individuality. The basic unit of society in the first century Mediterranean world was not the individual, but the kinship group.[523] The group accepted responsibility for the actions of its individual members

521. Cf. Pilch, "A Window," 101–13.
522. Mark 9:1; Dewey, "Feminist Reading," 31.
523. Dewey, "Feminist Reading," 32.

and the chief male member of the group determined what behaviour was appropriated.

In such a dyadic society, to deny oneself, meant to renounce one's kinship, which was not merely the main unit of consumption but also the main unit of production whether of the subsistence farm or the household industry. The kin was also the basic political unit. To step outside one's kinship, was therefore not merely a renunciation of one's family but also one's means to generate an income. It also placed oneself outside the accepted social order. To renounce one's kin was indeed a very radical move. If one did so, and one had any kind of following, one would be perceived as a threat to the social order.

Therefore, in the Gospel of Mark, if one became a disciple of Jesus, one renounced one's kinship in order to become a member of the circle of Jesus. A new community or fictive kinship is thus established around the person of Jesus.[524]

The rejection of the kin was also the rejection of the social-political-economical structure of the first century Mediterranean society. Therefore, it is understandable that the rejection of the kin led to persecution. Societies are not supportive of those who challenge their rules.

Dewey concludes that when Mark 8:34 is read against the backdrop of the first century Mediterranean context and the greater narrative context of the Gospel it becomes clear that it is not an exhortation to suffering an victimage in general.[525]

Rather it is an exhortation to remain faithful to Jesus and to the community of the faithful in the face of persecution and with the inevitable possibility of execution.

Furthermore, the insights of the social scientific reading of texts taught exegetes to be sensitive to the fact that the New Testament is an androcentric and patriarchal text and a naïve reading of the text would necessarily lead to the perpetuation of androcentric and patriarchal values in modern society.

The author of Mark argues almost simultaneously on a Christological as well as an Ethical level, for especially in this pericope, the two are inextricably intertwined. This is however an excellent example of the author's ethics at work for it is indeed a reflection upon certain behaviour grounded within the perception of the suffering Christ. Therefore, Mark's Christology certainly is foundational to his ethics and an integral part of his paraneatic reasoning.

---

524. Ibid., 33; cf. Malina, *New Testament World*, 106–19.
525. Cf. Mark 3:33–35; 10:29–30.

## Suffering as the Christian Way of Life

First Peter 4:12–13

*Beloved, think it not strange concerning the fiery trial as a test for you as though some strange thing happened to you: inasmuch as you are partakers of Christ's sufferings; you may be glad so that in the revelation of his glory, you may be joyful and rejoice.*

### Literal and Discourse Analysis

Ἀγαπητοί adjective **no degree** masculine plural normal vocative masculine plural **no degree** of ἀγαπητός, ή, όν "beloved," "dear(est)"; is used commonly in the New Testament to address the recipients of a particular writings (cf. e.g., Rom 12:19; 1 Cor 10:14; 2 Cor 6:7; Phil 2:12; Heb 6:9; 1 John 3:2) and here it is intended to conclude the inclusio started in 1 Pet 2:11 expressing unity within the letter. The author opens a paraeneticalunit by addressing his audience intimately. This emphasises the affectionate bond that exists between author and audience isgrounded in the brotherhood of the faith, since the author probably never met his addressees personally. The very motivation behind the origin of the letter was the Christian brotherhood in Rome's desire to express their solidarity with the suffering brothers and sisters in Asia Minor. Once again the theme of innocent suffering is taken up. The author's address of his audience as "beloved" is in accordance with the letter's emphasis on fraternal love and family loyalty.[526]

Ξενίζεσθε second person plural present imperative passive of ξενίζω "surprise," "astonish" in this case does not present a sudden new situation in the lives of the addressees, but is an expression of an perpetual problem.[527] This is confirmed by the following two participles:

Γινομένῃ dative feminine singular present participle middle of γίνομαι "become," "be"; "happen," "take place," "arise" (aor. often impers. "it happened" or "came about"); "come into being, be" and συμβαίνοντος genitive neuter singular present participle active of συμβαίνω of "happen," "come about." There is a relation to be noted between this verse and 1 Pet 4:4, because the author uses the same word: ξενίζω. It is probable that the author wants to indicate that the Christians should have the opposite reaction to unbelievers as that of unbelievers towards them. The inevitability

---

526. Dewey, "Feminist Reading," 35.
527. Cf. 1 Pet 1:8, 22; 2:17; 3:8; 4:8; 5:14; Elliott, *1 Peter: New Translation*, 771.

of Christian suffering is a common concern in the writings of the New Testament.[528] The idea is only re-emphasised by our author by using a genitive absolute in ὡς ξένου ὑμῖν συμβαίνοντος. Margot notes that the surprise would rather be experienced by Gentile converts than by their Jewish counterparts, since the Jews were used to exclusion and suspicion and suffering because of Roman opposition.[529]

Achtemeier does not interpret πυρώσει noun dative feminine singular common of πύρωσις, εως f "burning"; "fiery ordeal" "fire" to have a literal meaning but rather a metaphorical meaning of "painful test" or "purifying fire."[530] This understanding is supported by πειρασμὸν accusative masculine singular common of πειρασμός, οῦm "period or process of testing," "trial," "test"; "temptation," "enticement." Feldmeier also agrees with this and sees a comparison between this verse and 1 Pet 1:6 where the same metaphor is used in the sense of the melting precious metals in order to purify them.[531] The reference to ξενίζω "surprise," "astonish" does however, according to Feldmeier, indicate a deepening in the suffering experienced, moving to inner distress.

This study does not agree with a comparison between this verse and 1 Pet 5:8: ὁ ἀντίδικος ὑμῶν διάβολος ὡς λέων ὠρυόμενος περιπατεῖ ζητῶν [τινα] καταπιεῖν because διάβολος nominative masculine singular common of διάβολος, ουm "the Devil"; does not have a literal meaning here either as Achtemeier's understanding of the Satan as being the force behind the evil persecution of the Christians by their unbelieving neighbours.[532] Rather, this study opts for a metaphorical understanding indicating that the Christians are tempted, precisely because of their suffering on behalf of their faith, to abandon the faith altogether. In order to avoid this suffering, Christians would rather return to their previous pagan existence—an occurrence that our author wants to avoid. Διάβολος therefore rather evil or temptation personified. Therefore the suffering that the Christian communities have to endure is a test for their faith and their ability to resist the temptation to return to their former pagan existence.

Μὴ ξενίζεσθε second person plural present imperative passive of ξενίζω "surprise, astonish": Earlier, the author used the same verb to refer to the unbelievers surprise (1 Pet 4:4) because of the believer's disassociation

---

528. Achtemeier, *1 Peter*, 305; cf. De Villiers, "Joy in Suffering," 80; Kelly, *Peter and Jude*, 184.

529. E.g., cf. 1 Thess 3:3; 2 Tim 3:12; 1 John 3:13; John 15:18–21; Matt 10:24–25.

530. Margot, *Les Epîtres*, 76.

531. Achtemeier, *1 Peter*, 305.

532. Feldmeier, *First Letter*, 224.

of them. Now the believer's astonishment at the persistence and intensity of their suffering is in focus. The point the author is making is that the intensity and reality of their suffering should not come as a shock to them, since they are followers of the suffering Christ.[533] In what follows, the author provides reasons for why suffering should come as no surprise to the followers of Christ, but as something which they should regard as valuable.[534]

Firstly: τῇ ἐν ὑμῖν πυρώσει πρὸς πειρασμὸν ὑμῖν γινομένῃ: πυρώσει dative feminine singular common of πύρωσις, εως f "burning; fiery ordeal, painful test": Here it most probably refers to the process of exposing metal ore to extremely high temperatures in order to separate it from impurities (cf. Prov 27:21: δοκίμιον ἀργύρῳ καὶ χρυσῷ πύρωσις ἀνὴρ δὲ δοκιμάζεται διὰ στόματος ἐγκωμιαζόντων αὐτόν).

It may be concluded with relative certainty that since the author used πύρωσις in the same metaphorical meaning in 1 Pet 1:6–7. In both passages the purifying function of fire is equalled to innocent suffering, in order to give it a positive meaning; namely the divine testing of the consistency of one's faith. Πύρωσις according to Elliott, is an umbrella-term encompassing all the hostility, slander and abuse that the faithful have to endure.[535]

Γινομένη participle present middle dative feminine singular of γίνομαι "become, be; happen, take place." The dative participle modifies ὑμῖν in order to indicate the persons affected.

Πρὸς πειρασμὸν: πειρασμὸν accusative masculine singular common of πειρασμός, οῦ m "period or process of testing, trial, test" indicates the purpose of fiery ordeal. Just as fire tests the purity and genuineness of metal, so suffering tests the sincerity of faith as loyalty and commitment to Christ. This is confirmed by 1 Pet 1:6–7.

The meaning in 1 Peter differs from Matt 6:13/ Luke 11:4 where πειρασμός, οῦ is associated with the devil as the one who tempts. James 1:13–14 understands πειρασμός, οῦ to come from within the persons self, originating within his sinful nature. However in 1 Peter, since it has a positive meaning here, God is implied as the one who tests. Kühn points to the use of πειρασμός, οῦ in order to describe the daily situation of believes.[536]

Ὡς ξένου ὑμῖν συμβαίνοντος is a genitive absolute construction with ξένου functioning substantively as the subject of the participle συμβαίνοντος. Συμβαίνοντος present participle active genitive neuter singular of συμβαίνω "happen, come about" also echoes the language of 1 Pet 4:4 and forms the

---

533. Achtemeier, 1 Peter, 306.
534. 1 Pet 2:21–24; 3:18; 5:1.
535. Elliott, 1 Peter: New Translation, 771.
536. Ibid., 772.

contrasting parallel to ὑμῖν γινομένῃ so that both participles emphasise the fact that it is the addressees, the believers who are affected.

The present tense of συμβαίνω and γίνομαι also suggests a continuation of the current situation rather than a new or sudden crisis. The three fold use of ὑμῖν shows that the author is not simply talking in general put he is addressing the suffering of his audience specifically.

The causative clause, introduced by ἵνα: ἵνα καὶ ἐν τῇ ἀποκαλύψει τῆς δόξης αὐτοῦ χαρῆτε ἀγαλλιώμενοι indicates that the Christians' present suffering is conditional for their future glory. Future vindication and sharing in Christ's glory is only possible for those how successfully sustained the test of suffering. Or, put differently, sharing in Christ's suffering ἀλλὰ καθὸ κοινωνεῖτε τοῖς τοῦ Χριστοῦ παθήμασιν χαίρετε is the only way to share in his glorification. The future joy will occur when Christ's glory is revealed.

Ἀλλὰ καθὸ κοινων εἴτε τοῖς τοῦ Χριστοῦ παθήμασιν believers suffered because their Lord Jesus Christ suffered. Suffering is something not alien to those who "follow in the footsteps" of Christ. Therefore, the meaning of καθὸ here is "since." Believers should rejoice because of this commonality for their solidarity with Christ manifests in this way. The author no longer views the suffering of the believers to those of Jesus Christ, but he now speaks of them "sharing in" κοινωνεῖτε second person plural present indicative active of κοινωνέω "share, take part, participate; contribute, give a share."

Τοῖς τοῦ Χριστοῦ παθήμασιν the same phrase occurs in 5:1 and a similar expression is found in 1:11. By mentioning Christ the phrase becomes directly associated with the Messiah and within the Israelite tradition the suffering of the righteous and great tribulations formed part of the Messianic age and the end time. Christianity's unique and creative spin on the tradition is that the Messiah himself becomes the suffering righteous one. Israel never expected the Messiah to suffer but rather that he will be the victorious deliverer of his people from the oppression of their foreign governors. However, early Christianity transformed this idea to include the Messiah and his followers among the sufferers.[537]

Furthermore, the use of "Christ" without an article denotes the gradual development in early Christianity to use Χριστός not as a title, but as a personal name. For our author "Christ" and "the Christ" are equivalent designations for the same person, namely Jesus the Messiah.[538]

Χαίρετε second person plural present imperative active of χαίρω "rejoice, be glad": Because their innocent suffering unites them with their

---

537. Kühn, "*Peirasmos-Hamartia-Sarx*," 202–3; Luke 8:13; 1 Cor 7:5; 10:13; Gal 4:14; 6:1; 1 Thess 3:5.

538. Cf. Mark 8:13; 9:31, 32–34; Mark 13:7–27.

## CHRISTOLOGY AS FOUNDATION FOR ETHICS    269

Lord, believers ought to rejoice. The vocabulary of the verse echoes 1 Pet 1:6–8. The author's is of the present tense is meaning full since the believers ought to rejoice in the here and now. Joy should not only be a future hope, but a present reality, χαίρω is seldom used in conjunction with suffering in the NT—however the author is probably echoing a tradition found in Matt 5:11–12.[539]

Ἐν τῇ ἀποκαλύψει τῆς δόξης αὐτοῦ this temporal clause does not reflect Matt 5:11–12 or Luke 6:22–23 but rather another Christian tradition.[540] It echoes 1 Pet 1:8 where the same connection between present and future rejoicing is made. In the case of Jesus Christ suffering was followed by glory.[541] The argument therefore is that believers who shared in the innocent suffering of Christ can likewise look forward to sharing in his exaltation and glory Jesus Christ's glory involves his divine election (1 Pet 2:4), his resurrection (1 Pet 1:3, 21; 2:4; 3:18, 21) his ascension to God's right-hand (1 Pet 3:22). All he above constitute Jesus divine vindication by God.

### Traditions–and Theological "Wirkungsgeschichtliches" Background

This passage is indicative of a Christian tradition that adapted the Israelite idea of the suffering righteous in order to interpret suffering positively as divine testing and as a reason to rejoice.[542] To rejoice in the present amidst the suffering and not merely in the future is a distinctive Christin emphasis on this tradition viewing it as an experience of divine blessing with Christological focus.[543]

### Social and Historical Context

Because of the terminological and thematic similarities between 1 Pet 1:6–7 and 1 Pet 4:12–13 this study rejects the suggestion that 1 Pet 4:12 introduces a new actual crisis. The only difference is that 1 Pet 4:12–13 describes the circumstances of the suffering as well as how believers are supposed to behave amidst these circumstances.

---

539. Elliott, *1 Peter: New Translation*, 775.

540. Ibid., 776.

541. As found in Rom 8:17; 2 Cor 1:5–7, 4:17; Phil 3:8–1; Heb 2:9–10, 10:32–39, and 12:1–11.

542. 1 Pet 1:11, 19–21; 2:4; 3:18–22; 5:1.

543. Macc 6:28, 4 Macc 7:22; 9:29; 11:12, Tob 13:13–14, Jdt 8:25–27.

Once again the absence of the mentioning of organised persecution as well as the lack of extra-biblical evidence to that effect leads to view πειρασμός not as a persecution initiated by Rome or as an allusion to Nero's execution of Christians by fire.[544] Rather, this imagery is traditional in describing the tribulations and suffering endured by Christians in general.[545]

Converts of Gentile origin might have found suffering for the sake of one's religious convictions strange and unusual and not something known to their frame of reference.[546] This would not have been the case for Jewish Christians, for suffering was an integral part of Israel's religious experience and tradition especially as far as the suffering righteous is concerned. It is this tradition that our author is falling back upon in order to indicate that similar to Jesus who suffered as the righteous one, his righteous followers will suffer as well.

### Theological Implications

Following the will of God inevitably entails suffering—a thought known to Jewish as well as New Testament literature.[547] This again displays our author's familiarity with Jewish as well as early Christian tradition. However, ironically, Christ's glory is revealed in his suffering.

As Achtemeier states:

> Although suffering with Christ promised eschatological vindication and joy, that joy was already a reality for those who shared his suffering. As a result that future reality has already transformed the present reality of suffering from sorrow to joy, providing in that way an indication of the fact that the transformation of reality to be completed in the future has already begun for the Christians.[548]

Feldmeier sees the author's development of his argument in three phases: a) suffering by following in the footsteps of Christ, confirms the believers' solidarity with the suffering of Christ on their behalf; b) because of their sharing in his suffering, they will also share in his ultimate glorification;

---

544. Nauck, "Freude im Leidem," 76–77, Brox, *Petrusbrief* (2nd ed), 214, Millauer, *Leiden als Gnade*, 165–87, Goppelt, *Der erste Petrusbrief*, 316–21.

545. Contra Beare, *First Epistle*, 190; Leaney, *The Letters*, 65.

546 Elliott, *1 Peter: New Translation*, 773.

547 Elliott, *1 Peter: New Translation*, 773; Windisch and Preisker, *Katholische Briefe*, 77.

548 Cf. 2 Macc 6:28–30; 4 Macc 7:22; Jdt 8:25–27; Matt 5:11–12, etc.

c) because of this future expectation, the Christians may rejoice within their current situation.[549]

In Mark 8:34 (Κα ὶπρος καλεσάμενος τὸν ὄχλον σὺν τοῖς μαθηταῖς αὐτοῦ/ εἶπεν αὐτοῖς εἴτις θέλει ὁ πίσω μου ἀκολουθεῖν, ἀπαρνησάσθωέ αυτὸν καὶ ἀράτω τὸν σταυρὸν αὐτοῦ καὶ ἀκολουθεί τω μοι) the idea of solidarity with suffering Christ is expressed in terms of discipleship—to take up one's cross and to experience the same fate as Christ. In 1 Peter it stresses the solidarity believers ought to have with the suffering Christ. Once again the positive value of innocent suffering is emphasised.

As J. N. D. Kelly writes: ". . . (F)or the writer the joy of the end overflows into the present, irradiating the wretched plight of those to whom he writes."[550]

## Martyrs in their Everyday Lives

The choice of the early Christian figure of Peter as the author who was considered by early Christian tradition to be a martyr and became a symbol of the unity within the Christian church makes the claim of 1 Peter with its *"alletagsmartyrologischen"* position for a place in Christianity clear.[551]

In the opening of the letter the theme of the letter is stated in terms of ἐκλεκτοῖς and παρεπιδήμοις which constitutes that the addressees are elected by God and therefore they became estranged from their society. Both these words are descriptive of the situation of the addressees: they do not belong to their society anymore and they became disintegrated from the Greco-Roman society to which they previously belonged.[552]

The situation of the addressees is one of suffering caused by discrimination and ostracism from society. Nowhere in the text is it mentioned that the author expected the killing or physical harm of his addressees. Slaves may have had to endure physical punishment from their owners, something slaves had to endure under all circumstances, but now this kind of suffering has Christological meaning with reference to the passion narrative.

First Peter 2:18–25 indicates a willingness to endure suffering and injustice. Their current suffering should be understood eschatologically. The author does not prepare them for martyrdom, but admonishes them to stay faithful to Christ and their Christian way of life. When the author mentions the blood of Christ, it has the cultic meaning of salvation and is

---

549 Achtemeier, *1 Peter*, 307.
550. Feldmeier, *First Letter*, 224.
551. Kelly, *Peter and Jude*, 57.
552. Guttenberger, *Passio Christiana*, 8.

not an indication that the audience should be prepared to endure violence. However, sporadic executions of Christians did occur as mentioned in the correspondence of Pliny with Emperor Trajan. Pliny wanted to know from the Emperor if he should persecute Christians simply on grounds of the name *nomen ipsum*. Interestingly the author admonishes his addressees to be proud of bearing the name.[553]

One cannot assume that the situation of the addressees worsened in any way, because there is no extra-biblical evidence of a full scale Christian persecution.

The author of 1 Peter constructs the identity of his addressees as a minority who has to endure discrimination by making them aware of their elect and holy status with God. This identity ought to manifest in their behaviour within their hostile environment. They should do this by separating themselves from the non-believers and by conducting themselves well (cf. 1 Pet 4:2). This good conduct also has a missionary goal: non-believers should be lead to conversion by the behaviour of Christians so that they may share in the eschatological glory. The majority should be convinced that the Christian minority as value in order to alleviate conflict. This is especially important in terms of the believers' relationship with the government. Christians should be clear that they are by no means malicious or violent. They should rather be characterised by their good behaviour.[554]

The author of 1 Peter has a positive evaluation of civil authority. The author makes the point that although the state supports systems that cause the believers to experience their environment as hostile, the believers should use the maintenance and law and order function of the state to their own advantage. Christian freedom does not mean lawlessness. The New Testament does not interpret freedom in political terms. Obedience to God does not mean disobedience to the state, for that would be an abuse of freedom. Disobedience to the authorities would only cause more hostility.[555]

As far as the domestic sphere is concerned non-believing husbands should be moved to conversion by the behaviour of their believing wives. This is especially achieved by their modest behaviour. Their calm and gentle attitudes should become their strongest attributes following the example of the arch mother Sarah.

The author of 1 Peter does however make wives responsible for the eschatological fate of their husbands, or put differently, they have a missionary responsibility towards their husbands. Such a situation could cause conflict,

---

553. Guttenberger, *Passio Christiana*, 11; cf. Horrell, *1 Peter*.
554. Cf. 1 Pet 4:16; see Chapter 1 of this study.
555. Guttenberger, *Passio Christiana*, 34; cf. Wilde, *Social Description*.

for men possessed the authority to determine the religion practised in the home. Consequently, wives had to find their way through their marital and faith obligations. It would be problematic for a modest wife to stay away from her home the entire evening before Easter Sunday or to greet another man who is her brother in Christ with a kiss.[556]

Against this background it becomes clear that the author of 1 Peter had very high expectations of his female audience.[557] Their position within society was practically powerless, yet he encourages them to manipulate those in power positions. Consequently this argumentation of the author was controversial. It is interesting to note that the author does not fear the apostasy of female believers. He trusts them with so much pressure and he is not concerned that they will forsake the Christian faith.[558]

The next exhortation is aimed at the slaves who in the case of 1 Peter are the household servants who were part of the family. With the exhortation to the slaves the passion metaphor is placed in the centre. The paraenetic texts in 1 Peter differs significantly from other *Haustafelen* found in the New Testament in that only the socially most vulnerable are addressed, namely slaves and women. There is no exhortation directed at men or slave-owners. Furthermore, it is not a general paraenetic text, but it is specifically addressed to believing slaves owned by non-believing masters and as such the household servants form a *pars pro toto* in order to identify the powerless minority against the powerful majority as well as the conflict the Christian way of life has with the Greco-Roman culture in general. It signifies two opposite standings.[559]

The command given to the household servants later serves as a command given to all of the addressees (cf. 1 Pet 2:19). To admonish slaves to be submissive is superfluous for slaves did not have any alternative but to be submissive. If slaves were not submissive they were threatened with violence and rebellions among slaves were not tolerated. Therefore, the command makes more sense if addressed to the entire Christian community.

The suffering Christians had to endure, was undeserved suffering and should be viewed as a form of God's grace and should be understood with reference to the suffering of Christ. This is applicable in as much as the believers do not commit any wrongdoing. Suffering is only laudable if they have to endure it because of their commitment to Christ and the faith and their refusal to renounce Christ and to worship the Emperor.

556. Guttenberger, *Passio Christiana*, 36–37.
557. Guttenberger, *Passio Christiana*, 41; see Green, *1 Peter*.
558. See Popp, *Die Kunst*; Gielen, *Tradition und Theologie*.
559. Guttenberger, *Passio Christiana*, 43.

Guttenberger writes:

> Einerseits steht die Sklavenparänese eng mit der Aussageintention des gesamtes Briefes in Verbindung, so dass an zu nehmen ist der Verfasser betracht das Interpretationsmodell "Leiden als Gnade" als sein eigenliches Anliegen.[560]

To become foreigners is no foreign concept to the Christian believers. Their difficult circumstances were nothing extra ordinary (cf. 1 Pet 4:12–19). The fiery ordeal recalls the metaphor of their faith which is more precious than gold which is purified by fire (1 Pet 1:6). They should rejoice because of the privilege to share in the suffering of Christ, for it has the consequence that they will also share in his glorification.

Suffering is not only a possibility for the faithful, it is essential to the faith. As such their suffering has meaning and it gives meaning to the believers's understanding of their reality. To share in the suffering of Christ necessarily means that they will also share in his eschatological glorification and with this in mind it becomes possible to them to endure their suffering with composure.[561]

Peter wants his audience to be separated from their pagan Greco-Roman neighbours without becoming ascetic. The church is taking over the true identity of Israel, as God's people. The author does not want his audience to practise aggressive separation nor partake in militant actions. Rather he wants his audience to focus on the fact that although they are treated as an outsider group, they should make themselves acceptable to their hostile neighbours. The author tries to think from the perspective of the non-believers and to change the status of the stigmatised out-group to that of the normal in-group. Despite having a new valuable identity in Christ, they will still be rejected by the in-group. Therefore their best chance at survival is to behave themselves and not to resist. By doing so, they will not provoke any violence against them, and will not become complete outcasts from society. Furthermore it is very difficult to heal an identity that has become spoilt.[562]

## Concluding Remarks

This study attempted to highlight the Christological affinities between the Gospel of Mark and 1 Peter in order to indicate that the authors of both

560. Ibid., 45.
561. Ibid., 49.
562. Ibid., 57.

these New Testament texts used their Christology as foundation for their ethics. The influence of a common tradition, which probably originated in Rome, manifested in both texts as was indicated by the pericopes discussed in this study; for example, as far as 1 Pet 2:22-25 is concerned, there is a general consensus among scholars that the author used an early Christian liturgical tradition in the form of a "Christ hymn" or "Passion hymn."[563] The use of the tradition is indicated by the occurrence of similar kerygmatic, liturgical and creedal material.[564] In 1 Peter elements of the Christological passion hymn as well as redactional additions were employed to elaborate on the statement made in 1 Pet 2:21 to confirm the vicarious nature and the consequences for salvation that the suffering and death of Jesus Christ had. This Christ hymn or passion hymn belongs to a tradition upon which the Synoptic Gospels also relied. Goppelt traces it back to the primitive ὑπὲρ formula which is found in the words of Jesus concerning his immanent passion.[565] The motifs used here are derived from the suffering servant song of Isa 53. This Old Testament passage played a key role in the formation of early Christology. It is also the author's reliance upon the Suffering Servant passage, which he uses to unite the suffering righteous believers *passio iustorum* with their suffering righteous Lord *passio iusti*, which relates 1 Peter with the Gospels and especially with the Gospel of Mark.

"In Mark as well as in 1 Peter the suffering of the righteous community is inseparably linked with and based upon the suffering of Jesus Christ, the righteous One."[566] This study elaborates on the suggestion made by Elliott in reliance upon Nauck that Isa 53 together with certain Psalms provided motifs for a primitive Christological tradition upon which 1 Peter also draws.[567] According to Pesch the entire second half of the Gospel of Mark (Mark 8:27-16:8) incorporates a pre-Markan passion narrative and basic to this theme is the suffering righteous one, *Passio Iusti*.[568] This study elaborated on the similarities between Mark and 1 Peter especially in terms of their theologies of suffering which is based upon a larger pre-synoptic tradition.[569] The affinities between Mark and 1 Peter are not the result of literary dependence, but rather of reliance upon a common tradi-

---

563. Ibid., 59.

564. Elliott, "Backward and Forward," 190; cf. Goppelt, *Der erste Petrusbrief*, 204-207.

565. Cf. Deichgräber, *Gotteshymnus*, 142.

566. Goppelt, *Der erste Petrusbrief*, 206-207; cf. Mark 10:45; 14:24.

567. Elliott, "Backward and Forward," 190.

568. Elliott, "Backward and Forward," 192; Nauck, "Freude im Leidem," 68-80.

569. Pesch, *Markusevangelium 1*, 63-68.

tion which embraces not only the theme of "joy in suffering" but also of "solidarity in suffering."

First Peter 2:21 also has affinities with Mark. The case for the relationship between Mark and 1 Peter is further strengthened by their common origin in Rome.[570] According to Elliott: "If there is merit to this proposal, then local oral tradition shared by various groups in Rome, together with their social situation and socio-religious perspectives, would account for numerous points of contact between both documents, including their interpretation of solidarity in suffering and its link with the calling to follow Jesus."[571] This study hopes to have illuminated this proposal in support of an *Imitatio Christi*-ethic especially in terms of the Suffering Christ.

---

570. Cf. Selwyn, *The First Epistle*, 90–101; Lohse, *Märtyr*, 182–87 ; Schelkle "Das Leiden," 14-16; Goldstein, "Die Kirche," 38–54.

571. Cf. Elliott, *A Home*, 181–94.

# Bibliography

Achtemeier, Paul J. "1 Peter." In *HBC*, 1276–85.
———. *1 Peter: A Commentary on First Peter*. Hermeneia. Minneapolis: Fortress, 1996.
———. "'He Taught Them Many Things': Reflections on Marcan Christology." *CBQ* 42 (1980) 478–80.
———. "Newborn Babes and Living Stones: Literal and Figurative in 1 Peter." In *To Touch the Text: Biblical and Related Studies in Honour of Joseph Fitzmyer, SJ*, edited by Maura P. Horgan and Paul J. Kobelski, 207–36. New York: Crossroads,1988.
———. "Suffering Servant as Suffering Christ in 1 Peter." In *The Future of Christology: Essays in Honour of Leander E Keck*, edited by Abraham J. Malherbe and Wayne A. Meeks, 176–88. Minneapolis: Fortress, 1993.
Allen, W. C. *The Gospel according to St. Mark*. New York: Macmillan, 1915.
Annas, Julia. *The Morality of Happiness*. Oxford: Oxford University Press, 1993.
Arnold, Edward V. *Roman Stoicism*. Cambridge: Cambridge University Press, 1911.
Ashcroft, Bill, Gareth Griffiths, and Helen Tiffin. *The Empire Writes Back: Theory and Practice in Post-Colonial Literature*. New Accents. London: Routledge, 1989.
Bacon, Benjamin W. *Is Mark a Roman Gospel?* HTS 7. 1919. New York: Kraus, 1969.
Balch, David L. *Let Wives be Submissive: Domestic Code in 1 Peter*. SBL Monograph Series 26. Chico, CA: Scholars, 1981.
Balch, David L., and Carolyn Osiek, eds. *Early Christian Families in Context: An Interdisciplinary Dialogue*. Religion, Marriage and Family. Grand Rapids: Eerdmans, 2003.
Balz, Horst, and Gerhard Schneider. *Exegetisches Wörterbuch zum Neuen Testament*, 3rd ed. Stuttgart: Kohlhammer, 2011.
Barclay, John M. G. *Jews in the Mediterranean Diaspora from Alexander to Trajan (323 BCE—117 CE)*. Edinburgh: T. & T. Clark, 1996.
———. "Universalism and Pluralism: Twin Components of both Judaism and Early Christianity." In *A Vision for the Church: Studies in Early Christian Ecclesiology in Honour of J P M Sweet*, edited by Markus Bockmuehl and Michael B. Thompson, 207–24. Edinburgh: T. & T. Clark, 1997.
Barr, John. "'Abba' Isn't Daddy." *JTS* 39 (1988) 28–47.
Barth, Karl. *Church Dogmatics* I/1: *The Doctrine of the Word of God*. Translated by GeoffreyW. Bromiley. Edinburgh: T. & T. Clark, 1975.
Barton, Stephan C. *Discipleship and Family Ties in Mark and Matthew*. SNTSMS 80. Cambridge: Cambridge University Press, 1994.

———. *Life Together: Family, Sexuality and Community in the New Testament and Today*. Edinburgh: T. & T. Clark, 2001.
Bauckham, Richard. *God Crucified: Monotheism and Christology in the New Testament*. Grand Rapids: Eerdmans, 1999.
Bauman, Richard A. *Crime and Punishment in Ancient Rome*. New York: Routledge, 1996.
Baumann-Martin, Betsy. "Speaking Jewish: Post-Colonial Aliens and Strangers in 1 Peter." In *Reading 1 Peter with New Eyes: Methodological Reassessments of the Letter of First Peter*, edited by Robert L. Webb and Betsy Bauman-Martin, 146–77. London: T. & T. Clark, 2007.
Beasley-Murray, George R. *Baptism in the New Testament*. New York: St. Martin's, 1963.
Beard, Mary, John North, and Simon Price, eds. *Religions of Rome*. Vol. 1: *A History*. Cambridge: Cambridge University Press, 1998.
Beare, Francis W. *The First Epistle of Peter: Introduction and Notes*. 3rd ed. Oxford: Blackwell, 1970.
Bechtler, Steven R. *Following in His Steps: Suffering, Community and Christology in 1 Peter*. SBLDS 162. Atlanta: Scholars, 1998.
Bellah, Robert N., Richard Madsen, William M. Sullivan, Ann Swidler, and Steven M. Tipton. *Habits of the Heart: Middle America Observed*. New York: Harper & Row, 1985.
Berger, Adolf. *Encyclopaedic Dictionary of Roman Law*. Philadelphia: Fortress, 1953.
Berger, Klaus. *Historical Psychology of Identity and Experience in the New Testament*. Translated by Charles Muenchow. Minneapolis: Fortress, 2003.
Berger, Peter. *Questions of Faith: A Skeptical Affirmation of Christianity*. Oxford: Blackwell, 2004.
Berger, Peter, and Thomas Luckmann. *The Social Construction of Reality: A Treatise in the Sociology of Knowledge*. New York: Doubleday, 1966.
Bertram, Georg. *Die Leidensgeschichte Jesu und der Christuskult*. Forschungen zur Religion und Literatur des Alten und Neuen Testaments 15. Göttingen: Vandenhoeck & Ruprecht, 1922.
Beskow, P. "Mission, Trade and Emigration in the Second Century." *SEA* 35 (1970) 104–14.
Best, Ernest. *1 Peter*. NCB. Grand Rapids: Eerdmans, 1971.
———. "1 Peter and the Gospel Tradition." *NTS* 16 (1969) 95–113.
———. *The Temptation and the Passion: The Markan Soteriology*. SNTSMS 2. Cambridge: Cambridge University Press, 2005.
Biale, Rachel. *Women and Jewish Law: An Exploration of Women's Issues in Halakic Sources*. New York: Schocken, 1984.
Bieder, Werner. *Die Vorstellung von der Höllenfahrt Jesu Christi*. ATANT 19. Zurich: Zwingli, 1949.
Bigg, Charles. *A Critical and Exegetical Commentary on the Epistles of St. Peter and St. Jude*. International Critical Commentary. New York: Schribners, 1901.
Bock, Darrell L. *Blasphemy and Exaltation in Judaism and the Final Examination of Jesus: A Philological-Historical Study of the Key Jewish Themes Impacting Mark 14:61–64*. WUNT 2/106. Tübingen: Mohr/Siebeck, 1998.
Boismard, Marie-Emile. "Baptême et renouveau." *LV* 27 (1956) 103–18.
———. "Une liturgie baptismale dans la Prima Petri, II: Son Influence sur l'épître de Jacques." *RB* 64 (1957) 161–83.

Bolt, Peter G. *Jesus' Defeat of Death: Persuading Mark's Early Readers*. SNTSMS 125. Cambridge: Cambridge University Press, 2003.
Bonhoeffer, Dietrich. *The Cost of Discipleship*. Translated by R. H. Fuller. London: SCM, 1948.
Borg, Marcus J. *Conflict, Holiness and Politics in the Teachings of Jesus*. Studies in the Bible and Early Christianity 5. New York: Mellen, 1984.
Boring, M. Eugene. *1 Peter*. Abingdon New Testament Commentaries. Nashville: Abingdon, 1999.
———. "The Christology of Mark: Hermeneutical Issues for Systematic Theology." In *Reading the Present in the Qumran Library: The Perception of the Contemporary by Means of Scriptural Interpretations*, edited by Kristin de Troyer and Armin Lange, 125–53. SBLSymS 30. Atlanta: Society of Biblical Literature, 2005.
———. *Mark: A Commentary*. New Testament Library. Louisville: Westminster John Knox, 2006.
———. "Narrative Dynamics in First Peter: The Function of the Narrative World." In *Reading First Peter with New Eyes: Methodological Reassessments of the Letter of First Peter*, edited by Robert L. Webb and Betsy Bauman-Martin, 5–40. London: T. & T. Clark, 2007.
Bornemann, W. "Der erste Petrusbrief: Eine Taufrede des Silvanus?" *ZNW* 19 (1919) 143–65.
Böttrich, Christfried. *Petrus: Fischer, Fels und Funktionär*. Leipzig: Evangelische Verlagsanstalt, 2001.
Brandon, S. G. F. *The Fall of Jerusalem and the Christian Church: A Study of the Effects of the Jewish Overthrow of 70 AD on Christianity*. London: SPCK, 1978.
Brent, Allen. *A Political History of Early Christianity*. London: T. & T. Clark, 2009.
Britzer, Lloyd F. "The Rhetorical Situation." *Ph&R* 1 (1968) 1–18.
Broadhead, Edwin K. *Naming Jesus: Titular Christology in the Gospel of Mark*. Sheffield: Sheffield Academic, 1999.
Broughton, Thomas R. S. "Roman Asia Minor." In *An Economic Survey of Ancient Rome*, vol. 4, edited by Tenney Frank, 499–918. Baltimore: Johns Hopkins University Press, 1938.
Brown, Raymond E. *The Death of the Messiah: From Gethsemane to the Grave: A Commentary on the Passion Narratives in the Four Gospels*. New York: Doubleday, 1994.
———. "The First Epistle of Peter." In *Antioch and Rome: New Testament Cradles of Catholic Christianity*, edited by Raymond E. Brown and John P. Meier, 128–39. New York: Paulist, 1983.
Brown, Raymond E., Karl P. Donfried, and John Reumann. *Der Petrus der Bibel: Eine ökumenische Untersuchung*. Stuttgart: Katholische Bibelwerk, 1976.
Brox, Norbert. *Der Erste Petrusbrief*. 1st ed. EKKNT 21. Zurich: Benzinger, 1979.
———. *Der Erste Petrusbrief*. 2nd ed. EKKNT 21. Zurich: Benzinger / Neukirchen-Vluyn Verlag, 1986.
———. "Der erste Petrusbrief in der literarischen Tradition des Urchristendums." *Kairos* 20 (1978a) 182–92.
———. "Zur pseusodographischen Rahmung des ersten Petrusbriefes." *BZ* 19 (1975) 78–96.
———. "Situation und Sprache der Minderheit im ersten Petrusbrief." *Kairos* 11 (1977) 1–13.

———. "Tendenz und Pseudepigraphie im ersten Petrusbrief." *Kairos* 20 (1978b) 110–20.
Bruce, Frederick F., and Eberhard Güting. *Außerbiblische Zeugnisse über Jesus und das frühe Christentum*. Basel: Brunnen, 2007.
Buell, Denise K., and Caroline Johnson Hodge. "The Politics of Interpretation: Rhetoric of Race and Ethnicity in Paul." *JBL* 123 (2004) 235–51.
Bultmann, Rudolf. *The History of the Synoptic Tradition*. Translated by John Marsh. New York: Harper & Row, 1976.
Calloud, Jean, and François Genuyt. *La Première épitre de Pierre: analyse sémiotique*. LD 109. Paris: Cerf, 1982.
Cameron, Averil. *Christianity and the Rhetoric of the Empire: The Development of Christian Discourse*. SCL 45. Berkley: University of California Press, 1991.
Campbell, Barth L. *Honor, Shame and the Rhetoric of 1 Peter*. SBLDS 160. Atlanta: Scholar, 1998.
Carleton Paget, James N. "Jewish Christianity." In *The Cambridge History of Judaism*. 3: *Early Roman Period*, edited by William Horbury, William D. Davies, and John Sturdy, 731–75. Cambridge: Cambridge University Press, 1999.
Carrington, Philip. *The Primitive Christian Catechism: A Study in the Epistles*. Cambridge: Cambridge University Press, 1940.
Cassidy, Richard J. *Four Times Peter: Portrayals of Peter in the Four Gospels and at Philippi*. Interfaces. Collegeville, MN: Liturgical, 2007.
Catchpole, David R. "The Answer of Jesus to Caiaphas." *NTS* 17 (1971) 213–26.
Cervantes Gabbaron, Jose. "El pastor en la teologia de 1 Pe." *Estbib* 49 (1991b) 331–51.
———. *La pasión de Jesucristo en la Prima Carta de Pedro: Centro literario y teologico de la carta*. ISJ 22. Estella (Navarra): Verbo Divino, 1991a.
Charlesworth, James H. "A Caveat on Textual Transmission and the Meaning of *Abba*: A Study of the Lord's Prayer." In *The Lord's Prayer and Other Prayer Texts from the Greco-Roman Era*, edited by James H. Charlesworth, Mark Harding and Mark C. Kiley, 1–14.ForgeValley, PA: Trinity, 1994.
Clemen, Carl. "Die Einheitlichkeit des 1 Petrusbriefes verteidigt." *TSK* 78 (1905) 619–28.
Colish, Marcia L. *Stoicism in Classical Latin Literature*. Vol. 1: *The Stoic Tradition from Antiquity to the Early Middle Ages*. SHCT 34. Leiden: Brill, 1985.
Collins, Adela Y. *The Beginning of the Gospel: Probings of Mark in Context*. Minneapolis: Fortress, 1992.
———. *Mark: A Commentary*. Hermeneia. Minneapolis: Fortress, 2007.
Colwell, Ernest C. "Popular Reactions against Christianity in the Roman Empire." In *Environmental Factors in Christian History*, edited by John T. McNeill, Matthew Spinka, and Harold R. Willoughby, 53–71. 1939. Reprint, New York: Kennikat, 1970.
Cothenet, Édouard. "Les Orientations actuelles de l'exégèse de la première lettre Pierre." In *Etudes sur la première lettre de Pierre*, edited by Charles Perrot, 13–42, 269–74. LD 102. Paris: Cerf, 1980.
Cranfield, C. E. B. *I and II Peter and Jude*. TBC. London: SCM, 1950 / New York: Harper & Row, 1971.
———. *I and II Peter and Jude: Introduction and Commentary*. TBC. London: SCM, 1960.

———. *The Gospel According to St. Mark*. Cambridge Greek Testament Commentary. Cambridge: Cambridge University Press, 1959.
Cross, Frank L. *1 Peter: A Paschal Liturgy*. London: Mowbary,1954.
Crossan, John Dominic. *The Birth of Christianity: Discovering What Happened in the Years Immediately after the Execution of Jesus*. San Francisco: Harper & Row, 1998.
———. *In Parables: The Challenge of the Historical Jesus*. New York: Harper & Row, 1973.
Cullmann, Oscar. *The Christology of the New Testament*. Rev. ed. Translated by Shirley C. Guthrie and Charles A. M. Hall. New Testament Library. Philadelphia: Westminister, 1963.
Dalton, William J. *Christ's Proclamation to the Spirits: A Study of 1 Peter 3:18—4:6*. 2nd rev. ed. AnBib 23. Rome: Pontifical Biblical Institute, 1989.
———. "Christ's Victory over the Devil and the Evil Spirits." *TBT* 2 (1965) 1195–200.
Danby, Herbert. *The Mishnah*. Oxford: Oxford University Press, 1933.
Daniel, Jerry L. "Anti-Semitism in the Hellenistic-Roman Period." *JBL* 98 (1979) 45-65.
Danker, Frederick W. "1 Peter 1:24—2:17, A Consolatory Pericope." *ZNW* 58 (1967) 93–102.
———. *Invitation to the New Testament: Epistles*. Vol. 4: *A Commentary on Hebrews, 1 and 2 Peter, 1, 2 and 3 John and Jude, with Complete Text from the Jerusalem Bible*. DNTC. Garden City, NY: Doubleday-Image, 1980.
Davids, Peter H. *The First Epistle of Peter*. New International Commentary on the New Testament. Grand Rapids: Eerdmans, 1990.
Davies, William D., and Dale C. Allison Jr. *A Critical and Exegetical Commentary on the Gospel according to Saint Matthew*. International Critical Commentary. Edinburgh: T. & T. Clark, 1988.
Davis, David B. *The Problem of Slavery in the Age of Revolotion 1770–1823*. London: Cornell University Press, 1975.
Davis, Philip G. "Mark's Christological Paradox." *JSNT* 35 (1989) 3–18.
Dawson, Anne. *Freedom as Liberating Power: A Socio-Political Reading of the Exousia Texts in the Gospel of Mark*. Novum Testamentum et orbis antiquus 44. Göttingen: Vandenhoeck & Ruprecht, 2000.
De Jonge, Martinus. *Christology in Context: The Earliest Response to Jesus*. Philadelphia: Fortress, 1988.
De Villiers, Jan L. "Joy in Suffering in 1 Peter." *Neot* 9 (1975) 64–86.
Deichgräber, Reinhard. *Gotteshymnus und Christushymnus in der frühen Christenheit: Untersuchungen zu Form, Sprache und Stil der frühchristlichen Hymnen*. SUNT 5. Göttingen: Vandenhoek & Ruprecht, 1967.
Deissmann, Adolf. *Light of the Ancient Near East: The New Testament Illustrated by Recently Discovered Texts of the Graeco-Roman World*. Translated by Lionel R. M. Strachan. Rev. ed. New York: Doran, 1927.
Derrett, J. Duncan M. *Law in the New Testament*. 1970. Reprint, Eugene, OR: Wipf & Stock, 2005.
———. "The Reason for the Cock-Crowings." *NTS* 29 (1983) 142–44.
Dewey, Joanna. "'Let Them Renounce Themselves and Take Up Their Cross':A Feminist Reading of Mark 8:34 in Mark's Social and Narrative World." In *A Feminist Companion to Mark*, edited by Amy J. Levine, 23–36. Feminist Companion to the New Testament and Early Christian Writings 2. Sheffield: Sheffield Academic, 2001.

Dibelius, Martin. *From Tradition to Gospel*. Translated by Bertram L. Woolf. New York: Scribners, 1965.

Dickey, Samuel. "Some Economic and Social Conditions of Asia Minor Affecting the Expansion of Christianity." In *Studies in Early Christianity*, edited by Shirley Jackson Case, Frank C. Porter, and Benjamin W. Bacon, 393–416. New York: Century, 1928.

Dinkler, Erich. "Die Petrus-Rom-Frage." *TRu* N.F. 25 (1959) 189–230; 289–335.

———. "Die Petrus-Rom-Frage." *TRu* N.F. 27 (1961) 33–64.

Doering, Lutz. *Schabbat: Sabbathalacha und -praxis im antiken Judentum und Urchristentum*. Texts and Studies in Ancient Judaism 78. Tübingen: Mohr/Siebeck, 1999.

Donahue, John R. *Are You the Christ? The Trial Narrative in the Gospel of Mark*. SBLDS 10. Missoula, MT: Society of Biblical Literature, 1973.

———. *The Theology and Setting of Discipleship in the Gospel of Mark*. Milwaukee: Marquette University Press, 1983.

Donahue, John R., and Daniel J. Harrington. *The Gospel of Mark*. Sacra Pagina 2. Collegeville, MN: Liturgical, 2002.

Douglas, Mary. *Purity and Danger: An Analysis of the Concept of Pollution and Taboo*. New York: Routlegde, 1966.

Dowd, Sharyn E. "Reading Mark, Reading Isaiah." *LTQ* 30/3 (1995) 133–44.

Downing, F. Gerald. "Pliny's Persecution of Christians: Revelation and 1 Peter." *JSNT* 34 (1988) 105–23.

Dryden, J. de Waal. *Theology and Ethics in 1 Peter: Paraenetic Strategies for Christian Character Formation*. WUNT 2/209. Tübingen: Mohr/Siebeck, 2006.

Dschulnigg, Peter. *Petrus im Neuen Testament*. Stuttgart: Katholische Bibelwerk, 1996.

Dube, Musa W. *Postcolonial Feminist Interpretation of the Bible*. St. Louis: Chalice, 2000.

Duling, Dennis C. *The New Testament: History, Literature and Social Context*. Toronto: Thompson Wadsworth, 2003.

Dunn, James D. G. *The Partings of the Ways between Christianity and Judaism and Their Significance for the Character of Christianity*. London: Fortress, 1991.

Edwards, Catharine. *Writing Rome: Textual Approaches to the City*. Roman Literature and Its Contexts. Cambridge: Cambridge University Press, 1996.

Elliott, John H. *1 Peter: A New Translation with Introduction and Commentary*. AB 37B. New Haven: Yale University Press, 2000.

———. *1 Peter: Estrangement and Community*. HBB. Chigaco: Franciscan Herald, 1979.

———. "1 Peter, Its Situation and Strategy: A Discussion with David Balch." In *Perspectives on First Peter*, edited by Charles H. Talbert, 61–78. NABPRSS 9. Macon: Mercer University Press, 1976.

———. "Backward and Forward 'In His Steps': Following Jesus from Rome to Raymond and Beyond: The Tradition, Redaction and Reception of 1 Peter 2:18–25." In *Discipleship in the New Testament*, edited by Fernando F. Segovia, 184–209. Philadelphia: Fortress, 1985.

———. *Doxology: God's People Called to Celebrate His Glory: A Biblical Study of 1 Peter in 10 Parts*. St. Louis: Lutheran Laymen's League, 1966.

———. *The Elect and the Holy: An Exegetical Examination of 1 Peter 2:4–10 and the Phrase "basileion hierateuma."* NovTSup 12. 1966. Reprint, Eugene, OR: Wipf & Stock, 2006.

———. *A Home for the Homeless: A Sociological Exegesis of 1 Peter, Its Situation and Strategy*. 1990. Reprint, Eugene, OR: Wipf & Stock, 2005.

———. "Peter, Silvanus and Mark in 1 Peter and Acts: Sociological-Exegetical Perspectives on a Petrine Group in Rome." In *Wort in der Zeit: Neutestamentliche Studien: Festgabe für Karl Heinrich Rengstorf zum 75. Geburtstag*, edited by Wilfred Haubeck and Michael Bachmann, 250–67. Leiden: Brill, 1980.

———. "The Rehabilitation of the Exegetical Stepchild: 1 Peter in Recent Research." In *Perspectives on First Peter*, edited by Charles H. Talbert, 3-16. NABPRSS 9. Macon, GA: Mercer University Press, 1986.

———. "Salutation and Exhortation to Christian Behavior on the Basis of God's Blessings (1 Pet 1:1—2:10)." *RevExp* 79 (1982) 415–25.

———. "Social-Scientific Study of the Bible and the Biblical World." Paper presented at an MDiv Seminar at the Department of New Testament Studies, University of Pretoria, on 4 April 1989.

Elliott, John H., and Ralph A. Martin. *James, 1–2 Peter, Jude*. ACNT. Minneapolis: Augsburg, 1992.

Erlemann, Kurt. *Jesus der Christus: Provokation des Glaubens*. Neukirchen-Vluyn: Neukirchener Theologie, 2011.

———. *Unfassbar? Der Heilige Geist in Neuen Testament*. Neukirchen-Vluyn: Neukirchener Verlag, 2010.

Evans, Craig A. "In What Sense 'Blasphemy'? Jesus before Caiaphas in Mark 14:61–64." In *Jesus and His Contemporaries: Comparative Studies*, 407–34. AGJU 25. Leiden: Brill, 1995.

———. *Mark 8:27—16:20*. WBC 34B. Nashville: Nelson, 2001.

Feldmeier, Reinhard. *Die Christen als Fremde: Die Metapher der Fremde in der antiken Welt, im Urchristentum und in 1. Petrusbrief*. WUNT 64. Tübingen: Möhr/Siebeck, 1992.

———. *Der erste Brief des Petrus*. Theologischer Handkommentar zum Neuen Testament 15/1. Leipzig: Evangelische Verlagsanstalt, 2005.

———. *The First Letter of Peter: A Commentary on the Greek Text*. Translated by Peter H. Davids. Waco, TX: Baylor University Press, 2008.

———. *Der Krisis des Gottessohnes: Die Gethsemaneerzählung als Schlüssel der Markuspassion*. WUNT 2/21. Tübingen: Mohr/Siebeck, 1987.

Filson, Floyd V. "Partakers with Christ: Suffering in First Peter." *Int* 9 (1955) 400–412.

———. "Peter." In *IDB* 3:749–57.

Finley, Moses I., ed. *Slavery in Classical Antiquity. Views and Controversies about Classical Antiquity*. Cambridge: Heffer, 1968.

Fiore, Benjamin. *The Function of Personal Example in the Socratic and Pastoral Epistles*. Rome: Editrice Pontificio Istituto Biblico, 1986.

Fitzmyer, Joseph A. "*Abba* and Jesus' Relation to God." In *According to Paul: Studies in the Theology of the Apostle*, 47–63. Maryknoll, NY: Orbis, 1993.

Flesher, Paul V. M. "The Bread of the Presence." In *ABD* 6:780–81.

Flesseman-Van Leer, Ellen. "Prinzipien der Sammlung und Ausscheidung bei der Bildung des Kanon." *ZTK* 61 (1964) 404–20.

Fowl, Stephen E. *The Story of Christ in the Ethics of Paul: An Analysis of the Function of the Hymnic Material in the Pauline Corpus*. JSNT 36. Sheffield: JSOT Press, 1990.

France, Richard T. *The Gospel of Mark: A Commentary on the Greek Text*. NIGTC. Grand Rapids: Eerdmans, 2002.

Gager, John G. *Kingdom and Community: The Social World of Early Christianity.* Prentice-Hall Studies in Religion Series. Princeton: Prentice-Hall, 1975.

Gamble, Harry Y. *The New Testament Canon.* Guides to Biblical Scholarship. 1985. Reprint, Eugene, OR: Wipf & Stock, 2002.

Gammie, John G. "Paraenetic Literature: Towards the Morphology of a Second Genre." *Semeia* 50 (1990) 49–50.

Garleff, Gunnar. *Urchristliche Identität in Matthäusevangelium, Didache und Jakobusbrief.* Münster: Lit, 2004.

Garnsey, Peter D. R., and Richard Saller. *The Roman Empire: Ecomomy, Society and Culture.* London: Duckworth, 1987.

Gerhardsson, Birger. *Memory and Manuscript: Oral Tradition and Written Transmission in Rabbinic Judaism and Early Christianity.* Acta Seminarii Neotestamentici Upsaliensis 22. Lund: Gleerup, 1961.

Gerstenberger, Erhard S. *The Psalms: Part 1 with an Introduction to Cultic Poetry.* Forms of the Old Testament Literature 14. Grand Rapids: Eerdmans, 1988.

Gielen, Marlis. *Tradition und Theologie neutestamentlicher Haustafelethik: Ein Beitrag zur Frage einer Christlichen Auseinandersetzung mit gesellschaftlichen Normen.* AthenMTh 75. Frankfurt: Hain, 1990.

Gnilka, Joachim. *Das Evangelium nach Markus.* Evangelisch-katholischer Kommentar zum Neuen Testament 2. Zurich: Benzinger, 1978.

Goffman, Erving. *Stigma: Notes on the Management of Spoiled Identity.* Englewood Cliffs, NJ: Prentice-Hall, 1963.

Goldstein, H. "Die Kirche als Schar derer, die ihrem Leidende Herrn mit dem Ziel der Gottesgemeinschaft nachfolgen: Zum Gemeindeverständnis von 1 Pet 2:21–25 und 3:18–22." *BibLeb* 15 (1974) 38–54.

Goodman, Martin. *Rome and Jerusalem: The Clash of Ancient Civilizations.* New York: Knopf, 2007.

Goppelt, Leonhard. *A Commentary on 1 Peter.* Edited by Ferdinand Hahn. Translated and augmented by John E. Alsup. Grand Rapids: Eerdmans, 1993. [Translation of *Der erste Petrusbrief.* 8th ed. KEK 12/1. Göttingen: Vanderhoeck & Ruprecht, 1978].

———. *Der erste Petrusbrief.* 8th ed. KEK 12/1. Göttingen: Vanderhoeck & Ruprecht, 1978.

———. "Der Staat in der Sicht des Neuen Testaments." In *Christologie und Ethik: Aufsätze zum Neuen Testament*, edited by Leonhard Goppelt, 190–127. Göttingen: Vanderhoeck & Ruprecht, 1968.

Grassi, Joseph A. "Abba Father." *TBT* 21 (1983) 320–324.

———. "Abba Father, (Mark 14:36): Another Approach." *JAAR* 50 (1982) 449–58.

Green, Bernard. *Christianity in Ancient Rome: The First Three Centuries.* London: T. & T. Clark, 2010.

Green, Joel B. *1 Peter.* Two Horizons New Testament Commentary. Grand Rapids: Eerdmans, 2007.

Gruen, Erich S. *Heritage and Hellenism: The Reinvention of Jewish Tradition.* Berkeley: University of California Press, 1998.

Guelich, Robert A. *Mark 1—8:26.* WBC 34A. Waco, TX: Word, 1989.

Gundry, Robert H. "Recent Investigations into the Literary Genre 'Gospel.'" In *New Dimensions in New Testament Study.* Edited by Richard N. Longenecker and Merrill C. Tanney, 97–114. Grand Rapids: Zondervan, 1974.

———. *Mark: A Commentary on His Apology of the Cross*. Grand Rapids: Eerdmans, 1993.
Guthrie, Donald. *New Testament Introduction*. 4th ed. Downer's Grove, IL: InterVarsity, 1990.
Guttenberger, Gudrun. *Die Gottesvorstellung im Markusevangelium*. BZNW 123. Berlin: de Guyter, 2004.
———. *Passio Christiana: Die alltagsmartyrologische Position des Ersten Petrusbriefes*. SBS 223. Stuttgart: Katholisches Bibelwerk, 2010.
Hagner, Donald A. *The Use of the Old and New Testament in Clement of Rome*. NovTSup 34. Leiden: Brill, 1973.
Hall, Randy. "For to This You Have Been Called: The Cross and Suffering in 1 Peter." *ResQ* 19 (1976) 137–47.
Haubeck, Wilfridand Michael Bachmann, eds. *Wort in der Zeit: Neutestamentliche Studien. Festgabe für Karl Heinrich Rengstorf zum 75 Geburtstag*. Leiden: Brill, 1980.
Hays, Richard B. "Christ Prays the Psalms: Paul's Use of Early Christian Exegetical Convention." In *The Future of Christology: Essays in Honor of Leander E. Keck*, edited by Abraham J. Malberbe and Wayne A. Meeks, 122–36. Minneapolis: Fortress, 1993.
Hengel, Martin. *Crucifixion in the Ancient World and the Folly of the Message of the Cross*. Translated by John Bowden. Fortress: Philadelphia, 1977.
———. "Entstehungszeit und Situation des Markusevangeliums." In *Markus-Philologie: Historische, literaturgeschichtlichen und stilistische Untersuchungen zum Zweiten Evangelien*, edited by Hubert Cancik, 1–45. WUNT 33. Tübingen: Mohr/Siebeck, 1984.
———. *Saint Peter: The Underestimated Apostle*. Translated by Thomas H. Trapp. Grand Rapids: Eerdmans, 2010.
———. "'Sit at my Right Hand!' The Enthronement of Christ at the Right Hand of God and Psalm 110:1." In *Studies in Early Christology*, 199–225. Edinburgh: T. & T. Clark, 1995.
———. *Studies in Early Christology*. Edinburgh: T. & T. Clark, 1995.
———. *Der Unterschätze Petrus: Zwei Studien*. 2nd ed. Tübingen: Mohr/Siebeck, 2007.
Hengel, Martin, and Roland Deines. "E. P. Sanders' 'Common Judaism,' Jesus, and the Pharisees: A Review Article." *JTS* 46 (1995) 1–70.
Herzog, William R., II. *Parables as Subversive Speech: Jesus as Pedagogue of the Oppressed*. Louisville: Westminster John Knox, 1994.
Heussi, Karl. *Die römische Petrustradition in kritischer Sicht*. Tübingen: Mohr/Siebeck, 1955.
Hiebert, D. Edmond. *First Peter*. Chicago: Moody, 1984.
Hirschfeld, Yizhar., and Miriam Feinberg Vamosh. "A Country Gentleman's Estate." *Biblical Archaeological Review* 31/2 (2005) 18–31.
Horbury, William. "The 'Caiaphas' Ossuaries and Joseph Caiaphas." *PEQ* 126 (1994) 32–48.
Horrell, David G. *1 Peter*. New Testament Guides. London: T. & T. Clark, 2008.
———. *Becoming Christian: Essays on 1 Peter and the Making of Christian Identity*. Early Christianity in Context. London: Bloomsbury T. & T. Clark, 2013.
———. *The Epistles of Peter and Jude*. Epworth Commentaries. Peterborough, UK: Epworth, 1998.

———. "Social-Scientific Interpretation Thirty Years On: Prospect (and Retrospect)." Paper presented at the Social Scientific Criticism section of the Society of Biblical Literature Meeting at Philadelphia, 20 November 2005.

Horsley, Richard A. *Hearing the Whole Story: The Politics of Plot in Mark's Gospel*. Louisville: Westminster John Knox, 2001.

———. *Jesus and the Spiral of Violence: Popular Jewish Resistance in Roman Palestine*. 1987. Reprint, Minneapolis: Fortress, 1993.

Hunzinger, Claus-Hunno. "Babylon als Deckname für Rom und Datierung des 1 Petrus-briefes." In *Gottes Wort und Gottes Land: Hans-Wilhelm Hertsberg zum 70. Geburtstag am 16. Januar 1965 dargebracht von Kollegen, Freunden und Schuelern*, edited by Henning Graf Revent-low, 67–77. Göttingen: Vanderhoeck & Ruprecht, 1965.

Hurtado, Larry W. *One God, One Lord: Early Christian Devotion and Ancient Jewish Monotheism*. Philadelphia: Fortress, 1988.

Hutchison, John, and Anthony D. Smith. *Ethnicity*. Oxford: Oxford University Press, 1996.

Jenkins, Richard. *Social Identity*. 4th ed. London: Routledge, 2004.

Jeremias, Joachim. "'Abba' in the Prayers of Jesus." In *The Prayers of Jesus*, 35–59. SBT 2/6. Naperville, IL: Allenson, 1967.

———. *Jesus and the Message of the New Testament*. Edited by K. C. Hanson. Fortress Classics in Biblical Studies. Minneapolis: Fortress, 2002.

———. *The Parables of Jesus*. 2nd rev. ed. New York: Scribner, 1972.

———. *The Central Message of the New Testament*. Philadelphia: Fortress, 1981.

Johnson, Luke T. *The Writings of the New Testament*. Rev. ed. Minneapolis: Fortress, 1999.

Johnson, Sherman E. "Asia Minor and Early Christianity." In *Christianity, Judaism, and Other Greco-Roman Cults: Studies for Morton Smith at Sixty*. Vol. 2: *Early Christianity*, edited by Jacob Neusner, 77–145. Studies in Judaism in Late Antiquity 12. Leiden: Brill, 1975.

Jones, Arnold H. M. *The Cities of Eastern Roman Provinces*. Rev. ed. Oxford: Clarendon, 1971.

Jones, Russel B. "Christian Behaviour under Fire." *RevExp* 46/1 (1949) 56–66.

Jones-Haldeman, Madelynn. *The Function of Christ's Suffering in 1 Peter 2:21*. ThD diss., Andrews University, 1988.

Jossa, Giorgio. *Dal Messia al Cristo: Le origini della Christologia*. Studi Biblici 88. Brescia: Paideia, 2002.

———. *Jews or Christians? The Followers of Jesus in Search of Their Own Identity*. Translated by Molly Rogers. WUNT 202. Tübingen: Mohr/Siebeck, 2006.

Joubert, Stephan J. "Van werklikheid tot werklikheid: Die interpretasie en interkulturele kommunikasie van Nuwe Testamentiese waardes." *Scriptura* 41(1992) 55–65.

———. "Wanneer die onmoontlike moontlik word: Paulus as verkondiger en bouer van 'n nuwe universum." *Nederduitse Gereformeerde Teologiese Tydskrif* 33 (1992) 301–10.

Juel, Donald H. *Messiah and Temple: The Trial of Jesus in the Gospel of Mark*. SBLDS 31. Missoula, MT: Scholars, 1977.

Käsemann, Ernst. "Das Problem des historischen Jesus." *ZTK* 51 (1954) 125–153.

———. "The Problem of the Historical Jesus." In *Essays on New Testament Themes*, 41–43. Translated by W. J. Montague. SBT 41. London: SCM, 1964.

Kee, Howard C. *Community of the New Age: Studies in Mark's Gospel.* Macon, GA: Mercer University Press, 1983.
Kelber, Werner H. "Conclusion: From Passion Narrative to Gospel." In *The Passion in Mark: Studies on Mark 14–16,* edited by Werner H. Kelber and John R. Donahue, 153–80. Philadelphia: Fortress, 1976.
Kelly, J. D. N. *Commentary on the Epistles of Peter and Jude.* BNTC. London: A. & C. Black, 1969.
Kendall, David W. "The Literary and Theological Function of 1Peter 1:3–12." In *Perspectives on First Peter,* edited by Charles H. Talbert, 103–20. NABPRSS 9. Macon, GA: Mercer University Press, 1986.
Kennedy, George A. *New Testament Interpretation through Rhetorical Criticism.* Chapel Hill: University of North Carolina Press, 1984.
Kermode, Frank. *The Genesis of Secrecy: On the Interpretation of Narrative.* Cambridge: Harvard University Press, 1979.
Kertelge, Karl. *Die Wunder Jesu in Markusevangelium: Eine redaktionsgeschichtliches Untersuchung.* SANT 23. Munich: Kösel, 1970.
Kilian-Dirlmeier, Imma. *Nadeln der frühhelladischen bis archaischen Zeit von der Peloponnes.* Prähistorische Bronzefunde 18. Munich: Beck, 1984.
Kingsbury, Jack D. *The Christology of Mark's Gospel.* Minneapolis: Fortress, 1983.
Kirk, Gordon E. "Endurance in Suffering in 1 Peter." *Bibliotheca Sacra* 138 (1981) 46–56.
Klauck, Hans-Josef. *Hausgemeinde und Hauskirche im frühen Christentum.* SBS 103. Stuttgart: Katholisches Bibelwerk, 1981.
Knoch, Otto. *Der erste und zweite Petrusbrief; Der Judasbrief.* Regensburg: Pustet, 1990.
Knopf, Rudolf. *Die Briefe Petri und Judae.* 7th ed. KEK 12. Göttingen: Vandenhoeck and Ruprecht, 1912.
Knox, John. "Pliny and Peter: A Note on 1 Peter 4:14–16 and 3:15." *JBL* 72 (1953) 187–89.
Koester, Helmut. *History, Culture and Religion in the Hellenistic Age.* 2nd ed. New York: de Gruyter, 1995.
Koskennniemi, Heikki. *Studium zur Idee und Phraseologie des griehischen Briefes bis 400 n. Chr.* Helsinki: Akateeminen Kirjakuppa, 1956.
Kraus, Hans-Joachim. *Psalms: A Commentary.* 2 vols. Translated by Hilton C. Oswald. Continental Commentaries. Minneapolis: Augsburg, 1988–1989.
Kraus, Manfred. "Enthymemes in Pauline Argumentation: Reading between the Lines in 1 Corinthians." In *Rhetorical Argumentation in Biblical Texts: Essays from the Lund 2000 Conference,* edited by Anders Eriksson, Thomas H. Olbricht, and Walter Übelacker, 99–111. Emory Studies in Early Christianity 8. Harrisburg, PA: Trinity, 2002.
Krodel, Gerhard. "1 Peter." In *The General Letters: Hebrews, James, 1–2 Peter, Jude, 1–3 John,* 42–83, 146–47. Rev. ed. ProcC. Minneapolis: Fortress, 1995.
———. "Persecution and Toleration of Christianity until Hadrian." In *The Catacombs and the Colosseum: The Roman Empire and the Setting of Primitive Christianity,* edited by Stephen Benko and John J. O'Rourke, 255–67. Valley Forge, PA: Judson, 1971.
Kühn, Karl Georg. "*Peirasmos-Hamartia-Sarx* im Neuen Testament und die damit zusammenhängenden Vorstellungen." *ZTK* 49 (1952) 200–222.

Lampe, Peter. *From Paul to Valentinus: Christians at Rome in the First Two Centuries.* Translated by Michael Steinhauser. Edited by Marshall D. Johnson. Minneapolis: Fortress, 2003.

———. "The Language of Equality in Early Christian House Churches: A Constructivist Approach." In *Early Christian Families in Context: An Interdisciplinary Dialogue*, edited by David L. Balch, and Carolyn Osiek, 73–83. Religion, Marriage and Family. Grand Rapids: Eerdmans, 2003.

———. "The Roman Christians of Romans 16." In *The Romans Debate*, edited by Karl P. Donfried, 216–30. Rev. ed. Peabody, MA: Hendrickson, 1991.

———. *Die stadtrömische Christen in en ersten beiden Jahrhunderten.* 2nd ed. WUNT 2/18. Tübingen: Mohr/Siebeck, 1989.

Lampe, Peter, and Ulrich Luz. "Nachpaulinisches Christentum und pagane Gesellschaft." In *Die Anfänge des Christentums: Alte Welt und neue Hoffnung*, edited by Jürgen Becker, 185–216. Stuttgart: Kohlhammer, 1987.

Le Roux, Elritia. "Levitikus as agtergrond van Markus 5:25–34, geïnterpreteer in terme van eer-en-skaamte." *HvTSt* 67/3 (2011), Art. #911, 8 pages. DOI: 10.4102/hts.v67i3.911.

Leaney, A. R. C. *The Letters of Peter and Jude: A Commentary on the First Letter of Peter, the Letter of Jude and the Second Letter of Peter.* Cambridge Bible Commentary. Cambridge: Cambridge University Press, 1967.

Lee-Pollard, Dorothy A. "Powerlessness as Power: A Key Emphasis in the Gospel of Mark." *SJT* 4 (1987) 173–88.

Lieu, Judith M. *Christian Identity in the Jewish and Greco-Roman World.* Oxford: Oxford University Press, 2004.

Lohfink, Gerhard. *Jesus and Community: The Social Dimension of Christian Faith.* Translated by John P. Galvin. Philadelphia: Fortress, 1984.

Lohmeyer, Ernst. *Das Evangelium des Markus.* KEK 2. Göttingen: Vandenhoeck & Ruprecht, 1963.

Lohse, Eduard. *Märtyrer und Gottesknecht: Untersuchungen zur urchristlichen Verkündigung vom Sühntod Jesu Christi.* Forschungen zur Religion und Literatur des Alten und Neuen Testaments n.F. 64. Göttingen: Vandenhoeck & Ruprecht, 1963.

———. "Parenesis and Kerugma in 1 Peter." In *Perspectives on First Peter*, edited by Charles H. Talbert, 73–85. Translated by John Steely. NABPRSS 9. Macon, GA: Mercer University Press, 1986.

Losada, Diego. "Sufrir por el nombre de Cristiano la Primera Carta di Pedro." *RevistB* 42 (1980) 85–101.

Lössl, Josef. *The Early Church: History and Memory.* London: T. & T. Clark, 2010.

Lövestam, Evald. *Jesus and "This Generation": A New Testament Study.* ConBNT 25. Stockholm: Amqvist & Wiksell, 1995.

Lüdemann, Gerd. "The Successors of Pre-70 Jerusalem Christianity: A Critical Evaluation of the Pella Tradition." In *Jewish and Christian Self-Definition* . Vol. 1: *The Shaping of Christianity in the Second and Third Centuries*, edited by E. P. Sanders, 160–173. London: SCM, 1980.

Luther, Martin. *De servo arbitrio Mar. Lutheri ad D. Erasmum Roterodamum.* Wittenberg: Lufft, 1525.

———. *D. Martin Luthers Epistel-Auslegung.* Edited by Hartmut Günther and Ernst Volk. Göttingen: Vanderhoek & Ruprecht, 1983.

———. *Word and Sacrament I*. Edited and Translated by E. Theodore Bachmann. Luther's Works 35. Philadelphia: Fortress, 1960.

Luz, Ulrich. *Das Evangelium nach Matthäus*. 3 vols. Evangelisch-katholischer Kommentar zum Neuen Testament 1. Zurich: Benzinger, 1985–2000.

———. *Matthew: A Commentary*. Translated by James E. Crouch. Hermeneia. Minneapolis: Fortress, 2001–2007.

———. "The Secrecy Motif and Marcan Christology." In *The Messianic Secret*, edited by Christopher Tuckett, 75–96. Issues in Religion and Theology 1. Philadelphia: Fortress, 1983.

MacIntyre, Alasdair. *After Virtue: A Study of Moral Theory*. London: Routledge & Kegan Paul, 1995.

MacMullen, Ramsay. *Enemies of the Roman Order: Treason, Unrest, and Alienation in the Empire*. Cambridge: Harvard University Press, 1966.

Magie, David. *Roman Rule in Asia Minor*. 2 vols. Princeton: Princeton University Press, 1950.

Malbon, Elizabeth S. "The Christology of Mark's Gospel: Narrative Christology and the Markan Jesus." In *Who Do You Say I Am? Essays in Christology*, edited by Mark A. Powell and David R. Bauer, 33–48. Louisville: Westminster John Knox, 1999.

———. *Mark's Jesus: Characterization as Narrative Christology*. Baylor University Press, 2009.

Malherbe, Abraham J. *Moral Exhortation: A Greco-Roman Sourcebook*. LEC 4. Philadelphia: Fortress, 1986.

Malina, Bruce J. *The New Testament World: Insights from Cultural Anthropology*. Rev. ed. Louisville: Westminster John Knox, 1993.

———. *The New Testament World: Insights from Cultural Anhtropology*. 3rd ed. Louisville: Westminster John Knox, 2001.

———. *On the Genre and Message of Revelation: Star Vision and Sky Journeys*. Peabody, MA: Hendrickson, 1995.

Malina, Bruce J., and Jerome H. Neyrey. *Calling Jesus Names: The Social Value of Labels in Matthew*. Foundations & Facets: Social Facets. Sonoma, CA: Polebridge, 1988.

———. "Honor and Shame in Luke–Acts: Pivotal Values of the Mediterranean World." In *The Social World of Luke-Acts: Models for Interpretation*, edited by Jerome H. Neyrey, 3–23. Peabody, MA: Hendrickson, 1991.

Malina, Bruce J., and Richard L. Rohrbaugh. *Social Science Commentary on the Gospel of John*. Minneapolis: Fortress, 1998.

———. *A Social Science Commentary on the Synoptic Gospels*. Philadelphia: Fortress, 1992.

Marcus, Joel. *Mark 1–8*. AB 27A. New York: Doubleday, 2000.

———. *The Way of the Lord: Christological Exegesis of the Old Testament in the Gospel of Mark*. Edinburgh: T. & T. Clark, 1993.

Margot, Jean-Claude. *Les Epîtres de Pierre*. Geneva: Labor et Fides, 1960.

Marshall, Christopher D. *Faith as Theme in Mark's Gospel*. SNTSMS 64. Cambridge: Cambridge University Press, 1989.

Marshall, I. Howard. *1 Peter*. IVP New Testament Commentary Series. Downers Grove, IL: InterVarsity, 1991.

———. *New Testament Theology: Many Witnesses, One Gospel*. Downers Grove, IL: Intervarsity, 2004.

Martin, Ralph P. "1 Peter." In *The Theology of the Letters of James, Peter and Jude*, edited by Andrew N. Chester and Ralph P. Martin, 87–133. New Testament Theology. Cambridge: Cambridge University Press, 1994.

Martin, Troy W. *Metaphor and Composition in 1 Peter*. SBLDS 131. Atlanta: Scholars, 1992.

———. "The Rehabilitation of the Rhetorical Stepchild: First Peter in Classical Rhetorical Criticism." In *Reading First Peter with New Eyes: Methodological Reassessments of the Letter of First Peter*, edited by Robert L. Webb and Betsy Bauman-Martin, 41–71. Library of New Testament Studies 364. London: T. & T. Clark, 2007.

Marxsen, Willi. "Der Mitälteste und Zeuge der Leiden Christi: Eine martyrologische Begründung des 'Romprimats' im Petrusbrief." In *Theologia crucis, Signum Crucis: Festschrift für Erich Dinkler zum 70. Geburtstag*, edited by Carl Andresen and Günter Klein, 377–93. Tübingen: Mohr/Siebeck, 1979.

McDonald, J. Ian H. *The Crucible of Christian Morality*. London: Routledge, 1998.

McDonald, Lee M. *The Formation of the Christian Biblical Canon*. Rev. ed. Peabody, MA: Hendrickson, 1995.

McGrath, Alister E. *Luther's Theology of the Cross*. Oxford: Blackwell, 1985.

McWilliams, Warren. *The Passion of God: Divine Suffering in Contemporary Protestant Theology*. Macon, GA: Mercer University Press, 1985.

Meeks, Wayne A. *The Origins of Christian Morality: The First Two Centuries*. New Haven: Yale University Press, 1993.

———. *The First Urban Christians: The Social World of the Apostle Paul*. New Haven: Yale University Press, 1983.

Mell, Ulrich. *Die "anderen" Winzer: Eine exegetische Studie zur Vollmacht Jesu Christi nach Markus 11,27—12,34*. WUNT 77. Tübingen: Mohr/Siebeck, 1995.

Mercado, Luis F. "The Language of Sojourning in the Abraham Midrash in Hebrews 11:8–19: Its Old Testament Basis, Exegetical Traditions and Function in the Epistle to the Hebrews." ThD diss., Harvard University, 1967.

Messelken, K. "Zur Durchsetzung des Christentums in der Spätantike." *Kölner Zeitschrift für Soziologie und Sozialpsychologie* 29 (1977) 261–94.

Metzger, Bruce M. *The Canon of the New Testament: Its Origen, Development and Significance*. New York: Oxford University Press, 1987.

Meyers, Carol L., and Eric M. Meyers. *Zechariah 9–14*. AB 25C. New York: Doubleday, 1998.

Michaels, J. Ramsey. "Eschatology in 1 Peter 3.17." *NTS* 13 (1967) 394–400.

———. *1 Peter*. WBC 49. Waco, TX: Word, 1988.

Millauer, Helmut. *Leiden als Gnade: Eine traditionsgeschichtliche Untersuchung zur Leidenstheologie des Ersten Petrusbriefes*. EuroH 23, Th 56. Frankfurt: Lang, 1976.

Moffatt, James. "The First Epistle of Peter." In *An Introduction to the Literature of the New Testament*, 318–44. 3rd rev. ed. Edinburgh: T. & T. Clark, 1918.

Molthagen, Joachim. "Die Lage der Christen in römischen Reich nach dem 1 Petrusbrief." *Historia* 44 (1995) 422–80.

Moltmann, Jürgen. *Crucified God: The Cross of Christ as the Foundation and Criticism of Christian Theology*. Translated by R. A. Wilson and John Bowden. New York: Harper & Row, 1974.

———. *Der gekreuzigte Gott: Das Kreuz Christi als Grund und Kritik christlicher Theologie*. Munich: Kaiser, 1972.

Moule, C. F. D. "Some Reflections on the 'Stone' Testimonia in Relation to the Name Peter." *NTS* 2 (1956) 56–58.

Mouton, Elna. "The Transformative Potential of the Bible as Resource for Christian Ethos and Ethics." *Scriptura* 2 (1997) 243–57.

Myers, Ched. *Binding the Strong Man: A Political Reading of Mark's Story of Jesus.* Maryknoll, NY: Orbis, 1990.

Nanos, Mark D. *The Mystery of Romans: The Jewish Context of Paul's Letter.* Minneapolis: Fortress, 1996.

Nauck, Wolfgang. "Freude im Leidem: Zum Problem einer urchristlichen Verfolgungstradition." *ZNW* 46 (1955) 68–80.

———. "Probleme des früchristlichen Amtverständnisses (1 Ptr 5:2f.)." *ZNW* 48 (1957) 200–220.

Neusner, Jacob. *A History of the Mishnaic Law of Holy Things: Arakhin, Temurah.* Studies in Judaism in Late Antiquity 30. Leiden: Brill, 1979.

Neil, Stephen. *The Interpretation of the New Testament 1861–1961.* London: Oxford, 1964.

Neugebauer, Fritz. "Zur Deutung und Bedeutung des 1. Petrusbriefes." *NTS* 26 (1979) 61–86.

Neyrey, Jerome H. "The Idea of Purity in Mark's Gospel." *Semeia* 86 (1986) 91–128.

———. "The Symbolic Universe of Luke–Acts: 'They Turn the World Upside Down.'" In *The Social World of Luke–Acts: Models for Interpretation*, edited by Jerome H. Neyrey, 272–304. Peabody, MA: Hendrickson, 1991.

Ngien, Dennis K. P. *The Suffering of God according to Martin Luther's "Theologia Crucis."* American University Studies. Series VII, Theology and Religion 181. Bern: Lang, 1995.

Niebuhr, Reinhold, and Karl T. Jellinghaus. *Christlicher Realismus und politische Probleme.* Vienna: Verlag für Geschichte und Politik, 1956.

Nisbet, Robert A. *The Social Philosophers: Community and Conflict in Western Thought.* New York: Cromwell, 1973.

Nussbaum, Martha C. "Therapeutic Arguments: Epicurus and Aristotle." In *The Norms of Nature: Studies in Hellenistic Ethics*, edited by Malcolm Schofield and Gisela Striker, 31–74. Cambridge: Cambridge University Press, 1986.

Ogden, Schubert M. *The Point of Christology.* San Francisco: Harper & Row, 1982.

Omanson, Roger L. "Suffering for Righteousness' Sake (1 Pet. 3:13–4:11)." *RevExp* 79 (1982) 439–50.

Osborne, Thomas P. "Guide Lines for Christian Suffering: A Source-Critical and Theological Study of 1 Peter 2,21–25." *Bib* 64 (1989) 381–408.

Osiek, Carolyn. "The Apostolic Fathers." In *The Early Christian World*, edited by Philip F. Esler, 1:503–24. London: Routledge, 2000.

———. *What Are They Saying about the Social Context of the New Testament?* New York: Paulist, 1984.

Osiek, Carolyn, and David L. Balch. *Families in the New Testament World: Households and House Churches.* Family, Religion, and Culture. Louisville: Westminster John Knox, 1997.

Paget, James Carleton. *Jews, Christians and Jewish Christians in Antiquity.* WUNT 251. Tübingen: Mohr/Siebeck, 1999.

Perdelwitz, Emil R. *Die Mysterienreligion und das Problem des 1 Petrusbriefes: Ein literarischer und religionsgeschichlicher Versuch.* RVV 11/3. Giessen: Töpelmann, 1911.

Perkins, Pheme. *Peter: Apostle for the Whole Church.* Studies on Personalities of the New Testament. 1994. Reprint, Minneapolis: Fortress, 2000.

Perrin, Norman. "Mark 14:62: The End Product of a Christian Pesher Tradition?" *NTS* 13 (1966) 150–55.

Pesce, M. "Il Vangelo di Giovanni e le fasi guidaiche del giovonnismo: Alcuni aspetti." In *Versus Israel: Nuove prospettive sul giudeocristianesimo,* edited by Giovanni Filoramo and Claudio Gianotto, 47–67. Brescia: Paideia, 2001.

Pesch, Rudolf. *Das Markusevangelium.* Vol. 1: *Einleitung und Kommentar zu Kap 1,1—8,26.* Herders theologischer Kommentar zum Neuen Testament 2. Freiburg: Herder, 1976.

———. *Das Markusevangelium.* Vol. 2: *Einleitung und Kommentar zu Kap. 8,27—16,20.* Herders theologischer Kommentar zum Neuen Testament 2. Freiburg: Herder, 1977.

Peterson, Norman R. *Rediscovering Paul: Philemon and the Sociology of Paul's Narrative World.* 1985. Reprint, Eugene, OR: Wipf & Stock, 2008.

Philipps, Karl. *Kirche in der Gesellschaft nach dem 1 Petrusbrief.* Gütersloh: Gütersloher, 1971.

Pieper, Annemarie. *Einführung in die Ethik.* Tübingen: Francke, 2000.

Pilch, John J. "'Beat His Ribs While He Is Young' (Sir 30:12): A Window on the Mediterranean World." *BTB* 23 (1993) 101–113.

———. *Introducing the Cultural Context of the New Testament.* 1991. Reprint, Eugene, OR: Wipf & Stock, 2007.

———. "Understanding Healing in the Social World of Early Christianity." *BTB* 22 (1992) 26–33.

Placher, William C. *Narratives of a Vulnerable God: Christ, Theology and Scripture.* Louisville: Westminster John Knox, 1994.

Poirier, John C. "Why Did the Pharisees Wash Their Hands?" *JJS* 47 (1996) 217–33.

Popp, Thomas. *Die Kunst der Konvivenz: Theologie der Anerkennung im 1. Petrusbrief.* ABG 33. Evangelische Verlagsanstalt, 2010.

Pokorný, Petr. *Der Gottessohn: Literarische Übersicht und Fragestellung.* Theologische Studien 109. Zurich: Theologische, 1971.

Price, Simon R. F. *Rituals and Power: The Roman Imperial Cult in Asia Minor.* Cambridge: Cambridge University Press, 1984.

Prostmeier, Ferdinand-Rupert. *Handlungsmodelle im ersten Petrusbrief.* FB 63. Würtsburg: Echter, 1990.

Rabin, Chaim. "Historical Background of Qumran Hebrew." *ScrHier* 4 (1958) 144–61.

Radermacher, Ludwig. "Der erste Petrusbrief und Silvanus; mit einem Nachwort in eigener Sache." *ZNW* 25 (1926) 288–290.

Reichert, Angelika. *Eine urchristeliche Praeparatio ad martyrum: Studien zur Komposition, Traditionsgeschichte und Theologie des 1 Petrusbriefes.* BBET 22. Frankfurt: Lang, 1989.

Reicke, Bo. *The New Testament Era: The World of the Bible from 500 B.C. to A.D. 100.* Philadelphia: Fortress, 1968.

———. *The Epistles of James, Peter and Jude.* AB 37. Garden City, NY: Doubleday, 1964.

———. *The Disobedient Spirits and Christian Baptism: A Study of 1 Peter 3:19 and Its Context*. Acta Seminarii neotestamentici Upsaliensis 13. Copenhagen: Munksgaard, 1946.

Reinbold, Wolfgang. *Der älteste Bericht über den Tod Jesu: Literarische Analyse und historische Kritik der Passiondarstellungen der Evangelien*. BZNW 69. Berlin: de Gruyter, 1994.

Richard, Earl J. "The Functional Christology of First Peter." In *Perspectives on First Peter*, edited by Charles H. Talbert, 121–39. NABPRSS 9. Macon, GA: Mercer University Press, 1986.

Richardson, Peter. *Israel in the Apostolic Church*. SNTSMS 10. Cambridge: Cambridge University Press, 1969.

Roitto, Rikard. "Behaving like a Christ-Believer: A Cognitive Perspective on Identity and Behaviour Norms in the Early Christ-Movement." In *Exploring Early Christian Identity*, edited by Bengt Holmberg, 93–114. WUNT 226. Tübingen: Mohr/Siebeck, 2008.

———. "Identity in Christ and Household Identities in Pauline and Deutero-Pauline Texts." In *Identity Formation in the New Testament*, edited by Bengt Holmberg and Mikael Winninge, 141–62.WUNT 227. Tübingen: Mohr/Siebeck, 2008.

Ritter, Adolf M. *Alte Kirche*. Zurich: Neukirchener Verlag, 1994.

Roloff, Jürgen. *Die Kirche in Neuen Testament*. GNT 10. Göttingen: Vandenhoeck & Ruprecht, 1993.

Roskam, H. N. *The Purpose of the Gospel of Mark in its Historical and Social Context*. NovTSup 114. Leiden: Brill, 2004.

Rostovtzeff, Michael. *The Social and Economic History of the Roman Empire*. 2 vols. 2nd ed., rev. by Peter M. Fraser. Oxford: Clarendon, 1957.

Ruppert, Lothar. *Jesus als der leidende Gerechte? Der Weg Jesu im Lichte eines alt— und zwischentestamentlichen Motivs*. SBS 59. Stuttgart: Katholisches Bibelwerk, 1972.

———. *Der Leidende Gerechte und seine Feinde: Eine Wortfelduntersuchung*. Würzburg: Echter, 1973.

———. *Der Leidende Gerechte: Eine Motivgeschichtliches Untersuchung zum Alten Testament und zwischentestamentlichen Judentum*. FB 5. Würzburg: Echter, 1972.

Sander, E. T. "PYROSIS and the First Epistle of Peter 4:12." PhD diss., Harvard University, 1966.

Sanders, E. P. *The Historical Figure of Jesus*. London: Penguin, 1993.

———. *Jesus and Judaism*. Philadelphia: Fortress, 1985.

Sänger, Dieter. *Die Verkündigung des Gekreutzigten und Israel: Studium zum Verhältnis von Kirche und Israel bei Paulus und in frühen Christentum*. WUNT 75. Tübingen: Mohr/Siebeck, 1994.

Schaefer, H. "Paroikoi." In *Paulys Realencyclopädie der classische Altertumwissenschaft* 18/4 (1949) 1695–707.

Schäfer, Peter. *The Bar Kokhba War Reconsidered: New Perspectives on the Second Jewish Revolt against Rome*. Texte und Studien zum antiken Judentum 100. Tübingen: Mohr/Siebeck, 2003.

Schelkle, Karl H. *Die Petrusbriefe, der Judasbrief*. 3rd ed. Freiburg: Herder, 1970.

———. "Das Leiden des Gottesknechtes als Form christlichen Lebens (nach dem 1. Petrusbrief)." *Bibel und Kirche* 16 (1961) 14–16.

Schenke, Ludger. *Studien zur Passionsgeschichte des Markus: Tradition und Redaktion in Markus 14:1–42*. FB 4.Wurzburg: Echter, 1971.

Schlatter, Adolf. *Petrus und Paulus nach dem Ersten Petrusbrief.* Stuttgartt: Calwer, 1937.
Schmidt, K. L., and M. A. Schmidt, R. Meyer. "paroikos." In *Theological Dictionary of the New Testament*, edited by Gerhard Friedrich, 5:841–53. Translated by Geoffrey W. Bromiley. Grand Rapids: Eerdmans, 1967.
Schnelle, Udo. *The History and Theology of the New Testament Writings.* Translated by M. Eugene Boring. Minneapolis: Fortress, 1998.
Schrage, Wolfgang, and Horst R. Balz. "Der erste Petrusbrief." In *Die Katholischen Briefe: Die Briefe des Jakobus, Petrus, Judas und Johannes*, 59–117. 11th ed. NTD 10. Göttingen: Vanderhoeck & Ruprecht, 1973.
Schrenk, G. "The Messiah as the Righteous." *TWNT* 2:186.
Schüssler Fiorenza, Elisabeth. *Jesus: Miriam's Child, Sophia's Prophet: Critical Issues in Feminist Christology.* New York: Continuum, 1994.
Schutter, William L. "1 Peter 4:17, Ezekiel 9:6 and Apocalyptic Hermeneutics." In *SBL 1987: Seminar Papers*, 276–84. SBLSP 26. Atlanta: Scholars, 1987.
———. *Hermeneutic and Composition in 1 Peter.* WUNT 2/30. Tübingen: Mohr/Siebeck, 1989.
Schweizer, Eduard. "The Son of Man." *JBL* 79 (1960) 119–29.
Scott, James C. *Domination and the Arts of Resistance: Hidden Transcripts.* New Haven: Yale University Press, 1990.
Seland, Torrey. "'Conduct Yourselves Honourably among the Gentiles' (1 Peter 2:12): Assimilation and Acculturation in 1 Peter." In *Strangers in the Light: Philonic Perspectives on Christian Identity in 1 Peter*, 147–89. Biblical Interpretation Series 76. Leiden: Brill, 2005.
Selwyn, Edward Gordon. *The First Epistle of St. Peter: The Greek Text with Introduction, Notes and Essays.* 2nd ed. London: St. Martin's, 1947.
———. *The First Epistle of St. Peter.* London: MacMillan, 1955.
Senior, Donald. *1&2 Peter.* NTM 20. Wilmington, DE: Glazier, 1980.
———. *The Passion of Jesus in the Gospel of Mark.* Wilmington, DE: Glazier, 1984.
Sherwin-White, Adrian N. *Fifty Letters of Pliny: Selected and Edited with Introduction and Notes.* 2nd ed. Oxford: Oxford University Press, 1969.
Sherwin-White, Susan M. *Ancient Cos: An Historical Study from the Dorian Settlement to the Imperial Period.* Hypomnemata: Untersuchungen zur Antike und zu ihrem Nachleben 51. Göttingen: Vanderhoeck & Ruprecht, 1978.
Siker, Jeffrey S. "Christianity in the Second and Third Centuries." In *The Early Christian World*, edited by Philip F. Esler, 1:231–57. London: Routledge, 2000.
Smith, Terence V. *Petrine Controversies in Early Christianity: Attitudes towards Peter in Christian Writings of the First Two Centuries.* WUNT 2/15. Tübingen: Mohr/Siebeck, 1985.
Snodgrass, Klyne R. "The Parable of the Wicked Husbandmen: Is the Gospel of Thomas Version Original?" *NTS* 21 (1974) 142–44.
Sommer, Urs. *Die Passionsgeschichte des Markusevangeliums: Überlegungen zur Bedeutung der Geschichte für den Glauben.* WUNT 58. Tübingen: Mohr/Siebeck, 1993.
Sordi, Marta. *I Cristiani E L'Impero Romano.* Milan: Jaca Book Spa, 1983.
Spicq, Ceslas. *Notes de Lexiographie Néo-Testamentaire.* Orbis biblicus et orientalis 22. Göttingen: Vandenhoeck & Ruprecht, 1978–1982.
———. *Theological Lexicon of the New Testament.* 3 vols. Translated by James D. Ernest. Peabody, MA: Hendrickson, 1994.

Spitta, Friedrich. *Christi Predigt an der Geister (1 Petr 3,19ff). Ein Beitrag zum neutestamentlichen Christologie.* Göttingen: Vanderhoeck & Ruprecht, 1890.
Spohn, William C. *Go and Do Likewise: Jesus and Ethics.* New York: Continuum,1999.
Stark, Rodney. *The Rise of Christianity: How the Obscure, Marginal Jesus Movement became the Dominant Religious Force in the Western World in a Few Centuries.* San Francisco: HarperSanFrancisco, 1996.
Stibbs, Alan M., and Andrew F. Walls. *The First Epistle General of Peter.* TNTC. Grand Rapids: Eerdmans, 1959.
Stone, John. "Max Weber on Race, Ethnicity and Nationalism." In *Race and Ethnicity: Comparative and Theoretical Approaches,* edited by John Stone and Rutledge M. Dennis, 28–42. Oxford: Wiley-Blackwell, 2003.
Strange, James F. "First Century Galilee from Archeology." In *Archaeology and the Galilee: Texts and Contexts in the Greco-Roman and Byzantine Periods,* edited by Douglas R. Edwards and C. Thomas McCollough. South Florida Studies in the History of Judaism 143. Atlanta: Scholars, 1997.
Streeter, Burnett H. "The Church in Asia: The First Epistle of St. Peter." In *The Primitive Church,* 115–36. New York: Macmillan, 1929.
Stuhlmacher, Peter. *Biblische Theologie des Neues Testaments.* 2 vols. Göttingen: Vanderhoeck & Ruprecht, 1992.
———. "Das Christus-bild der Paulus Schule eine Skizze." In *Jews and Christians: The Parting of the Ways A.D. 70 to 135,* edited by James D. G. Dunn, 159–75. Tübingen: Mohr/Siebeck, 1992.
Sugitharajah, R. S. *The Bible and the Third World: Precolonial, Colonial and Postcolonial Encounters.* Cambridge: Cambridge University Press, 2001.
Suhl, Alfred. *Die Funktion der alttestamentlichen Zitate und Anspielungen im Markusevangelium.* Gütersloh: Gütersloher, 1965.
Talbert, Charles H. "The Educational Value of Suffering in 1 Peter." In *Learning through Suffering: The Educational Value of Suffering in the New Testament and in Its Milieu,* 42–57. Collegeville, MN: Liturgical, 1991.
Tannehill, Robert C. "The Gospel of Mark as Narrative Christology." *Semeia* 16 (1980) 57–96.
Taylor, Vincent. *The Foundation of the Gospel Tradition.* London: Macmillan, 1933.
Telbe, Mikael. "The Prototypical Christ-Believer: Early Christian Identity Formation in Ephesus." In *Exploring Early Christian Identity,* edited by Bengt Holmberg, 115–38. WUNT 1/226. Tübingen: Mohr/Siebeck, 2008.
Thomas, C. H. "The First Epistle of Peter."In *The Interpreter's One-Volume Commentary on the Bible,* edited by George A. Buttrick and Charles M. Laymon, 921–30. Nashville: Abingdon, 1968.
Thompson, Michael. *Clothed with Christ: The Example and Teachings of Jesus in Romans 12:1—15:13.* JSNTSup 59. Sheffield: JSOT, 1991.
Thorsen, Donald A. "Gethsemane." In *ABD* 2:997-98.
Thorsteinsson, Runar. "The Role of Morality in the Rise of Roman Christianity." In *Exploring Early Christian Identity,* edited by Bengt Holmberg, 139–58. WUNT 1/226. Tübingen: Mohr/Siebeck, 2008.
Thornton, T. C. G. "1 Peter, a Paschal Liturgy?" *JTS* 12 (1961) 14–26.
Thurén, Lauri. *Argument and Theology in 1 Peter: The Origins of Christian Paraenesis.* JSNTSup 114. Sheffield: Sheffield Academic, 1995.
Tolbert, Mary Ann. *Sowing the Gospel: Mark's World in Literary-Historical Perspective.* Minneapolis: Fortress, 1996.

Toolan, Michael J. *Narrative: A Critical Linguistic Introduction*. 2nd ed. London: Routledge, 2001.

Treblico, Paul. *The Early Christians in Ephesus from Paul to Ignatius*. WUNT 166. Tübingen: Mohr/Siebeck, 2004.

Turner, John C. "Towards a Cognitive Redefinition of the Social Group." In *Social Identity and Intergroup Relations*, edited by Henri Tajfel, 15–40. European Studies in Social Psychology. Cambridge: Cambridge University Press, 1982.

Van Aarde, Andries G. "Inleiding tot die sosiaal-wetenskaplike kritiese eksegese van Nuwe Testamentiese tekste: Die metodologiese aanloop in die navorsingsgeskiedenis."*HvTSt* 63/1 (2007) 49–79.

———. "Die Sosiaal-wetenskaplike kritiese eksegese van Nuwe Testamentiese tekste: 'n Kritiese oorsig van die eerste resultate." *HvTSt*63/2 (2007) 515–42.

———. "Sosiaal-wetenskaplike kritiese eksegese van Nuwe Testamentiese tekste: 'n Voortgaande debat sonder einde." *HvTSt* 63/3 (2007) 1119–47.

———. "The *Evangelium infantium*, the Abandonment of Children, and the Infancy Narrative in Matthew 1 and 2 from a Social Scientific Perspective." *Lovering* (1992) 435–53.

Van Bruggen, Jacob. *Commentaar op het Nieuwe Testament Afdeling Evangeliën: Marcus*. Kampen: Kok, 1988.

Van Eck, Ernest. *Galilee and Jerusalem in Mark's Story of Jesus: A Narratological and Social- Scientific Reading*. HvTStSup 7. Pretoria: University of Pretoria, 1995.

Van Iersel, Bas M. F. "'To Galilee' or 'In Galilee' in Mark 14,28 and Mark 16,7." *ETL* 58 (1982) 365–70.

Van Staden, Pieter. *Compassion—The Essence of Life: A Social-Scientific Study of the Religious Symbolic Universe Reflected in the Ideology/Theology of Luke*. HvTStSup 4. Pretoria: Tydskrifafdeling van die Nederduitsch Hervormde Kerk, 1991.

Van Unnik, Willem C. "Christianity according to 1 Peter." *ExpTim*68 (1956) 79–83.

Vanhoye, Albert. "1 Pierre au carrefour des théologies du Nouveau Testament." In *Etudes sur la première lettre de Pierre*, edited by Charles Perrot, 97–128. LD 102. Paris: Cerf, 1980.

Verheyden, Jozef. "The Flight of the Christians to Pella." *ETL* 66 (1990) 368–384.

Vielhauer, Philipp. "Die Apokryphen und die Apostolischen Väter." In *Geschichte der urchristlichen Literatur: Einleitung in das Neue Testament*, 580–89. De Gruyter Lehrbuch. Berlin: de Guyter, 1975.

Vogels, Heinz-Jürgen. *Christi Abstieg ins Totenreich und das Läutering an den Toten*. FTS 102. Freiburg: Herder, 1976.

Volf, Miroslav. "Soft Difference: Theological Reflections on the Relation between Church and Culture in 1 Peter." *ExAud* 10 (1994) 15–30.

Vouga, François. *Les premiers pas du Christianisme: Les écrits, les acteurs, le débats*. Le Monde de la Bible ; no 35. Geneva: Labor et Fides, 1997.

Waetjen, Herman C. *A Reordering of Power: A Socio-Political Reading of Mark's Gospel*. 1989. Reprint, Eugene, OR: Wipf & Stock, 2014.

Walsh, Peter G. *Pliny the Younger: Complete Letters*. New York: Oxford University Press, 2006.

Weber, Max. "Religion of the Non-privileged Classes." In *The Sociology of Religion*, 95–117. Translated by E Fischoff. Beacon Series in the Sociology of Politics and Religion. Boston: Beacon, 1964.

Weder, Hans. *Neutestamentliches Hermeneutik*. Zürcher Grundrisse zur Bibel. Zurich: Theologische Verlag, 1986.

Wiarda, Timothy. *Peter in the Gospels: Pattern, Personality and Relationship*. WUNT 2/127. Tübingen: Mohr/Siebeck, 2000.

Wifstrand, Albert. "Stylistic Problems in the Epistles of James and Peter." *ST* 1 (1948) 174–88.

Wilcox, Max. "'Upon the Tree' in Deut 21:22–23 in the New Testament." *JBL* 96 (1977) 97–99.

Wilde, James A. "A Social Description of the Community Reflected in the Gospel of Mark." Ann Arbor, MI: Xerox University Microfilms, 1974.

Wilson, Bryan R. *Sects and Society: A Sociological Study of the Elim Tabernacle, Christian Science and Christadelphians*. Berkeley: University of California Press, 1961.

———. *Patterns of Sectarianism: Organization and Ideology in Social and Religious Movements*. London: Heinemann, 1967.

———. *Religious Sects: A Sociological Study*. London: Weidenfeld & Nicolson, 1970.

———. *Magic and the Millennium: A Sociological Study of Religious Movements of Protest among Tribal and Third-World Peoples*. New York: Harper & Row, 1973.

Wilson, Stephen G. *Gentiles and the Gentile Mission in Luke-Acts*. SNTSMS 23. Cambridge: University Press, 1973.

Wilson, Walter T. *The Hope of Glory: Education and Exhortation in the Epistle of the Colossians*. NovTSup 88. Leiden: Brill, 1997.

Windisch, Hans. *Die Katolishe Briefe*. 2nd ed. HNT 4/2. 3rd rev. augm. ed., with appendix by Herbert Preisker. Tübingen: Mohr/Siebeck, 1951.

Winn, Adam. *The Purpose of Mark's Gospel: An Early Christian Response to Roman Imperial Propaganda*. WUNT 2/245. Tübingen: Mohr/Siebeck, 2008.

Winter, Bruce W. "The Public Honouring of Christian Benefactors: Romans 13.3–4 and 1 Peter 2.14–15." *JSNT* 34 (1988) 87–103.

Witherington, Ben, III. *The Gospel of Mark: A Socio-Rhetorical Commentary*. Grand Rapids: Eerdmans, 2001.

Wolff, Hanna. *Neuer Wein, alte Schläuche: Das Identitätsproblem des Christentums im Lichte der Tiefenpsychologie*. Radius-Bücher. Stuttgart: Radius, 1981.

Wolter, Michael. "Die ethische Identität christlicher Gemeinden in neutestamentlicher Zeit." In *Woran orientiert sich Ethik?* Edited by Wilfried Härle and Reiner Preul, 61–90. MJT 13. MThSt 67. Marburg: Elwert,2001.

Worchel, Stephen, et al., eds. *Social Identity: International Perspectives*. London: Sage, 1998.

Woyke, Johannes. "Der leidende Gottesknecht (Jes 53)." In *Verheißung des Neuen Bundes: Wie alttestamentliche Texte im Neuen Testament fortwirken*, edited by Bernd Kollmann, 200–225. BThS 35.Göttingen: Vandenhoeck & Ruprecht, 2010.

Wrede, William. *The Messianic Secret*. Translated by James C. G. Crieg. Cambridge: James Clark Ltd., 1971.

———. *Das Messiasgeheimnis in den Evangelien: Zugleich ein Beitrag zum Verständnis des Markusevangeliums*. Göttingen: Vandenhoeck & Ruprecht, 1901.

Yoder, John H. *The Politics of Jesus: Vincit Agnus Noster*. Grand Rapids: Eerdmans, 1972.

Zimmermann, Heinrich. *Neutestamentliche Methodenlehre: Darstellung der Historisch-kritischen Methode*. 4th ed. Stuttgart: Katholisches Bibelwerk, 1974.

Zimmermann, Ruben. "The 'Implicit' Ethics of New Testament Writings: A Draft on a New Methodology for Analysing Ethics." *Neot* 43/2 (2009) 399–422.

Zwierlein, Otto. *Petrus in Rom: Die literarischen Zeugnisse. Mit einer kritischen Edition der Martyrien des Petrus und Paulus auf neuer handschriftlicher Grundlage*. Untersuchungen zur antiken Literatur und Geschichte 96. Berlin: de Gruyter, 2009.

www.ingramcontent.com/pod-product-compliance
Lightning Source LLC
Chambersburg PA
CBHW050622300426
44112CB00012B/1617